CLEAR AND PRESENT

GAME
CHANGERS

To : Ben Glass
Thank you for sharing your
wisdom on my podcast !

STRATEGIES TO
TURNAROUND
& TRANSFORM
YOUR BUSINESS

[signature: James Karl Butler]

JAMES KARL BUTLER
BEST-SELLING AUTHOR OF
THE SYSTEM IS THE SECRET

This publication is designed to provide accurate and authoritative information in regard to the subject matter covered. It is sold with the understanding that the publisher is not engaged in rendering legal, accounting, or other professional service. If legal advice or other expert assistance is required, the services of a professional should be sought.

Butler, James K.,
    Clear and Present Game Changers: Strategies to Transform and Turnaround Your Business

ISBN 978-1537657776
    1. Business 2. Success

Printed in the United States of America

**To three mentors who have helped me
become a better entrepreneur:**

Dan Kennedy

No one can teach like you. I have devoured your
teachings, insights, and ideas and have sought to
implement them in my life and business.

Bill Glazer

No one can lead and inspire like you. A chance plane
ride with you changed my life and the trajectory of
my business. I will always be grateful for your help,
your teachings, and your leadership.

Lee Milteer

No one can motivate and encourage like you. I'm
grateful for your friendship, your teachings, your
kindness, and all that I've learned from you.

What Others Are Saying about Clear and Present Game Changers:

"Without a doubt James Butler is one the smartest marketers and implementers that I have ever met. He is a voracious student of marketing and uses that knowledge to massively improve his own businesses. This book is packed with practical, tried, true and tested information that will have a huge impact on your business. You would be well advised to not only learn from what he has to say but to place this information into immediate action to stand out from your competition and to grow your revenue."--Grant Miller, CEO, Cool Renew MedSpa

"Coming from a niche in retail where I help independent retailers profitably and efficiently convert inventory and assets to fast cash, AND knowing what got these retailers in this position in the first place, I found this book captivating. The thinking that got you to where you are right now cannot be the same thinking that is going to take you where you want to be and that is what this book tells you how to do. All businesses have a lifecycle, but if you take the time to read every single page of this book, internalize it, study it, then read it again I can guarantee you -from 2 decades of experience- that you will extend your lifecycle as a business owner."--Travis Walker, Founder, Retail Sales PRO, Renowned Retail Exit Strategy Specialist, Author of *Liquidation Secrets Revealed,* www.RetailSalesPRO.com

"I would recommend *Clear & Present Game Changers* to any thoughtful business owner. In this book, James Butler lays out a practical and applicable Master's level understanding in each chapter. Whether you are a business veteran, as the author is, or you are just starting out your entrepreneurial career, you are going to want the wisdom in this book to help you grow and future proof your business."-- Mark Day, MBA, CEO Remarkable Home Loans

"As a small business coach, I've seen tremendous change in the way business is done in the past decade. *Clear and Present Game Changers* is an exceptional book on how to cope with the new realities of business today and come out on top, even in hyper-competitive markets. I highly recommend studying and implementing the principles in this book so you can soar to new heights with your business and achieve your dreams."--Patrick Snow, Professional Speaker, International Best-Selling Author of *Creating Your Own Destiny* and *Boy Entrepreneur*

"*Clear and Present Game Changers* outlines ten of the most challenging situations facing entrepreneurs today and how to overcome them to build a successful and profitable business. I have interviewed James for my Millionaire Smarts program for several of his books and have found his experiences and advice insightful. He even did a session for our Peak Performance members on writing and publishing a book and our members found that very helpful. His new book outlines how entrepreneurs can stay focused on what really matters and will help you build more value, stay on top of changing trends in your industry, and how you can better compete and win in today's marketplace. I highly recommend this book." --Lee Milteer, author of *Success is an Inside Job*, www.milteer.com

"James Butler has done it again and with the release of his latest book, *Clear & Present Game Changers*, he offers a comprehensive road map to out-market and out-smart your competition. This is a book that is not merely meant to just be read and put on the shelf. It is a workbook which can guide you to new levels of success if you follow James' smart advice. Chapter 8 is pure gold for all business owners!" --Mike Capuzzi, publisher, author and business coach, MikeCapuzzi.com

"James Butler has written a resource manual for any business person looking to solidify and grow their business. With solid advice and provocative questions seemingly on every page, this isn't a read it once book, but one that becomes your trusted advisor for the rest of your business life." --Kevin Eikenberry, best-selling author and Chief Potential Officer of the Kevin Eikenberry Group

"The author teaches the reader why and how to profit from specialization, yet this book itself is a tour-de-force, soup-to-nuts instructional guide on how to tremendously improve every single aspect of any business. Bravo!" --Steve Sipress, Founder and CEO, Successful Selling Systems, Inc.

"I first met James Butler after hearing him compete for marketer of the year for Glazer Kennedy Insider's Circle. I walked right up to him in a nearby restaurant and told him his presentation detailing all he did with his bridal company was absolutely amazing. I was in awe of all he accomplished with his marketing. He went on to win this highly competitive event that year. I then read his book, *The System is the Secret*, which was a masterful look at the systems needed to run a successful business. I said at that time that he could teach a master class on this subject. Fast-forward a number of years. he reached out to me and asked if I'd be willing to read and review his newest book *Clear & Present Game Changers* and I immediately said "Yes!" After having read his newest book, I have to say that every entrepreneur should read this book, study it, implement the ideas, strategies and advice in this book and then re-read it again. This is really a master guide to marketing. He constantly uses real-life analogies and case studies to help you understand concepts. He makes it simple to understand and importantly, asks critical questions that will help you evaluate where you are and where you want to be. Two important questions for any entrepreneur to answer, which he identified immediately were: "1) Do your prospects feel like they are at the center of the experience in your business, or do they feel like they are just part of a transaction? and 2) In what ways specifically can you enhance the emotional connection they feel when they arrive in your business?" The importance of an emotional connection a consumer/customer needs to have must be emphasized repeatedly. I appreciated the reminder I had learned long ago, but seemed to have forgotten. I really think this book deserves a James Butler training seminar to supplement the content to get entrepreneurs to delve deep into his wisdom and experience. This was an excellent read from a top-notch marketer and I'm proud to call him a friend."--Gerry Oginski, Esq., Founder, Lawyers Video Studio, NY Medical Malpractice & Accident Attorney

"This book is absolute gold for any serious entrepreneur. The Business Checkup section is invaluable for any entrepreneur looking for big business expansion or for getting a business back on course. James brings his wealth of experience and innovative ways of thinking that take emotion, influence and persuasion and transform them into useable and valuable business growth tools."—Maritza Parra, author of *Heartwork Journaling*

"In selling today, there can be a big disconnect between the prospect's process and what the seller does or wants to do. *Clear and Present Game Changers* outlines how you can push for the sale without being pushy and what you can do to be more persuasive in the sales process. James Butler is an expert on systems and this book is full of practical solutions to the most challenging issues that entrepreneurs are dealing with today. I highly encourage you to read and apply the valuable lessons contained in this book.'" –Eric Lofholm, sales trainer and best-selling author of *The System*, *Focus*, and *Leverage*

"Coming from consistent study and years of real world business experience, James Butler's business writings are an unusual treat. Whenever he gets focused on something it's impressive to watch. He is committed, tenacious and prolific! Whenever he writes another book, I dig in as fast as I can. This book is filled not only with key success tactics you need to know and implement but inspiration as well."--Jay Henderson, CEO, Real Talent Development, Inc., Author of *The Ultimate Small Business Guide To Hiring Super-Stars*

CONTENTS

INTRODUCTION

The book you are reading contains the most important lessons I've learned about what it takes to turnaround or transform a business. I've observed and lived these lessons first hand through successes and failures both running my own businesses and coaching many top entrepreneurs in today's competitive environment.

Business today is in an era of tremendous change. There are clear and present game changers that are changing the way business is done. Technology is making it easier for customers to bypass traditional distribution channels. As a result, customers are in charge and armed with information that can dictate what they will pay (and if and when they will buy). Prospects enter a potential deal today with much more information than their counterparts five or ten years ago ever dreamed of having. To succeed in this environment, smart entrepreneurs must learn how to better position what they sell in a way that helps them lower costs and increase profits.

This book explores the clear and present dangers you're facing in the marketplace and the game changers you must employ to continue winning in a changing marketplace.

Throughout its pages, I'll share strategies that will help you sell more profitably in an unprofitable world and give you specific game changing strategies so you can achieve greater success in your business.

When you become successful in business, it is easy to be seduced into expanding into other areas that aren't your core competency and where it is perceived that competitors are doing well. These forays into new areas can create new revenues, but sometimes they can slowly lead you away from the core business that helped you become successful in the first place. I was talking recently with a successful entrepreneur who told me that she had seen this lesson first hand in her business. She had built a very successful and profitable business, but thought that adding a few new product lines (that didn't have the same margin) would help her appeal to a new customer she didn't already have. The reality was that she sold the new products, but at a lesser profit margin for the same amount of work.

It is so easy to be seduced by the persuasive power of new without thinking about how it really integrates with the successful core parts of your existing business. Allowing new to cannibalize old at the expense of your core profitability is a big mistake that may not be fully understood until time passes and it is too late to correct. Many are able to course correct to the core before it is too late. Other businesses are not as fortunate.

Here is the reality: You cannot transform your company if you don't lead and excel in your core business. It is critically important to be perceived as the undisputed authority for what you do better than anyone else in your market niche. So, with that in mind, ask and answer these four questions:

1) What are you the undisputed authority on to prospects and clients in your market?

2) What is your core business (what drives everything else)?

3) How can you better tell your story so prospects seek you out and want to do business with you *before* they arrive at your web site or place of business?

4) Are there other ways you can be in touch with the prospect throughout the sales process that will reinforce your authority?

Answering these questions should help you realize whether you are currently leading and excelling at your core business before you begin launching into new areas. Remember why customers come to you in the first place. If your client acquisition is dropping, what is happening?

It is wise to periodically ask yourself this question: What do people come to your business for? The answer is not just a product or service. They come for the fulfillment of their desires. You sell dreams or outcomes, not products or services. The deeper you and everyone on your team understands that, the more successful your business will be.

Here are four more questions you should consider as you think about where your business is now and what you can do to grow to the next level:

1) Do your prospects feel like they are at the center of the experience in your business, or do they feel like they are just part of a transaction?

2) In what ways specifically can you enhance the emotional connection they feel when they arrive in your business?

3) If you are considering adding something new, ask: What else can we offer to our clients that complements the experience they're already having?

4) Are there market niches that you could add that would complement what you are already doing and not distract from your specialization and focus? If it distracts you from your core, is it wise?

This is obviously the most important thing in any business. You have to have a profitable AND sustainable model. Without this, you won't be able to grow or sustain what you are doing very long.

How often are you evaluating the profitability of what you are selling?

When something isn't profitable anymore, do you have the courage to stop offering it and replace it with something that is?

As you go through this book, I invite you to act on the ideas I'll share with you. Decide what you'll do and be clear about what every member of your team must do to make this new vision of success a reality.

It is easy to be busy. It is much more difficult to be disciplined to be focused on what matters most.

In tough economic times, it is much easier to hold on to what you have than to make changes that can get you back on track or to achieve rapid growth. It is easier to cower and hide than it is to face the music and do what needs to be done.

Let me share an example of a lesson I learned first hand from the success and failure of my business. After a few years of working for others and seeing their success, my wife and I decided to start our own business. We grew our first business, a retail bridal store, from $0 to over $1,000,000 a year in sales in three years. A few years later, we reached $1 million a year in sales in another retail business in eighteen months. My wife designed the dresses we sold and we operated a wholesale company selling dresses to stores throughout the United States and Canada. We worked directly with manufacturers overseas and learned the import business. We sold these designs to other retail stores throughout the United States and Canada. This wholesale company did millions of dollars in sales each year.

We ended up working with nine factories in mainland China. It was scary going into a country we hadn't been to before, but my desire to learn about the industry and find the right manufacturers drove me to discover who the top factories were through public import shipping records. I didn't speak any Chinese, but I was able to set up numerous appointments with these factories through email. Then, when we arrived in China, we had the concierge at a hotel in Zhongshan, China write numerous notes in Chinese which we could give to drivers with directions to take us to visit these factories for our appointments. For a few years, we spent nearly a month a year in China working on dress designs which we then sold in our own and to other stores.

We grew to three retail stores and had twenty-eight employees. We won the prestigious GKIC Retailer of the Year Award out of sixty finalists nationwide and I was often asked by many store owners to help them grow their businesses. I spoke at retail associations and market gatherings. I started a training and consulting company to help other bridal store owners and wedding professionals on how to grow their businesses. I wrote several business books and had hundreds of stores enrolled in online courses detailing aspects of selling, marketing, and the keys to managing a successful store. Store owners from around the world flew to our stores to meet with us and see how our operations were set up. It was very fulfilling to help others succeed.

In 2008, the market began shifting. Customers started buying direct from factories for less than what it took to design, import, and stock the dresses in our retail stores. Our sales plummeted. With that shift, there were many challenging times. Laying off employees and closing stores one by one was a crushing blow as we struggled to survive. My consulting clients had their own struggles with their retail stores and weren't able to pay me to consult with them. Several store owners who bought dresses from us and that our company was importing into the country charged back hundreds of thousands of dollars for dresses they had ordered so they could pay their own bills. Our merchant accounts were frozen. We were unable to pay our bills or bring in more money. We switched merchant accounts, but the dominos had begun falling. We scrambled and hired an attorney to help us deal with lawsuits from vendors and landlords. We closed the last of our stores in 2015 and ended up filing bankruptcy.

Losing everything was beyond depressing and discouraging. I had never felt so low. I felt like a failure as I struggled to provide for my wife and five children. We lost our home and most all of our material possessions. My wife became a high school history and English teacher. I ended up working in California on straight commission selling solar panels and returning to Utah when I could. In the midst of my discouragement, I applied my hungry mind to learn a new industry. I became one of the top salespeople in my regional office and was promoted to help manage a team of twenty sales reps. I helped run this office until I was offered a position managing a team of reps in Utah. I was later promoted to be the Vice President of Sales for another company.

I continued to sell solar and started a sales training organization to help solar companies train their sales teams to succeed. I helped my wife start a new business, conducted interviews, and started/edited three podcasts.

I currently work in the franchise industry helping entrepreneurs get started and succeed with proven systems and help. The process of getting back on top in new industries, being in the trenches while selling, and doing what it takes to run successful businesses has taught invaluable lessons.

Along the way, I continued to work on the outline for this book. I talked with and asked questions of business owners about what they were doing to succeed in their changing business environment. They shared similar experiences and what they had done to rise above industry challenges to succeed. I took notes on our conversations, read widely, and consumed media in many formats sifting through mountains of information to distill the most important and usable strategies to turnaround and transform businesses in a variety of different industries. I wrote what I discovered and outlined what I felt were the biggest challenges of businesses today and what could be done to overcome them.

This book is my answer to these challenges and what businesses must do to succeed today. Here are ten of the biggest challenges and problems that have caused and are causing big changes in virtually every industry:

1. *Hypercompetition.* There is an explosion of choice and every market is saturated with offerings and promotions that make it very difficult for companies to stand out in a sea of sameness. It is even more difficult for consumers to understand what they actually get when they buy something from one company over another. We'll talk about these specific challenges and how to overcome them in chapters 1, 2, and 3.

2. *Speed to market.* If you have a successful business today, it won't be long before someone else copies your idea and tries to offer what you sell for less. Financially backed entrepreneurs can scale quickly and offer similar products faster than a small, boot strapping company can. In chapter 4, I'll discuss how you can speed up your process to convince prospects to take action now so you can beat your competitors in the last steps of the sale by pre-selling prospects to buy now.

3. *Price shopping via the Internet.* When people are sold on a product and can find it with a few keystrokes online for less, there is little to no chance to build value. In chapter 5, we'll discuss how you must shift to selling experiences, instead of just products to counteract this trend.

4. *Up and down markets* cause paralysis and fear in investors and entrepreneurs. Threats of new tariffs and shifts in where and how products are manufactured causes uneasiness. Skepticism is high and confidence in sales is low. I'll talk about the best ways to build trust and value in chapters 6 and 7.

5. *People are more resistant to sales people and being sold.* Many people are hesitant to give up their personal information for fear of being contacted and being sold something (even if they are looking for it). They don't like the sales process and would rather pay more for something if they can escape dealing with a salesperson. There is a big disconnect between the prospect's process and what they seller does or wants to do. We'll address how you can push for the sale without being

pushy in chapter 8 and how you can overcome resistance and be more persuasive as a result.

6. *Distraction.* It is more difficult to focus now because of the sheer number of distractions with addictive phones and apps. There is always a shiny, new object that can easily take your focus off what you were doing. On top of that, a lot of time is spent worrying about things you can't control. That worrying takes your focus away from what can be done. When you are not focused on your overall strategy in the midst of your daily actions, it is easy to get off track and end up somewhere that you don't want to be. I'll talk about how you can avoid these distractions to stay focused on what you can control in chapter 9.

7. *Lack of leadership to deal with growing employee problems.* Employee mentality has shifted. Many have diametrically opposed ideals to their employer. Trust and loyalty are rare. Some want something for nothing. I'll talk aout how you can avoid destructive management mistakes that will stop and hinder your growth in this changing workplace in chapter 10.

8. *Huge amounts are spent on lead generation and building value in a company, yet there is a huge lack of follow-up/follow through to ensure that deals are closed.* I'll talk about how you can leverage your strengths in chapter 11.

9. *Customer expectations are higher than ever and disgruntled customers have the platform to discourage future sales by broadcasting their unhappiness or displeasure.* We'll talk about how you can navigate these frightening trends in chapters 9 and 12.

10. *Businesses weaken their market position by offering products or services that distract from the core of what is already working.* Many struggling businesses are able to get back on top by eliminating non-core items from their business. We'll talk about this principle throughout the book and finish by talking about the importance of taking action in the midst of defeats and failures.

When you consider this last challenge about seeking the new while neglecting the core business, I think about how Starbucks has navigated this challenge over the past several years. When Howard Shultz took back over the day-to-day operations of Starbucks in January of 2008, the company was in trouble. After 16 years of 5 percent growth or better, store traffic was decreasing and their sales had only gone up by one percent in the first three months of the fiscal year. Retailers such as Home Depot and Nordstroms were announcing similar drops in revenue.

One of the first decisions Schultz made was to discontinue warm breakfast sandwiches, which at the time were accounting for approximately 3% of the revenue of each store. The sandwiches were also getting in the way of their core competency as the smell of burnt cheese from the ovens overpowered the experience of the smell of their coffee. Stores had also added all kinds of products to sell that would help them increase their store numbers from quarter to quarter.

Schultz says:

"Once I walked into a store and was appalled by a proliferation of stuffed animals for sale. 'What is this?' I asked the store manager in frustration, pointing to a pile of wide-eyed cuddly toys that had absolutely nothing to do with coffee. The manager didn't blink. 'They're great for incremental sales and have a big gross margin.' This was the type of mentality that had become pervasive. And dangerous." – *Onward*, p. 90.

This is a good example of how seductive it can be to begin selling things that take you away from your core competency. If you have products that take up space that account for a very small percentage of your overall sales, but detract from your mission of being the best business in your market niche, you may need to make a decision similar to what Schultz did. He cut out what was cutting into the perceptions and experience of Starbucks. He retooled the experience to get back to his core competency (coffee, in his case).

This is something all entrepreneurs must be honest about with themselves. When my wife and I opened our first bridal business, we carried wedding invitations for a short while because I thought it added to what brides could get from us. In reality, it took time to explain what to do and the profitability on the invitations was very low compared to how much time it took to explain, write, and place the order. We cut out the invitations and threw away the numerous books we had been sent by the invitation suppliers. You may need to make a similar decision to focus on your core competency.

The ups and downs of the economy in recent years have had an interesting effect on many businesses for this reason. Business owners have had to get back to the core of what really matters. Some ignored these realities during the great recession. They really struggle or have gone out of business. Others have have gotten back to what they do best. Those who have stayed focused on their core have seen their sales rise as the economic outlook has continually improved and gotten better.

All entrepreneurs need to take more time to think and plan strategically about where their business is going. This skill is critically important to what you actually get done and where you will end up. Getting outside of the constraints of what you have always done and thought can be freeing in a lot of ways.

If you want to make a turnaround in your business or grow rapidly, you have to know what you stand for and what makes you unique from any other business in your market niche. If you are the same (or are perceived to be the same), you will never grow until you get past that hurdle. Sometimes it takes a new way of looking at things in order to get back on track to where you need to be.

One of the things that happens quite frequently in any business is that when things get tough, business owners look for a single solution that will pull them out of the difficulties they are experiencing.

Starbucks was no different when they began their turnaround. Shortly after Schultz took back over the company, they found an Italian-made beverage that was not ice cream or sorbet or a smoothie but when mixed with milk, fruit, or yogurt tasted delicious. This new product was dubbed Sorbetto and Schultz believed it was the answer to increase revenues. Unfortunately, when they finally received the product from Italy to make the drinks, they found that their margins had shrunk. On top of that, the employees didn't enjoy the process that took nearly an extra hour and a half to clean the drink machines each night. They lost enthusiasm even though they figured out how to reduce the process to 45 minutes. They ended up eliminating the product and cutting their losses.

Schultz says: "I'd brashly embraced Sorbetto as a silver bullet. But there is no such thing. Not growing our store count. Not new coffee blends. Not loyalty or value programs. Not healthier food and drinks. Yes, opportunities to transform Starbucks for profitable, sustainable growth existed everywhere, but no single move, no product, no promotion, and no individual would save the company. Our success would only be won by many. Transforming Starbucks was a complex puzzle we were trying to piece together, where everything we did contributed to the whole. We just had to focus on the right, relevant things for our partners, for our customers, for our shareholders, and for our brand." –p. 169.

This is a common attitude amongst entrepreneurs. I am often asked what the one thing is that a company needs to do in order to be successful. There is no *one* single thing that will propel a business to be successful. It is a myriad of things that work together in concert to make the business work. It is a simultaneous approach of actions instead of a step-by-step sequential process.

It is understanding and implementing great systems as I outlined in my book *The System is the Secret*. In this book, I outline the factors that are most important for making game changing moves in business, but you can't look at them independently as if they are the only single thing that will make you successful. There is no single silver bullet.

When you first start a business, you are working with customers every day. You are in the mud of the marketplace: You know what they are looking for, what you don't have, what you need and what is selling in your area of specialty better than anyone else. As your business grows, you may find that you are not working everyday with customers. This is dangerous ground because you can lose your touch with what is going on in the marketplace very quickly if you are not careful. If you do delegate this to someone else, be sure you understand what is going on in the daily details of your business.

It is much better to get into the mud of the marketplace as much as possible so you can better understand what needs to be done and what is happening with the attitudes and preferences of your prospects and existing clients. Keeping your ear low to the ground can help you anticipate where trends are moving. Acting on these observations quicker than your competitors can give you a big advantage.

The passion behind what you do everyday must never be diminished by the challenging experiences you go through and endure as an entrepreneur. Rather, you must use those challenging moments to reignite and redefine what makes your business great. What you do daily must put more meaning into the lives of those on your team and the clients you serve each day.

The biggest game changer in business has been to build a business around a new concept or idea. Throughout history, we've seen visionary leaders who transformed their industries and saw explosive growth in their businesses as a result. Here are a few notable ones:

- Henry Ford and the invention of the assembly line

- Ray Kroc and the revolution of the fast food industry via

franchising

- Jeff Bezos and the revolution of buying things online instead of in traditional retail environments. This affects your business in more ways than one even if you are not a retailer.

- Larry Page and Sergey Brin who completely changed the game of advertising and marketing with Google.

- Mark Zuckerberg and the revolution of changing the way we interact with one another socially through Facebook and Instagram which virtually connects everyone who has access to a computer and the Internet.

- Steve Jobs who changed the way we buy and consume media online with the iPod, iPhone, and iPad.

All of these business leaders started with a new concept or idea. They stood up for something in order to stand out. I think this rule should permeate every aspect of your business as well. Your systems, setup, organization, and everything you do should set you apart from your competitors. Don't try to be a copycat business. It will never create the enthusiasm you will create simply by being different, unique, and new. You want to get customers talking about how your business _is_ the place all prospects who need your product or service must visit.

The little things make a huge difference in how well you run your business <u>and</u> how you are perceived in the marketplace. Trying to be all things to all people is a big mistake. It is much better to specialize in a few things and then seek to build more and more value around those few things.

Barry Schwartz, a Swarthmore professor and author of _The Paradox of Choice_ says: "Customers may think they want variety, but in reality too many options can lead to shopping paralysis. People are worried they'll regret the choice they made....People don't want to feel they made a mistake.' Studies have found that buyers enjoy purchases more if they know the pool of options isn't quite so large. Trader Joe's organic creamy unsalted peanut butter will be more satisfying if there are only nine other peanut butters a shopper might have purchased instead of 39. Having a wide selection may help get customers in the store, but it won't increase the chances they'll buy.... 'It takes them out of the purchasing process and puts them into a decision-making process,' explains Stew Leonard Jr., CEO of grocer Stew Leonard's, which also subscribes to the 'less is more' mantra."—*Fortune*, Volume 162, Number 4, p. 92, 94.

It is difficult to stand out when you have the same product offerings as everyone else. Be different and unique. Having more often confuses the prospect instead of helping him or her get out of a decision making process and into the buying process.

What can you do to simplify the choice so that your prospects aren't overwhelmed? The concept is simple. The execution is more difficult. Simply put, you've got to help them make a choice instead of being overwhelmed with all of your options.

The way in which you choose to set up your buying options is your choice. Focus on simplicity and the experience the prospect will have that will make them want to talk with their friends and family about you. If you do this, you will be much farther ahead of a business owner who hasn't thought in depth about how to simplify the process on the other side of the transaction. Being unique and standing out will help you spread the word about your business much faster than trying to blend in with every other competitor you have.

What is unique about your business?

What is the one thing that you have that no one else does?

The truth is that the only thing that you have that is truly unique is yourself. Your competitors can't copy you. You are one of a kind. You will gain a unique and unfair advantage when you build your brand around yourself and promote that distinct difference to those in your market niche.

What do your customers associate with you?

What are you doing to stand out?

What is unique about you that will help you stand out and that your prospects won't be able to help but notice? That is where you should put your focus if you want to be truly unique and succeed today.

Competitors who copy you is a big challenge for any business today. Business owners get extremely frustrated when competitors try to copy instead of building their own unique advantage. They try to gain business by offering a better price or overall value in an attempt to persuade prospects to buy from them instead of from you.

Many businesses have a very low cost barrier to entry. Someone can start with low start-up costs that can be paid for with a few gigs. The highest paid entrepreneurs I know promote their difference by the experience they create with their customers, not the product they deliver. This is an important distinction. It is much harder to duplicate an experience than it is to duplicate a product. This is why your focus should be on selling experiences, not products

What is your distinct advantage in your marketplace?

Do your prospects and customers know that you have that advantage?

Doing what everyone else is doing will never allow you to build a sustainable, long term advantage. You must have at least one (and preferably more) big difference between you and anyone else in your marketplace that is distinguishable to your prospects and customers. Without this, you will be unable to sustain the growth of your business for a long period of time.

The biggest challenge you will encounter when selling is your prospect's status quo. If a prospect is already happy with their life without your product or service, you have to lower resistance before you can get someone to make a commitment of any kind now.

How are you dealing with your prospect's skepticism and fear? If you can address these issues while simultaneously pointing out your advantage, your likelihood of getting the sale goes up dramatically. Prospects make decisions because of the psychological trigger of contrast. If they can see a distinct advantage to doing business with you, they will. If they can't, they will continue to look until they find the best deal for them.

If you're dealing with customers who are seemingly happy with their current status, you'll benefit greatly from the practical strategies I'll share with you throughout this book.

The only thing scarcer than a business with a truly unique advantage is a business owner who *implements* what they know they must do to have such an advantage. If you don't already know your advantage, now is the time. You aren't going to get ahead being a copycat business. You'll only grow when you have a distinct and sustainable advantage that helps you stand out and rise above the rest of the pack.

It is not about what you're going to do. It is about what you're doing. Execution or implementation is the difference between an average or mediocre income in any business and an extraordinary one. If you want to accelerate the rate of referrals you get, be sure you deliver on what you say you will as a bare minimum. That allows you to keep the business you already have. To get the approval and recommendation of others, you must take it up a notch and wow your customers. Most game changers in any industry can be identified by this point. They didn't just come up with an advantage, they spread the word to increase the speed of utilization.

Are you implementing what you must do to stand out in a crowded marketplace?

If not, when will you start?

You have to understand what your competitor's strengths and

weaknesses are so you can exploit those to bring prospects over to do business with you. Remember, you aren't the only one who is trying to take market share away from the leader in your market. The more focused you can be on the weaknesses of your biggest competitor and look to exploit those areas, the more successful you will be in beating them. You've got to step out to stand out.

What is your value offering?

Is it your ability to provide benefits to prospects far beyond just the product or service you offer?

What do your customers value about working with you the most?

What are you doing to provide more of that to them?

In this book, I'll show you specific ways to build your value so that you can sell at higher prices and have your prospects love you for it.

Your advantage in business will likely change over the years as your competitors attack what you have defined. If you can't ride your sustainable advantage for several years, it makes it challenging for you to create the momentum necessary to get to the wave of the next unfair advantage. You have to continually reinvent yourself in any business. You are only as good as what you did last. Hanging onto the past for too long can be fatal.

Failing to do communicate your advantage is a one way ticket to mediocrity and a slow death at the hands of competitors who get this point and make it happen. If there is a gap between what the market wants and what you can actually provide, you won't be able to reach larger sales revenues or create the momentum necessary to make that a reality.

Apple produces amazing products, but if they can't keep up with the demand (as was evident upon the initial launch of the iPhone) because of the inability of the manufacturers to make the product, they will lose market share if another competitor can come into that space and offer a similar product faster. Apple has learned their lesson and are much more strategic and precise as they launch new products.

A great idea or a great product isn't enough today. Competitors can knock off your best ideas quickly, and if you can't deliver to the marketplace rapidly, you will lose. Being able to rapidly expand and shift your marketing focus and direction with a hot new product or idea is critical to succeeding in business today. I'll share secrets to accelerating trust and connecting with customers throughout this book so they'll rush to buy from you.

One of the reasons why Apple continually reinvents itself and comes out with a new version of its products every six months to year is because it is very difficult for the competition to catch up if the leader is always changing the game and increasing their advantage. There are so many things you have to always be looking at because things change quickly in business.

For example, what would happen if your biggest competitor announced a similar advantage that you have developed? What would you do to compete against this new information?

Here is a good way to think about this: What would you do if you owned a software company and a reporter called you and told you that Microsoft just announced a product that was virtually the same as yours? Thinking about how you would respond gives you a powerful, sustainable advantage that will help you stay ahead of the game. Ignoring these types of scenarios will cause you to wake up in the future shocked, surprised, and dismayed as you learned that some of your biggest customers went somewhere else.

What are you doing to be a moving target?

What are you doing to stay in the lead?

You can't lead if you are always responding to what your competitors are doing. You want to do things that make them have to respond to you. It is naïve to think that your advantage in your business niche will stay that way. Competitors will attack your advantage and may even overtake it with their own twist on it.

As the leader, you have to be the one who sees what is coming and looks to the future to adapt and change. Only you can create the advantages that will propel your business forward. Waiting for others to lead the way (until it is safe) is a sure way to lose market share and begin the slow decline towards decay and death.

I talk in depth about what you can do to create your vision and your long-term plan in my book *The System is the Secret*.

You want a lot of customers, but the way you get there seems counterintuitive to many people. To have a truly unique advantage and be able to aggressively promote it and defend it, it needs to be on as narrow of a front as possible.

Advertising expert Peter Montoya says: "Specialization is the single most important personal branding strategy in your arsenal. You simply cannot build an effective brand without being a specialist....Specializing lets you pick a few lucrative, in-demand areas of your business and build your brand around them. Specialization offers many important benefits to any business." – *There's Always a Way*, p. 111.

An important part of successful retailer Trader Joe's strategy is specialization. Here is what reporter Beth Kowitt says about how they leverage this strategy at their store. She says:

"Typical grocery stores can carry 50,000 stock-keeping units, or SKUs; Trader Joe's sells about 4,000 SKUs, and about 80% of the stock bears the Trader Joe's brand. The result: Its stores sell an estimated $1,750 in merchandise per square foot, more than double Whole Foods. The company has no debt and funds all growth from its own coffers."

She then makes this observation which I think is at the heart of being unique and standing out. She says:

"A closer look at its selection of items underscores the brilliance of [founder Joe] Coulombe's limited selection, high turnover model. Take peanut butter. Trader Joe's sells 10 varieties. That might sound like a lot, but most supermarkets sell about 40 SKUs. For simplicity's sake, say both a typical supermarket and a Trader Joe's sell 40 jars a week. Trader Joe's would sell an average of four of each type, while the supermarket might sell only one. With the greater turnover on a smaller number of items, Trader Joe's can buy large quantities and secure deep discounts. And it makes the whole business—from stocking shelves to checking out customers—much simpler."— *Fortune*, Volume 162, Number 4, p. 92.

There is a great lesson here that I hope you haven't missed. If you have fewer items (and have truly specialized), you will know what is selling best and can bring more of those items in to sell through. This is also a very important point of profitability. Find out what the best sellers are and promote those more in order to maximize your sales and productivity.

Throughout this book, I'll show you how to build a unique and sustainable advantage that will help you get to the next level. Here are four great questions to identify and exploit your competitive advantage:

1) Where else can your prospects get that is exactly like what you sell?

2) How easily can your "advantage" be copied?

3) How hard is it to maneuver and change to gain another advantage in your market area?

4) Do you respond quickly or more slowly to change?

In business today, the game board is shifting underneath the pieces you're moving. Pieces no longer move and have the same effect they once did. Competitors and market conditions are not predictable. When change happens, some entrepreneurs panic and adopt a move in all directions approach to discover what will work.

If those on your team see that you are out of your depth and that you're losing the game you *were* playing, they'll lose confidence in you and your strategy. Money will dry up from investors, employees will sluggishly go through the motions. No one likes to play on a team where they are getting beat so bad that morale is hurting. Yet, if they believe in their coach and have a few new plays up their sleeves, they'll line up again and again at the line as their small wins turn into bigger wins and they move forward toward the goal line.

It is time for you to step up as a leader and start calling better plays. It is time for you to understand how the rules to the game have changed. It is time for you to focus on what really matters and get back on track, marching forward with resolute determination to the goal in front of you.

On the pages that follow, I'll outline a plan you can utilize in your business and share what I would encourage you to do if we were sitting down to discuss how to turnaround or transform your business face-to-face. It's your time to make this your best year ever. To start, I would like you to answer a few questions to assess where you are now. If you want to create a road map and outline where you are going, it is critical to understand where you are starting from. On the pages that follow I have put together a 10 area, 101 question self-assessment quiz that can help you see where your business is at right now. It doesn't matter whether you are a one person operation or have a team with thousands of sales reps. Answer each of the questions honestly. At the end of the exercise, I'll show you how you can score it to see what grade your business currently has. After reading the book and implementing what I'll teach you, you should take the test again to see how you are doing at implementing these fundamentals into your business. Let's get started.

BUSINESS CHECKUP EXERCISE
MISSION/VISION/PURPOSE

Mission / Vision /Purpose	Oops	Sometimes	Mostly	Always
1. We have our finger on the pulse of our market niche at all times.				
2. We are moving in a clear direction and every strategic decision supports that direction.				
3. We have a good knowledge of our competition and their practices and how we stand out from them.				
4. Our business is going in the direction that we originally intended and /or in a direction we are happy with.				
5. Vision, mission, goals, and strategies are well known and acted upon by all in our organization.				
6. Everyone owns their part and knows what to do to make goals happen. There is clarity and consistency in our daily work.				
7. I am proud of myself as both a business owner and as a person.				
8. I am happy with the amount of money I make.				
9. I do not stay awake at night worrying about my business.				
10. The prospects we talk with about our product/service have a positive perception about our mission and purpose.				

"Everyone has his own specific vocation or mission in life; everyone must carry out a concrete assignment that demands fulfillment. Therein he cannot be replaced, nor can his life be repeated, thus, everyone's task is unique as his specific opportunity to implement it."—Viktor E. Frankl

SALES

Sales	Oops	Sometimes	Mostly	Always
1. We analyze our mistakes when sales don't happen and learn from them.				
2. Sales information is readily available and closely monitored.				
3. We track our appointments with qualified prospects, our close ratios, and the number of transactions continuously. If our consultants aren't where they need to be (closing percentages), we help them become better or replace them quickly.				
4. Every sales consultant knows and achieves their individual sales goals per day, week, and month.				
5. Every member of the team recognizes and works to help achieve daily, weekly, and monthly team sales goals.				
6. Our sales consultants follow a system that allows them to stay in touch with prospects in the marketing funnel if they don't buy on the first visit.				
7. Consistent sales training is offered to every member of our team and it is implemented.				
8. Our sales consultants have a system in place to prioritize the prospects they are working with.				
9. Our sales consultants are professional, have the experience necessary to excel at selling, and don't make false claims or promises to make the sale.				
10. We evaluate and make changes to our sales training based on changes in the marketplace.				

MARKETING

	Marketing	Oops	Sometimes	Mostly	Always
1.	We have a complete marketing plan for the year.				
2.	We adhere to the marketing plan throughout the year (with some adjustments).				
3.	Our marketing plan is a result of input and involvement from key managers and team members.				
4.	Our marketing plan guides the actions of our team to achieve our financial goals and objectives.				
5.	We have a contingency plan to adjust for external changes that can affect our business (what our competitors do, etc.).				
6.	Our marketing plan contains specific and measurable objectives for each sales event to schedule appointments.				
7.	We track the effectiveness of our marketing collateral, promotions, and all lead generation activities to ensure that advertising expenditures are wisely made.				
8.	We only advertise when we can test and measure results.				
9.	Our marketing pieces are evaluated carefully before they are sent out to ensure that they will grab / hold the attention of our prospective prospects and cause them to act.				
10.	There is accountability for implementation of our marketing plan.				
11.	We have a system that helps us schedule qualified appointments.				

LEADERSHIP

Leadership	Oops	Sometimes	Mostly	Always
1. Our executive team, leaders of operations, and sales leaders all have strong leadership capabilities.				
2. We have a strong culture of developing leaders around us at our business.				
3. We provide learning resources to our team members to help them develop their leadership qualities.				
4. I continuously offer hope and encouragement in our team's ability to reach our business goals.				
5. I set and enforce high standards at our business.				
6. I reward production and results, not laziness and mediocrity.				
7. I foster an environment where rotten attitudes, selfishness, and gossip cannot take root and spread.				
8. I stop investing in team members who aren't growing.				
9. I create new opportunities that motivate and excite each member of our team based on their motivational style.				
10. I evaluate our team members often and replace 'C' players with 'A' players.				

"Fuel gets your rocket ship moving, but people determine where it goes."

—Michael Stelzner, *Launch: How to Quickly Propel Your Business Beyond the Competition*

"The best executive is the one who has sense enough to pick good people to do what he wants done, and self-restraint to keep from meddling with them while they do it."

—Theodore Roosevelt

TEAM

	Team	Oops	Sometimes	Mostly	Always
1.	There is a synergy among all of the members of our team.				
2.	Everyone is listened to and encouraged to speak up and make recommendations.				
3.	The team always remains positive and does not tolerate negativism among its members.				
4.	The team sees change as positive and is always ready for challenges.				
5.	My team members are accountable and never make excuses for performance.				
6.	Deadlines are taken seriously and managed by the team leaders.				
7.	Every member of the team enjoys their work.				
8.	Every member of the team does complete work (nothing is redone or substandard).				
9.	Team communication is effective and duplication of work does not occur.				

CUSTOMER SERVICE

	Customer Service	Oops	Sometimes	Mostly	Always
1.	We follow an overall team approach to create loyal customers who refer us to their friends.				
2.	We evaluate the timeliness and efficiency with which we handle customer complaints and make adjustments.				

	Oops	Sometimes	Mostly	Always
3. Important business performance information from all of our systems is readily available and easy to retrieve.				
4. Our systems give me the information I need to make important decisions about our business.				
5. Our systems are reliable and there are minimal customer service issues as a result.				
6. Our critical computer data is properly backed up and safe and can be recovered quickly in the event of a disaster.				
7. Our systems are in place and each member of our team adheres to them.				
8. We have an ongoing system to regularly communicate our orders with our suppliers.				

OPERATIONS

Operations	Oops	Sometimes	Mostly	Always
1. No one area of our business is dependent upon a single supplier.				
2. Our suppliers and vendors are true partners to our business.				
3. Our internal financial statements are prepared without errors.				
4. Our financial statements help relationships with our lenders.				
5. I get accurate projections about taxes. I plan and pay them on time.				
6. I look at our financial statements monthly, at the very minimum. With the information I gather from those statements, I'm able to make good short and long-term decisions.				

7. Profit margins have increased over the last three years.				
8. Suppliers and service provider's invoices are routinely paid on time.				
9. Our profits are measured regularly. Profits will increase this year by no less than ___%.				
10. The ratio of the company's total debt to equity has decreased over the last year.				
11. We have the cash flow to achieve our objectives.				

FINANCIAL AND INVENTORY MANAGEMENT

Financial and Inventory Management	Oops	Sometimes	Mostly	Always
1. I have a good control over our inventory at all times.				
2. Each category of what we sell at our business is profitable.				
3. We systematically eliminate unprofitable inventory items from our business.				
4. Through reports and surveys, I have an accurate pulse on what is selling and what is not at all times.				
5. I am aware of our best selling products and purchase inventory accordingly.				

"The achievement of financial independence will require a tremendous number of small efforts on your part. To begin the process of accumulation, you must be disciplined and persistent. You must keep at it for a long, long time. Initially, you will see very little change or difference, but gradually, your efforts will begin to bear fruit. You will begin to pull ahead of your peers. Your finances will improve and your debts will disappear. Your bank account will grow and your whole life will improve."

—Brian Tracy, *The 100 Absolutely Unbreakable Laws of Business Success*, p. 180.

	Oops	Sometimes	Mostly	Always
6. Inventory is closely monitored to ensure maximum turnover and minimal financial outlay.				
7. Terms are negotiated with all suppliers including early payment discounts.				
8. Debt service as a percentage of gross profit decreased last year.				
9. I have and utilize a budget when making inventory expenditures.				
10. I stay on top of the hottest trends in our market niche and make sure they are available to sell.				

How to Score Your Business Checkup

	Oops	Sometimes	Mostly	Always
Scoring	0	1	2	3
Your Totals				

TOTAL SCORE: _____

Total up points from each category

303 highest possible score

Now that you've taken this quiz, you've probably seen several areas you need to work on to improve. I would encourage you to take one category per month and work on that in your business so that you can focus on improving your skill in each one of these areas.

Successful business owners think about **what they want and how to get it.** They analyze current performance and look to the future. They refuse to consider the possibility of failure. They say things like:

- We're going to increase our sales 15% this month over what we did last year.

- I have the best team in our industry and our sales are improving every day.

- We are the most profitable business in our area.

- I set two appointments every day, run two appointments every day, and close new sales every week that help us hit our goals.

On the other hand, pessimists think about **what they don't want and why they've got it.** They think about people they don't like, problems they're having and who is to blame for their situation. They are heard saying things such as:

- My leads aren't very good. All of the decision makers are never together at my appointments so they can't decide now.

- Our team isn't selling.

- I can't seem to get the sale, but luckily they were there for the appointment.

- Our competitors seem to be getting all of the sales. Their cost and price is lower than ours.

- We're doing worse than we were last year.

- Everyone seems to be making more money than me.

- I seem to be working harder than ever before with little results.

What do you think about most of the time? Do you think about the future? **or** Do you think about what has already happened in the past?

Instead of beating yourself up about the past, write your own future. Think about a clear, exciting future vision of what is possible and make it happen. This book is designed to help you make changes to succeed so the goals you've set for your business can become a reality.

CHAPTER 1

OUT-MARKET AND OUT-SMART YOUR COMPETITORS

"If the rate of change outside your business is greater than the rate of change inside your business, you're out of business." –Cameron Herold

C ompetition today is more ruthless than it has ever been. Years ago, prospects used to go to a few companies in their own town to find the perfect product or service they needed. Now, there is an explosion of choice with the proliferation of Internet vendors, big box retailers, and other dominant players who are marketing to your prospects all around the world. With all of these choices, prospects today are overwhelmed. They are literally bombarded with choices for the product or service you offer.

Unfortunately, choice can limit a prospect's motivation to buy since one usually feels like they need to see more or all of the options before the best decision can be made. As Swarthmore College sociology professor Barry Schwartz wrote in *The Paradox of Choice*: "People are so overwhelmed with choice that it tends to paralyze them. Too much choice makes people more likely to defer decisions. It raises expectations and makes people blame themselves for choosing poorly. You don't expect much if there are only two pairs of jeans to choose from. If there are hundreds, you expect one to be perfect."

Because of this explosion of choice, you have to be smarter about how you market and position yourself against your competitors. The reality is that many discounters, Internet vendors, and local competitors are cutting into your sales. To combat these competitors, you have to think differently about your business and implement new tactics and strategies to come out on top. To successfully grow your business in today's new economy you will have to outsmart, outmaneuver, and outsell your competitors. In this chapter, I'll share ten ways you can do just that.

1. Learn from other competitive battles. Study the principles of warfare to understand how to define your difference to the prospects in your market niche and beat your competition.

If you're going to be successful in the battle to make and keep a sale, it is a good idea to understand warfare. Karl von Clausewitz was a great philosopher of war and a Prussian general. He wrote a book in 1832 that outlines the strategic principles behind all successful wars. It is titled simply, *On War*. It is still studied today at West Point. Marketing experts Jack Trout and Al Ries say that this book is the best book on marketing ever written. They say:

"War has changed dramatically since *On War* was first published. The tank, the airplane, the machine gun, and a host of new weapons have been introduced. Yet the ideas of Clausewitz are still as relevant today as they were in the nineteen century. Weapons change, but warfare itself, as Clausewitz was first to recognize, is based on two immutable characteristics: strategy and tactics. His clear exposition of the strategic principles of war are likely to guide military commanders well into the twenty-first century." –*Marketing Warfare*, pp. 1-2.

In order to gain a competitive advantage in your business, you need to understand the basic strategies and tactics of war. This means that you view and do battle with different competitors in different ways. To help you better understand how you should do battle with your competitors (depending on where you fall in the marketplace), consider the four ways to fight a marketing war before deciding which type of warfare you should engage in. The four types of war are:

1) **Defensive warfare** – this is a game for the marketing leader. Who is the leader in your market niche? If you are the leader of a specific niche in your industry, you want to fight this war to hold onto the leadership advantage you have gained. If you are not the leader, you will want to consider one of the other options until you become the leader.

Your business doesn't create its leadership in the market. Instead, those that buy from you do. The perception of customers (and who they perceive is the leader) in your market is the reality, not what you think. Many marketing wars are lost on this battlefield, because entrepreneurs have the perception that they are the leader when the customers in that market category don't have that same belief or perception.

Apple, Gilette, and Intel are masters maintaining their leadership by attacking themselves. They invent or create a new product that replaces an old one. If you want to maintain your market position, you have to be willing to constantly reinvent yourself so that your competitors can't catch up. As the saying goes, "a moving target is much harder to hit than a stationary one." How can you continually reinvent your best selling products instead of solely relying on what has historically been selling? If you aren't continuously attacking yourself, your competitors will and they will become the market leaders.

A great example of this principle in action is Gilette and their Mach 3 razor. Shortly after the Mach 3 was introduced, Gillette's primary competitor, Schick introduced the Quattro (the first four bladed razor). Gillette blocked this move by introducing a five bladed razor (Fusion) in 2006 which made the four bladed razor that Schick introduced irrelevant for a time. Schick eventually released their own five bladed razor called Hydro four years later. Was their response too little, too late? Schick is currently second to Gillette in razors globally, but is currently the top razor in Japan. Sometimes, in warfare, it is wise to pick the battles in which you fight.

Most business owners (with some exceptions in specific niches) can't take on the dominant business in their market head to head. The amount of money they spend on advertising and marketing is staggering compared to the advertising budget of the average business owner. Instead, you have to employ different marketing tactics and strategies. Which one and how you should use it depends on your position in the marketplace.

2) **Offensive warfare** – this is a game for the #2 or #3 competitor in a given market niche. This is a company strong enough to mount a sustained offensive against the leader. These companies should mount and sustain an offensive attack over a period of team if they want to succeed.

In order to be successful at taking market share away from the leader of the marketplace, you have to look for areas where they are weak and then seek to dominate those areas. The more focused you can be on the weaknesses of your biggest competitor and look to exploit those areas, the more successful you will be in beating them. In war, the leader of the offensive attack is always looking for weaknesses in the defense. Then, they focus their objective on beating the enemy there as they seek a way to break their line of defense.

Another way to launch a successful attack on a competitor is to look at what a competitor does well (but doesn't recognize or promote) and attack at that area to get a competitive advantage. Avis is a classic example of the #2 competitor who has used Hertz's strength to wage war. Avis ads used to say, "Rent from Avis. The line at our counter is shorter." They were also very successful using the campaign, "We're #2. We try harder." That worked well until Hertz started saying, "For years, Avis has bragged about being #2. Then, they identified their flaws and weaknesses.

Look for your competitor's weaknesses and point out why your option is superior. Every competitor has an Achilles heel which can lead to their downfall and loss of market share.

Entrepreneurs make a big mistake in competing against big competitors by trying to do all of the same things that the market leaders do. They try to compete on all fronts and as a result they lose more since as Clasewitz says, "the odds favor the defender." Instead, you want to use the principle of force and attack at a single weakness or unrecognized strength, to gain the competitive edge. If you study marketing, you'll notice that the most successful companies have focused their battle on a very narrow front. They aren't trying to be all things to all people. They are specialists in a specific area and then beat their competitors in specific niches.

3) **Flanking warfare** – this is the game for smaller competitors who go around a major competitor instead of attacking them head on. Probably the greatest example of flanking in modern business is how Apple beat Sony with the iPod. Instead of going head to head with Sony, they created iTunes, an innovative way for people to digitize their music and play on their .mp3 player, the iPod. This sleek gadget took the music industry by storm and surprised Sony.

Flanking is different than offensive marketing into an occupied space because there is no established market for the new product or service. Carrying a product that no one else has is an example of a flanking move (especially if it meets the needs of customers that no one else is servicing and if no one else can really provide the product). However, it can be risky as the leader can quickly adapt and offer the product more competitively (more options, better pricing, better fianancing, etc).

The most successful flanking attacks are ones that are totally unexpected. The more surprise that there is, the harder it is for the leader to react and recover. Surprise in today's marketplace is difficult to achieve because many marketers expose their strategy to their competitors too early. Apple is a great example of a company you should study for how they keep new announcements under wraps until they are ready to launch them. Then, they use curiosity and excitement to get people talking about the products once they are already available in the store or the same day they are available to order. Apple's launch of the iPhone and the iPad (and their subsequent upgrades) are good examples of how Apple has kept new products secret until they were ready to be launched. Then, the launch happens in a synchronized way so that is all consumers can talk about. When everyone is talking about your product, it makes it very difficult for a competitor to respond.

Most flanking attacks fail because there is not enough thought and resources put into how the attack will be sustained over time. For example, if you choose to get into a specific market segment and no one in your area was doing this as well, would you slack off once you made your first sale, or would you have the ability to continue until you became a dominant player in the marketplace? Big gains in market share can be obtained through flanking, though it is difficult to successfully execute, since your competitors will likely respond to what you do. It is best to have a well thought out plan to surprise, beat, and sustain your competitive advantage over time.

4) **Guerilla warfare** – For the most part, this is where independent businesses have to focus their marketing efforts to successfully beat the market leaders. Most small businesses have much smaller budgets to advertise with so they have to get in and get out and make the biggest impact. The best way to do this is to utilize a guerilla approach. A guerilla seeks to reduce the size of the battlefield in order to make themselves appear bigger than they really are. This analogy can best be conveyed by looking at the wars in Iraq and Afghanistan. Small guerrilla forces or insurgents competed with a large military force by

setting up roadside bombs that derailed the military's progress in those areas. You can operate like a guerilla force against large competitors by concentrating on a niche or market segment that you can defend against those market leaders.

What small area or market niche can you best defend in the minds of prospects and customers in your area? You can specialize in areas big competitors may not think is a very important specialty. Your specialization can help you build a powerful brand and may even become your core business.

The key point here is to have everyone at every level in your business focused on selling. Big companies and organizations get mired down in bureaucracy quickly. Instead, be focused on selling all of the time. Regardless of how successful your business is or becomes, always have the attitude of thinking big and acting small as Jason Jennings points out in his excellent book *Think Big, Act Small*. Never lose touch of what is going through the prospect's mind and what is happening in the marketplace.

As a small business, you can change and make adjustments to product lines and offerings simply by making the decision and making the change. This is not really possible in large companies where many people are involved and it takes a lot more time to make a change.

You can also jump into a market if you see a need that a big competitor is not meeting. A guerilla can never forget what helped them achieve success in the first place. Southwest Airlines is a good example of a guerilla approach as this is how they grew their business when they started. They have consistently focused on growing their business with a no frills strategy.

Think carefully about your long term strategy with regard to how you will fight with your entrenched competitors in certain market segments. Look for openings where you can come in and redefine the marketplace. Being a 'me-too' company that has what everyone else has severely limits your ability to stand out in the marketplace. When you look at other businesses through the paradigm of war, you better understand why some companies are gaining ground in their marketing and why some are losing the battle.

When you really understand how you are perceived in the marketplace, you can build a successful marketing strategy around the tactics that will help you get where you want to be. If you have your eyes on dominating your market, you need to understand what type of marketing approach you will utilize to succeed. Then, you can put together an unbeatable combination which prospects and customers will respond to and that your competitors will have to react to. Continually ask yourself this question: Are my competitors reacting to me or am I reacting to them? The answer will tell you a lot about what strategy you are really employing.

2. Know your competitors and what they are doing.

The truth is that if you don't know what your competitors are up to it is awfully difficult for you to beat them. It is critical to know how each one of your competitors is perceived in the marketplace, what they are doing, and if possible a little about where they are heading. Such information will only come from some reconnaissance activities that will require some time and effort on your part. Ignoring competitors (especially those that you don't feel pose much of a threat) is a sure way to find yourself being passed up by more aggressive marketing campaigns and approaches. For example, Blockbuster ignored Redbox and Netflix and no longer exists.

Don't allow yourself to become arrogant about your competitors. Always be respectful of them and watchful of what they are doing. They could try to flank you at any moment. Remember, arrogance is always the first step to a downfall. Paul Allaire, past president of Xerox once made this statement: "We were fairly arrogant, until we realized the Japanese were selling quality products for what it cost us to make them."

All entrepreneurs have experienced the challenges that come from aggressive competitors who have slashed prices to get the sale. Stay on top of what is going on in your market, what customers are seeing, and how you will change your marketing focus so that you don't have compete solely on price.

Sam Walton, the founder of Wal-Mart, was constantly learning from his competitors as he built his business. In his book, *Made in America*, he wrote a chapter entitled "Meeting the Competition." I would highly recommend that you read this book and particularly that chapter. Walton would frequently go to Kmart stores with a tape recorder and ask questions to their employees. This was back when Kmart had five hundred stores while Wal-Mart only had sixty stores. He was a student of his successful competitors and you should be as well. Today, Kmart is struggling to survive while Wal-Mart has flourished and is quite successful. Never become arrogant. Always remain humble and learn from what your competitors are doing.

Sam Walton said this about how competition improved Wal-Mart and why ignoring competitors is not a good idea:

"Our competitors have honed and sharpened us to an edge we wouldn't have without them. We wouldn't be nearly as good as we are today without Kmart, and I think they would admit we've made them a better retailer. One reason Sears fell so far off the pace is that they wouldn't admit for the longest time that Wal-Mart and Kmart were their real competitors. They ignored both of us, and we blew right by them." – *Made in America*, p. 190.

Knowing what your competition is doing and learning from other companies in other industries *will* make you a better competitor. As Bud Walton says in *Made in America*:

"Competition is very definitely what made Wal-Mart from the very beginning. There's not an individual in these whole United States who has been in more retail stores—all types of retail stores too, not just discount stores—than Sam Walton. Make that all over the world. He's been in stores in Australia and South America, Europe and Asia, and South Africa. His mind is just so inquisitive when it comes to this business. And there may not be anything he enjoys more than going into a competitor's store trying to learn something from it."--p. 190.

When was the last time you visited another business (not in your industry) and thought about how you could implement what you found?

What are you doing to constantly be learning about what works to use in your own business?

Sun Tzu, an ancient Chinese general made this statement in *The Art of War*:

"Know the enemy and know yourself; in a hundred battles you will never be in peril. When you are ignorant of the enemy but know yourself, your chances of winning or losing are equal. If ignorant both of your enemy and of yourself, you are certain in every battle to be in peril."

Brian Tracy says: "Your goal is to win customers in a competitive market. Your goal is to be superior to your competitors. Your goal is to achieve victory against whatever odds you are facing. This means that you must continually examine and re-examine every part of your competitive posture continually looking for ways to achieve superiority relative to your competitors."—*Victory*, p. 115.

Be inquisitive. Learn what your competitors know and what they are doing. Knowing your competitors will help you outmaneuver and outmarket them to the prospects and customers you want to attract into your business.

3. Know your prospects /customers better and know what they are looking for.

If you are not selling every day and in front of what customers are asking for, it can be easy to lose touch with what is going on in your market. By being there and listening, you are able to determine what prospects are asking for and what your competitors have and don't have. As the old saying goes: "Listening is the way to gain wisdom because everything you say you already know."

Another challenge that can cause your competitors to pass you by is to trust more in your own instincts than in what prospects are asking for. When you've been in your business for a while, it can be easy to think more of your opinion than you do of the opinions of customers who buy from you every day.

You can beat this tendency by always being on your toes. When you follow up with prospects and they say they say they made their purchase somewhere else, find out where and the reason why. Find out if you had something similar or if it was a type of product or service that you don't even offer. By continually interacting with your customers, you'll have a much better sense of what you should be offering in the future.

Norman Brinker, the late Chairman of Chili's Restaurant (one of the nation's five best-run food service chains according to *Restaurants and Institutions* magazine), says that he spen[t] time each month listening to both employees and customers. As a result, almost 80 percent of the Chili's menu came from suggestions.

When you are in tune with what your customers want, you will always have a competitive edge over a competitor who trusts in their gut instinct. Stay close to your customers and you'll always have this edge.

4. Reposition your competition to prospects and customers in your market niche.

Today, the proliferation of choice and competition has caused many products to become commoditized. You can combat this by repositioning your product in the mind of your prospects. A great example of the power of repositioning a category is that of Löwenbräu beer. Brian Tracy tells this story in his book *Victory*. He says:

> "Many years ago, the makers of the German beer Löwenbräu tried
> to break into the U.S. market by competing against American
> beers. But no matter how much or how clever the advertising, the
> sales of Löwenbräu remained low. Then one day, a copywriter for
> the advertising agency came up with an idea. Why not reposition
> the beer, choose a different competitor, and change the entire
> strategy of the marketing campaign. The next month, the first new
> advertisements for Löwenbräu appeared. They said, 'When you
> run out of Champagne, order Löwenbräu.' The sales of Löwenbräu
> took off from that day forward and Löwenbräu has been a top
> selling imported beer in the United States ever since. By changing
> the focus and defining Löwenbräu as a drink that has the same
> status as Champagne rather than as a competitor with lower-
> priced American beers, they created a multi-million dollar market
> overnight." –*Victory*, pp. 106-107.

Unfortunately, most businesses try to reposition what they are selling by
being at a lower price. I really like Jack Trout's advice on this principle in
his book *Repositioning*. He says:

> "Trying to reposition the competition as being more expensive
> usually is not a very good strategy to pursue. Price is often the
> enemy of differentiation. By definition, being different should be
> worth something. It's the reason that supports the case for paying a
> little more for a product or service, or at least the same amount.

> But when price becomes the focus of a message or a company's
> marketing activities, you are beginning to undermine your chances
> to be perceived as being unique. What you're doing is making price
> the main consideration in picking you over your competition. That's
> not a healthy way to go.

> Few companies find happiness with this approach, for the simple
> reason that every one of your competitors has access to a pencil.

And with it, each of them can mark down its prices any time it wants to. And there goes your advantage."—*Repositioning*, pp. 39-40.

Consider the difference between a $0.50 glass of lemonade and $5.00 glass of lemonade. Here are four ways that you can create demand for a lemonade stand (so you can charge more):

1) Change the place where you serve your lemonade. Depending on your location, you can charge more. You pay more at Disneyland for a drink of lemonade than you do at the gas station or if you make it yourself. If you developed a lemonade delivery business based on paying attention to when your neighbors are out working in their yard, you or your kids could deliver lemonade to them *when* they are thirsty. If you make it convenient for them, when they want refreshment the most, they are more likely to buy. You are more likely to build a successful lemonade business if you are in an area with more affluent individuals and they like your kids and their initiative.

2) Change or add to the product that you offer.

Lemonade served over shaved ice is sold at a a higher price at Six Flags or a local amusement park. You can also get a higher price by adding to what you sell. For example, you could add berries to lemonade, sell a collectible cup with your lemonade, or offer a customized, hand-painted glass that your lemonade is served in. In each case, the value and the price at which you can sell lemonade increases with customization or adding something of value to the transaction.

3) Explain the process by which your lemonade is made or served.

Can you tell a better story about where you get or where you import your lemons from in order to make your lemonade?

Can you change something to how the lemonade is prepared that will make it more appealing? (low sugar, no sugar, etc.)

Starbucks has grown a massive business by explaining the process by which they import, process, and make coffee from their coffee beans. You can do the same.

4) Add an experience to the product to make it have more value.

Can you add an experience or give extra bonuses that make buying from you more fun? For example, could you offer entertainment to those who buy your lemonade by singing a song or doing a dance so that makes it more fun and enjoyable to buy from you?

Could you offer to wash the car windows of your customers when they stop at your stand and while they are enjoying your lemonade?

It takes time to think about how you can incorporate this kind of value into your offering. Businesses that are only focused on selling volume won't utilize these ideas and are doomed to compete solely on price. Instead, create more demand and sell more overall product at a higher price. What you are really doing by analyzing and acting on these four areas is creating your own weather. In other words, you are making it so that the customer *wants* what your are selling because you are targeting the prospect when they are thirsty. In addition, the environment you choose to sell in and your marketing approach reminds a prospect that it is hot and they need a drink.

Take the time to think about how you can shift the perceptions about place, product, process, and the overall experience can help you better position what you sell to create more demand and value.

We'll talk more about how to build value in contrast to your competitor's offers in chapter 7.

5. Better utilize the data you gather from your current customers.

Too many entrepreneurs gather information from their prospects / customers, type it into a computer, or have it on a registry form and then never utilize the information ever again. Beat your competitors by better engaging with those that are coming into your business and actually follow up with the prospects who have already entered your marketing funnel. How well are you following up with the leads you are generating from each of your marketing efforts? Simply following up better than your competitors with those who are considering your product or service can give you a great competitive advantage.

Offer value in the form of education and information and then put each lead in a systematic funnel that addresses the next step. For example, you should have at least two sequences: 1) if the prospect buys and 2) a separate approach if the prospect doesn't buy. You can determine what these sequences will be, but if you don't follow up, it is very likely that your competitors will. We'll talk more about the specifics of this process in chapter 4.

For example, when brides stopped by for an appointment or visit at our bridal store, we would ask specific questions on our bridal registry. We would write down information that they would tell us on our registry form and we would refer back to it when writing a personalized thank you note. Each bridal consultant was responsible for their own leads and separated the lead into one of two sequences (depending on what happened at the first visit). If the bride bought a dress, she went into a sequence to invite her back to buy bridesmaid dresses or other accessories she still needed for the wedding. If she didn't buy, then the bride went into a separate marketing funnel to ensure that she was invited back into the store to get her dress from us through a series of postcards, emails, or personal contacts. Each of our bridal consultants followed a system to go through those marketing sequences to follow up and make every effort to ensure that a sale would happen.

If you want to sell more, you have to track the numbers of prospects and customers you are working with and ensure that the follow up steps are being followed. Then, you can meet with your sales consultants individually to evaluate their performance with following up with these leads and set goals for improvement. In this evaluation meeting, you can look through the consultant's notebook or database together and discuss areas of improvement and specific courses of action for prospects they may have questions about.

When you see one of your team members excelling at follow up, reward them in front of the other members of your team. Let everyone know you value and reward excellent follow up. You may even want to pay a specific bonus out to the sales consultant who has the best follow up sequence and number of customers returning per week who buy more from you. As Michael LeBoeuff says in his book, *The Greatest Management Principle in the World*, "The things that get rewarded get done."

6. Position and leverage yourself to gain power in your chosen specialty with a powerful pre-sales strategy. Look for new segments or niches of the market where you can sell and build a powerful brand.

Always remember that no one is forcing you to sell exclusively to the market to which you are currently selling. Look for opportunity to sell to another market in your area and you can increase your higher end sales and your profits.

One of the most important aspects of positioning and leverage is that it is all about perception. What types of perceptions do your customers have about your business and your overall price and value? If you want to attract customers at a higher price point, you have to raise your price and value in the minds of those you serve because in the mind of a prospective customer, a higher price equals greater quality.

I first became exposed to this idea in the sale of furniture and have seen it since as I have studied other businesses in a myriad of industries. When a price is higher, the buyer assumes that the quality is higher. However, when you look inside of furniture being sold at a high or low price, there is a "Made in China" stamp on much of the furniture. I've driven by many of the factories in China where most of the furniture is made that is sold around the world. Just like the majority of products in the retail industry, most furniture is made by a handful of manufacturers and sold to wholesalers who in turn sell it to retailers. The real difference between the prices between one furniture retailer and another is how they are positioned and perceived in the marketplace.

Even though no one likes to admit this, we all inherently believe that a higher price indicates higher quality. A study conducted at Stanford and MIT proves this point. Their findings were published in the November 2005 *Journal of Marketing Research*. This group of researchers found that a customer's overall satisfaction could be shaped by price and their beliefs about the price for an energy drink based on how it was positioned and sold.

This study revealed that perception about price influenced how people felt after they used a product. In one test, two groups of bodybuilders were given an energy drink. One group was told the product was sold at a discounted price and the other group was told that the drink was sold for a premium price. Those who viewed the drink as a discount product reported having a less intense, effective workout.

They also did a test with two groups of consumers who were told that the drink improved mental function. Those who believed that the drink was sold at a discounted price were less effective at solving the same word puzzles as those who were told the drink was a premium priced product. --*Journal of Marketing Research*, Vol. XIII (November 2005), pp. 410-414.

What lessons can you learn and apply from this study?

One immediately applicable lesson is that you should analyze and think carefully about how you are pre-selling your prospects. Does your marketing collateral help your prospects value what your business does and see it in a way that favors your strengths (in comparison with your competitors)? If not, how can you immediately start doing this?

To beat your competitors, you have to position yourself in such a way that the prospect sees you and your product as the best choice (and even better as the *only* choice) as they go on their search for a solution to what they are looking for or need. Failing to consciously communicate your value and your unique difference leaves the prospect to his or her own impressions. Unfortunately, these impressions may or may not be favorable to you, your business, and how you can help him or her find the product or service they'll end up purchasing.

The biggest mistake you can make when pre-selling your business is to talk about how great you are in your own words. You want others to do this for you because this is what will make the strongest impression. Remember, people are coming to your web site looking for information. The more information you can provide them about why you are the best place to acquire your product that is said in words by others who are also their peers, the better off you will be.

Get out there and let prospects know why they should come see you. If you can't or aren't able to do this effectively before the show, look for creative ways to grab attention to make your booth the talk of the show and the place to be. This excitement will carry over to your store and bring prospects into your marketing funnels to buy if you do it right.

In summary, here are five principles to help you better position your business so that you have more power than your competitors:

- Understand the customer's perceptions about your business in connection with other businesses in your market niche.

- Understand your competitive difference and articulate it to your prospects.

- Position yourself as an authority with valuable expertise. When you are an authority, you can charge more (because the experience of dealing with you) is perceived as being more valuable.

- Position yourself as the preferred source in your market niche –

use written and video testimonials to validate your claims.

- Improve your systems so that you can run your business more effectively and smoothly. Improving your sales and marketing systems is especially important.

7. Do the things your competitors aren't willing to do and do them now. Don't wait. Always be looking for ways you can implement and get things done faster.

George Cloutier in his book *Profits Aren't Everything, They're the Only Thing* says: "[If your sales and profits are down], it's easy to blame the economy but the underlying cause is the business owner's unwillingness to do the obvious: get out there and hustle." Doing the hard things is what separates those who achieve greatness and those who settle for mediocrity. There are great opportunities all around for those who commit to making it happen and give a little bit more every day, especially in areas where your competitors aren't willing to put forth the effort. If you see an opportunity and don't act, you may be left in the dust. Abraham Lincoln once observed: "Good things may come to those who wait, but only those things left behind by those who hustle."

Here are some characteristics of those who are willing to do the tough things and implement more (even at the risk of making mistakes and failing):

- They get things done. They do what they say.

- No one around them can outwork them.

- They don't let their failure define them. They seek to fail as quickly and as early as possible to learn what doesn't work. Consider some of the early failures these individuals had that didn't stop them from becoming what they are known for today:

    - Henry Ford forgot to put a reverse gear on his first automobile.

- Michael Jordan was cut from his high school basketball team.

- Elvis Presley didn't make the glee club.

- Napoleon finished near the bottom of his military school class.

- The Beatles were turned down for a recording contract by Decca Records

- John Grisham's first novel was rejected by sixteen agents and a dozen publishers.

- Post-It Notes, Jell-O, and Timex watches were all failures until perfected or reformulated.

• They aren't paralyzed by decision paralysis. They decide and do. You can measure a person's ability to hustle and implement by the time that passes between decision and action.

• They are accountable to themselves and accept responsibility for what needs to be done. Things are delegated, but never abdicated. In other words, those who get things done don't get so busy running on the treadmill of business that they forget the big picture. They constantly look for ways to improve training and system implementation.

• They don't take no for an answer. They keep looking for new ways to get something done until it is.

Author James Dale makes this note in his book *The Obvious:* "The average entrepreneur fails 3.8 times before achieving success. Clearly, he or she learns something in those first three plus busts that lead to the ultimate success."

If you hustle and act quickly when you resolve to do something, you don't have to be the smartest competitor in your market. The ability to take action and implement is one of the most powerful ways to ensure that you will beat your competitors. Be one who is known for always tackling new projects with fervor and enthusiasm and being committed enough to work until they are done. It is very difficult for even a very entrenched competitor to beat you if you are smart about how you work and work harder than they are willing to. You can't afford to be complacent. You must be willing to do the hard things and do them now. Don't delay.

I remember talking with an entrepreneur once who asked me several questions about how we did a marketing event. On a subsequent visit, I asked if she had scheduled a time and date for her marketing event. She told me that she didn't think she had enough time and that it would have to wait until next year. I told her that wasn't acceptable—that if she wanted to grow her business, she needed to put together that event now and do it no matter what it took – so she would gain the competitive advantage in her market. She ended up putting the event together and had a good turnout and increased her sales as a result. Action matters.

8. Sell and market where you are already good. Get better at your strengths instead of trying to improve your weaknesses. You will always be most competitive when you get better at what you already do well.

Garrison Wynn makes this point in *The Real Truth About Success: What the Top 1% Do Differently, Why They Won't Tell You, and How You Can Do It Anyway*:

"From our surveys, we learned that the top 1 percent understand this secret: *Do very little of what you do badly and a lot of what you do well.* If you don't do something well, stop doing it in front of the people you're trying to influence....The overriding concept is that you're most competitive when you get better at what you already do well. It's an important conclusion drawn from a Gallup study of 80,000 managers and 1 million employees. The study results, presented in the book *First, Break All the Rules* by Marcus Buckingham and Curt Coffman, aligned tightly with responses that showed up consistently in our interviews with the top 1 percent: Successful people do very little of what they do badly and a lot of what they do well."

He continues: "As simple as that sounds, people forget that. I've seen lots of strugglers over the years—people who do all the right things and still don't succeed. They suck at what they do, and still they do it everyday. They think, 'If I can just improve my weaknesses, then I'll be successful." No, that's why they're your weaknesses. You're no good at it. Go where you're good. No one ever became a professional ice-skater by practicing the shot put. People become professional ice-skaters because they are really, really good at ice-skating." –p. 64.

You should already be able to answer these questions: What are you the best in your market at in your business? Why do customers tell you that they come to you over your competitors?

If you can't answer these two questions, you will have a difficult time succeeding against entrenched competitors. Without expertise in some area, you don't have a competitive advantage.

Unfortunately, most of us were taught our whole lives that we should work on our weaknesses. Yet, in business, it is better to work on your strengths.

A simple analogy about swimming may help you understand what I'm trying to communicate. Who would win a swimming competition between you and Michael Phelps (when he was competing competitively in the Olympics from 2000-2012)? The answer is so obvious that it seems silly that I'm even asking the question.

We all know that Michael Phelps would win. For most of us, he would beat us today even though he is retired from competitive swimming. In this race, he starts from a position of strength. He has a body built for swimming and he has honed his skills through years and countless hours of practice. If you were going to find someone to compete against Michael Phelps at the Olympics, you wouldn't begin with someone who begins flailing their arms about and screaming when they jump in the pool. You look for someone who is already great at swimming (it is *already* a strength) and then look to improve his or her strengths to be even more competitive.

This seems like such an obvious concept, but it is amazing how many individuals in business ignore this concept. You won't beat your competitors if you compare your weakest area of business (what you are not good at) against where your competitors are strong (what they are the best at).

Instead, to successfully compete, you have to know where you *are* the best and compete there. The battle should be fought on terrain where you have the advantage, not where you are weakest.

Focus on improving your strengths. Overcome your limitations and weaknesses by surrounding yourself with talented individuals who can help you be strong in those areas.

You won't be able to beat your competitors when you try to be all things to all people. Those who specialize get better at what they do and improve their strengths. This is why specialization is the key to success in beating your competitors in any business.

Jim McCormick and Maryann Karinch make this observation in their book *Business Lessons from the Edge*:

"Knowing what you do well and what you show potential to do better will get you a lot further than trying to be superior at everything you attempt. You would be better off spending that extra effort finding people whose talents complement yours and getting them in your corner."—p. 23.

Here is an assignment for you. Write down what you perceive to be your greatest strength in your market against all of your competitors in your region.

Then, compare how that "strength" compares to two different areas: 1) how customers *perceive* you in your market area and 2) how you *really* compare with your competitors by answering the questions below:

How You Are Perceived By Customers in Your Business (in comparison with your competitors):

1. Is what you sell at your business perceived by customers to be unique enough to ask a premium price and get it?

2. Can customers get the same products or services you sell from a local or Internet competitor for less? Or are you perceived to be the only provider of the product lines you offer?

3. Do customers perceive you to be an authority figure in your market? Do they look to you for advice and follow it?

4. Do customers perceive you to be a better value overall than what your competitors offer? What do customers perceive is the most valuable aspect of what you are offering?

5. Do customers perceive you to be a lower risk provider than your competitors as they consider the solution they seek?

6. Are your customers loyal to you once they've purchased from you (or are other competitors more persuasive in their marketing to pull these customers away from you into their businesses)?

7. Are you perceived to be a generalist or a specialist by customers in your area?

8. Do customers perceive your marketing materials to build your brand or the brand of the vendors you offer?

9. Do customers feel assured by their peers that your business is the best place to get what you offer? Are your video and written testimonials persuasive?

10. What reputation does your business have online (Better Business Bureau, online reviews, and specific industry review sites) and how do

you respond to negative reviews?

As you look at these questions, you probably see some areas where you can improve. If you aren't able to successfully answer any of these questions, you may not have been considering your true strength in the marketplace.

Here are twelve more questions to consider how you actually compare with your competitors. As you read through these questions, you can rate yourself on a scale of 1-10 with how you compare with each specific competitor you want to compare yourself with. This exercise may also help you realize an area of strength that you didn't realize you had.

How You Compare With Your Competitors (Your Areas of Strength):

1. Do you have any economy of scale advantage in how you purchase what you sell? (For example: are you able to buy your product lines for less (because of volume discounts allowing you to maximize your profitability?)

2. Do you occasionally or regularly cut your prices and lower your profit margin to match or beat a competitor's price to get the sale?

3. Do you have operations advantages (better fixed costs) that help you have an advantage over your competitors?

4. Do you have relationships with individuals in specific niche channels that your competitors don't have that you are able to monetize?

5. Do you have territory protection with certain vendors to give you exclusivity to stand out from your competitors? (If so, rate your strength 1-10 based on what percentage of the total vendors you carry that give you this advantage)

6. Do you have a better follow up sequence than your competitors to get additional sales from those who have purchased (or get the initial sale from those who haven't purchased) than your competitors?

7. What advantages do you have over competitors at trade shows (bigger booth space, more sales consultants, better offers, etc.)?

8. How does your social networking presence compare with that of your competitors (Facebook, Twitter, Instagram, blogging, etc.)?

9. How does your web site compare with that of your competitors?

10. How do your sales closing percentages compare with those of your competitors? Do you have a sales training regimen that you use to keep your consultant's sales skills sharp?

11. How well do you ask for and get referrals from those you sell to as compared with your competition?

12. What is extraordinary about your business as compared with your competitors? Do customers perceive this difference?

What did you learn from asking yourself these questions? Did you identify your strengths? If so, focus on these strengths and make them stronger. This will help you better compete in the marketplace and beat your competitors.

These questions have likely given you a wake up call about where your strengths really lie. Analyzing where you *really* compare with your competitors can help you do the things that you need to do that aren't easy. This can help you be sure you are focusing on your strengths. Remember, doing the things that others are unwilling to do is often the key to being successful.

Garrison Wynn points this out in *The Real Truth About Success*. He says:

"What it takes to get to the top may be something that a lot of us are unwilling to do. When people find themselves in a circumstance in which they feel an emotional need to succeed, they'll tend to find a way to do it. They didn't just try harder or rely on their natural intelligence or follow the advice of their forebears. They looked deep inside themselves to find any possible advantage they could and then used that advantage the best they could. The truth is that there are plenty of people with a lot of knowledge who aren't doing a whole lot with it. Then you've got a guy who knows only two things, but he uses what little he knows to consistently become ultra-successful. It's not necessarily what you know or how smart you are; it's about your willingness to use the resources around you, take a look at who you are, and use everything you've got. *Everything.*" –p. 196.

If you are still struggling to determine what your strengths are, ask yourself the following questions. They will help you identify your strengths, differentiate your business, and beat your competitors:

- What makes me different from my competitors?

- If I ceased to exist, why would my customers miss me?

- What do customers ask for that I don't have?

- What need do I fill that no one else in the market fills?

- What need could I fill for the prospects entering my marketing funnels if I wanted to?

- Have I segmented my market precisely enough?

- Who are my best customers? Why? What need of theirs do I fill?

- Do customers buy everything I offer? What part of what I sell is the most popular? What is most profitable?

- Where are the customers that I want to capture?

Remember to focus on *your* strengths. Choosing this approach will help you beat your competitors on the battlefields *you've* chosen. It will help you stand out to the prospects in your marketplace and provide a superior experience to your customers allowing you to gain even more ground against your competitors.

9. Better promote your difference.

Being better than your competitors is one thing. Being better at promoting your difference so that customers *perceive* and *believe* that you are the best is the real goal.

To beat your competitors, you have to differentiate yourself and communicate to customers why your offering is superior, different to and better than what your competitors are offering. If you can articulate this difference **and** be persuasive in the way you communicate this message (especially with testimonials), you will have a huge advantage in your marketplace.

Several years ago, marketing expert Jack Trout wrote an excellent book entitled *Differentiate or Die*. In his book he makes the following statement about the explosion of choice in the world today and why this necessitates defining and articulating your difference in order to be noticed. He says:

"What has changed in business over recent decades is the amazing proliferation of product choices in just about every category....The big difference is that what used to be national markets with local companies competing for business has become a global market with everyone competing for everyone's business everywhere."

He continues:

"If you ignore your uniqueness and try to be everything for everybody, you quickly undermine what makes you different."—Jack Trout, *Differentiate or Die*, pp. 2-8.

Throughout this book, Trout articulates nine ways that you can differentiate yourself from your competitors. If you haven't read this book, you should get it and study it to help you define your point of difference. Here is a brief summary of these nine strategies with some thoughts for you to consider:

1) Being First - *What areas can your business claim they are first in?*

It is better to be first than it is to be better. If you can't be first, is there another category you can create in the minds of prospects in your area where you *can* be first?

2) Attribute Ownership - *What attributes do you want to position your business to own in prospect's mind?*

When you own an attribute in a prospect's mind, you can use this to position yourself against your competitors. BMW has done this successfully for years by repositioning Mercedes using an attribute they own (the ultimate driving machine). In their ads, they seek to reposition their competitor as the ultimate sitting machine. When you know what you stand for, it is much easier to reposition your competitors. However, if you are trying to be all things to all people, it is easy for your competitors to reposition and beat you. Choose to be the one who repositions by being clear about what it is that you stand for.

3) Leadership - *What areas can your business claim leadership in? What are you the best at?*

This goes back to the idea of being first. It is easiest to be the leader in your market niche. This is especially true when you are perceived as being an expert at something or being the first or best one to specialize in a certain market niche. Always ask yourself this question: Is there a category that my business can own in the minds of prospects and customers in my area?

4) Heritage – *How long have you been offering what you do best to customers in your market niche?*

Heritage is all about telling your story. You should tell your story about how long you have served customers in your market and how you got started in your business in such a way that you truly connect with the prospect who hears it (so that they want to do business with you). As Trout says: "...recognize that being around a long time...gives prospects the feeling that they are dealing with an industry leader. If not the biggest, they certainly are a leader in longevity."--p. 116.

Here are four types of heritage you can promote: 1) Your location and how long you've served the community; 2) Anyone else in your family who has served customers (multi-generational businesses can do this quite well); 3) Being a landmark in your city or area (businesses in historic downtown locations or areas can do this very well); and 4) Being known for what you stand for (your area of specialty or expertise in a certain market niche). Which one of these areas can you *best* use to promote your difference in the marketplace?

5) Market Specialty - *Is there a particular segment of the market that you can specialize in?*

Don't just strive to be a specialist. Strive to be a celebrity authority figure specialist. A celebrity authority figure specialist is someone that everyone knows about and *trusts* his or her opinion. What is something that everyone says that you are experts at doing? What you want is for everyone around you to recognize you as the expert. This type of strategy works best if you have a specific market niche that you can tap into that highlights your strength. Know what you are best at and promote that to your prospects and customers.

6) Preference - *What specific preference strategy could your business tap into? Do you have any celebrity customers or individuals who have endorsed your business? Do you display written testimonials or videos highlighting the great experiences customers have had as a result of doing business with you?*

Preference is a very powerful way to communicate your point of difference and your strength. You do this by helping future customers see what others have found and why they preferred you over your competitors. Tylenol has positioned their difference very effectively with their message that they are the "pain reliever that hospitals prefer". Lexus has done this very well with their constant promotion of how

J.D. Powers & Associates and their customer surveys prove that Lexus owners are more satisfied than other luxury car owners. Science Diet, which is a premium priced cat and dog food, has done a great job of using preference by promoting that they offer "what vets feed their pets".

The best way you can do promote your preference in your market is to have numerous written and video testimonials on your web site or marketing materials. Each of these testimonials should promote you and what made each customer's experience wonderful when they did business with you.

7) **How Product is Made or Brought into Your Business** – *Is there something about how the products or services you offer are made or brought into your business that can give you a distinct edge?*

For example, Vera Wang promotes her custom-made wedding dresses as being made in the United States (although her White line at David's Bridal is not). Justin Alexander promotes their Pure line as eco-friendly, organic, and biodegradable. Kleinfeld Bridal promotes their retail store by saying: "We travel the world twice a year... to bring you the latest European bridal gowns which can only be seen in the United States at Kleinfeld... *No passport or travel expenses required!"*

Your business also travels to trade shows, markets, or conferences every year. Let your customers know how you decide what products or services you bring to market for them.

8) **Being the Latest** – *What market trends do you offer that no one else in your area does?*

How can you offer more value than their competitors with new product offerings that other competitors haven't even considered yet? What's new? How do you stay ahead of the market and what your customers want and need?

9) **Hotness** – *Is there something about what customers are saying about you or your sales that defines you?*

This is the one area that you can really promote to customers by positioning yourself as a celebrity authority figure. Identify why customers are choosing to do business with you and *why* you are the hottest business in your market. This might be based on sales, a new and exclusive product that you offer, or any other type of promotion that your business is running that is newsworthy to your local market.

Use these nine strategies to better position your business in the marketplace. When you do, customers will *perceive* and *believe* that you are the best in your market niche.

10. Offer more value.

Consumers today are looking for better deals and many businesses are lowering prices to compete with struggling competitors who have slashed prices. This causes pricing wars. Savvy prospects are looking for the best deal. Many prospects wait longer to buy today because they are looking for more value for their dollar. Those business owners who get better at offering value are the ones who will thrive in the years ahead.

Understanding the difference between the value prospects expect and what you actually deliver is critical if you are to increase and maximize your overall value in the eyes of your prospects.

Making a shift to building higher levels of value as opposed to what is expected is a big shift for many business owners. Typically, when a business owner enters a new industry, they look at what everybody else is doing and do the same thing. They do the same type of advertising, try to offer similar products, go to the same trade shows, etc. However, the most successful businesses in any field are those who create value based on what their customers want and value, not on what the owner thinks something should be valued for.

For example, consider the difference in attending a Broadway performance and a high school production of the same play. In both cases, the audience is watching a theatrical performance with actors and actresses and hearing the same lines of dialogue. So, why is there such a drastic difference in what an audience will pay to see a play on Broadway versus seeing the same play at their local high school? Could the drama students command the price of a Broadway play for their performance? The answer obviously is no, but the reason *why* is the essence of what creates value in the mind of those who will pay the higher price for the Broadway performance.

In both cases, there is an intrinsic or face value of experiencing the play. In both cases, you will have watched the same lines repeated and spend roughly the same amount of time at the event. The difference is in the personal and customized aspects of the play and *that* makes all of the difference in the world. Unless it is your son or daughter in the leading role of the high school play, I think we can all agree that the performances, the props, and the production values (lighting, music, etc.) will all be superior at the Broadway performance. The reality is that these differences translate into a 10 or 100 x increase in ticket price for essentially seeing the same play. What creates the *value* is something that you should carefully think about as you develop value for your prospects and customers as compared to your competitors.

How do most businesses establish value? They usually do it through one of four ways. If they want to add value, they will typically add more of something into one of the following value areas:

1) **By a specific unit of time** – many businesses determine how much something will cost to their customers based on the rate it will cost to produce it over time. The only way to increase the value is to increase the expertise behind what is done in a specific amount of time. For example, anyone who is paid by the hour like attorneys or graphic artists charge based on what they feel they can charge. This rate is usually based on how long they have been working in the marketplace, their own skill level (which a potential client can rarely correctly calculate), or what they feel their time is worth. Those who charge the most money per hour have arrived at that status level

through a focused specialty and through creating authority and celebrity.

Most of how business owners charge is often determined by this type of valuation for any business activity where you are trading time for money. The cost is usually determined by figuring out what something will cost you per hour or what you feel the time to complete that activity is worth plus your profit. The customer on the other hand asks: "Can I have someone else do the same work for less? Or is it really worth that price?" If you can't answer those questions to the satisfaction of the prospect, they will take their business somewhere else.

There are three challenges with this type of value:

- *Your rate may go up or down based on demand or your popularity.* For example, someone who may have been a celebrity at one point in their career can go down in value over time. A string of misses instead of hits will have this effect. It is especially true if a celebrity doesn't continually promote himself or herself or if they fall out of favor in the public eye.

- *Your customers may not value your time the same way you do.* Just because you get more training or add value to what you are doing doesn't mean that the customer will understand the value in the same way. You have to position the value by building authority and celebrity **and** then brand what you do that way. Another way to look at this is to ask: Is there any more value in having a wedding put together by the wedding planner who coordinated a celebrity wedding or an experienced, skilled, well-respected wedding planner who has the same connections who doesn't have any celebrity clients? The answer is no but the wedding planner who does the weddings of celebrities can charge much more (because there is perceived value that those who do the weddings for the well-known and well-connected are worth more).

- *Most entrepreneurs don't value their time accurately.*

Harry Beckwith in his book *The Invisible Touch* tells a great story about Picasso:

"A woman was strolling along a street in Paris when she spotted Picasso sketching at a sidewalk café. Not so thrilled that she could not be slightly presumptuous, the woman asked Picasso if he might sketch her and charge accordingly.

Picasso obliged. In just minutes, there she was: an original Picasso.

'And what do I owe you?' she asked.

'Five thousand francs,' he answered.

'But it only took you three minutes.' She reminded him.

'No,' Picasso said. 'It took me all my life.'"

Beckwith ends with this advice:

"Don't charge by the hour. Charge by the years." —pp. 137-138.

Here's another example:

"A man was suffering a persistent problem with his house. The floor squeaked. No matter what he tried, nothing worked. Finally, he called a carpenter who friends said was a true craftsman.

The craftsman walked into the room and heard the squeak. He set down his toolbox, pulled out a hammer and a nail, and pounded the nail into the floor with three blows. The squeak was gone forever. The carpenter pulled out an invoice slip, on which he wrote the total of $45. Above that total were two line items:

Hammering, $2
Knowing where to hammer, $43

Beckwith's advice:

"Charge for knowing where." –*Selling the Invisible*, p. 138.

You are the only one who can place an accurate value on your time and work. Your clients won't value what you do in the same way. Be sure you charge for your experience *and* for knowing where.

2) **By quantity, volume, or size** – many businesses build value by how big or small something is. For example, many restaurants serve huge amounts of food when you go to their restaurant. The sheer volume in portion sizes has gone up astronomically in recent years. I recently visited a restaurant where I ordered a grilled chicken caesar salad. The salad that came out was nearly as big as my entire chest cavity. This insane way of valuing food size has happened because businesses have increased the size to justify an increase in price. On the other hand, there are restaurants that I have gone to where the price for a very small portion of food is 5 to 10 x what an entire meal may cost at a fast food restaurant. I was happy to pay it because it tasted so good and the experience at the restaurant was so amazing. Think carefully about this. Are you trying to raise your value by offering more in terms of size or are you shrinking the size (or leaving it the same) and raising the experiential value of what it means to do business with you? The answer to this question can help you raise your value and your prices.

3) **By comparison with others in the marketplace** – Many people set their prices and their value based on what their competitors offer or offer a lower price. For example, if competitor XYZ down the street or Internet competitor ABC prices a product at keystone (double the cost) or less, many stores will offer their pricing for the same amount because that is all they feel they can charge. In reality, by increasing your overall value, you can raise your price and have your customers ecstatic about paying it because of the overall value they get when they do business with you.

internationally, many hotels only have one iron and ironing board for the entire floor. So, you have to deal with the inconvenience of asking room service to bring you one. In one case at a hotel in China, I asked for an iron and ironing board and they told me, "Sorry, we are all out." It was a big inconvenience and I had to wear a wrinkled shirt that day. When your expectation is violated, your frustration escalates. This hotel may have thought they were doing their guests a favor by having one iron and ironing board per floor, but for one of their guests it was a disappointing experience (and that disappointment was compounded by the language barrier).

What things do you promote at your business (through your advertising) that prospects *expect* today? Unfortunately, most of the things businesses promote as differentiators (such as customer service) are things that your people already *expect* you to have. They aren't true differentiators.

For example, the Starwood Hotel chain or Westin hotels have made their differentiating claim on their Heavenly Bed and Heavenly Shower. They have taken something that most hotels take for granted and marketed the perception of these things as more upscale and luxurious for those who stay at their hotels.

Here are four questions that I want you to seriously consider as you think about your value to your prospects and customers:

1. What areas of your business that are taken for granted could you slightly tweak to make you even more valuable?

2. What can you do to raise your value?

3. How can you raise the perception of the value that a prospect gets from doing business with you?

4. If prospects only see what you sell as commodities and you don't differentiate what you do, can you really blame them for deciding where they will buy based on the cheapest price?

Take time to carefully analyze and think about these questions. They *will* help you take action to raise your value in the eyes of your prospects and customers.

Add more value to what you do. For example, many Broadway plays now include an option for a pre-play party and the opportunity to get autographs and meet the cast following the performance.

Many locally owned independent drug stores are competing against large national chains like CVS and Walgreen's. In addition to these two large chains, there are also supermarket drugstore departments and independent drugstores, and Internet providers of drugs.

Edgar Falk in his book *1001 Ideas to Generate Retail Excitement* makes this point about independent drugstores:

> "With low profit margins on prescriptions, especially those covered by insurance plans, the independent has to develop a significant nonprescription business and additional revenue-producing services to stay in business. The prescription business may bring people into the store but if a pharmacy cannot develop other business from these customers, it is in big trouble.
>
> One pharmacist who has been successful in developing this additional business is Beverly Schaefer, the owner of Katterman's Sand Point Pharmacy in Seattle. She developed a plan of action to prove that being bigger is not a substitute for the knowledge and expertise customers want when they visit a pharmacy. 'People seek advice and information when they shop in a drugstore, and they don't get it from reading the ingredients and claims on the label,' the veteran pharmacist said. 'They have questions and they want answers from a knowledgeable source.' That was the thinking behind Ms. Schaefer's plan. Since 80 percent of her volume was from products whose price is determined by a third party, namely prescription plans, she decided she would concentrate on the other

20 percent of her volume, which includes lucrative over-the-counter products about which big store employees seemed to know little.

The number of Americans who favor vitamins, herbal remedies, neutraceuticals, and other alternative forms of medicine is growing and represents an increasingly important market. Ms. Schaefer realized that customers had many questions about these wellness drugs, and wanted to discuss them with a pharmacist. She was told that it was often difficult to find a chain pharmacist who had the time or expertise to discuss them with a customer. So she positioned herself as the problem solver for her customers, an expert who could advise them on preventative medicine as well as on the multitude of nonprescription products available for everything from colds, allergies, and flu symptoms to minor pains and constipation, as well as medical equipment. Whether it is a conventional or homeopathic product, a testing device or orthopedic product, or advice on what medications to take on an African safari, Ms. Schaefer dispenses the knowledge customers urgently want and usually cannot get elsewhere.

It is this knowledgeable personal service that draws customers to Katterman's. They trust the owner and her staff and come in not only for medications but also for their immunizations, and even to have blood drawn for cholesterol, PSA, and other tests, which Washington State pharmacists can administer. The customers look upon Katterman's as their wellness center.

Katterman's Web site provides additional information on the store's products, including a section on nonprescription drugs, which customers might need for the current season, as well as its health care services, line of quality gifts, and new additions to its book section.

As for the big store competitors? It may be one of the best things that happened to Katterman's, who picks up a lot of their dissatisfied customers."—pp. 235-236.

Another important thing Katterman's has done is to create their own private line of products. Here are several other things they're doing to increase their value to their customers:

- Setting up space so customers can be counseled by pharmacists in privacy. In other words, you don't have to tell everyone behind you in line what potentially embarrassing health problems you are having.

- Hold a 'check your medication day' in which customers bring in their prescription and non-prescription drugs so pharmacists can check to see if taking any of them concurrently is dangerous.

- Offer expertise in specific areas: fertility, diabetes, newborns, respiratory ailments, H1N1 viral infections and immunizations, etc.

- Distribute a newsletter on new products and new offerings and the latest research on newly available drugs in language that everyone can understand

To more successfully compete with your competitors, you should always be asking: "What can I do to raise my overall value?" and then have the courage to act on the answers. We'll talk more about this in chapter 7.

To help you in this endeavor, I want you to think about every interaction you have with customers who come into your business through the following stages of the sales process. The very best businesses are always looking for ways they can raise their value at each interaction with prospects at each step. As you read through each of these areas, consider how you can raise your value at each level.:

1) Before the prospect comes in first contact with your business

2) The first 30 seconds after the prospect enters your marketing funnel or sits down with you for a first appointment

3) The needs analysis process

4) Educating the prospect on what you do and how it can meet their identified needs

5) Presenting the solution

6) Closing the sale

7) Add on options

8) Follow-up

9) Referral process

Don't blow this assignment off. You should seriously think about what you will do to add value in each of these areas and implement these ideas as quickly as you can. When you do, you will build great contrast between your business and every competitor in your area. When a customer perceives that you have the most overall value, they will choose to do business with you and you will beat your competitors.

CHAPTER 2

DEFY CHANGES IN YOUR INDUSTRY AND COME OUT ON TOP

"Every revolution begins with a single act of defiance."—Mahatma Gandhi

There is constant change in business. This doesn't come as much of a surprise, but the big lesson I hope to share with you in this chapter is found in what you have to keep doing to defy the forces, shifts and changes that would drag you backwards and how you can beat them to make more sales and more money.

One of the big challenges today is that you must shift with what your competitors do and what your employees don't or won't do to beat the gravitational forces that constantly seek to pull you down and prevent you from soaring to new heights and accomplishing what you really want.

Before we get into the strategies and actions you must take to rise above these challenges, I'd like to first discuss some of the forces that pull you back from what you could be. These forces are serious threats that you must adapt to in order to survive and thrive in the ever-changing marketplace.

A big challenge in all businesses today is that the behaviors and habits of consumers change and continue to evolve. Expectations are higher, choices are everywhere, and people are comfortable buying online. Traditional sales channels have been wildly disrupted and things will never go back to what they were. It costs a lot to acquire a new customer today and in some industries, people don't return to buy a product every year (such as in the solar and wedding industries). In other industries, such as with monthly subscriptions or monthly fees such as in the property management industry, customers return month after month. If you do a good job creating effective promotions, you can capture additional sales revenue from customers month after month and year after year. The challenge is that most businesses don't follow up very well. To follow up correctly, you've got to be in front of prospects with your offer when they are ready to buy.

Another challenge with consumers today is that the way they gather information and are influenced about the products you offer happens largely before they ever arrive on your radar. This means that you must better understand what they are willing to buy and insert yourself into the dialogue of the conversation long before you used to. It isn't enough anymore to start this dialogue when someone shows up. In most cases, they have already made the decision about a product need before they meet with you.

Hypercompetition shrinks the available pool of prospects searching for your product before many are even aware that these prospects are in the market for what is being sold. You can't succeed in today's marketplace by reactively waiting for disappointed and unhappy prospects who weren't pleased with another proposal or poor customer service to come into your orbit.

Jack Mitchell, who runs Mitchells, a profitable high-end clothing business that was originally founded in Connecticut in 1958 wrote a book entitled *Hug Your Customers* that details this philosophy. In 1958 when Mitchells started, they did $50,000 worth of sales and were thrilled. Today, they have seven locations around the United States and do more than $100 million annually in sales.

In the book, Mitchell makes this statement: "In the 1970s and early 1980s, sales associates stood around and waited for people to come into the store. ou waited and you reacted: "May I help you?" And we did. But that doesn't work any longer. Now you need to be proactive. You can't stand idly twiddling your thumbs until someone walks in the door. You have to take actions that will bring the customers through that door. In other words, you need to initiate the sale, not simply complete it."--pp. 15-16.

Many businesses today still have a reactive approach to selling. They wait to see who comes into their orbit each day. The best businesses have a proactive approach with their marketing and sales efforts so they initiate the sale and follow through to close the sale.

Mitchell makes this observation:

"It's obvious to me that many leading businesses, whether they sell clothes or cornbread, are all about product. If they're in the clothing business like us, they're interested in whether it's a so-called Super 100 wool fabric or a Super 180. Is it handmade or machine-made? Is it a light gray or olive? Two-or three-button? Short or long shirt?"

He then makes this observation: "At Mitchell's, clothes are not our priority. It's not the first thing we think of, nor the last. Don't get me wrong. We like fabulous product, and we search the world to get it, but we're all about customers. Now that may sound amazing. A clothing store that isn't about clothes? But it's true. And if we were a restaurant, we wouldn't be about food. If we were an electronics store, we wouldn't be about [electronics].

"Businesses have lost sight of the idea that customers, not product, are the most important priority. Most companies think all you have to do is have plenty of great product and the right value and customers will

descend like locusts on their stores....Many stores have those things...
[but] it's how you treat customers that defines your long-term success....
Far too many business managers have no idea who their customers are,
or what their customers want, or what their perceptions are, and haven't
a clue as to how to find out."--*Hug Your Customers*, pp. 19-20.

Consumers are so skeptical in today's marketplace that a mere marketing
message (no matter how good it is) and whether it is a social media post,
a postcard, email, phone call, or contact at home, in a business, or at a
trade show will do little by itself to persuade. Consumers aren't likely
to drop everything in their busy lives simply because you invite them to
check out the product you sell.

With all of the commotion of the marketplace, it is easy to see why your
marketing message is getting buried in the clutter and ignored.

According to Daniel Seeburg in his book *The Digital Diet*, the
average online user now visits 40+ web sites a day, checks and updates
[social media], email, texts, and is distracted by other online content
more than 100 times a day. His thesis is that "human beings are
being neurologically re-programmed by their tech addiction" to the
point that they are constantly distracted. With all of the distraction
consumers experience today, it is no wonder that your message isn't
getting noticed or getting through to the prospects you're trying to
reach. On top of that, your business isn't the only one that is trying to
contact your prospects. All of your competitors are marketing to the
same narrow niche and every other vendor in your market region is
trying to convince them why *they* are the best option. Fortunately, many
competitors aren't very good marketers and don't have a consistent
message that draws prospects into their businesses. However, they are
getting better our of necessity.

Consider the graphic on the next page that shows the sales process
from the point of view of your prospects and your sales professionals.
Prospects today enter the sales process *you are aware of* later than you
think. Think carefully about how, when, and what you're doing at each
stage of the process. Those who are best at each stage will make the sale.

	Process for Deciding on Your Product *(Perspective of a Prospect)*		Process for Selling Your Product *(Your Perspective As Sales Pro)*	
	Process / Sequence	Where/When	Process / Sequence	Where/When
Before prospect meets with sales professional	**The Search** *(I'm interested in a particular product – where should I go to get it?)*	Online, Interaction with Online Chat, Reading Reviews	**Marketing** *(Interested in this product? We have the perfect....)*	Interaction with Web Site, Your Marketing Funnel
	Getting Educated *(Checking out pictures, web sites, reading reviews)*	Online, Friends, (those who have already purchased from you or someone else who sells your product)	There is a big gap here today. Prospects are getting educated online or by talking with others (who are likely not trained professionals).	
	Assessing Budget vs. Value *(The product or service I want is how much?)*	Online, Talking to friends and neighbors who have purchase product		
After prospect meets with sales professional	**Validating Decision** *(Do I like this _____ I saw online or at another business? If I have seen it at multiple locations, what is the best price?)*	Online, in-person meeting	- **Approaching the Prospect** - **Building Rapport & Trust** - **Needs Assessment** - **Building Value / Presenting Product**	Online, in-person meeting
	Justification *(I haven't seen this configuration anywhere else and this seems to be a good value/price) or (I like this idea or design but I saw it online for $- or I want to see if I can get it for less)*	Home, Online, In Person Meeting with You or Another Sales Rep	*Prospect is likely going through this process on their own without any input from a sales professional.*	
	Decision *(looking at pictures, searching for lowest price and/or lowest risk provider)*	Home, Online, In Person Meeting with You or Another Sales Rep	**Answering Objections**	Home (In-Person Meeting), Online
	Buy the Product *(online or with a sales rep who talked with them about a proposal)*	Online, In Person Meeting	**Finalizing Transaction**	In Person Meeting

The reality of what this illustrates is that prospects are controlling the steps of the sale more than your sales organization. People are buying online *after* they choose what they want. We'll talk more about how you can successfully compete in this new sales environment in Chapter 3.

This number of online sales will increase. There isn't a very efficient way to track what the effect of the Internet on shopping for your product really is on a nationwide or worldwide basis. In my opinion, most of the statistics about consumers who buy online are under-reported. This is a significant concern to you. You must brand your business instead of relying on manufacturers (whose products are also sold online either by themselves or other online competitors) to do it for you. If you don't, you will be at the mercy of prospects who decide to shop for the best price. In their mind there is no difference between a product purchased from you or the same product bought online (except for an overall better price) since they don't have to pay sales tax in many states (although this is changing). Online businesses usually offer a free premium when customers buy on their web site as well.

Those businesses who position themselves well with social media and mobile applications will be the ones who direct prospects into their marketing funnels and make sales. Those who ignore these trends or downplay them (since they aren't sure what to do about them) will suffer declining revenues and shrinking numbers of customers who choose to buy from online instead.

The average cost of products today continues to rise. The purchasing power of the dollar is declining and with inflation is resulting in higher prices across the board for raw materials. In addition, new labor laws in countries like China have caused the average worker's salary to rapidly increase over the past few years. This trend will continue and we will all pay higher prices for the products we buy and sell.

The bottom line is that if you want to increase your sales and maintain your profit margins, you must market to more affluent markets who will be able to afford these price increases and you must get better at selling to the prospects that you attract into your business on the first visit. You likely won't have a second chance. Trying to wing it when you sell will result in declining close ratios. You have to continually train and support your sales consultants so they are getting better at selling.

Michael LaFido is a great example of this with his luxury real estate training seminars. He is helping realtors focus on working with more affluent clients. You can see and learn from his approach at www. luxurylistingspecialist.com.

The rising cost of inventory is not the only concern entrepreneurs have going forward. Business owners also have to worry about increased costs of customer acquisition, shipping, healthcare, and other increased employee costs. With costs rising so rapidly, sales must also rise too. If not, your business will be in trouble very quickly.

With all of the sales offers consumers have seen over the years for virtually every product they buy, they expect more today than they ever. This means that you have to get better at building more and more value into what you sell in ways that don't increase your expenses. If you don't do this and your sales revenues remain flat, you will fall behind very quickly.

Those who will do the best in today's changing marketplace are those who can focus on niche markets where they have exclusivity (thus protecting their profit margins) and who focus on increasing their celebrity and specialization so they are better known through referrals and recommendations as the best place to get their offered products and services. You've also got to stay up with supply and demand. This requires changing products and changing systems.

Several years ago, Bill Gates made the following statement: "In 3 years every product my company makes will be obsolete. The only question is whether we will make it obsolete or someone else will." This statement really got my attention. This should get your attention too.

Parenthetically, every time a very successful business owner makes a statement that seems to contradict what most people in any industry think or do, I think it is critically important to pay attention to what they are saying. Peter Drucker reinforced what Gates said by saying: "Every 3 years, each product and process should be put on trial for its life, otherwise the competition will pass you by." With the speed of business today, three years may actually be too long of a period of time before this work should be done.

Imagine for a minute that a judge comes to your business tomorrow and sets up his courtroom in your conference room. The trial has been set up to analyze every single product you currently offer. One by one each offering you sell is brought before the judge and analyzed.

If this scenario happened in your business, would you have anything left to sell? Or would the judge and the customers who are called to testify announce the verdict that your business is relying on products from three and four years ago to make the bulk of your sales when in most cases they aren't what today's prospects are even looking for anymore?

The harsh reality is that if this scenario played itself out in businesses across the country, there would be a lot of guilty verdicts pronounced and countless products condemned. You should convene your own court and act as the judge, jury, and executioner eliminating products that should no longer be offered. Dead products should be priced to move (if you have physical inventory) and product options that are selling now should be brought into your business as quickly as possible.

If you will have the discipline to put each product and process on trial at your business for its life, you'll be able to prune back dead and dying areas and make room for proven and promising products that will propel your growth to the top of your market niche.

General George S. Patton adopted this philosophy of constantly advancing during World War II. He never wanted his subordinates to inform him that they were holding their positions. "Let the Germans do that," he said. "We are advancing constantly and we are not interested in holding onto anything" other than what they could wrest from the enemy. "Our basic plan of operation," he said, "is to advance and keep on advancing regardless of whether we have to go over, under, or through the enemy." --*The 21 Irrefutable Laws of Leadership: Tested by Time*, p. 216.

Remember, you are in business to make a profit. If you aren't currently making a profit with a product (regardless of how successful it has been in the past), you are digging a slow grave, one loss at a time. Don't let the force of bad and unprofitable products hold you back from soaring to new heights. Mark it down and get rid of it.

Additionally, the sales skills of those selling your products must be continually developed. None of us can remain static. You must continually train and help your best sales consultants hone their skills so they become unstoppable.

I view training as a way to plug the slow leaks that develop in the skills of those who sell for you. If you are continually training your sales consultants with the best ways to overcome the objections they're facing, your consultants will get better and your sales will increase.

I once fired a sales consultant who had a 62% close ratio over a previous 30 day period. Why would I do this? Why would I let go of a consultant who many would be thrilled to have selling at that level? The reason is two fold. First, I was looking at what she wasn't doing that one of our consultants who was closing at 80 to 85 percent was doing. Secondly, she was overall a 'B-' player. I didn't want our top performers and 'A' players to feel like they were being pulled down from reaching our sales goals. When such a decision is made, the other sales consultants also see I'm serious. In fact, the day and the day after this decision was made, sales skyrocketed at our business. The consultants were happier to sell without the added stress of dealing with this "B-" player as well.

She was also trying to invent her own sales strategies (which weren't working), but she was convinced that they were. She was buying into the excuses and objections that prospects were giving. She wasn't paying attention to the training I was offering, instead thinking that what she was doing was working, but over the long-term it was obvious that it wasn't.

My question for you: Are you aware of the sales consultants who need to receive more training whose skills have been slowly leaking out over time?

What are you doing to ensure that your consultants are always prepared and full of the best sales strategies and techniques to ensure high closing ratios?

Take an inventory of your sales consultants. Ask yourself the following questions about each of them. Then, think about where you are going. Will you be able to get there with the team you currently have or will you need to make adjustments?

Here are six questions for you to ask:

Does this sales consultant:

• Put me at ease or am I on edge when I think about him and the results he is getting?

• Listen well to the prospects she works with?

• Get along with the other members of the team? Do they enjoy doing things together outside of work?

• Would you trust this consultant to help the son or daughter of your very best friend to find the right solution to their needs? Do you have confidence in his or her ability to help a prospect find the perfect solution with your product?

• Continually improve and have a desire to learn how to sell better?

• Have consistent results (a high close ratio, high sales results consistently every week / month, high follow-up conversions, etc.)?

Once you've asked yourself these questions, determine whether you should invest more resources into developing that sales consultant or whether you would be better off to channel your attention and focus into a different consultant that can help you get where you want to go. When you ask yourself these types of questions, you'll find out what really matters. Then, have to have the courage to act on what you've discovered.

Many of the changes and forces that are affecting your results are depressing and discouraging. Others are areas that you have to be vigilant about so you don't lose ground that you've worked hard to gain.

When you consider all of these shifts and changes in the marketplace, it is no wonder that you may feel like going crazy every now and then. So, what do you do about all of these forces, shifts and changes that are dramatically affecting the way you do business? That is the essence of what we'll cover in this book.

The reality is that all of these challenges can cause us to question what we are doing more often and many succumb to what Cameron Herold calls a crisis of meaning in his book *Double Double*. He says:

"When you start feeling yourself sliding into this Crisis of Meaning stage, you really do have to reach out for help....We all need to understand the feelings we're having as we're moving down the roller coaster. For women entrepreneurs, this can be a little easier since they know how to tap into that emotional intelligence and intuition from years of practice, and, frankly, it's more socially acceptable for them to do so. They're also more likely to talk to others about their feelings, whereas guys tend to think through stuff silently from our little caves. The bottom line? We all need to listen to our bodies and brains more." –p. 172.

He continues: "When you're moving toward Crisis of Meaning, you need to be able to communicate. Say, 'Hey, I'm feeling stressed, terrified, completely anxious.' And don't feel ashamed of it; every single business owner out there goes through this stuff. I promise!"—p. 173.

Instead of getting overwhelmed with a crisis of meaning, choose to put your focus on efforts to make more sales and more money.

For starters, look for ways you can add additional revenue streams in your business that strengthen your financial position.

This doesn't mean that you need to add new product lines or new product categories. When you introduce a new product category, you have another set of challenges within the business you already have and a learning curve as well.

A big revenue stream that most entrepreneurs miss out on is the one that comes from good follow-up. There is a cost for acquiring qualified prospects who are ready to buy on their first appointment. There is also a big opportunity cost that results when you refuse or resist marketing to customers who have already purchased one thing (that could purchase another). Since costs of acquiring prospects and doing business will continue to rise in the future, you need to have ways to have others help you defer these costs.

To sell more today, you may have to expand your boundaries of how and what you sell. You can do this by attracting customers from farther distances or by better marketing to different cultural segments of your business. There are likely cultural segments in big cities near your business that aren't being served that you could tap into and do well with.

For example, when I was in the bridal business, I met with the owners of a Thai foot massage, Vietnamese furniture, and Filipino fashion business who were interesting in partnering with our store to promote our bridal gowns to that specific niche. I discovered that there is a very large Thai, Vietnamese and Filipino market in our area that I wasn't even aware existed. We worked out a referral program where they referred their customers to us for a referral bonus. There was an Asian shopping center less than five minutes away from our business. After our initial meeting, those business owners introduced to me to many of their friends and we generated multiple sales as a result.

We also looked for ways that we could expand the referral program into the evening dresses we sold to create a new pageant. The owners selected members of their clientele to compete in the pageant and we provided the formal wear for the contest. The owner of the Vietnamese furniture store was very involved in a similar pageant contest and worked with us to create an event that was a fun experience and contest for her high end affluent customers. I guarantee that there are cultural segments of your business that you could sell to if you would just expand your vision to the possibilities. What cultural segments of the population could you investigate, market to, and benefit from with your business?

You may be hesitant to get into different geographic or cultural niches that you may not be familiar with, yet many of these sub-niches have very affluent populations within them. If you can meet the right connector within these niches, you can create new revenue opportunities for your business. Always be on the lookout for new niches you can dominate in your business.

The focus on creating new and better experiences to your current niche markets can help you grow new and better revenue opportunities within your current business and may be valuable for you to consider.

Enhance the experience prospects will get when they buy from you. You could include a membership with unique experiences that they'll only get when they buy from you. For example, I've coached clients who started offering a breakfast club experience to their customers. Since there aren't any other businesses who are offering this type of experience in their markets, it effectively repositions them into categories of one that customers are drawn to (since they can't get the networking opportunities or experiences unless they participate in these programs – which sneakily require a purchase in order to be a part of them). You would do well to carefully consider ways in which you can reposition what you are selling within such a context.

Analyze your business where you are making the most net profit in your business and look for ways to create enhanced or better experiences. I'll talk more about how you can do this in Chapter 5. Going into depth in these profitable areas can help you counteract some of the forces, shifts and changes in today's marketplace so you can make more sales and more money.

When I met the owners of the Thai, Vietnamese and Filipino markets, they showed me a thick monthly publication that was was mailed to all of the homes within their niche. We advertised and aligned our business with their list by designing a promotion they could send out to their customers. We were able to leverage that relationship in a way that allowed both of us to profit from that cooperation. You can do the same. The professionals in other market niches in your area all have Facebook, Twitter, and Instagram followers and other ways they stay in touch with their customers. You can ask these business owners to share an article about your business with their customers and draw business from this. You can do the same to help them increase sales.

Every business has hidden money in it. Some thought about the assets of your business can help you uncover opportunities where you can convert them into cash. For example, when you pay to promote your business, can you look for ways to get paid as well? Can you get any and all advertising venues you currently spend money with to promote your business to each of their customers? What incentive could you create for these other professionals so they want to promote you and get their list of customers to consider your offer? Some serious reflection on this could create new opportunities for you to grow your current business.

Cameron Herold tells this story in his book *Double Double* about how they found hidden money in their business that is very instructive. He said:

"Years ago, one of my sales teams was working with a large client called Public Storage. We were doing about $180,000 of business with them annually. When we asked them how much total spending they did with us and with competitors of ours, they said they'd have to check. The following week they came back and reported that overall, company wide, they spent about $2 million. Wow! And we were getting a mere 9 percent of that!

"Imagine how the conversation changed at that point to this: 'How can we get more of your business? What do you need to see from us to spend 50 percent of that figure with us?' We knew they had the money because they told us they were spending it! Now we just had to work closely with them to have them spend it with us instead of our competitors."

He continues: "Figure out which of your clients or prospects are doing well. Do your research, really focus on those prospects, and you'll land them without any problem. Ask your clients how much of their current business you are currently getting. Spending time with your top clients to increase revenues is easier than finding new ones. They've got money, remember, and more of it could be yours." –pp. 156-157.

It is very valuable to focus on the 20% of your customers who provide 80% of your business.

Another way you can generate more revenue now is by incentivizing existing customers to refer their friends to do business with you. One solar company I worked with offered to pay a year of a customer's power payments for referring three of their friends to meet with us. Another offered a $500 bonus for every sale they made from a referral. You could also offer an additional bonus when a customer emails you a copy of a testimonial that they posted online. Remember, the things that get rewarded get done.

If you are slow and aren't doing anything to convert leads, you are making a big mistake. Discuss ways with your team in which you could invite customers back to do business with you again. Make specific offers to schedule appointments in empty time slots. Test offers by marketing to your customer list or a list of leads from a recent trade show. Find out which offer pulls buyers in better. Then, adapt what you've learned to continue working through the list in the days and weeks ahead. Instead of mailing to your entire list in one fell swoop, test the waters with two different offers. Find out which one pulls in the most business and then focus more on that promotion with the other customers on the list.

Educational offers are a great way to market to prospects today. If you can provide information that helps each prospect, they will trust you quicker than by just sending out a specific offer.

To market better to prospects today, you must relate to prospects and target what they want most. Prospects will suspend their disbelief about the experience of buying from you if they feel like you relate to them and if you target what they want most. If you don't quickly build trust and relate to a prospect, they will be very skeptical about whether you can actually solve their problem of finding the perfect solution. When prospects aren't confident, they have to get their confidence from you. Prospects desperately want what they seek but they are scared that they can't have those results now – that it really isn't affordable or possible. You can change all of this by being more certain and expressing that confidence through the helpful information that you share.

To better relate to prospects and express your confidence, create educational videos that speak to the prospect and their concerns.

These videos should be designed to answer questions you've been asked by prospects (and a few that they should be asking that they might not have thought of) so you can build each prospect's confidence that you are simply the best choice to find the solution they seek.

Gerry Oginski, a New York medical malpractice attorney, has created and uploaded over 3000 videos that he uses to answer legal questions his prospects have about common and complex questions. Check out his website at oginski-law.com and his You Tube channel to see the masterful way in which he educates his prospects and pre-sells them on why they should hire him as their attorney. He also has several books that he has written (available on Amazon) that promote his expertise and celebrity.

Here are some questions for you to carefully consider as you put your videos together:

• What is the biggest problem that prospects considering your product face?

• How can you better describe your solution to that problem in the advertising and marketing you do?

• How can you tell your story in such a way that prospects feel that they are like you?

Enter into a conversation that is already occurring in the mind of your prospects. Do your best to talk to them about what's on their mind and what they are worried about. Never forget where a prospect is in the process of buying. They should be marketed to differently depending on where they are.

Post your videos on different areas of your web site. They should only be accessible to prospects based on where they are at in the sequence of process of the sale. You should do this for two reasons:

1) You don't want your competition to see everything you're doing, especially on the back end.

2) You don't want prospects to see your videos out of sequence or to address issues that they might not even be worried about until it matters to them. As your sales consultants find out where they are at in different steps of your marketing sequence, they should send the next link to that

prospect with a video explaining what they should do next. These videos are covertly positioned as educational information, but include specific marketing recommendations designed to get a prospect to take the next step in your sales process.

Remember, your business doesn't exist in a vacuum. You must build contrast. When advertising does cut through and gets noticed, remember that your ad is only one of the many messages that they are seeing. Prospects make decisions about what to do, which businesses to check out, and when they should go all based on what they see and hear. Be sure you have a compelling message that stands out so that they see why they need to take action now.

To build contrast in a hypercompetitive environment, you have to be aware of what your competitors are doing and compete in a way that highlights your differentiating point and value. How are you standing out? How many marketing methods did you use to bring in prospects in the last 30, 60, or 90 days? What is working best?

If you are in a hypercompetitive market (and all of us are), you have to stand out in unique ways. What does it take to get *you* out of your house or business to go into a business that is marketing to you? If you are honest with yourself, it likely takes a pretty dramatic offer to incite you to action.

Your prospects are no different. They are busy living their lives. Considering your product may be an interruption to an already stressful day. It would be so much easier to grab and hold their attention if you didn't have any competitors also trying to get them to come into their businesses instead of yours.

In order to properly plan and execute great marketing campaigns, you have to have them planned out in advance and you have to delegate each task to a dedicated team who will work together to make them successful.

One of the reasons why I plan my marketing calendar out a year in advance is that I always know I have a specific strategy or promotion coming up in the next week or two to get more prospects into a marketing funnel and in a position to buy. If you don't plan ahead, it is easy to stop promoting your business and get into a mindset and behavior (of little to no action) that is not healthy. This type of planning requires tremendous focus and discipline.

Always ask questions of others to find out what is working and look carefully at what others in unrelated industries are doing to bring customers into their businesses. Never be content with how things are. Constantly seek to be learning and improving your marketing.

Use multiple offers. All of us are busy and consumed in the multifaceted aspects of our lives. In addition, we all procrastinate. We all should do more than we do to improve key areas of our businesses. Your prospects are no different. Many prospects may have been considering your product or service for weeks or months and still haven't begun the process of shopping. And, this isn't because they haven't been invited to do so. They have likely been invited repeatedly by your competitors, and probably even your own marketing offers. The problem is that unless there is a compelling reason to act, people rarely do. When urgency and scarcity are combined, you can interrupt the daily pattern and routine they find themselves in and inspire them to get into your business to buy from you.

You can't take anything for granted today. Every communication matters now more than ever if you are going to get the sale. You have to use urgency and scarcity in covert ways to get prospects to pay attention to you and act on your promotions. Since all of us procrastinate, scarcity and urgency combined with consistency and sequenced marketing encourage decision.

Perception is reality. Perceived quality matters more than actual quality. If you've ever spent time looking at your largest competitor's offerings, you may noticed that the quality of their products is different than the quality you offer. If you notice that their quality is less than what you offer, remember that they are still bringing prospects into their business and selling them their "lower quality" merchandise. They may continue to sell products of lesser quality year after year because they do a better job of creating a perception in the marketplace that they are the best place to buy the producte they're selling.

I've seen business owners who become infuriated because they know that the quality of what they sell is so much higher than that of what is sold by their biggest competitor. However, perceived quality is much more important than actual quality in the mind of your prospects. It isn't right, but that is the way it is. You can fight these perceptions or you can go out and create your own perceptions.

To do this, you have to use a mix of marketing mediums to grab and keep your prospect's attention. The best way to ensure your promotions get results are to be sure that they appeal to emotion and employ psychological triggers.

The more I study how the human brain reasons, the more convinced I am that the science of neuromarketing should be mastered and studied by every entrepreneur.

Since 95% of why a prospect buys from you is based on a subconscious decision, it is critical to understand how to utilize these psychological triggers to get better results in your marketing and sales efforts. When you study how and why selling works, it is amazing to see how little triggers actually activate the buy switch in the brain. When you understand this and use it in your marketing and selling processes, you will see dramatic results.

A valuable exercise is to watch infomercials to see if you are motivated to act or buy something. You should particularly observe and notice why and consciously determine which psychological triggers were used to create a particular emotional response in you (especially when you do want to buy what is being sold). When you understand how emotion is triggered in you, you'll be better prepared to start using these triggers on a daily basis.

Joe Sugarman says in his book *Triggers*:

"The real underlying psychological triggers that motivate, inspire and influence a prospect to make a buying decision are often unknown to even the most experienced salesperson. Knowledge of these triggers can be a powerful weapon in the battle for your prospect's business. Many of the triggers are very subtle, many are exactly the opposite of what you would expect, and still others you are probably using yourself right now but don't even realize it." --p. 1.

One powerful trigger you should employ more often is the reason why. Prospects know that you want their money, but they really want there to be another reason – so address it when you write your marketing copy. You can do this by asking and answering questions like:

• Why are we going to such an extent to make it easy for you to get what we're offering?

• You may be wondering why we are offering such a great deal on....

It is very important to have a reason why answer to those questions. If you don't, a prospect will not trust what you have to say. Strive to include this in every promotion that you do. When you employ psychological triggers that increase desire and prompt the decision to buy, you will be more successful.

Barry Callen in his book *Perfect Phrases for Sales and Marketing Copy* says:

"Behavior is the result of fear and desire. When the desire exceeds the fear, people act. Your goal in writing sales and marketing copy is to increase desire and reduce fear." Because this is true, it is important that everything we write as we put together marketing campaigns uses powerful emotional words that get to the heart of the matter and trigger an emotional response.

A powerful reason why is to allow prospects to discover why others decided to buy from you. The business with the most social proof wins. Skepticism in the marketplace looms large (and will continue to increase). Those who capture and showcase the most persuasive testimonials will overcome this skepticism to win the battle of perceptions in your market area.

You get testimonials because you ask for them. If your prospects are feeling fear and skepticism, the only way they'll get past those feelings to consider your offer is if they see massive quantities of testimonials from their peers who have purchased from you and who can reassure them that they can trust you as a professional to help them get the results they seek.

When I talk with business owners about this, many of them sense the need to do this, but very few are actually implementing systems in their businesses to capture and disseminate these testimonials to the eyes and ears of the public.

If you haven't started capturing testimonials, today is the day to begin. You can't afford to let another customer who has purchased from you leave without capturing either a written or video testimonial of their experience of buying from you and how the experienced compared to the other competitors they visited or considered.

It is no secret that people would rather watch a movie than read a book. People today would rather watch a short video featuring one of her peers over reading a testimonial any day of the week. Are you providing this easily accessible experience for prospective clients to view on your blog and social networking platforms? If not, start now. The businesses that will grow quickest will be those who have the most social proof.

Every area of your business should promote how you have helped customers using their words. Don't ignore this critical area of your marketing. You can never have too much social proof. Never stop gathering these video and written testimonials and you will be rewarded with customers who are persuaded by their peers to do business with you.

As we conclude this chapter, ask yourself: What is weighing *you* down? What forces, shifts, and changes do you need to make in your business so you can be more competitive and make more sales and more money? I hope this chapter has opened your eyes to the problems you face today, what you must do going forward to take more control, and what you should be focusing on to maximize your results.

CHAPTER 3

COMPETE AND WIN AGAINST AMAZON AND THE GIANTS IN YOUR INDUSTRY

"All David had was faith and a rock and he defeated a giant."—Anonymous

G iants dominate every industry. Corporate takeovers and buyouts have built massive companies that have tremendous buying power and who make competing difficult. Amazon has profoundly transformed the retail industry and the company continues to change how transactions are done worldwide.

Today, more than twenty-five years after Amazon.com began, they have completely altered the consumer landscape.

Here is a brief rundown of Amazon.com's operations today:

• 175 fulfillment centers worldwide (with 110 in North America)

• In partnership with USPS, currently offering Sunday deliveries in select cities. Someday, Bezos hopes to deliver packages via drone.

• More than 100 million AmazonPrime members worldwide ($109/

year membership fee)

• 100 million+ eligible AmazonPrime products (free 2 day shipping - recently changed to 1 day shipping on many of these items)

• AmazonPrime instant video offers tens of thousands of movies and TV episodes, including PBS, FX, NBC, CBS, HBO programming, kids' programming like Spongebob SquarePants and Dora the Explorer and original programming (launched less than a decade ago to compete with what Netflix is doing in the same space).

• Amazon bought Whole Foods in 2017 in a deal valued at $13.7 billion and now has 450 physical locations from which to deliver groceries and other items

• Amazon bought and owns Zappos, but Amazon Fashions, which they've grown from scratch is also booming. Their 40,000 square foot fashion photography and web production studio in Brooklyn, New York shoots an average of 14,000 photos everyday.

• Total full time and part time employee count: more than 750,000 at the end of 2019

• Amazon.com currently has more than 310 million active customers. Jay Greene of The Seattle Times writes that while Google and Facebook get all the attention for their potential to attract online advertisers, the data that Amazon has on "its [310] million active customer accounts... puts Google to shame." He's right. While Google and Facebook can tell advertisers what its customers like, Amazon can tell them what they actually buy...and when...and how frequently...and to a certain extent why." (Sources: Money.com, Google, Time.com, Seattle Times)

Competition continues its relentless attack on business owners in many shapes and fashions, but the effects that will continue to be felt by Amazon.com will be profound. Consider this statement by Amazon founder Jeff Bezos:

"We are genuinely customer centric, we are genuinely long-term oriented and we genuinely like to invent. Most companies are not those things. They are focused on the competitor, rather than the customer. They want to work on things that will pay dividends in two or three years, and if they don't work in two or three years they will move on to something else. And they prefer to be close-followers rather than inventors, because it's safer. So if you want to capture the truth about Amazon, that is why we are different. Very few companies have all of those three elements."—Brad Stone, *The Everything Store*, p. 12.

What does all of this mean? I think there are three main things to recognize about the rapid growth of Amazon.com and the future of your business.

First, Amazon.com has a huge amount of customers who trust their brand. Think about what this means for retailers who are selling branded merchandise in their stores that is NOT their own brand. With one and two day free shipping for Amazon Prime members, the reality is that the business landscape has fundamentally shifted because Amazon.com has the ability to market far better than the average business today.

What does this mean for your business? Think about the changes made by Amazon.com in the past twenty-five years. What will the future of business look like twenty-five years from now?

Manufacturers are going to sell their products where they can sell the most of what they offer. If Amazon.com can deliver more customers to them than a retail store, a manufacturer will either open their own retail stores or move to sell online with Amazon. Amazon has already opened a few of their own retail stores. This is what a Wal-Mart executive said is one of their greatest fears. With their own grocery stores and a delivery force, they can have groceries delivered to a home within an hour of an order.

When I think about the future, I truly believe that every business owner MUST brand themselves and their business. Your competitors (and this includes Amazon) can't copy you and they can't exactly duplicate your brand and the relationship you have with your customers. However, if you are a generalist and offer the same things they carry (and if Amazon. com starts offering products in your industry) you can be sure that many will go out of business because they won't have adapted to specialize in what is truly unique about their business. If you haven't already started building your own celebrity brand, I hope this prediction motivates you to get up and get going. I also think more specific customization will be an important piece that wholesalers and retailers need to work on together so they can better figure out how to create even more powerful experiences for shoppers.

Secondly, Amazon.com has a fascinating portal program that provides the ability to sell directly to their customers for a percentage of each sale. You can learn more about that on their web site at: https:// sellercentral.amazon.com. In other words, you can set up your own storefront on Amazon.com and offer products to your prospects. Businesses who recognize the power of branding themselves and offering services directly to their prospects through this platform will bypass those who aren't willing to learn how to utilize this technology or ability.

The challenge with businesses that align themselves with Amazon as its transactor is that Amazon may enter the business directly when they see a large volume of profitable transactions. There is value in aligning with Amazon's seller central program. Yet, long-term, it may prove to arm Amazon with valuable intel as to the worth of your business.

Third and most importantly, every business owner must learn how to use as much of what Amazon offers to promote themselves, their business, their products, and their E-book platform to present themselves as an expert. You can learn more about that option on their web site: https://kdp.amazon.com.

The most valuable aspect of Amazon is your ability to use it to connect with their customers and build your expertise at the same time. Every entrepreneur MUST learn how to use Amazon.com as a source to generate leads for their business.

I've coached many entrepreneurs to write a book that prospects can download on the Amazon site when they search for your product and service. You can have a book entitled "The Ultimate Insider's Guide to Get *Your Product and Service*". Use Amazon to build your expertise and authority by writing your own book that educates your prospects about why they should do business with you.

Now you likely have no interest in growing a business that has 750,000+ employees. Just hearing or reading the statistics I shared about Amazon.com's startling growth over the past twenty-five years may give you tremendous anxiety and fill you with fear regarding the future. I am not sharing these details to scare you. I am sharing them with you so that you can think differently about your business and so that you can respond proactively in a way that will benefit your business instead of reacting after your business has already gone somewhere else. Previously successful businesses like Blockbuster and Hollywood Video learned that in today's economy, it isn't enough to have a great retail location. They've been beaten and destroyed by forward thinking entrepreneurs who have capitalized on trends and possibilities that their competitors hadn't thought about or responded to well.

I believe that learning how successful entrepreneurs think and what they do with their time is critically important. This is one of the big reasons why I read so many business biographies and strive to listen to and learn from business leaders in other industries. I share my findings in Chapter 5 of my book *The System is the Secret.*

I had a conversation with a mentor and coach of mine who talked with me about his routine for taking time to think for at least an hour each and every day. This allows him to better define and look at how to utilize the opportunities within his own business. I believe that you and I must learn to do this better as well instead of being so busy that we end up just going with the flow.

Mindy Grossman, previous CEO of the Home Shopping Network (and current CEO of Weight Watchers International Inc.) said in the *New York Times* on June 14, 2010 that "the days of trying to get a customer to come to you are over. You really have to be in the consumer's world, wherever, whenever and however." That is a pretty fascinating statement.

What are you doing to be in your prospect's world so that you can sell to him or her wherever, whenever, and however they please? The reality is that retailers aren't doing this very well and so customers are finding online options where they can shop as they please once they believe they've found exactly what they're looking for.

Apple has changed the expectations that customers have when they open a new product (especially in regards to packaging). Are you creating an amazing experience when your customers buy something from you? What surprises and fun packaging options do your customers receive after they purchase a product from you?

Remember, there is an actual endorphin rush that comes with opening a package that has been ingrained in you since childhood when you anticipated and opened presents on Christmas morning. Smart entrepreneurs create packaging and surprises that tap into these emotional triggers. Deliver more value and better packaging to your customers. It is one more way that you can stand out in an Amazon.com world.

Set up and position your business for success on your first visit by creating an E-book detailing information that introduces you, positions your business as a leader in your market niche, and offers other helpful information that will help prospects see the benefit of choosing your business as the place to buy what they need. Prospects can download this E-book through a special link on Amazon.com for free.

Post information on your web site so that prospects can download special reports and checklists right off your home page when they give you their email address.

You can have someone convert your Word file to a .mobi file (which is the format that Amazon.com utilizes for their Kindle readers) and to design your ebook cover at http://www.fiverr.com/ and by searching for "Convert Word file to .mobi file)" Once your file has been converted, you can upload it to amazon.com on their site: https://kdp.amazon.com after you set up your own account.

Here are a few examples of E-books you could create:

• What to Expect at Your First Visit

• The Most Common Mistakes Made by People Searching for Product X and How to Avoid Them

• The 10 Commandments of Shopping for Product X

• The Ultimate Insider's Guide to Finding the Perfect Solution to Challenge XYZ

Put these together in an E-book and have the .mobi file created so you can upload it to your kdp.amazon.com page.

When writing your E-book or your presales collateral, remember, the biggest mistake you can make when pre-selling your business is to talk about how great you are in your own words. You want others to do this for you. Remember, prospects are coming to your web site looking for information and the more information you can provide them about why you are the best place to get Product XYZ that is said in words by his or her peers (other customers who had the same challenge), the better off you will be. Convert your testimonials into a video to put on your web site and your ebook to showcase to prospects of what their peers think of your business who have actually purchased from you.

Offer something for free that you can use to convert lookers into prospects that you can market to. This can be a contest for a drawing for free merchandise or having informational articles that inform prospects.

The goal is to capture their email address and contact information so you can send them more information and invite them to schedule an appointment. A free E-book filled with coupons and links to your site is a great way for you to set you apart from your competition, teach prospects what they should expect from their buying experience, how to know if a business is the best place to buy your product, etc. The goal is to help the prospects by giving them information that makes them feel more comfortable about you because you are helping them make a good decision.

Amazon and the giants of your industry will eat you alive if you don't change what you are doing and adopt game changers that will put you back on top. Here are ten big lessons and strategies that business owners must better employ to compete with Amazon and win against the giants of their industry on a local level:

1. Fight industry giants on unfamiliar ground and where they don't want to risk losing a battle with you.

Stephen Denny talks about this principle in an excellent book entitled *Killing Giants*. The basic premise is that if you lure a giant onto an area of thin ice, you'll be much more successful battling him there, since his weight will cause him to fall through the ice. Instead of risking losing, the giant will usually retreat and choose not to fight.

In Denny's words, "thin ice" is "dangerous to companies who are too big to venture far from the relative safety of familiar ground. The giant's weight shifts and the ice cracks and groans underneath its feet. It's dangerous out here. Better to retreat than to risk everything. But you know the ice can support your weight. You made this patch of ice in the first place. So taunt the giant all you want. When we create our own 'thin ice', we change the environment to suit our needs. We move the public dialogue to a place where the giant is unprepared to go. Rather than risk the loss of face that will come from such a fight, the giant will likely choose to simply not fight at all." –*Killing Giants*, p. 17.

A great example in the book is the online search engine Baidu. Baidu is a Chinese web search engine that competes with the giant Google, but does so by pointing out why they are superior in their mastery over the Chinese language (an area that Google doesn't have dominance in). This is a great illustration of the principle of moving your marketing battle to unfamiliar ground to the giant:

There are four points that Denny makes in the book that I think bear some thought about how you compete against the giants in your industry. Denny's points are in italics, followed by my observations:

1) Act like a local. In the case of Baidu, they focused on something (language) that the giant Google (who is based in the U.S.) can never really command like the natives who run the Chinese site Baidu.

What things can you highlight at your business that highlight your unique differences and contribution to the community?

To do this, you must promote your local ties (how long you've been in the community, how you contribute back to the community, share, and promote your self-generated PR that shows why you are different and a valuable resource to your community.

When we opened our first business, my wife and I invited several media outlets to come and do a story on a specific niche that we served that our biggest competitors didn't. We were able to highlight our difference and use language that showed to our target niche that we really understood their needs. I also called up a target publication that was sent directly to that niche and did advertising there (which the big box retailers weren't even aware existed) and then I wrote an article about our store and submitted it to the editor. I told her she could attach her name to it and even take credit for writing the article. When the article came out, the editor only changed 2 or 3 sentences of the article I wrote (which promoted us in a 3rd person endorsement). We then framed the article and hung it in our business where all of our customers could see it and promoted it to brides who came into the store. It helped us to stand out and get recognition from that market niche very quickly. In most cases, big national or global competitors aren't familiar with your local community and operate outside of it. If you can tap into the local community with your own clever marketing strategies, you can stand out in ways that the larger competitor can't.

2) Ask: What argument can the giant in your industry never win?

In my opinion, there are three main areas:

- Attention to niche market areas that they don't see as important or meaningful

- Attention to follow up detail (Most giants are primarily interested in getting prospects into their business first – their follow up if the prospect doesn't buy is good, but you can be different and better)

- Customer service (Giants will never care about a customer as much as you will) – if you can develop and promote this difference in a clever way, you can really stand out (For example, a bridal retailer I coached promotes this difference in their marketing. They say: "We care as much about your wedding as you do. When you purchase your dress here, you will always be a friend, not just a number or a sale." How can you point out your difference in a similar way?

3) Point out how you are like those you serve and can identify with the challenges they are facing. It never ceases to amaze me how asking questions and listening can build trust and help prospects really feel like you are on their side. Many times, sales consultants at larger competitors only view what they do as a job and the difference shows. There is a lot of turnover with employees and it is hard to build momentum when everyone is constantly new and learning how to talk with prospects about their needs.

Affinity matters. When someone can identify with you, the speed at which trust develops accelerates. Let your prospects get to know you before they meet with you for the first time with a welcome video link emailed to them when they schedule an appointment and a "What to Expect" pre-sales sequence.

Most big competitors promote themselves as being all things for all people. How are you standing out in contrast to this? Are you building your brand so that it means something to buy your product from you? Build your brand around you and the overall experience that the customer will get from you that they can't get anywhere else. Promoting yourself, your individual brand, and your ties to the local community can be a great way to re-position a larger competitor who doesn't offer the top notch experience and treatment they'll get when they buy from you.

In the bridal business, the industry leader, David's Bridal, oftens highlights their leadership expertise. For example, in their ads promoting their bridesmaid colors, they say: "Lots of places have lots of colors, but when it comes to the latest in fashion, David's leads the way. Only the hottest colors make it to our showrooms."

A question I once asked a bridal retailer I coached is a good one for you to consider as well. I asked: What are you the leader of in your market? Then I asked: What are you doing to pick the colors that make it into your store? I told her that her biggest competitor really misses the mark in their advertising by not romancing the story about how the colors and the dresses actually made it into their store. As a result, she started saying in her promotions: "Last year, my staff and I traveled 3,421 miles to bring you 14 brand new colors in addition to the 49 stunning colors we already offer to the most fashionable brides in our area." She marketed that difference and it improved her perception amongst her target customers. You can do the same.

Specificity (especially with numbers is a very powerful way to position your expertise). In this case, pointing out exactly how many miles she travels to markets and to factories overseas to bring those colors into her store makes a more compelling case than the generic advertising of her biggest competitor.

A story can be even more meaningful if you talk about how you helped a specific customer and give a testimonial of how they praise you for going the extra mile to get what they were looking for.

4) Aim at the underserved. Giants have so many different product lines and offerings (and brands) that it can be easy to confuse the prospect. How can you position yourself as speaking directly to a prospect who may feel overwhelmed and confused by all of the options? How can you reassure a prospect that you are there for them and will take care of them throughout every step of the customer experience in ways that your competitors can't or won't?

When you can point out these differences, you force the big competitors to come onto the thin ice where you have the advantage. Your competitors will never be able to offer the personal touch that you can as an independently owned business. It is critically important that you exploit this difference in your marketing. They may have more marketing muscle in terms of dollars and cents, but they will never have as much personal heart and intense focus on the needs of customers than you do. If you aren't promoting those differences, prospects will be swayed by the persuasive and slick marketing of these big competitors and you will miss out on a lot of sales that you could otherwise have.

Giants in any industry (and your industry is no different) have different problems than you do. Their focus is more on supply and logistics than it is on truly creating a unique experience for prospects who come into their businesses. This is a big opportunity for the independent business owner if you will recognize it and capitalize on it.

In the solar industry, I see the biggest competitors fail most often on delivering memorable experiences to their customers. By offering a personal touch that wasn't just focused on putting panels on roofs (and how to lower the cost per watt to satisfy investors), smaller competitors sell circles around the biggest companies. A personal touch and better experience has helped them rise above the giants with more referrals and and it will do the same for you.

2. Industry giants are often slow to move and can't hit what they can't catch. Be more nimble and win on speed.

Your competitors are doing a lot of things right and they are focusing on a lot of the right things. However, this doesn't mean that they are perfect. The key is for you to look at weaknesses that you can exploit and take advantage of that speak to their weaknesses and that speak to your strengths.

The old saying "The bigger they are, the harder they fall" is one that lots of small business owners would like to believe about their competitors and industry giants, yet more often than not, they are doing very smart things with their social media and advertising that you must pay attention to.

The movie *Ford v. Ferrari* starring Matt Damon as American car designer Carroll Shelby and Christian Bale as British race car driver Ken Miles illustrates a great example of this principle.

In 1963, Ford made an offer to buy struggling car manufacturer Ferrari. Just before the deal was to close, Enzo Ferrari pulled out of the deal and sold a majority stake in Ferrari to car manufacturer Fiat. Henry Ford II, the grandson of Henry Ford, decided to take revenge by building his own car to race against Ferrari in the 24 Hours of Le Mans race. After losing to Ferrari in 1964 and 1965 at Le Mans, Ford put Carroll Shelby in charge of designing a car that could win. Ford ended up humiliating Ferrari in 1966 by winning the first, second, and third spots while Ferrari didn't even finish the race. Ford won Le Mans in 1966, 1967, 1968, and 1969. The ingenuity and resourcefulness with which Shelby and Miles overcame challenges on the track and with the car is a very inspiring story. Being nimble and figure out what works with speed made the difference between defeat and winning. The same is true with the industry giants you compete with in your market as well.

3. Win in the last few feet where you make the sale. Your competitors and industry leaders may be winning the advertising

and marketing battle, but all battles are really decided in the last few feet where the sale is made. Are you winning there?

If you are going to compete and win against those that dominate your industry, you have to fight to win in the last few feet. You have to fight to win by having a better sales approach and incentive that will tip prospects over the edge to buy from you instead of continuing to look at other places. You also want prospects to come visit you first so they have a point of comparison if they do go look at the other offerings later on. I know many smart entrepreneurs who encourage prospects to meet with them first so prospects can get in and experience what their business is like first. That way, if they do end up going to a competitor (if they didn't get the sale the first time), they will come back because of what a different experience they had with you first.

The challenge with taking on any giant in any industry is that they have more resources with money and people than you do. They are very good at starting lots of things. They spend a lot of money to build awareness. A great push for a new product line may be made for a new product, yet in most cases, there are only a limited number of actual products to buy as the giant tries to hedge their bets to see how the product will sell first before they stock it in any depth. Some ideas fail and some are wildly successful. Most new ideas come and go. Few are executed well. To compete against this, you have to create your own buzz worthy events that promote you and your brand.

Do you stay on top of your competitor's sales and promotions?

Do you know what they are starting and aren't following through with?

When you see gaps, are you pouncing on these opportunities or are you so caught up in your day to day drama that you forget to look for opportunities?

Work on your persuasion skills in the last few feet. I think studying how to be more persuasive when you sell is a critically important characteristic that can help you be much more successful.

Also, ask: Where doesn't my biggest competitor think to compete?

I think this is a great question that would give you some great insights if you would think about it. Most industry giants try to be all things to all people. They are focusing on so many different specialties that they really aren't taking the time to be great at any of them. They begin things well, but don't consistently follow through well.

The real opportunity to beat your competitors is to focus on areas where they don't think to compete and specialize in those areas better than they can or will.

The key point is this: The industry giants will always be good at product launches. They have the marketing budget to run TV and online advertising with numerous steps along the way. But, they don't sustain those ideas for a long period of time. Look for their weaknesses in these areas and then strike.

Industry giants are usually so busy putting periods after each market segment and moving on to a new category that they won't really notice if you are putting question marks behind those statements and point out why you are different and why what they are promoting really isn't what your prospect wants or needs.

To win in today's hyper-competitve markets, you must *know* your prospects and customers. When you know at least three things more about a prospect and how they are planning to use your product and the experience they're trying to create, you'll be more successful than your competitors. Knowing more details means the prospect trusts you more which also means that you are on track to make the sale. Never get so far away from your prospects and customers that you aren't aware of what is going on. A quick glance at a lot of the reviews of industry giants indicates that they aren't really in touch with what their customers want or what they are experiencing when they go through their journey in pursuit of the product you offer. Be sure to monitor your own reviews as well to catch issues that your customers are concerned about.

There is a lot of anger and frustration voiced online today. I once heard an executive foolishly say that he didn't care about bad reviews because he could bury those bad reviews with more good reviews. That attitude of burying complaints instead of listening is an opportunity for a competitor to gain a competitive upper hand. Don't let that happen to you.

Remember that there is also a point in every sale when prospects are open to persuasive suggestions. Are you in front of prospects when they are open to suggestion? If not, what can you do to be there (and win)?

4. Fight back. Don't be content with allowing industry giants to take a large percentage of the prospects in your market niche. Fight back to maintain your competitive edge.

Some companies will fight dirty to win business without considering the cost. I'm not one who endorses fighting dirty. I just don't think you can't fight this way without becoming a little bit of what you were fighting in the first place. But, I do believe you should fight back. There is no excuse for letting another competitor define you and saying nothing about it. Sometimes, you may have to use guerrilla tactics to win the fight, but you should do so tactically so that you end up where you want to. Sometimes you can fight the wrong fight and win and you end up someplace that you didn't think you would.

The best way to fight and win is to narrow the niche and become the best in the world in that area. It is difficult to defend something that is too big. What small area or market niche can you best defend in the minds of prospects who are considering your product or service? Remember, there are riches in niches. You can specialize in certain areas or offer certain products that big competitors may not think is a very important area. Your specialization in these areas can help you build a powerful brand and may even become your core business.

Think carefully about your long-term strategy with regard to how you will fight with your entrenched competitors in certain market segments.

Look for openings where you can come in and dominate the marketplace for your customer. Being a 'me-too' business that offers what everyone else does severely limits your ability to stand out in the marketplace. Choose to stand out with your unique difference.

When you look at other businesses in other competitive industries through the paradigm of war (and where individual competitors are at), you'll see why some companies are gaining ground in their marketing and why some are losing the battle.

Hershey dominated Nestle in the candy wars with their Krackel bar over the Crunch bar by focusing on winning in the vending machine niche. They gave better incentives to the owners of the vending machines that Nestle wasn't willing to (and so they got better placement) and as a result more sales.

Disney shifted the battlefield to position themselves to win the streaming wars with Disney+ by first buying companies with great intellectual property (Pixar, Marvel, Lucasfilm, and Twenty-First Century Fox) and then developing value out of great characters and stories. They are focused on telling great stories with their characters instead of just putting out content (whether it is good or not) to fill their platform.

Internet vendors have shifted the battlefield against independent retailers who carry the same product lines they do by offering products without sales tax, free shipping, and other incentives with purchase. Many retailers complain that this isn't fair. It may not be fair, but they are winning because they have shifted the battlefield in their favor.

What are *you* doing to shift the battlefield so the odds are stacked in your favor?

Carrying the same product lines that everyone else has stacks the odds in favor of Internet vendors and you will be used as a try on business where the prospect can find out what they like (and in many cases the manufacturer and SKU number) so they can buy online.

Building your own brand over the manufacturer's brand stacks the odds in your favor. It is a way to fight dirty without getting dirty. If you are losing sales to local competitors and industry giants (and you are), think about what you can do to get the upper hand in the battles you are fighting.

5. Do the unthinkable. Do what the big box retailers or industry giants can't or won't do well.

What is the unthinkable that the industry leader in your market can't or won't do?

This is where your opportunity lies. No matter how big your business is, you can build your brand. No one can compete with that. There is only one you. Tying yourself to a celebrity is a great marketing strategy, but the best marketing strategy of all is to turn yourself into a celebrity and promote yourself (thus building trust and creating a unique experience that will be completely different from the experience your biggest competitors are promoting). What customers who buy from the industry giants really get is this: They buy a non-unique product that customers all across the country will use. If you can position their experience as average and generic while simultaneously positioning yourself as an approachable celebrity they can truly get to know and work with, you will have a huge advantage.

Giants in your industry won't take risks with some new trends because they have to duplicate the product for hundreds of locations. Making mistakes with inventory are much more costly for them than they are for you, especially if they are under contract to put so many products in their stores. If the products aren't very good or don't sell, they have a lot of money tied up in inventory that may not come back very quickly. This is where you can compete and win since you can respond much quicker to trends that are happening in the marketplace than they can. You can bring in a few product offerings and afford to make small mistakes to find out what is really selling, whereas a mistake on their end can be very costly and slow to recover from.

Here are five things you could do that your biggest competitors may not be willing to do:

1) Share your knowledge in a way that builds a relationship with the prospect. Any information that is shared by industry giants is typically done in a sterile, non-relationship building way. You can share special reports that build your authority and celebrity and that build a one-on-one relationship with your prospects. Always look for ways you can share information that will be meaningful to them and that will help them get answers to questions and challenges they are facing.

2) Address the fears a prospect may be facing head on in a personalized way that opens a relationship. This is best done through written and video testimonials. Incentivize customers to share their experiences with you by offering them an incentive for sharing their thoughts on paper or in a video format that you can use to answer a new prospect's most common questions. Do this in a way that allows prospects to overcome their fears of buying the product you are offering. Make a list of questions that prospects have and create a series of videos where you answer each of those questions in a way that allows prospects to get to know you personally. Even if industry giants were to do this (which they likely won't), prospects won't have the added benefit of meeting the person in the video like they can if you are to do these for your business.

3) Offer an outrageous incentive when customers refer their friends. You can do this in tiered levels or even offer the customer their money back if they refer a certain number of their friends. I've seen retailers refund purchases up to $1,000 to those customers who referred eight or more new customers who also bought from that store. I've seen solar companies pay for up to a year of a customer's power bill just for referring people who sit down with a member of their sales team for an appointment with a qualified homeowner. Big box giants would likely never attempt such a program because the red tape of something like

that with hundreds of locations would be very challenging to track on a corporate level. This is an advantage you can tap into.

4) Think hard about where industry giants can't go and put together your own road map of how you could go there and prosper in that uncontested area. Also think about what you can do that they can't. This is where you true opportunities lie. What contracts or supply arrangements are they locked into that may be a disadvantage to them? Look at your biggest competitor's web sites and think about this question in comparison with your own strengths and specialties. What opportunities do you see? What are they taking for granted that you could exploit? Bureaucracy really limits how much creative thinking giants can do. Don't limit yourself by thinking small in these areas.

5) Look at what really brings in the money for giants of your industry. Since, the giant's business model depends on volume, what could you do that would disrupt that volume and bring it into your business instead? Ask yourself: How do they really make money? What problems arise as a result of focusing more on volume than on an individualized, personalized experience?

Choose to do more unthinkable things that an industry giant would never conceive or dream of doing. There may be big opportunities for you in those areas.

6. Make the inconvenient argument about why buying from you is better.

Most business owners don't really think about why they are unique and different. They don't promote their differences very well. If you can articulate why you are better and make the inconvenient argument that positions your business as a better buy than your competitors, you will win the sale. If they do this better than you, they win the sale. How do you win in this scenario? By putting the math in front of your prospects and helping them to see that you are clearly the best choice.

I once talked with a bride who came into our store who loved a dress but just couldn't commit to buy the dress on her first visit. I stepped back and said, "I know you love this dress. What is it that is holding you back from going ahead and getting the dress you love?" She finally opened up and told me the reason that was holding her back (she had been offered a package deal at another bridal salon that she had just been to). When she finally opened up and shared this detail with me, then we were able to have an honest conversation about how our total offer compared with what she would get from the other store. It was amazing to see her face and her shoulders physically relax when she finally told me what the real concern was. It was an emotional fear of losing out (because of the total package of what she would get including flower girl dresses that we didn't offer). When I told her of a place in town where she could get flower girl dresses with the money she was saving on her dress and by giving her a $100 discount for purchasing from us on her first visit, I could see that she was open to be persuaded. If I wouldn't have known what her concern was and I kept pushing for the sale, I would have lost it (and probably never known why). As it turns out, we had a great discussion about the dress and she bought it and spent the money she saved by buying on her first visit towards the flower girl dresses at the store I told her about.

Are you putting the math in front of your prospects and showing them that you are the best overall value? If not, you are making a big mistake. If not, your prospects are only looking at the total price of what you are selling (which is never an indicator of the best total overall value).

Consider the difference between two scenarios:

1) A product offered for $1,000 (or whatever the average amount of your product or service is).

2) A product for $1,000 (or whatever the average amount of your product or service is) with an incentive if a customer buys on their first visit or appointment, over $1,000 in coupons from local vendors they

can't get anywhere else, and the opportunity to get the first year of their payments paid simply for referring three friends to meet with one of your sales consultants.

That type of contrast helps prospects decide emotionally AND rationally since it makes all of the sense in the world to buy from the place that will save you money and time and give you a chance to get back the money you have spent.

Industry giants won't put together packages like that with local vendors and the logistics of a referral program with multiple locations can be so staggering that it likely won't even be attempted.

Not only will a promotion like that spread like wildfire through social media and traditional media outlets, it can also create tremendous testimonials afterwards. You can use those testimonials to invite other new prospective customers to experience your competitive difference.

Here are two great questions for you to ponder (as an assignment):

What things could you do or offer during slow seasons at your business that would get the attention of the social media channels or traditional media channels you are in (or aren't in yet)?

What can you do to eliminate fine print or worries that prospects may have that can help you make the argument that buying from you is the best choice they could ever make?

Think about these two questions. Put the math in front of your prospects and you'll be amazed at how they'll respond. Letting prospects know how much they'll save if they buy on their first visit before they even sit down for their first appointment is a big part of this strategy that will help you compete against and win against your biggest competitors.

7. Thrive by drawing attention to your differences. Help prospects make the decision to buy from you now by polarizing these differences.

Part of being different is knowing what you stand for and eliminating everything that doesn't match that. Emphasizing your difference is an exercise in subtraction—where you prune out anything and everything that no longer matters. This kind of discipline is difficult, especially when you are operating out of fear because you've just lost a series of sales to a new, larger competitor. You will have to decide what will work best for you, but the key point is that you can't panic when you see sales drop.

As much as you would love to operate your businesses in a vacuum without any competition, you become a better business person because of competitors. They force you to think differently about your businesses and this makes all of the difference in the world. Positioning yourself against the competition allows you to compete and grow against them. You have to find your niche and specialize instead of trying to be all things to all people. To some, this seems counterintuitive, but it is the best strategy for beating a giant at their own game. Study what successful businesses in other industries do to compete with their giants. Use your ability to adapt quicker to succeed.

Put the math in front of your prospects and help them win the argument about why buying from you is the best overall value. If you don't aggressively promote your difference, your prospects won't know. If they don't know, they can't contrast what they see at your business versus what they see at another competitor. This is the same for Internet vendors who compete with you. If you are trying to compete on price, you will lose that battle. The reality is that you can't sell the same product for the same price (because they can always beat you with no sales tax, no shipping, or some other special offer they have) even if the product is sold at the same price. Build your value in other ways above and beyond price. Offer products that aren't sold online. It is a lot easier to build value if prospects can't compare apples to apples.

It is no fun to be stressed out all of the time. Your prospects can sense this. It is much better to laugh, to have fun, and to truly enjoy the experience of working with those prospects you meet with. When you and your sales consultants are excited and happy, you'll sell more. Part of being a great leader is to recognize when the morale of your sales consultants is down and do whatever it takes to get it back up and soaring again. Let your team members know how much you appreciate their efforts and what they contribute each day.

Your ability to get to know a prospect on a personal level is what will always set your independent business apart from bigger competitors. Employees of big competitors will never be as invested as you are in taking care of prospects and providing that little bit extra that goes a long way in their mind. What are you doing to get to know prospects better? Do they sense your commitment to them and helping them get the results they seek? When you are committed do doing what is right for those you serve, they'll sense the difference and do business with you over a larger competitor who doesn't offer the same level of attention to detail.

You decide what you will offer in your business. You can choose to offer products and services that you lose money or break even on, but why? Why not invest in product lines that give you a better margin and that aren't available anywhere else? Set yourself apart from your competitors by finding your speciality and your niche. Remember, it is your business and you can be as flexible as you want by how you choose to buy and sell your merchandise. No one is forcing you to offer products that you can't make a healthy margin on. Only you can decide what you will offer and what you won't. At the end of the day, that decision will make all of the difference in how successful you are at competing against and winning against the giants of your industry.

Choose which battles you will fight. Trying to offer everything that a competitor does is a recipe for disaster. You'll never be able to compete with them on that level and with that kind of overhead in inventory expense. Instead, you have to look at profitable areas you can focus on that can give you the edge you want and need. Look again at what the giants are unwilling to do and see if you can offer things to your prospects that they can't or won't and that can be profitable for you. This is so important. Deciding what you will stand for and sticking to this is as important as a strategy as any to successfully compete with the giants in your industry.

How often are you looking at the web site and social media for your biggest competitors? Do you know what they are doing? Since you don't operate in a vacuum you had better be aware of what they are doing. As the old saying goes, 'Keep your friends close, and your enemies closer.'

Sun Tzu, an ancient Chinese general made this statement in *The Art of War*:

"Know the enemy and know yourself; in a hundred battles you will never be in peril. When you are ignorant of the enemy but know yourself, your chances of winning or losing are equal. If ignorant both of your enemy and of yourself, you are certain in every battle to be in peril."

Be aware of what is going on. Get competive flyers at trade shows. Study what they are doing. Put together an outline of their marketing calendar to help you plan your offensive attack against them. Study what they do and think about how you can and will respond.

Invent media if you have to promote your difference to the community and your contribution back into the community. Big box retailers typically don't have this type of involvement in the local communities in which they are located. Choose instead to stand out in this area.

When we opened our first business, I introduced myself to the manager at the closest David's Bridal (the giant in the bridal industry) and told her that we specialized in sleeved wedding dresses (which they didn't carry). We got a lot of referrals from that store manager who would send brides who were looking for sleeved dresses simply because I had the courage to introduce myself and tell her of a service we offered that brides in our area are looking for. Make a goal that you will introduce yourself to your competitors at your next trade show. Now, I know that there may be some terrible competitors out there with whom you could never imagine having that kind of conversation. Sometimes, a fresh approach can yield big dividends. Look for ways to make friends out of your competitors.

Get to know what your competitors are doing and it is much easier to point out your differences and help prospects see why you are the best choice.

8. Lead the conversation. Step up and lead. People are looking for a leader.

Here are some questions for you to reflect on:

• What are you doing to capture the imagination of prospects? Is the atmosphere of your business fun (so that prospects get emotionally caught up in what they are doing)?

• Are you pointing out your differences? If you don't know what they are, your prospects don't either. Step up and control the conversation so that prospects know how fun the experience of buying from you will be.

• Are you building your celebrity? Are prospects drawn to your comments (blog posts, video posts, special reports) and do they believe that you are an authority in your industry? What can you do to be the conversation and take up all of the oxygen in the room?

• Are you appearing everywhere that prospects are looking for help with their challenges and your product solution?

• What have you done today to let prospects know about you and your business?

In most areas, there is no designated spokesperson for your customers. You need to become that person. This will set you apart from your bigger competitors and let prospects know that they must check out your offering before they decide.

There are so many tools today that make is so easy to speak directly to your prospects including online networks, podcasts, and videos. You can be the dominant spokesperson in your market by making the decision to direct and control the conversation in a way that promotes you and your business.

9. Be a fearsome competitor and no one wants to fight you. Choose your battles carefully by specializing in areas only you can win. This makes you more fearsome to battle in the future.

One of the ways you can be even more fearsome to your competitors is to be more in tune with what the market wants. Do the dirty work that will give you clues into what is happening in the market. Ask: What are you doing to make yourself indispensible to prospects who are considering what you offer? Are you in the room when the prospect is thinking about what they'll do to achieve the results they want with your product or service? If not, how can you be there?

If you have what prospects are asking for, you'll be able to draw them into your marketing funnels better and close the sale. How well are you staying on top of what is happening in your market? Remember, listening closely to what your customers are saying can give you the edge. Here are some suggestions to help you do this better:

• Stay in touch with what is going on in your market. Listening is the way to gain wisdom because everything you say you already know.

• Don't trust your instincts more than what prospects are actually asking for.

• When you lose the sale, find out why. Find out if you had something similar to offer or if it was a product that you don't currently offer. By continually interacting with your customers, you'll have a much better sense of what you should buy and offer.

• Stay on top of trends. Get feedback from your social media channels about what people are looking for.

• Ask your customers why they bought from you.

• Ask those who didn't buy why they chose to buy from someone else. That means you have to have an open dialogue with them. Stay on top of what customers want. If you do, you'll be more in tune with what the market is asking for and you'll win more sales.

Bottom line: Stay close to your customers and you'll always have an edge.

10. Psyche out your competitors by showing off your strengths. Promote why you are the best choice loud and clear.

A big part of any fight is the psychological one. Most fighters try to psyche out their competitors long before they get in the ring. If you are going to fight a competitor, you have to let them see your teeth once in while. You have to let them know that you are confident that you will win the battle.

There are many areas where you should be showing off your strengths. Put written and video testimonials in different areas of your web site. Your testimonials are your best way to instill fear into your competitors, especially if they don't have any. Great testimonials are the best way you can show your strength, because they are said by others, not you. It proves to the prospect considering your product that you are the real deal because they will believe what their peers say about you more than they'll believe what you have to say.

Do your promotions show your strength? How do your strengths stack up and compare with what your bigger competitors are promoting to prospects? Be creative and aggressive. Flex your marketing muscles. Let your competitors know that you are showing up with your "A" game by how you market and promote your business.

Shock and awe your prospects with your pre-sales materials. Let them know that they aren't dealing with a novice, but a bona fide expert who can help them find the perfect solution with your product or service.

Ads that tell prospects only where you are, when you are open, and what lines you carry are weak. They don't show any strength. They don't show *why* you are truly different. Remember, your location, hours, and what you offer (especially if you are a generalist trying to be all things to all people) are rarely persuasive in and of themselves.

I once had to redo a successful print ad before the local publication would print it. They had to rewrite their rules for their entire publication because my competitors were complaining about my ad to them. If your ads aren't creating controversy like this, your ads don't have strength. When competitors complain, it means that they are scared and that you are winning the battle.

How can you better show your difference and show your strengths with the next marketing piece you send out?

If you do TV or radio advertisements, be sure to infuse them with your own personality and a clear differentiating idea that can set you apart from your competitors. You want your competitors to hear your promotions and get scared a little bit. See if you can't lower the cost of doing advertising in these mediums by joining forces with other vendors to offer contest prizes that you can give away and promote.

It takes persistence to get well placed publicity. But, there is little that can scare your competitors and show your teeth better than having great articles written about you, being on podcasts, and having informative videos about you and your business. Be on the lookout for inexpensive and creative PR opportunities to promote your business. If you don't have any publicity being done at your business, my guess is that you don't have the phone numbers and email addresses of the the top publications, podcasts, and social media influencers handy and that you aren't actively working to develop a better relationship with these contacts. Remember, this is an area where you can beat big competitors who take this kind of coverage for granted when they first move into a market and do little to continue those promotional efforts after they've opened their doors. Don't ever take this for granted. You have to work at it if you want to be newsworthy and promoted in this way.

When your competitors see you show up and set up your booth and signs at a trade show, how do they respond? If they start copying you, your booth and your promotions have teeth. If not, and you are copying them, you are running from them. Go on the offensive. Get out there and let prospects know why they should come see you. If you can't or aren't able to do this effectively before the show, look for creative ways to grab attention to make your booth the talk of the show and the place to be. This excitement will carry over to your business and bring prospects into your marketing funnels to buy if you do it right.

One last area I'll mention is your sales effectiveness. The most powerful thing you can do to show your teeth is to show how much better you are than your competitors by getting really good at closing sales. If prospects come into your marketing funnel and leave with your product or service, you've shown your teeth and you are taking back your market one customer at a time. If a prospect leaves without buying, you haven't shown that you are a good fighter. Fight for every sale. Get good at building trust, analyzing needs, presenting your solution, and closing sales.

The essence of what I have tried to communicate about how you must compete in an Amazon.com world is that you need to pre-sell your prospects better utilizing technology and tools that are available today in everything that you do. This is becoming more and more important. Take the ideas I've shared here and put them into action. It will make a world of difference. It will give you a jump on your competition and help you get on track to achieving your business goals.

It takes courage to continue on when you hear about some of the advances that Amazon and other industry giants are making. You have a choice: be upbeat or be beat down.

"Walt Disney once said, "All our dreams can come true—if we have the courage to pursue them." So have faith in yourself. Be a person of courage. Stand erect and move forward into the storm; the winds will subside and the sun will shine. Keep your eye on your dream and stay a steady course. Let your persistence, your pit-bull determination, see you through to your goal. As you move forward, be guided by the words of Winston Churchill: 'Never, never, never give up.'"—*It's a Jungle In There*, pp. 145-147.

Thousands of other entrepreneurs across the country are persisting and making their businesses work day in and day out. Some give in, and some have failures. But the ones that succeed in the end are those who persist through the difficulties because of their passion and commitment. It takes passion and persistence to push through the challenges and the pain to emerge victorious. When you become frustrated and start to lose faith in what you are doing, remember that "the person who can drive himself or herself once the effort gets painful is the person who will win" as Roger Bannister once observed.

What will motivate you to persist through whatever challenges you are facing and emerge victorious on the other side? Only you know the answer to that question. My hope is that you'll hold onto that through the pain and difficulty and someday you'll have your own story you can share with others that can inspire them to persist through their own difficulties. It's all a matter of perspective and choice. Choose to persist and make it happen for you and your business.

In conclusion, if you are going to beat a giant in battle, you have to study their weaknesses and fight them in ways that will allow you to win. I hope the ideas I've shared in this chapter have been helpful to show you the areas you must focus on if you are going to successfully compete and win against the industry giants who are coming into your market with the goal to take your customers away from you.

You can successfully compete and win against the giants if you focus on the right areas. Be more proactive about your success. You may not be able to be bigger than the giants in your industry but you can be better, faster, and more creative than they are. Study the gaps. Where are the giants in your industry weak? Where do they not currently participate? At what point do they assume the sale is already made? Is this a point which you can enter and dominate the conversation? Choose to get on the offensive. Play to win AND you will.

CHAPTER 4

PRE-SELL THE PROSPECT SO THEY WANT TO BUY FROM YOU AFTER THEIR FIRST INTERACTION WITH YOUR BUSINESS

"The trust the customer has in your company and you strongly outweighs the techniques you use to sell."--Mike Puglia

To be more successful in your marketing, you need to understand the overall sequence of what happens when a prospect buys your product or service or doesn't buy anything from you at all.

A good way to do this is to create a flow chart where you look at what typically happens when a prospect makes a purchase or doesn't buy anything and how that individual is treated based on those decisions (and most importantly what happens next). For example, you may have six follow-up sequences if a prospect buys your product and three follow-up sequences if the prospect doesn't buy anything from you (to get them back into your marketing funnel) so they will eventually buy something from you. I won't share the specifics of all of these sequences here, but I will give you a brief overview so you can devise your own sequence. Amongst other things, there should be a thank you sequence, a bounce back sequence inviting prospects to return to talk with you, a referral sequence, a vendor sequence inviting prospects to do business with other businesses in you niche that you can refer them to, a sequence to gather pictures and videos you can use for testimonials and a sequence to sell items after their initial purchase. You should also have a completely different set of sequences if the prospect doesn't buy.

The reality is that most businesses don't think about this too much. They have one response if the prospect buys and then do little to nothing to get them back in if they don't buy. This lack of planning prevents the prospect from having any kind of meaningful experience with you leading to a purchase of some kind.

To help you think through this process, take the time to list all of the things you sell in your business. Then, list *when* a prospect typically buys them, and *how* you invite a prospect to do business with you (from the first moment they begin interacting with you).

Then, on a separate piece of paper or using the boxes in the illustration on the next page, outline this process in a flow chart and look for ways to anticipate and prepare marketing pieces to surprise and delight prospects and get them back to do more business with you.

Don't ignore the sequence of what should be done next and just assume it will happen. Instead, anticipate what the prospect will do (and you can do this even better when you've gathered information from them when they interact with you on the first occasion) and then choreograph your response accordingly.

You should have multiple sequences based on what the prospect does

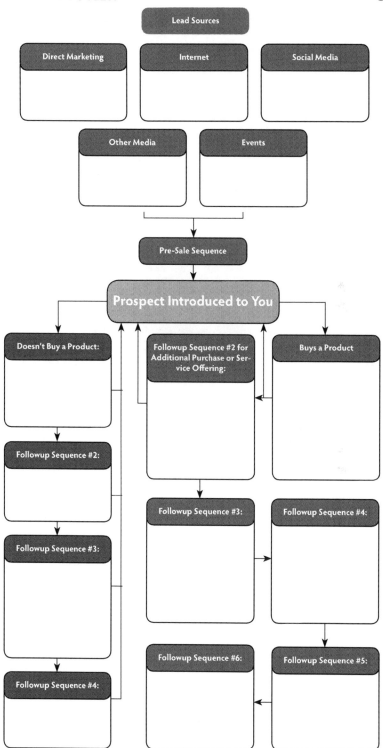

at the end of their interaction with you. For example, the follow up sequences on the right after your initial introduction to the prospect are designed for those who buy. You should have multiple follow up sequences to get those customers to return to buy more or to refer their friends and family to you. The follow up sequences on the left should invite prospects to return, to buy a secondary item (if they've already made an initial purchase somewhere else), and a request for referrals.

If you don't give prospects a reason to act today, they will not act today. An important thing that works well is to help prospects see the benefits of being decisive by emailing them a special report that details what to expect when they interact with you for the first time. This helps the prospect understand the reasons why you can offer a special offer to them on their first visit and explains why he or she should come with the intent to buy when they meet with you for the first time. You can also have these reasons illustrated on a brochure or flyer that is located where you sell so prospects are reminded of the benefits of buying on their first visit.

This is so important. If you don't articulate why prospects need to buy now, they won't. They have so many other things going on in their lives that they will not act unless there is a compelling reason and a strong benefit for them if they take action now. They will stay where they are at in their current, comfortable situation for as long as possible, unless the fear of loss or another compelling reason motivates them to pick up the phone to call and schedule an appointment to meet with you.

Now, analyze how well you are pre-selling prospects by asking these two questions:

1) Are you giving prospects a clear explanation of what they should do when they schedule an appointment?

2) Or do you just talk about what you do (hoping that prospects would connect the dots) and buy now?

Never take this step for granted. You must always give prospects directions and tell them what to do next. When you tie this to a specific benefit they will get for taking action now, you exponentially increase the likelihood that a prospects will find and buy your product or service when they first interact with you.

Lead with facts that indicate you clearly understand where the prospect is coming from and specific testimonials or evidence that support how you have helped other prospects actually get what they wanted. Then, you need to explain what benefits the prospect will get when they act now and buy your product or service from you.

In general, most prospects will follow the lead of someone who they feel clearly understands their problem and who they trust to help them come up with a clear solution to a problem they feel they need solved.

Do your prospects understand all of the benefits of doing business with you over a competitor?

Is there a compelling reason they should do this now? Do you explain this to each prospect in your marketing and pre-sale communications?

Is each prospect motivated to act NOW, schedule an appointment, and meet with you so they can take the necessary steps to get the solution they desperately want?

The most important part of helping prospects see the benefit of acting now is to tell them what will happen if they don't take action now. Every marketing promotion you send out should contain:

1) The specific benefit a prospect will get by scheduling an appointment, meeting with you, and buying now.

2) The lost opportunity and the continued problem the prospect will have of not owning your product or service (and being stressed out) if they don't get your product or service now.

Remember, your goal is to:

- Share with each prospect the benefits of getting your product/ service from you now.

- Detail how many specific benefits she'll get (even better if you can quantify this down to a specific amount of money or time they'll save, etc.)

- Why they need the experience of going through your process

- What kinds of other prospects have found solutions to their challenges from you

- What did these prospects get when they purchased a product or service from you? Using testimonials is a great way to communicate this.

- What happens to the prospect if they don't buy from you?

How clear are you currently being in your marketing? Are you helping prospects see the consequences of delaying their decision to buy now? Are you identifying the specific negative consequences that will happen if they don't buy now from you (in contrast with any of your competitors)?

Selling products today has changed dramatically. Unfortunately, most sales consultants have never gotten the message and are using sales tactics and techniques from the past that no longer work. The result is a bunch of very frustrated sales consultants and business owners who are panicking because they are not achieving their sales goals. On top of all that, the economic downturn shifted previous sales cycles and trends into upheaval. As the smoke has cleared and business has ramped up over the past several years, business owners have discovered that prospects are waiting longer to commit to large purchases and many sales consultants don't know what to do or where to turn to help prospects find the right solution to the challenges the prospect faces.

What has really changed is the mentality and psychology of prospects today. Prospects today are overwhelmed with choices. In addition, it has become increasingly noisy in the marketplace. Prospects are constantly hearing about the latest new thing as they are literally bombarded with choices to buy products and solve challenges they face. On top of that, prospects have in large measure become apathetic in today's market. In general, they lack trust in those who are selling them anything and because they have so many choices, they feel they need to wait to buy to figure out what is best for them.

With technology today and the Internet, prospects literally have instant access to shop around for better pricing on the products you are selling, see what your business reputation is, and see what actual customers are saying about you and your business practices. In order to succeed in this new marketplace, you have to give prospects a *reason* to believe that your business is the best choice and *accelerate the process of building and earning trust.* When you do this effectively, you can develop a relationship and help prospects buy now, not later.

Remember, pre-selling the prospect is all about building trust and how quickly and deeply you can build it so that any concern, objection, or obstacle that would otherwise stand in the way of you making the sale is completely eliminated. Since Amazon.com already has such a strong relationship with such a large percentage of customers and more importantly are doing things that will attract more and more people to utilize their services, this is opportunity for any and all business owners who recognize and capitalize on their platform and reach.

The big reason why you need to pre-sell prospects today before they come into your business is to pre-empt your competitors so that everyone else the prospect sees after you is seen within a frame of reference that highlights your differentiating strength. If you don't give prospects a reason why they should hold out to buy the product they need to achieve the results they seek UNTIL they come to see you, someone else will likely beat you to the sale.

The essence of this strategy is to persuade the prospect of your experience and expertise so that he or she wants to do business with you before they even meet with you.

To help you develop a better pre-sales strategy at your business, here are eight ways you can pre-sell prospects and get a jump on your competition:

1. Set up and position your business for success on your first visit by creating an Ebook detailing information that introduces you, positions your business as a leader in your market niche, and offer other helpful information that will help prospects see the benefit of choosing your business as the place to buy what they need. Prospects can download this Ebook and you can sell it for $0.99 to $2.99 or you can offer it to prospects through a special link on Amazon.com for free.

Post information on your web site so that prospects can download special reports and checklists when they give you their email address. You can have someone convert your Word file to a .mobi file (which is the format that Amazon.com utilizes for their Kindle readers) and to design your ebook cover at http://www.fiverr.com/ and by searching for "Convert Word file to .mobi file)" You can see the work of several designers who can convert your file for you so you can upload it to amazon.com on their site: https://kdp.amazon.com after you set up your own account.

Examples of Ebooks you could create:

• What to Expect at Your First Visit

• Mistakes Made by Those Shopping for (Your Product) and How to Avoid Them

• The 10 Commandments of Shopping for (Your Product)

• How to Get the Most out of (Your Product)

• Etc.

When writing your e-book or your presales collateral, remember, the biggest mistake you can make when pre-selling your business is to talk about how great you are in your own words. You want others to do this for you. Remember, prospects are coming to your web site looking for information and the more information you can provide them about why you are the best place to come that is said in words by their peers (other customers who had the same challenge), the better off you will be.

Convert lookers into prospects that you can market to by offering something for free. This can be a contest for a drawing for free merchandise or having informational articles that inform prospects. The goal is to capture their email address and contact information so you can send them more information and invite them to come into your business or marketing funnel. A free Ebook filled with coupons and links to your site is a great way for you to set you apart from your competition, teach prospects what they should expect from their buying experience, how to know if a business is the best place to buy what you sell, etc. The goal is to help the prospects by giving them information that makes them feel more comfortable about doing business with you because you are helping them make a good decision.

Let's take this a couple of steps further and actually have you evaluate how you are pre-selling your prospects with every interaction they make before she they enter your marketing funnel in six specific areas:

1) Your website

Prospects are tired of being 'sold to' and they get more and more tired of this as they get closer to actually buying your product or service. Consumers today are already very skeptical. Add to that the numerous sales pitches prospects they hear as they consider the right option for them, and they feel even more frustrated. They want to hear from an independent source who doesn't (in their opinion) have a vested interest in your business. When they hear from their peers (other prospects who have purchased from you) these testimonials are very powerful because they take away risk and concern and help accelerate the speed of trust.

I think it is a good idea to put testimonials in different areas of your site as well as your Ebook. If you just have them in one place, that is better than not having them at all, but if they can speak to why they are a good idea now, it is much better.

Here are other places you can put them on your site:

• As captions under photos of your customers enjoying your product or service

• Next to your differentiating factors to back up your claims

• Under specific products or offerings on your site

• At the top, bottom and inside of a box where you are highlighting a specific specialty of your business

2) Your direct marketing – phone calls, direct mail, emails, referrals

• Are you really preselling your prospects in every interaction you have?

• How could you do this better?

Here are three suggestions of how you can do this in all of your marketing mediums:

• Tell your story. But tell it the right way. Don't do it to build up yourself and make yourself sound unapproachable.

Build your celebrity status by talking about how you have helped customers, how you are known in the community, and strive to connect with the prospect so that they feel like they are dealing with a real person.

Let them have a chance to get to know you through your Ebook by having a link to your Facebook or Twitter account. This is a great way for people to get a chance to interact with you and find out more about you on a personal level. People buy from those they like, know, and trust. Be more transparent and your trust will increase more rapidly with those who enter your marketing funnels.

• Pre-Sell the next prospect with a story of a current customer who loves you and your business.

If you can do a video case study of a customer who came into your business and show how much they loved the total experience, you've uncovered a great way to build excitement, eliminate risk, and build massive trust.

• Write copy that builds desire. Don't be boring.

Don't make boring comments. Many web sites have lots of boring information and data on them that doesn't speak to prospects in a compelling and persuasive way. Instead, build desire so they want to pick up the phone, set an appointment, or request more information.

3) Your direct marketing pieces (postcards, etc.)

Do your direct marketing pieces have a compelling offer that your prospects will act on?

4) Social media posts

Are your social media posts fun and engaging?

Are you keeping your posts social and educational instead of constantly asking for the sale?

5) PR opportunities

What ways have you been able to use to promote your celebrity and build your brand?

Where do you need to appear so your audience will have more trust and excitement to meet you in the future?

6) Trade shows

Are you building anticipation for these events?

If you offer a promotion, do you stick top your deadlines for those who take action at the event?

2. Convert special reports into Ebooks to educate your prospects. In the articles, take away the big objections they have and turn them into positives and the reason why they have to buy from you. Build trust and take away their skepticism.

Write articles from a perspective of information that your prospects would like to know about. You don't have to write the articles yourself, but it doesn't hurt to write some things yourself.

In these special reports, include more testimonials and information about you that will help build your trust and experience. Since prospects today are so skeptical, how can you use more third party endorsement to reduce risk, build trust and get them to take action?

How can you build more proof at your business?

• Ask your customers to write down their experience when they make a purchase with you. Be patient, but ask.

• Gather and use video testimonials (Have three questions written on a card. Offer a gift card if they'll let you record their responses. Here are examples of three questions you can ask: 1) How did you discover our business? 2) How did our product or service compare with others you saw in the marketplace? 3) What did you love most about your experience with us?) Record the answers on your phone and post them to social media or on your website.

Some other sources that you may not have considered are:

• If you have won awards, ask the award sponsor to give you a testimonial which you can highlight on your web site.

• Charities you have donated to

• Podcasts you have appeared on or other notable individuals who have done business with you

• Manufacturers or suppliers you do business with

• Association owners you may belong to who can write about you

Remember to articulate your point of difference. Does your Ebook or website clearly explain to any prospect who visits how your business is different from any of your competitors?

If you can't articulate your difference, your prospects and customers can't either.

Explain why you are unique and different. If you are the same, prospects will make their decision based on price.

You have to be different – if you aren't – the decision to buy from you will be made solely on the basis of price.

3. Have and stick to a Pre-Sell Sequence.

• Pre-sale collateral (magazine, blog articles, "What to Expect..." sequence)

• Pre-sale interview (this should be choreographed)

For example, when we were in the bridal business, we would welcome a bride when she arrived at our store. We asked her to have a seat and had her fill out a registry form that helped us gather information about what she was looking for and her shopping experience up to that point. The receptionist would say: "Please have a seat while I personally tell your consultant that you are here."

While in the waiting area, she could look through our catalog or view a presentation about our store. The presentation had pictures of happy brides who purchased dresses from us and every three slides or so had bullet points about the benefits of buying at our bridal store. This presentation was loaded with testimonials and benefits of why brides from all over the area trusted our store . The video conveyed credibility while demonstrating social proof. Each bride saw information we wanted her to see in the first few minutes before she even started looking at and trying on dresses.

When the receptionist returned with her bridal consultant, she would say, "This is _____, your personal bridal consultant for your appointment. As she walked back to the dressing room area, she would see pictures of happy brides who had purchased gowns from us, and articles written about our store. The bridal consultant would say: "You may recognize some of these brides who entrusted us with their wedding attire. You've certainly come to the right place for finding your perfect gown." By doing this, we would reassure the bride and give her social proof once again.

I would encourage you to put together a video with interviews with key players in your business which then can be played in the entrance to your business or on your web site to build your credibility and expertise.

You should ask questions about what happens within the first 30 seconds after a prospect enters your business or marketing funnel. What happens? What do prospects see and feel?

Do they see pictures of happy customers on your web site with testimonials that all build your credibility and expertise?

If you are a homebuilder or service provider where construction is ongoing, could you have a magnetic board pointing out where (in your city, state, or country), your work is being done?

Could you have a Wall of Fame area detailing projects you've done or customers you've helped?

4. Improve your systems and build a better experience.

Systems help you see and track:

• What specifically customers will buy in the future

• How often they will buy

• How long they will continue to buy

To sustain and increase your growth, you must continually analyze, test, and perfect your systems.

Jay Abraham wrote: "If you're not strategic, then each month, you'll be putting out the same fires. Usually those fires are related to finances and cash flow....However, if you're strategic, every month sees your business bringing in clients and prospects...you have an unshakable system in place that progressively and sequentially moves your prospects down an evolutionary line." – *The Sticking Point Solution*, p. 82.

To succeed against online marketers, Amazon.com, and industry giants, you must build a better experience. In other words, in a service economy, the value is built around your experience. If the experience at your business is no different than what happens when someone buys your product online, you can see why people find it easy to make the decision to buy online. Your experience must be amazing if you are to help prospects see what they will be missing out on if they choose to buy anywhere else except from you.

5. Avoid mediocre marketing.

Jay Abraham wrote: "Most entrepreneurs fail to understand that the difference between mediocrity and making millions has more to do with effective marketing than with any other single factor....Marketing is the bedrock of virtually every enduring dominant business in every field. You must be a superior marketer."-- *The Sticking Point Solution*, p. 23.

Average and mediocre marketing appears everywhere. It doesn't stand out and it doesn't produce results. Here are some questions for you to consider:

• Is your marketing mediocre? Does it stand out from your competitors?

• In what way?

• Could you better articulate your difference and why prospects should buy from you?

6. Create a pre-sale persuasion package.

When someone sets and arrives for an appointment to meet with you, what are you giving to them that shows you are going to be different? Providing a gift when they arrive is a good example.

When we were in the bridal business, we had our receptionist give each bride who arrived for her appointment a customized pink box that said: A Very Special Gift for..._her name_

From: (_name of her consultant_)Your Caring Bridal Consultant at ___the name of our store____

When the bride opened the box, it read:

"You Found Your True Love...

And opened to:

"Now Fall in Love All Over Again with ___*the name of our store*____."

That small gift set the tone for the experience she would have at our store. How could you apply this idea to your business?

Here are some ideas for how you could build your pre-sales persuasion package:

1. Gifts

• Stress Busters or Chill Pills with a Thank You Note on Outside – These pills could be Jelly Belly candies in small prescription type bottles with prescription on outside with the prescription to take 2 chill pills each time you are feeling stressed out.

• Gift Bag with your business logo on it

• Wrapped candy or chocolate

2. Coupon Book – listing all of the great benefits they will get from local vendors you've set up when they buy from you.

3. What Others Are Saying About Your Business- testimonials highlighting their experience (even better with pictures)

4. CD with Planning Tips for Better Utilizing your Product or Service

5. DVD Highlighting Products You Offer, Testimonials, and a Tour of Business (you could also put the video on YouTube or have the video playing in the reception area while they wait for their consultant to arrive.

Your Pre-Sale Persuasion Package could also include:

• A small microwavable bag of popcorn and DVD with testimonials of your customers

• A little booklet filled with pictures of happy customers and their experiences working with you

You could also give or send a package to follow up with your customers who purchased from you. You personalized note inside could say:

Thank you so much for coming into our store and buying __*your product*__ today. We're so happy you've chosen to work with us and this gift is our way of helping you start off our relationship on the right foot as we seek to offer you an experience unlike any other with impeccable, world-class service. Our dedicated team will take care of all of the details in a way that will astonish you. We look forward to continuing to serve you and invite you to share your experience with us with those who could benefit from our services as well. Thanks again and we look forward to seeing you again soon!

You could also give or send a treat or cookie delivered with a Thank You note such as this one:

Thank you so much for purchasing our product! We are so excited to
have you be a part of our family as we work to take care of all of the
details of delivering a wonderful experience as you use __our product__.
Please enjoy this treat as a way of saying "Thank You" from the bottom
of our hearts. We look forward to continuing to astonish you as you use
our product going forward.

**7. Shift prospects to buyers faster by breaking the trance your
prospects are in. Then, persuade them why they should buy the
solution they love and need.**

Dave Lakhani in his book *How to Sell When Nobody's Buying* makes
this assertion:

"The reason you are not selling more right now is that you don't
understand how your clients really buy. They are being conditioned
and responding to that conditioning without even knowing it....The
problem you are experiencing is that people accept what they hear over
and over as being real and uncontrollable. When you hear that the
economy is in the toilet or you hear that your industry is experiencing
massive downturns, it is very easy to say, 'Well, I need to hunker down
and ride this out,' when in reality what you need to do is focus on
calming down your prospects in the face of fear and mass hysteria."
—p. 96.

Prospects today have gotten so bogged down by what they read or hear
in the news that they are in a kind of trance and it is your responsibility
to snap them out of the trance they are walking around in before you
begin to persuade.

In addition, many sales consultants are in a trance induced by their
own beliefs and prejudices or by the media. This keeps you from selling
more as well since it is easy to believe the negativity that is so pervasive
around you. We get into a mental flow that can prevent us from

thinking differently because we have conditioned ourselves to think a certain way (based on the input we are putting there – news we are listening to, watching, etc.).

If you are going to shift prospects from a trance of apathy to excited prospective customers who are ready to buy now, you have to break the trance they are in *before* you seek to persuade them to buy from you. The best way to do this is to use curiosity to help the prospect become consciously aware of the experience they will have when interacting with you. One of the reasons why you want to educate prospects is because this breaks the trance they were in and causes them to start thinking about which option will be best for them to solve the challenging situation they have in front of them.

When someone is curious, they are much more likely to be open to new ideas. On the other hand, if you attack their beliefs or their perception of what will happen when they look for the product you offer, you will encounter resistance. Curiosity opens the door to present new ideas and have prospects accept these ideas as well.

For example, using the words 'notice how' allows you to direct attention to what you want to point out. It also diverts the brain from what it was thinking about to what _you_ are pointing out.

"You'll notice as you use our product how easily and comfortably it is to do the work. Notice how…

Here are three suggestions on how you can get prospects talking and help them break out of the trance they are in and get them into the world of what you are offering:

1) *I'm curious about how you decided to investigate our product. Can you give me a little background about what you've been looking for and how you decided to check out ___name of product___ ?* This question helps a prospect open up and tell you details that help you understand their situation better. This

is also a great question to speed up trust. When you sincerely want to know more about the prospect in front of you and you are genuinely interested in their response, you will build trust. It also gives you important feedback for later in the sale that can help you be more persuasive.

2) *Point out something about the person you are meeting with.* When we were in the bridal business, we would ask: "Your ring is absolutely gorgeous. How were you able to determine that it was the one you wanted?" In the solar business, we would often ask about something we saw in their house. Maybe it was their car parked in front or something about the design of their home. For example, "I love your car. I've heard a lot about the Tesla. What made you decide to get that model?" This type of question can help you find out what is important to the prospect and can often give you clues into their criteria for making decisions. Then, when you are helping the prospect decide between two options, you can use these same criteria to persuade them how they like to decide.

3) *Tell me more about where and how you will be using this product. What is the ideal outcome you would like to achieve?* This question helps you identify the hopes and dreams the prospect has when using your product and how it will fit into that vision. Their answer will help you build emotional desire by helping them imagine the outcome they seek in the setting they are imagining.

Each of these questions will help you break the psychological state the prospect is in and help them enter an emotional state where a buying experience can be triggered. Never forget the importance of breaking prospects out of the psychological state they are in before you strive to persuade them to buy now. If you don't, you will encounter resistance and disappointment.

Don't seek to make a dollar without seeking first to make a difference in the prospect's life. To successfully set up a sale, you have to overcome their skepticism and accelerate the speed at which you build trust. Remember, if the prospect doesn't like you, know something about you, and trust you, they *will not* buy from you. Seek connection in order to build trust. Touch the prospect's heart with your kindness, your service, and your knowledge before you ask for the sale. That kind of connection will accelerate the speed at which the prospect feels they can trust you enough to go ahead.

Consistency is a core component of trust. Erratic behavior breaks down trust. Mood swings, lack of continuity, emotional outbursts, unpredictable personal and professional patterns, and broken promises are examples of inconsistencies that destroy trust. I once knew an individual who was different every time I saw him. People were very uncomfortable around him because they never knew what kind of mood he would be in. Consistency accelerates trust and you make or break the sale by how well you build trust.

Be a better listener. The only person who loses by having poor listening skills is you. You can learn a lot from your prospect if you will give them the chance to talk and express themselves. Many sales consultants are under the huge misconception that they have to *talk* a lot in order to sell something (discussing all of the points of a product, benefits, etc.) Nothing could be further from the truth. You must give the prospect a chance to buy. You must *ask* a lot in order to sell something.

The key is to know the products you sell well, but know your prospect better. The only way to do this is to listen more, and talk less.

8. Break out instead of break in. Try different approaches. Be unpredictable. Don't fall into boring routines.

Columnist Thom Singer asks: "Look at all the marketing, business development, sales and PR activities that your competition is actively pursuing. Advertising, events, seminars, direct mail, calling, networking, etc...Now look at what you are doing. Is it the same stuff? Stop doing marketing that is just like everyone else. Be different. Be unique."

He continues: "I have never understood why people observe the competition and instantly mimic their every move. Why would a prospective customer select one clone over the other? Don't be a clone! I have a sign on my desk that reads "Out-Think The Competitor Everyday". It makes me feel sorry for them, as I do not think they try to out-think me."

Instead, ask yourself, "What are our potential customers looking for they can't find elsewhere?" Offer that in a creative way and people will flock to your business.

Breakthroughs happen because of our mindset. People who make breakthroughs have an opportunistic approach and attitude to their business. I invite you to identify your biggest and easiest existing breakthrough opportunities by brainstorming for at least one idea each day over the next 30 days. Take 30 minutes each day and think about questions that will help you analyze and think about your business.

Here are seven questions to help you get started:

• How could the prospect's first few steps interacting with your business be better?

• How could your approach be more effective?

• How could your grab a prospect's attention better?

• How can you partner with other businesses in your market niche?

• How can you improve your marketing, sales, and follow up strategies?

• What overlooked opportunities are you sitting on?

• What creative offering could you construct to prevent prospects from wanting to keep shopping and buy from you now?

Your goal with this exercise is to come up with at least 30 ideas that you could test that would result in a major breakthrough.

All business owners face competitive challenges. Instead of moaning and complaining about them, figure out ways to work over, around, and through them. Make a list of breakthroughs you have noticed in other industries and keep adding to it over time. Create a file of some of the best marketing approaches you've seen.

Too often, you are too close to the little details and don't step back often enough to see the big picture. Take more time to think about where your opportunities lie now. When you take time to think about your business more, you'll see bigger and better opportunities.

Focus on one thing and only one thing at a time and you'll be amazed at the results you see. The more sucesssful you are at your pre-sale, the more successful your business will be.

Choose to begin each day with the attitude that when you meet with prospects each day, you will astonish them. Don't be boring. Don't be predictable. Be different. Take control of your business. Refuse to be controlled by fear. Stop internalizing your disappointments, defeats, and discouragement and letting those negative feelings prevent you from doing what you are capable of in your business. We all fail. Yet, we can rise from these failures to accomplish new and amazing things.

CHAPTER 5

SELL EXPERIENCES, NOT PRODUCTS

"You've got to start with the customer experience and work back toward the technology - not the other way around."--Steve Jobs

"There are many things I would do differently if I could do them over again."--Derek Bond, DDS

Entrepreneurs must sell experiences, not just products, to succeed in today's economy. People today will pay much more for experiences and memories than they will for mere products. Products become commoditized quickly by agressive competitors. Experiences on the other hand are much harder to replicate. What kind of experience are your prospects and customers having when they enter into a business relationship with you?

To help you build more value for your prospects and clients, here are five ways you can turn the products you sell in your business into experiences that differentiate you from your competitors:

1. Create a more immersive experience.

Businesses who focus on creating memorable experiences have found that their target audience will not only pay more for a more emotionally involved and thrilling experience, but they will also spread the word faster to their family and friends.

As an example, James Cameron's film *Avatar* began a resurgence of 3-D films in late 2009. People from all across the world went in droves to see Avatar and importantly, were willing to pay more for the experience. The desire to experience this movie in 3-D at the theater rocket-propelled it to the highest grossing film of all time in just a matter of months. That record held until Marvel's *Avengers: Endgame* crushed that record by brilliantly creating an event and follow up to a story that audiences were invested in discovering the outcome to with characters they had grown to care about.

One of the reasons why movies are released in the 3-D format is that the big screen experience cannot be replicated yet at home in the same way. In addition, a film is much more immersive in this format so the audience feels more involved in the story. While an overuse of this technology and poor conversion in some cases dampened the resurgence of 3-D, movie viewers generally perceive that there is an increase in value for what they will experience when seeing the film on an IMAX screen or in 3-D (or both).

Customers are willing to pay a higher price for an enhanced experience. Look at what you can do in your business to create more immersive and memorable experiences for your clients. To do this successfully, you must engage prospects by moving them from a passive state to an active state. Your job is to get your prospects immersed in the emotional side of the sale as quickly as possible.

Prospects are initially passive about their approach to getting a new product or service. They may even put off something they know they need (such as getting insurance or making an investment of any kind). As prospects become more physically involved, they become more mentally and emotionally involved as well. Their initial analysis of any product or service is analytical, yet proficient sales professionals quickly get prospects emotionally involved. This can be done with a product by either having them actually experience it or by getting them to visualize themselves using the product and feeling that it is what they want or need.

Until a prospect moves into the emotional aspect of a buying interaction, they aren't ready to make a buying decision. The experience (the one you provide or the one a prospect creates in their mind) is what triggers the decision to buy. Whether or not someone buys from you depends on the uniqueness of what you offer in comparison to what else they have observed, felt, and seen.

For example, if a prospect finds a product they want or need without getting emotionally involved, they will return to an analytical, rational state and ask: "Can I find this product / service somewhere else for less?" If they don't perceive that they can get the product / service they love most anywhere else for a better overall value, they will buy it from you. This is why it is so important to build your value in a prospect's mind so that they view the experience of buying something from you as a total value proposition, not just as a product or commodity that is being sold and purchased.

The most successful businesses embrace this concept of providing and creating experiences in how they set up what they do. For example, if you've ever been to Cabela's, you've experienced this concept. Cabela's is the world's foremost outfitter of hunting, fishing, and camping supplies. They currently have more than 80 locations. My two youngest boys love going to the Cabela's for the experience. The experience of going to Cabela's truly differentiates them from any other retailer who sells hunting, fishing, or camping gear.

At Cabela's, they immerse you in the experience of one of four different North American ecosystems as you go through the store. Their retail locations are huge and are designed around a thirty-five-foot high mountain with a waterfall. Three aquariums in the store hold a number of varieties of fish and literally hundreds of taxidermic animals which are placed in and around every department in the store. Owner Dick Cabela says of their store concept: "We're selling an experience."

The experience is so inviting that opening events at their stores usually attract over 35,000 people on their first day and they typically attract more than one million visitors to each store location each year.

The main attraction of the store is the thirty-five foot high mountain and waterfall. It is strategically placed at the back of the store so you have to walk through the merchandise to see the impressive display. It is obvious that a lot of time went into thinking about the layout of the store and how to immerse their customers into a wildlife experience.

What can you do in your business to draw prospects in and help them become more active participants in the sales process?

This is something you should carefully think about and act upon. Look for ways you can build more value in a prospect's mind throughout the sales process so that they become a much more active participant.

I consult with a lot of retail store owners. I often tell them that when we opened our first bridal store, we decided to create an immersive experience by setting up over 90 mannequins with dresses on them around the perimeter of the store. Most bridal stores just have a few mannequins in their windows. We wanted to be different and allow brides to interact more closely with our dresses instead of just going through rows and rows of dresses in plastic dress bags.

To accomplish this, we put up a bi-level platform around the store so the mannequins could be staggered up and down. We also had a lot of space in front of the mannequins so brides could stand in front of the dressed mannequins while looking closely at the detailed ornamentation and feel the fabrics. This allowed our bridal consultants to educate brides about the different types of fabrics, silhouettes, and ornamentation that go into making wedding dresses.

We also had the four silhouettes or cuts of dresses strategically placed by the front door so that when brides entered the store, we could educate them and help them evaluate the dresses they would try on using this criteria. It also helped the bride see that no matter how many pictures she sees, dresses she tries on, or stores she goes to, that there are only four types of dresses. This simplified the process in her mind and helped her realize that she would see all she needed to see at our store (as opposed to going to many other stores).

Pay more attention to the details that create an immersive experience. When you go into a retail environment, a restaurant, or any other business, notice how the best ones immerse you in an experience. Always be looking for ways you can turn the process of selling what you do into an experience your prospects and clients will never forget.

2. Stage surprises for your clients.

Are your prospects surprised at what you offer that your competitors don't? If not, why? Your answer will reveal how you really stand out from your competitors. This is why understanding your uniqueness is so important. If a prospect expects certain things from a business in your industry, will it really be a surprise when they find out you do it too? Obviously not. On the other hand, if you can stage surprises for your clients along the way that they do not expect, it raises your value and makes the experience of buying from you even more fun.

The best way to stage surprises for your clients is to shift how you think about the experience they will have when interacting with you. Typically, most business owners evaluate their performance around how well they are selling their products by asking questions such as, "How did we do?" instead of asking "What do our clients really want?" If you can anticipate and create offerings to clients (that they really want) and then surprise them along the way with something new, you create an entirely unique experience.

Several years ago, I attended a two-day leadership retreat called Exchange with John Maxwell, who is one of my favorite authors. I was there with 75 other leaders from across the country and we had leadership discussions and trainings over that period of time. One of the things that impressed me most about that experience was how they constantly sought to surprise us with talks by great leaders whom we knew and then got a chance to meet. Gifts were left in our hotel room to discover after returning from a full day of meetings. They also gave us surprise gifts during the meetings. There were at least eight surprises that happened to each of us during these two days. Each one of them was carefully planned to make the experience even more unique and special for us. The experience was fun because I never knew what to expect and the gifts were very nice.

The thing I learned most from that experience is that all of us like to have fun surprises in our life and those who consider doing business with you or who are already doing business with you are no different.

How can you use this principle to create better experiences for your prospects and customers?

Could you offer a free gift to your prospects when you meet for your initial consultation? The surprise they will get when they receive the gift will set a great tone for their experience in working with you and also utilizes the psychological trigger of reciprocity.

Carefully evaluate the interactions you have now with your clients and look at how you can add at least two surprises to the process that will endear them more to you. They will love it and that extra touch can often be the deciding factor that persuades a prospect to buy from you.

3. Collaboratively customize what the prospect receives by creating an exploratory experience.

More and more companies are creating value for their customers by offering customization that really gets to the heart of what their customers want.

Now, your product may be complex enough that it may be difficult to customize the product or experience. Yet, you can have great success at implementing some customization if you think and plan. For example, your preliminary consultation can help you identify ways in which you can customize your offer. If you can help a prospect see your expertise in what you do and then help them see exactly how you can help them exactly meet the result they are looking for, the likelihood you will make the sale increases dramatically. Focus on creating pre-sell materials or articles that prospects can read online that feature details about what you do.

Along with helpful information that makes the prospect's job of shopping for the result they are looking for easier, each article you write should feature your picture and a brief bio about how you've helped others who are just like them. You could create articles like this for your business and use them in your preliminary consultation in a way that would help you establish yourself as an authority-figure and celebrity and make the experience of getting to work with you even more special.

The goal is to do something that helps each prospect feel immersed in the process of doing business with you. Not only that, but you could give them a unique experience of dealing with you (and as an added bonus, you can give them a signed copy of your book as part of the value they gets from doing business with you). Think about the unique advantages that would give you in your market niche and the truly unique experience it would give to individuals who buy from you. This type of experience is also something that you could charge more for since no one else in your area would be doing anything like this.

Whatever you choose to do, be sure to set up the experience correctly by building yourself up as a celebrity and expert to the prospect before they arrive at your appointment. Plan and choreograph specific questions you will ask and the flow of how your interaction will go.

The questions should be designed to build trust and expertise and help you stay in control of the sale. You also need to set up the sale in ways that build contrast between you and your competitors and really help clients really see the value of doing business with you.

Look for specific ways you can customize the experience clients will have when they work with you. Know where your difference is and highlight that to prospects who visit you. This will help you stand out from your competitors in unique ways that will persuade them to buy from you.

4. View yourself and every member of your team as a performer on a stage for the clients you serve.

Disney has gone to great lengths to ensure that each employee views him or herself as a "cast member" who individually is part of creating a magical experience for guests who come into one of their theme parks.

What really creates value is the experience your prospect has when they see the talent of all that are involved in the production of helping them achieve the results they seek with your product / service. You need to carefully think about this in relation to how you view your business and how you develop your value, especially when compared with your competitors.

In what ways can you help your team members see how they interact with your prospects and clients?

A friend of mine, Brian Brooker, does a phenomenal job of creating an experience with his Brooker's Founding Flavors Ice Cream shop in Vineyard, Utah. His business is built around the American Founding theme of the Founding Fathers and heroes of the American Revolution. The servers teach history while you enjoy ice cream. He and his team each wear colonial clothing and explain the history of those after whom each flavor is named as you pick and enjoy your selection. He follows this principle of viewing himself and every member of his team as a performer on the stage where they serve ice cream. You can learn more about his business and see pictures of his menu and store at: www.brookersicecream.com

Be a leader in this area. Create experiences for prospective clients on the stage of your business. Help each member of your team to understand that they are players on this stage and their job is to create a memorable experience that the prospect will never forget while persuading them that your overall value is greater than anyone else.

5. Change the expectations clients have about the experience they'll have when working with you.

The expectation a prospect has about his or her shopping experience in large measure determines the value that he or she gives to you and to what you do in your business. Since this is true, you should be very cognizant of what expectations prospects typically have of businesses in your niche category. The perceptions others have of businesses in your industry are not always coming from positive sources.

If a prospect comes into your marketing funnel with a false perception or expectation, it can be very difficult to overcome.

You can change perceptions once a prospect enters your marketing funnel, but it is much more difficult at that point since they are in control. In addition, they hold those beliefs in their minds and don't typically share them with you. In other words, their intention may be that they won't be buying from you. If they truly intend to use you to learn about your product and then buy the product or service online or from a competitor (and they are empowered by you to do that), you will lose the sale since they won't be able to perceive any difference between the product you offer and what is offered by anyone else.

Many entrepreneurs today are awaking to the reality of this problem. They are finding that prospects are using their sales consultants as a place to have a free experience or get free information. Prospects are separating the product from the experience and then buying the commodity product online because they don't see any differences between what you sell and what they find somewhere else (and in most cases they are right). The best businesses who avoid this tendency have changed the expectations prospects have about how they will shop for your product / service and refuse to be used by buying private labeled merchandise that isn't sold online or by retagging / relabeling their merchandise.

Buying privately labeled merchandise or retagging products with different product codes may help you get some sales, but if the product is easily identifiable online, you will get backlash for doing this. I have seen bridal retailers who have retagged dresses and received tremendous online backlash. It is better to build your own brand. Regardless of how you sell a product, you have to create a memorable experience and build value so that the prospect sees the value of buying from you (as opposed to any of your competitors). The best way to do this is to change your perceptions in the marketplace by building your celebrity and authority and by using a pre-sales strategy. It needs to mean something to buy from *you*.

The important point is this: In order to build value, *you* have to view it differently first. If you view your value in an intrinsic way, that will come across in how you market, promote, and sell. If you can learn how to accurately assess value in terms of how the prospect entering your marketing funnel actually does, you will be much more successful in branding your business.

Jaynie Smith in her book *Creating Competitive Advantage* makes this sobering statement: "In my research with middle-market companies, I found only two CEOs out of 1,000 who could clearly name their companies' competitive advantages. The other 99.8% could offer only vague, imprecise generalities." –*Creating Competitive Advantage*, pp. 1-2.

She continues: "Your competitive advantages should be the

foundation of all your strategic and operational decisions. Ignoring them can be an expensive and even fatal mistake. After all, they're the reason customers choose to buy from you instead of the other guy. Without this edge, you will lose customers. Eventually, you will go out of business." --*Creating Competitive Advantage*, pp. 1-2.

Be clear about your competitive differences and advantage. Continually ask yourself: Do you know why clients really buy from you over one of your competitors? Remember, your goal is to see value how your prospects see value. When you have a clear difference you can articulate and prospects / clients perceive this difference, you will be successful in building value and selling experiences, not products.

6. Understand what a truly memorable experience should deliver to each client and look for better ways to acknowledge, appreciate, recognize, and create a sense of belonging for each one of them.

I think it is helpful to look at five definitions of experience as found on dictionary.com to get some insights about the types of experiences you should be delivering to your clients.

These definitions are in bold and the sentences in italics are examples of how this definition is used:

The first definition of experience is: A particular instance of personally encountering or undergoing something: *(My interaction with my sales consultant was the best experience I have ever had shopping for anything OR They were so rude to me OR That was the worst experience I've ever had and I'm shopping for_____ your product or service____!)*

The experience a prospect has with you and anyone else at your business will either be exhilarating, ho-hum, or downright disappointing (with many levels of satisfaction or dissatisfaction in between). The last thing you want a prospect to experience when they deal with you is to have an experience that was mediocre to disappointing in any way.

The next two definitions illustrate what a client gets from their continued experience over time whereas the first definition refers to a specific encounter or experience with you and your business.

The process or fact of personally observing, encountering, or undergoing something: *That consultant has great sales experience.*

The observing, encountering, or undergoing of things generally as they occur in the course of time: *to learn from experience; the range of the client's experience as they prepare to receive the benefit from your product / service.*

One of the reasons why many consumers are so jaded towards the experience of buying something is that they feel like they are wined and dined before they become a customer and then promptly forgotten after they become a customer.

To ensure a positive overall experience, you have to deliver throughout the client's experience of entering into a relationship with you. Since a client buys a product or service with a specific outcome in mind, there are a myriad of different experiences that they can have (the product works as advertised, the product doesn't work as advertised, the product works but it is a big hassle and frustrating to use, etc.).

Businesses that do a great job providing unforgettable experiences (Disney, Apple, American Girl, etc.) have obviously thought through what they want to have happen before, during, and after the moment you do business with them or interact with them in any way. Then, they choreograph the surprises, the fun, and the WOW into what will happen to enhance the experience even more. This is something you should think about in your business. Where can you choreograph more surprise and fun into what you do?

One of the reasons why these two definitions of experience are important to keep in mind is that even if a client has had a great first experience buying something from you, it can all unravel with a bad experience with the next step of the process (that may or may not be in your control). Think about how the individual parts of the experience you are creating and providing relate to the whole overall experience the client has in their interaction with you. The unfortunate reality is that a good experience can be ruined by one bad thing and your systems should be set up to maximize the positive overall experience the client has and minimize any potential hazards or variables that could detract from this end goal.

The fourth definition of experience is: **Knowledge or practical wisdom gained from what one has observed, encountered, or undergone:** *My best friend purchased a product / service from you a year ago. We have already had a great experience interacting with your business (or another business) OR I had a bad experience at another business.*

Parts of creating experiences is realizing how a client's past experiences will color or influence the experience they have with you. This is why it is important to market early to a prospect and invite them to go through your process first (before they have the chance to talk with someone else). The experience they have in your pre-sales sequence will also have a big impact on setting up expectations about what will happen next and the contrast they'll experience with competitors.

You should create a "What to Expect in Your First Interaction with Our Business" section of your web site or a brochure designed to set up the expectation for how long your initial interaction will be, what will happen, and also educate a prospect about specific things they should know about your product or service before they make the decision to buy. You could also have a questionnaire for a prospect to fill out and bring to the appointment. This helps you to build trust quickly and better understand what experiences they have already had as they has been searching for the solution to the problem they face.

The fifth and final definition of experience is: **Philosophy; the totality of the cognitions given by perception; all that is perceived, understood, and remembered.** *His bad experience buying something that broke quickly when he was five years old created skepticism and framed the way he views anything he purchases now.*

When you get right down to it, what is it that makes an experience memorable? Here are three aspects that I think are critical to consider about what happens in your business:

Being appreciated or acknowledged – When a client does business with you, do they feel like you roll out the red carpet? Or do they feel like they're interrupting a conversation you're having at with someone else? The first few moments after a client enters your orbit are really important. For example, a small gift given to a prospect when they first interact with you would create the start to a wonderful experience and relationship. Never underestimate the power of emotions and feelings especially around the need we all have to feel valued, acknowledged, and appreciated.

Being recognized as being important – The first time my wife and I took our children to Disneyland, we were amazed by the cast member who was dressed as Princess Aurora (Sleeping Beauty). She went out of her way to get down on my oldest daughter's level, signed an autograph to her, and talked to her in a way that made her feel special. My daughter Maddy walked away from that encounter beaming, full of excitement, and she clutched her autograph book close to her heart. Of course, as parents it made the experience and the fun of being there together even more wonderful. My question for you is this: What are you doing in your business to recognize your prospects and clients as being important? Do you or could you do something when you first meet with a prospect to acknowledge her and make her best friends and closest family members collectively say or think "awww" by how they were treated? Maybe, this means having a special VIP (very important prospect) designation. Perhaps you give, do, say, or offer something to a prospect that enhances the experience they will have as they interact with you like we were touched by the cast member who created a memorable experience for our daughter. You should really think about this: What can you do in your first interaction to help a client feel like the prince or princess they are? Another way to look at this: How would you respond if a daughter of a noted celebrity came into your business? How do you think you would treat her? What kind of preparation would you make for such a visit? Would it be different than how you are treating clients you work with now? In what ways can you shift the way you treat your prospects so that they feel as important at that celebrity's daughter would feel? Don't underestimate the power of recognizing each prospect as being important and treating them that way.

Having a sense of belonging or feeling like you are a part of something bigger than you – Several years ago, our family went on vacation to Washington D.C. during the fourth of July holiday. There is something about that experience and how we felt watching the fireworks display with our family that stands out as a powerful memory. You likely have had powerful emotions like this too as you have observed a fireworks show, watched a community parade, or found yourself in a group of people you identified with who made you feel like you belonged. This is the essence of what makes an experience memorable in your business as well. Do those you interact with feel like they are a part of something bigger than them just by working with you?

This is one of the reasons why brides from all over the world travel to Kleinfeld Bridal or choose to have a celebrity design their dress and a big part of why they are willing to pay more for that privilege. Kleinfeld's and celebrity designers have created the perception and experience that brides want to have through their television show *Say Yes to the Dress* and through their marketing efforts.

Work to create a sense of belonging in your business and have it mean something to the client to be associated with you.

Never forget what makes an experience truly memorable. Seek to put more elements of recognition, appreciation, and a sense of belonging into what clients experience when they interact with you. It will make all the difference in what they remember about you and will be the spark behind why they refer others to you.

7. Give customers WOW experiences and leverage their social network to get massive referrals.

Zappos.com is a great example of the power of WOW experiences. Zappos began in 1999 and has since become the largest online shoe store. In 2007, they grossed over $800 million in sales and over $1 billion in 2009. Amazon.com acquired Zappos for $1.2 billion in July of 2009. In 2015, Zappos passed $2 billion in annual sales.

The primary source of their growth has been repeat customers and rabid word of mouth recommendations. Nearly 75 percent of purchases are from returning customers and those repeat customers order at least 2.5 times more in the next 12 months. The average order size of their customers also increases every time they buy.

Their customers spread their excitement because of the experience of dealing with them. Here is a recent post from one of their customers on their Facebook fan page:

"I love Zappos!! The customer service is second to none...just got shoes from you yesterday, overnight!! ...Thank you so much for treating me like a VIP!!"

Zappos has ten core values which they let their fans and customers know about. The first value – Deliver WOW through service is posted all over their web page. They are:

Deliver WOW through service.

Embrace and drive change.

Create fun and a little weirdness.

Be adventurous, creative, and open-minded.

Pursue growth and learning.

Build open and honest relationships with communication.

Build a positive team and family spirit.

Do more with less.

Be passionate and determined.

Be humble.

Zappos has a stated goal to offer the "best service in the industry." Their company has three big differences that make them stand out from other online retailers in their niche. Zappos offers the following innovations:

1) Free shipping both ways

2) A 365-day return policy (you can return shoes in their original condition and original packaging up to 1 year after purchase)

3) A call center that is always open (in fact, their toll-free number is posted on every page – something that is rare for a company of their size)

Zappos also promises 4-day shipping free with all orders but often delivers next-day anyway, so as to pleasantly surprise customers.

Joseph Jaffe in his book *Flip the Funnel* makes this observation about Zappos:

"Getting people to make an initial purchase is one thing; getting them to return again and again is an entirely different nut to crack. At some point, Zappos made the successful leap from superior to sustainable customer service and in doing so, flipped the funnel from a transaction-based brand to an experience-based brand."

"A prime example is the 'I Heart Zappos' story in which blogger and Zappos shopper Zaz Lammar bought seven pairs of shoes for her terminally ill mother. When only two of the pairs fit because her mother had lost so much weight, Zaz was forced to return the rest. However, she was unable to make the shoe return a priority, given her circumstances. When Zappos emailed her, asking about the returns, she told them the story—and in an unprecedented gesture, Zappos took the initiative to send a UPS truck to pick up the shoes. But that's not all they sent; they also surprised Zaz with a bouquet of flowers from a florist."—*Flip the Funnel*, p. 89.

CEO Tony Hsieh (pronounced SHAY) believes that transparency, vision, repeat customers, and culture are the four keys that have been responsible for the rapid growth at Zappos. His philosophy is embodied in this phrase: "We're not a shoe company that happens to give great customer service; we're a service company that happens to sell shoes." This is not just a statement—it is what they really believe and do.

Zappos does many things very well – but I believe their ability to establish a lasting connection by how they follow up is their "secret sauce" that keeps customers coming back for more and more experiences with them. Most companies that I purchase something from or deal with very rarely follow up with me to find out how I am enjoying what I purchased from them. It is likely that you have experienced the same.

When was the last time that you received acknowledgement of some kind for any big ticket item that you have purchased? If you have had this experience, what kind of lasting impact did this have on you?

The unfortunate reality is that very few companies follow up and create a lasting connection. Why is this? Why not work harder to keep the fire burning? Unfortunately, many companies allow the light they've just created to be extinguished simply by doing nothing following the sale. It is much harder to reignite a relationship than it is to keep it burning. The game changer I'm trying to convey here is this: Don't be so consumed on getting the sale that you don't even pay attention to the tremendous growth that could come from better acknowledging those clients who have just made a purchase from you. I have seen many companies struggle with long-term growth because they ignore their current customers. Those that acknowledge clients well after the initial sale is completed will crush their competitors.

Don't let your clients fall into obscurity after they buy from you. When they fall through the cracks of your process, they are likely falling into the clutches of one of your competitors. To avoid this tendency, you have to have a better system that helps you follow up without you having to think about it.

Author Seth Godin says that "customers are essentially underused assets" for most companies. Since your business has more clients who have purchased from you than employees, shouldn't you be better leveraging their positive experience with an amplifier or megaphone to their friends and family? We all know that unhappy customers tell lots of people about their bad experience. People are just as willing to share amazing experiences, especially ones that surprise them and cause them to experience a WOW factor.

Two computer companies that do a great job in an industry that is not well known for its ability to handle technical issues with customer service are Dell and Apple.

"Dell now installs software on its customer's computers that makes contacting the company incredibly easy. In addition, the first thing you'll be asked when you get on the line is your telephone number— just in case you get disconnected. This is a far cry from the industry norm ('unfortunately, we're not able to dial out') or the probing, clarifying questions devoid of empathy care, or concern. Dell also utilizes software that allows the technician to take over your computer, that is, to see what you see. They can remotely access your PC and, in doing so, are able to troubleshoot as if they were there in the room with you."—Joseph Jaffe, *Flip the Funnel,* pp. 40-41.

I am a big fan of Apple. Recently, I took my MacBook to the Genius Bar at one of their Apple stores. If you've never been in an Apple store, it is an area at the back of the store where knowledgeable people answer specific questions you have about your computer, iPod, iPad, or whatever device you have purchased from them. They are very helpful and do amazing things. I scheduled an appointment online, had my appointment confirmed when I walked in (on one of their iPads), was introduced to a very nice and knowledgeable guy named Jared, and most importantly got my computer question answered very quickly. It was very impressive to me how they interacted with me. The "genius" I worked with that day even sent an email that thanked me for coming in and invited me to come back if I had any other questions. It was a WOW experience.

What are you doing to create WOW experiences for your clients? Are you innovative in at least three ways from any of your competitors? Do you point out this difference to your prospects and clients?

When you impress clients with WOW experiences, they can't wait to tell all of their friends – especially if you have an incentive in it for them like a referral card (such as an offer of cash gift cards for the first two referrals and an iPad for the third). Such incentives motivate your clients to refer others to you, not just because they had a great experience, but because there is also something in it for them. Remember, the things that get rewarded get done.

8. Shift the way you view the experience you are creating.

In his book *Minding the Store,* Stanley Marcus of Neiman Marcus speaks of his store as a home. When greeting clients who begin a relationship with you, do you see them as guests entering your home?

Do you welcome them as friends? Approaching clients with this mindset will make a huge difference in the speed at which you build trust and the outcome of their experience working with you.

Here are five more ways you can surprise and acknowledge the clients you work with and shift the experience to one where prospects and clients are truly WOWed.

1) Give a free gift when they arrive at your first interaction – At the stores of many retailers I coach, a free pair of pearl earrings or cufflinks inside a little gift box is given when a prospect arrives at their appointment to check out their products. Some people are surprised to hear that these stores give a prospect a gift when they first come in the door, but it has a magical effect of building trust and creating a WOW experience.

Should you do something like this with your clients? Why not? You want that prospect to love their experience with you from the first moment they contact you and before they interact with you or your sales team for the first time. When they talk with you about their needs and situation, you want to acknowledge their time and sacrifice to be there and to WOW them with the beginning of what will be a great experience as they gets results from your product / service. I've seen other companies offer movie tickets, gift cards to local restaurants, or $25 Amazon gift cards as a free gift at the start of a qualified appointment. What could you do to WOW your prospects?

2) Show your gratitude by welcoming them back. When someone purchases a second product from you, express with gratitude: "Welcome back! What has been your experience with us so far?" Show you value their input by asking and really listening to what they have to say.

I really like Joseph Jaffe's perspective on acknowledgement as expressed in his book *Flipping the Funnel*. He says: "[Thank you] is the simplest form of acknowledgement and the two most powerful words in any playbook. A company that recognizes a customer's patronage conveys a sentiment that can touch even the coldest heart. The problem today is that people have become jaded. Trust in companies has declined, and customers' default reaction is typically a guarded one; they are waiting for the catch, the trap, the fine print, or to be sold to. Prove them wrong, already."—p. 59.

3) Send a personal handwritten note from their sales consultant. This personal connection makes such a big difference. Are you doing this? If not, you should start now.

4) Make a personal phone call the following day just to express thanks and as a courtesy check-in. This can be a short 30-second to a minute long phone call. John Lee Dumas and Kate Erickson of Entrepreneur on Fire are great examples of this principle. They have a welcome package they send to new clients that includes a treat and a quick phone call. By doing this, you are able to subtly check up on your sales consultants (if you have them) and to make yourself available to answer any questions, address any concerns a new client may have, and to genuinely let her know that you value their business. Most importantly, such an interaction firmly establishes a lasting connection with the client that can help her spread the story of their experience with you.

5) Offer free beverages or candy. Mitchell's (a very successful menswear retailer) gives out free coffee and other beverages, free M&Ms, muffins, and bagels to those who come into their store. In one year, they gave out 20,613 cups of coffee, 80 pounds of plain M&Ms, and 1,065 pounds of peanut M&Ms. That is a lot of coffee and M&Ms! But, since their focus is having their store feel like a home, it seems natural to them. They also create unique experiences at their stores where customers can interact with designers of the many clothing lines they offer or be first to see brand new offerings. It is amazing how giving builds trust and causes buyers to feel more at home when making a significant purchase.

What could you do in your business to make clients feel more at home?

Little things make a big difference, but helping people feel at home will endear them to you and the experience they are having with you and your business.

Thinking more about the experiences you provide is a big shift for most people. Consider what Jack Mitchell says about this in his book *Hug Your Customers*:

"At Mitchell's, clothes are not our priority. It's not the first thing we think of, nor the last. Don't get me wrong. We like fabulous product, and we search the world to get it, but we're all about customers. Now that may sound amazing. A clothing store that isn't about clothes? But it's true. And if we were a restaurant, we wouldn't be about food. If we were an electronics store, we wouldn't be about [specific electronic products]. Businesses have lost sight of the idea that customers, not product, are the most important priority. Most companies think all you have to do is have plenty of great product and the right value and customers will descend like locusts on their stores....Many stores have those things...[but] it's how you treat customers that defines your long-term success....Far too many business managers have no idea who their customers are, or what their customers want, or what their perceptions are, and haven't a clue as to how to find out."

So, to successfully make this shift, you should work on the following three things:

• Personalize the relationship between your clients and your business in some way. Think about how you can do this based on how prospects and new clients interact with you.

• Be sure that everyone in your company at every interaction listens and learns from what clients say they love or dislike about their experience with you. Take notes and make adjustments where necessary.

• Strive to know your client's preferences before they do and have the ability to predict what they want.

Shift the way you view, set up and create experiences in your business and look for ways to surprise and delight your guests. This will help you shift the way you view your business and prepare your clients to be wowed with their interaction with you so they will tell everyone they know.

9. Have multiple experiences, themes, and stratification to give clients a sense of control. Don't be bland and boring.

In its first full year of operation (2006), Tao in Las Vegas (located inside The Venetian) was the highest grossing independent restaurant in the United States with $55.2 million in total revenue (as of this writing, they are still number one, with $42.5 million in sales in 2018). Tao (Las Vegas)went from zero to number one in just 12 months. This restaurant has 60,000 square feet, an average check of $90, is open 24/7, and has multiple experiences under one roof. Its creator, Richard Wolfe, indicated that this was one of its big draws and competitive advantages. He said, "The multiple experience strategy gives Tao a big competitive advantage...You never want to leave our premises to go somewhere else to do something different."

In other words, Tao has become so successful because they use the principle of stratification to give their customers tiered and price differentiated choices so each customer has a sense of control. Stratification is having different options with different price points that allow customers to choose. At Tao, there are different restaurant themes and experiences with a corresponding variety of price points. This is a smart way to include those who come in without having them feel excluded in any way.

Apple does this by setting their stores up with different themes and different products within the themes. They have a setup for computers based on how they will be used (home, business, video editing, etc.). They also have their products categorized by type (iPod, iPad, computers, watches, etc.) and then they are priced based on functionality or memory space (32 GB, 64GB, 132 GB), etc. Customers can pick their price point based upon functionality and storage. This allows customers to have a much more immersive experience by allowing them to interact with products and employees based on their area of expertise. Staff members are also stationed by product tables based on their area of expertise.

Disney has done the same thing with their theme-based parks (where they highlight certain themes—Adventureland, Frontierland, Fantasyland, Tomorrowland, and their new *Star Wars* themed Galaxy's Edge). They bring in different characters into each themed location for planned, staged, and surprise experiences. Disney also give customers options of a single day pass, two day pass, multi-day pass, etc. so customers can plan ahead and know what will work best for their situation. They can also bundle the experience with hotel stays for even better savings.

You should think carefully about how you can utilize stratification and themes in how you set up your business to give customers a more interactive and fun experience. Here are some questions to help you get started:

• How could you arrange your product offerings (in person or online) so that prospects never have to simply say yes or no and never have to feel excluded either?

• In what ways could you set up your business so that prospects feel like they are truly entering a different dimension or theme in comparison with other offerings you have?

• Do you have stratification within different themed areas of your business now? If not, how could you introduce this?

• What can you do to make prospects and clients feel included and valued so they feel like they belong to your business (refer to themselves as ___(your name's)___ clients) and that they have been inducted into your hall of fame?

The way in which you introduce and use stratification is such an important part of creating valuable experiences. Use it wisely.

10. It is not just the experience. It is also about what happens as a result of the experience.

The end result (whether the client loved their experience and achieved the desired outcome) is the big tipping point for creating an emotional experience. It is the single biggest influence of whether a client tells others about his or her experience in working with you.

You need to look at two parts of the experience clients will have when they interact with you. One is to consider the effect the experience will have on the client (being disappointed, satisfied, surprised, ecstatic, or feeling it was just another ho hum experience that didn't offer any lasting value). The other part of this is helping the client feel like they have experienced a result that matters to them.

Consider the opening of the Star Wars:Galaxy's Edge theme park at Disneyland in May of 2019. Disney carefully planned how to limit the number of people who could attend, but their overall attendance went down in the months that followed as a result. Disney has been so successful with packing their parks with guests that in some ways they have lost the magic they created in the first place. No one wants to wait in crowded, long lines all day long. We want our vacation experiences to be memorable and fun, not terrible, moving from one line to another to wait in the heat with impatient, unhappy people who are crammed into small spaces for a few minute ride. Never lose sight of the experience you are creating, or your own success may wind up creating a very different experience than you intended.

Another thing to keep in mind is that experiences like products can also become commoditized by prospects if they aren't unique or different enough. I think this is best embodied in the common phrase heard today, "Been there, done that." That phrase should frighten you since you want to always be delivering new value to a client that makes his or her experience more enjoyable and fun.

Don't be boring. Stand out. It takes commitment to create lasting experiences with clients.

In order to shift your business from transaction-based to experience-based, you have to have the right team. It takes a real commitment to create experiences that clients will be so ecstatic about that they will tell all of their friends. You can't create these types of experiences without true commitment on the part of each member of your team.

Joseph Jaffe makes this point in his book, *Flip the Funnel*. He says: "Marketing is not a campaign. It is a commitment. The same is true of customer bonds or the connections between a brand and its community. In today's marketplace, our relationships with customers seem to mirror the current divorce rate. There's an acute lack of patience and staying power when it comes to forging lifelong, inseparable ties with customers. Perhaps the reason for this is an insufferable focus on short-term results and the immediate gratification that comes from making the sale. It's really emblematic of what I call 'sales sickness,' an epidemic of sorts, where there is a wholesale abandoning of the ship at the exact moment the cash register chalks up the transaction. Call it after-sales support on its basic level, but it's more than that. Failing to close the loop is lack of follow-through or follow-up. It's an inability to stay the course, and stay connected in the process."—pp. 33-34.

Choose to embrace the changing economy by offering more value by giving your clients WOW experiences that truly differentiate you from any of your competitors. Stand out and be unique through the experiences you provide. There is a power in being different. Staying the same and not embracing the experience economy will cause you to blend in instead of break out. And blending in won't help you get your business to where it needs to go and where you want it to be.

CHAPTER 6

MANUFACTURE YOUR OWN CELEBRITY AND BRAND YOUR OWN BUSINESS

"Celebrity is no different from any other energy. It's a force for good or evil. It's no different from money. It's power."—Jerry Seinfeld

We live in a celebrity-obsessed culture. In order to combat today's price conscious and commodity driven market, you have to stand out by promoting yourself and creating a memorable experience that will grab attention. The most powerful way you can do this is to position yourself as a celebrity in your market niche. In this chapter, I'm going to outline the benefits of why you should undertake this approach and specifically what you can do to elevate your status to prospects and customers so they will pay more attention to you and your business, value your authority and expertise, and have experiences they'll tell their friends and family about (that raise their status and importance in the eyes of their friends).

In today's culture of celebrity, people love talking about how they saw or met a celebrity and the story that goes with it. People are willing to pay big money to have access to celebrities whether that is a simple video from a service like Cameo (https://www.cameo.com) or a big endorsement deal. Understanding this phenomenon is an important part of understanding why you should promote yourself in this way (which I'll add is counterintuitive and strongly resisted by most people).

Mark Earls makes this observation about celebrity in his book *Herd: How to Change Mass Behaviour by Harnessing Our True Nature:*

"[There is an] interesting paradox at the heart of the culture of celebrity with which we are currently swamped. We watch, we read, we gossip together about the lives, loves, and losses of the privileged few who live lovelorn lives in the glare of the paparazzi's flash bulbs. In order for this phenomenon to have any cut at all, we have to all know the individuals and at the same time be able to be interested in learning and sharing our knowledge about their lives."--*Herd*, p. 95.

He also points out:

"If a famous person wears a certain designer's clothes or uses a particular face cream or drives a certain car then – it is believed – the average individual consumer will follow the celebrity's behavior because they want to be or look like that celebrity." –*Herd*, p. 157.

This happens because in his words people believe that "It's what people I admire/respect buy" and "It's what people like me do/buy/wear/drive." –*Herd*, p. 157.

I think the definition of a celebrity is insightful for what it teaches about the power of promoting yourself in this way.

"A celebrity is a person who is easily recognized in a society or culture. Generally speaking, a celebrity is someone who gets media attention. There is a wide range of ways by which people may become celebrities: from their profession, appearances in the mass media, or even by complete accident or infamy. Instant celebrity is the term that is used when someone becomes a celebrity in a very short period of time. In the 21st century, the insatiable public fascination for celebrities and demand for celebrity gossip has seen the rise of the gossip columnist, tabloid, paparazzi and celebrity blogging. Celebrities have been flocking to social networking sites such as Twitter, Facebook, and Instagram. Social networking sites allow celebrities to communicate directly with their fans, removing the middle-man known as traditional media. Social media humanizes celebrities in a way that arouses public fascination as evident by the success of magazines such as *Us Weekly* and *People Weekly*. Social media sites have even catapulted some to fame."--http://en.wikipedia.org/wiki/Celebrity

Since most people resist the idea of purposefully becoming a celebrity, I want to share four benefits of why you should make this your quest:

1. **Branding you and your business helps you stand out from your competition and will increase your sales.**

People want to do business at a place where lots of others have done business (it gives us a sense of trust). The real reason why customers travel to a designer store in New York is because of the bragging rights they have ("I got 'X' at Kleinfeld where they make the *Say Yes to the Dress* TV show) and the experience they have ("I got to meet Randy or Mara"). Standing out in this way by becoming a celebrity really makes your competition irrelevant because you successfully reposition yourself into a category of one.

Many entrepreneurs to whom I've explained the concept of celebrity and authority really resist the idea. They haven't seen themselves in this way before and their natural inclination is to resist it. The reality is that becoming a celebrity in your market niche in your industry gives you a tremendous advantage over your competitors and is a way of highlighting the only truly unique thing about doing business with you over any other competitor.

Garrison Wynn makes this observation about this in *The Real Truth About Success*: "To create a personal advantage, you have to see the *real* business world, not the *ideal* one. This requires unconventional thinking and planning and a clear understanding of the most challenging aspects of business culture today." –p. 61.

We live in a celebrity obsessed culture. You can ignore this fact or you can use it to your advantage and stand out. My hope is that you'll use it to your advantage to increase your status and authority in the marketplace and watch your sales increase as a result.

Positioning yourself as a celebrity is really nothing more than letting people know what you are really good at. You have talents, abilities and strengths in your business that can help customers have unbelievable experiences. Prospects will never be able to become customers and use your amazing services unless they know about your talents and that means that you have to promote them. Positioning yourself as a celebrity is the easiest and best way to do this.

2.   You gain power in the marketplace.

Celebrities have power and authority over their fans. Fans of certain people want to look like, do, wear clothes, drive, and generally be like those they admire and respect. Don't ignore the strength and power of being an authority and celebrity when selling to your prospects. Rise to the top of your industry hierarchy by becoming an authority figure celebrity specialist. My friend Michael LaFido is a great example of this in the luxury real estate market. He has spent the past several years positioning himself as a celebrity in his market which influences why home owners choose him to list, market, and sell their homes. His web site: http://marketingluxurygroup.com is worthy of your study and emulation. He sells homes faster and for more money because of his positional authority. You must do the same in your market.

3.   Creating a celebrity experience helps people to spread the word quicker through their network of family and friends – people are excited to tell everyone they know about their interaction with a celebrity.

Think about this for a minute. If you had a chance encounter with a celebrity such as Tom Holland, Beyoncé, Brad Pitt, Dwayne Johnson, Michelle Obama, or Tom Hanks and got your picture taken with them, how many people would you call and show that picture to before the end of the day? The answer reveals the power that celebrity culture has. By establishing your own credibility as a celebrity in your market, you can create this experience as well and get a similar kind of attention and respect.

4. You can accomplish things much quicker.

Irregardless of what you think of him, Donald Trump understands and uses the power of celebrity. In his book, *How to Be Rich*, he says:

"I can get a project off the ground in no time now, whereas an unknown developer would require many months, if not years, to get something going. The number of people I employ to get a project finished reaches into the thousands, and those people would not have a building to work on without a developer to give them a job. Commerce and art cannot function independently—they must work together. That is the beauty of a successful brand name." –Donald J. Trump, *How to Be Rich*, pp. 52-53.

There is tremendous power in branding you and your business. I think the following experience Donald Trump had early in his career helped him understand the power of branding. Consider what he says:

"I was originally going to call Trump Tower by another name— Tiffany Tower, for the famous jewelry store next door. I asked a friend, 'Do you think it should be Trump Tower or Tiffany Tower?' He said, 'When you change your name to Tiffany, call it Tiffany Tower.'

"We have all seen the power of a brand name, especially quality brand names. Coco Chanel became world-famous eighty years ago by naming her first perfume Chanel No. 5, and it's still going strong in a fiercely competitive market. Her fragrance, as well as her name, has become timeless. She proved that the right ingredients can create a legend.

"Trump has become a great brand name, due to my rigorous standards of design and quality. We all admire Rolls-Royce cars, and I see every one of my ventures as being just that elite. Being a stickler has paid off, because my buildings are considered to be the finest in the world....In 2003, Chicago Tribune real estate columnist Mary Umberger attributed the sales for Trump International Hotel and Tower in Chicago to 'The Trump Factor.' Umberger reported: 'The sales velocity surprises even experienced real-estate players, who told me at the sales inaugural that they doubted Trump would gain enough momentum because Chicago's luxury market was—and is—in a lull.

"Some people have written that I'm boastful, but they're missing the point. I believe in what I say, and I deliver the goods. If you're devoting your life to creating a body of work, and you believe in what you do, and what you do is excellent, you'd better...tell people you think so. Subtlety and modesty are appropriate for nuns and therapists, but if you're in business, you'd better learn to speak up and announce your significant accomplishments to the world— nobody else will." –Donald J. Trump, *How to Be Rich*, pp. 51-52.

There is a lot you can learn from this statement. Two things I want to point out here:

- No one will value what you do *until* you value it first.

- You have to promote yourself <u>and</u> your business. You can't wait for others to do it for you. All great promoters promote themselves first and **then** get others to promote them too.

There is tremendous power in creating a celebrity brand that everyone in your market knows about. So how do you go about becoming a celebrity for prospects and customers in your market niche? Before I share with you 10 ways you can do this, I want to briefly explain the connection between status and celebrity (which are ideas that I originally learned from author Dan Kennedy).

According to the dictionary, status is the relative social, professional, or other standing of someone or something. It can also refer to a standing, rank, or official classification given to a person or organization.

Status is critical to develop as you become an authority figure celebrity specialist in your industry. In order to promote your status, you have to have some classification of ranking, have a third party who validates it (credibility), and it must be promoted so that your status is widely known.

How do celebrities promote their status? First, celebrities choreograph how they promote themselves when they promote movies to maximize their exposure and elevate their status. They have stories they are familiar with and have practiced to every conceivable question they might be asked as they go on talk shows and get pictures taken by the paparazzi. They know how to promote an idea or a story they are a part of that they want everybody to know about.

If you are going to promote your brand and your status, you have to work more on the product of you – you have to promote yourself and your business – You have to promote you and your story (how you got into your business and any and all interesting tidbits that help prospects and customers get to know you and your business better so they can help promote you to others).

Here are ten ways you can create and promote your status and position in your niche market:

1. **Stop waiting for someone else to elevate your status. Elevate and appoint yourself. Position yourself as an expert and well-known leader in your market.**

All celebrities and celebrity authority specialists have promoted themselves to a level of authority first. Then, they promote that they are an authority through carefully choreographed appearances. Once they have been there for a while, others will *then* actually give them an official ranking.

In order to appoint yourself, you need to do the things that people recognize as creating expertise and authority.

You can best do this by creating content that shows your expertise. Why wait for a TV station to come down and film you running your business? Create your own show and then promote it on YouTube, Instagram, Facebook, or Twitter. Then, just like celebrities, you will be contacted by the news media to promote you. This happens because you are promoting your expertise to those who utilize and need your product or service. When you create a following amongst prospects and customers based on your expertise, you will be recognized as an authority on the topic and your status and position in your market will increase. Don't just fit in. Stand out. This is the only way you'll be remembered in the hypercompetitive sea of choice that makes up your industry.

It is best if you can position yourself to be in a category of one, even if that means reinventing a new category so that you reposition your competitors. The person who creates a new category and names something is remembered. Those who follow what everyone else does are usually not remembered.

Isaac Newton is a great example of this. Seth Godin makes this observation: "Ask any elementary-school kid about Isaac Newton and you'll hear the same answer: 'He invented gravity!'

"Of course, Newton did no such thing. Newton certainly invented calculus. He also invented the reflecting telescope....[But why is he best remembered for gravity?]"

"Newton gets credit for inventing gravity because of a tree in his backyard. He was sitting in his garden, thinking about the moon, when he looked up and noticed that an apple on the tree nearby was precisely the same size (to his eye) as the moon. As an object gets farther away, it appears to be smaller. In a flash, Newton realized that the apple was proportional to the moon in size, and the effect of 'gravitas' on each much be proportional as well. Newton had figured out that gravity decreased over distance. More important to his reputation, he gave gravity its name. The apple never actually hit him on the head, but the term 'gravity' stuck."

Now, this important point:

"While Newton spent far more time on calculus and on alchemy, he's known for discovering gravity. Why? Because he named it.

"To the average person, Newton's contribution to science was a word. A word that described something that was already there, something that affected everyone, all the time. By naming gravity, he gave us power over it. He gave us a handle, which permitted both scientists and laypeople to talk about and interact with this mysterious force. Organizations change when you give something a name." –Seth Godin, *The Big Moo*, pp. 17-18.

Years ago, I coached a bridal retailer named Mary Feeley of Mary's Bridal in Annapolis, Maryland. When I spent a day in her store training her sales team, she told me how she named certain aspects of dresses (types of bustles, styles of dresses, ornamentation, etc.) and the effect this had on brides she worked with. She created unique names that were unique to her store. Think about this: If a bride leaves her store and goes somewhere else and uses the words Mary has taught her and the other bridal consultant has no idea what she is talking about, what impression does that leave with the bride? The reality is that Mary's status is elevated while the other bridal consultant is diminished because she doesn't know as much about the dresses. There is a big lesson to be learned from this. Mary is a great example of the power of positioning yourself as an authority.

Many entrepreneurs will never appoint themselves as an expert because they personally don't believe it. If you don't believe it, why should anyone else?

Donny Deutsch explains this principle in his book *Often Wrong, Never in Doubt*. He says:

> "The key to success is not purely who's the smartest, who's the best, but also who can say with conviction, 'I deserve it.' The entire concept is wrapped up in one phrase: why not me?"

He learned this principle from the first guy that he ever hired: Richie Kirshenbaum, who was younger than he was. Consider what he says and don't miss the important lesson:

[Richie] was maybe six months out of Syracuse University, working for a small agency called Korey Kay & Partners. After two years David Deutsch Associates was starting to make some inroads. We weren't seen as one of the hot shops, the sexy, bigger-name creative agencies like Chiat / Day or Ammirati Puris. We didn't have a lot of notoriety; we were this little boutique print house that had been around for fifteen years that was making more noise than we used to. We were a small, high-end creative shop and we were known as a small, high-end creative shop.

Richie [left] after two years to go work at J. Walter Thompson,...a bigger place, more money, more responsibility. Time to move on. No big deal. We remained friends.

About six months later I heard that Richie was going to start his own agency with some guy I'd never heard of. I laughed and dismissed it. 'Boy, he's certainly not equipped to start an ad agency.' 'Oh yeah,' I said to myself, 'that'll last a week.'

The first campaign they did was for Kenneth Cole shoes. Very controversial, political ads. Not about shoes at all; about the attitude behind the shoes. It was an immediate hit. They did a couple more controversial campaigns. In those days everyone read Bernice Kanner's advertising column in *New York* magazine. One week Kanner wrote a two-page spread about how Richie Kirshenbaum was running the agency of the moment. Here was this little *pischer*, a couple of months into it, he'd done a few nifty ads and positioned himself, and *he had the hot agency*!

I got insanely jealous.

That lasted about a minute. Then my jealousy turned to '*Ah ha!*' Wait a second, I figured; he's a guy who I actually know. Richie and I have worked side by side. I think I'm smarter than this guy. I think I'm a harder worker.....I lived with this guy for two years; now I'm reading about him. What's wrong with this picture? How did this happen? What's Richie got that I haven't got that's making him so hot?

No bells started flashing, no light bulb went on over my head, but it didn't take me long to figure it out. Richie had a fully developed sense of entitlement. He's clearly said to himself, 'Why shouldn't I have the next hot agency?' Richie was looking to make his mark on the world. His answer was, 'I should.'

What hit me was that Richie went into his new company saying, 'We're going to be the next hot agency,' and worked back from there. 'What do I have to do?' He's figured, 'If I want a hot agency, I've got to do a specific type of work that not only pleases my client but is also going to get a certain kind of attention.'

Me? I wasn't even dreaming that David Deutsch Associates would get written up in *New York*. We had been grinding all along but never thought it was possible. Million-dollar clients? Out of our league. If someone had asked me, 'Why shouldn't you have the next hot agency?' I'd have every answer in the world except the right one. Richie Kirshenbaum showed me I was wrong. Why *couldn't* we do work like I was reading about? That could be us. That *should* be us. We could pitch anybody. But first we had to own it. If we wanted to be written about, we'd first have to create the kinds of ads that garner attention. Why not me? From then on I started to do ads that would make waves."—Donny Deusch, *Often Wrong, Never in Doubt*, pp. 3-5.

Why can't you be the biggest and best-known business in your industry niche?

Why can't you be the biggest celebrity to the prospects and customers you serve in your market?

If you think about it, the only limitations are in your own mind. Don't limit yourself. Believe that you are worth it. You have great expertise and knowledge that can help customers in your area of expertise. Project this knowledge into your authority, celebrity and expertise. Own it. Figure out what category you want to dominate and be known for and work your way back from there. Figure out what you need to do to become recognized as a authority and a celebrity figure and do it.

2.   Choose an area of expertise and specialize.

The quickest way to promote your expertise and authority is to be an expert at something. It is much easier for a prospect or customer to remember you when you stand out as an expert in a category of one. People have a hard time remembering generalists or someone who tries to be all things to all people.

My father and younger brothers run Butler Professional Farrier School (butlerprofessionalfarrierschool.com) just outside of Chadron, Nebraska. I've observed my father become world renowned because of his focus and specialization in the farrier business. He is one of less than one percent of farriers in the United States to have a Ph.D., which he received from Cornell University in veterinary anatomy and equine nutrition. He is one of 550 Certified Journeyman Farriers in the U.S. He is one of 158 Fellows of the Worshipful Company of Farriers (FWCF) of Great Britain since 1356 A.D. He is one of 35 living FWCFs and the first American citizen to achieve it. He is the only person who is a Ph.D., CJF and FWCF. He won the North American Horseshoeing Competition in 1980 and has won many horseshoeing competitions over the years. He wrote *The Principles of Horseshoeing*, the most widely used textbook in the world on the subject, and numerous other books, has created dozens of training videos, and has spoken all over the world teaching and training new farriers on the craft.

When I was growing up, he repeated a lesson he had learned from Earl Nightingale, that if you would study for an hour a day on a subject, that you would be a foremost expert on that topic within five years. I've seen that principle to be true in his life. He has consulted with top owners, trainers, and veterinarians and has worked with many of the top horses across the world because he chose to specialize and focus. He is a great example of the kind of focus and specialization required to achieve true expertise.

Specialists are the ones who become well known and stand out. They are the ones who have the most power and control in whatever market they become the best in. Choose to be the best and be well known.

3. **Invent a new category where you can be first in the prospect and customer's minds.**

I really like what Donny Deutsch has to say about this. He says:

"Unless you're an exceptional human being from the get-go—which most people, including myself, are not—our entire social system is basically about putting people in boxes. School, in particular, should be educating children to their possibilities but instead serves just to standardize them. For my whole academic career, my behavior was 'unsatisfactory' because I had a creative mind and it wandered.

Dreams are vital—all I did was daydream—but I got penalized for mine. The world is littered with people who've been shoved back into boxes and didn't have the personal firepower to fight their way out. Maybe some kids in fourth grade are told, 'You're exceptional'—maybe their parents tell them constantly, which can add a whole other set of problems—but most are told to know their place. My parents knew I was bright and had leadership qualities. They had no clue as to my creativity.

When asked, I tell people to find their place. I don't have children, but if I did, I would tell them, 'You can be president of the United States.' I'd tell them, 'Follow your dream. You're entitled to your dream. If your dream is to be president of the United States, then why not you?'

Inside all of us, somewhere, is a dream. But no one is going to tap you on the shoulder; pluck you out of the chorus, and make you a star. First you've got to make the conscious decision to pursue that dream. You've got to put it in Drive. Want to be a chef? An investment banker? [A celebrity business owner]? What do you have to do to get there? What's the first step? Take it!

The older you become, the more your dreams get rationalized, the more you come to terms with your compromises; you know the corners you've cut better than anybody. In a Jewish family, what are we brought up to want to be? Doctor, lawyer. Make a good living. It's a pretty narrow box. We weren't brought up to be president or movie star, or to cure cancer. Most people want to please—our parents, our teachers, our clergymen—so rather than pursuing our own dreams, we follow a compendium of theirs. That rarely works. The happiest people are the ones who follow their own dreams most closely. The day your dream dies, a little part of you dies. And all of us want to live forever.

Pick your own dream. There are 20,000 advertising copywriters in

New York City right now. If I polled them, I'm absolutely positive that 19,990 would say they deserve to be a creative director. 'I'm working for them, I'm smarter than they are, I do all the work... 'Every one of them. But until they say, 'I should have that job, if not here, someplace else—and here's why,' they'll stay at their desks and begrudgingly meet their deadlines.

On one level or another, these people either don't think they deserve it or don't have the skills. If they did, they would make it happen. The math on that equation is, having the skills is necessary but doesn't guarantee success. For every person with the stuff, the one out of a hundred who goes to the very rarefied place is the one who says, 'Why not me?' and goes for it?" –Donny Deutsch, *Often Wrong, Never in Doubt*, pp. 6-7.

How many entrepreneurs across the world say that they deserve to have more success than they do? How many work long, hard hours and look at the success of others and say, "I should have a business that size. I should be more successful than them. I've been in this business longer or know more than they do"?

The reason they haven't already accomplished more is because of their self-limiting beliefs. Choose to be different. Specialize. Choose to be well-known in your market. Learn the steps to become a celebrity authority figure in your area.

The best way you can do this is to strive to be a big fish in a small pond or to specialize in a certain niche (instead of trying to be all things to all people where you blend in instead of standing out).

4. **Be visible to prospects and customers in places that are significant to them. Use the many tools and resources available today to build a following.**

Celebrities promote themselves on talk shows, in magazines, in TV or radio interviews, and on podcasts. In a similar fashion, you have to promote yourself to prospects and customers in places that are meaningful to them. Promote yourself on social media. Create helpful video tips that you can post on YouTube. Write blog posts. Be a guest on podcasts where your audience is already listening. Create your own podcast. Then, link or post this content across your social media platform.

YouTube is a powerful platform. You can broadcast your content and amass a huge following. It also positions you as an expert and celebrity. It is amazing what some people get known for. Decide you'll be the leader, the expert, and the dominant voice in your industry by posting helpful, relevant, and meaningful content to your audience.

The key is to be where your prospects are. Then, once you've created any kind of content, promote the content you've created so that prospects and customers can go back and see or hear it again (and most importantly, share it with those who follow them). You can say, "As seen in or on" and then list the places you've been featured or seen on such as "Such and such" trade show, publications where your promotions are featured, etc.

5. Align yourself and be seen with others who already have status in the mind of your prospects and customers.

Who is this for you?

- **Trade Shows** – at your next trade show, how can you position yourself to be seen as an expert by those who attend? Think carefully about this. Who can you align yourself with in your area who is already seen as an expert to those in your market niche?

- **Celebrities** – are there podcast hosts or other celebrities you can invite to interview and promote you?

- **Radio Host or Podcast Personalities** – See if you can't get a celebrity endorsement from a local radio or TV personality. Oftentimes, you can get this type of endorsement by paying for it or advertising with the station. Call the stations nearest you to find out what opportunities are available. Even if an opportunity doesn't immediately present itself, look for creative ways to be in front of those who could and should promote you.

- **Local celebrities** – Is there a local celebrity in your area that you could give something to in exchange for their endorsement? This type of alignment would be well worth what you would give to them because of the endorsement you would receive.

- **Use celebrity names as key word searches for Google Ad words** – This is a smart thing to look at closely and change on Google Ad Words from time to time if a celebrity does something that your business addresses. Then, when someone searches for what the celebrity has been up to that relates to your business, your ad will appear in their search results.

6. Create and promote dramatic demonstrations that illustrate your prestige in the marketplace.

A great example of this is during awards season for celebrities. Designers line themselves up with celebrities by having them wear their gowns and then they promote that certain celebrities were wearing their fashions. Consider how celebrity designers such as Monique Lhuillier, Badgley Mischka, and Oscar de la Renta promote themselves as dressing certain celebrities at award shows and then most importantly *how* they promote that fact to others. This is a great example of a dramatic demonstration in action.

To help you better understand the power of a dramatic illustration, let me share several examples from history and point out why the dramatic demonstration is so powerful.

The first example is that of magician Harry Houdini. Seth Godin makes this observation in his book, *The Big Moo,* which has an instructive lesson. He says:

"Historians of magic are in total agreement about this: Houdini did hackneyed mechanical tricks, showed little evidence of talent, and had almost none of the suave charisma that the great magicians of his era had.

And yet, when I ask you to name a famous magician, odds are you'll say, 'Houdini!'

So, how did he do it? How did a lousy magician become such a spectacular success?

Simple. *He wasn't a magician.*

Harry Houdini invented an entirely different sort of vaudeville attraction. He was not a magician at all, but an escape artist. Crowds didn't line up to watch him cut a lady in half. Instead, they were fascinated by his taunting of death, by the way he used himself as the most important prop in the act.

One of his breakthrough performances took place in England. Houdini was challenged (by a renowned locksmith—something you don't see very often) to free himself from a new kind of escape-proof set of handcuffs. At first he hesitated, but, motivated by the cry of the public, he accepted the challenge.

After half an hour in a tiny, isolated chamber onstage, Houdini came back before the audience and asked that the cuffs be removed so that he could take off his heavy wool coat (he was sweating from the heat) and then replaced. The crowd angrily refused—Houdini would not be permitted to trick them....With a grimace, he returned to his chamber. An hour later, he emerged triumphant, holding the opened handcuffs over his head.

When Houdini made the decision to focus on escapes instead of magic tricks, it was considered professional suicide. There wasn't a market for escape acts. There wasn't a demand for it. It had never been done before. No one knew what it was worth and no one could tell him how long or how demanding his acts should be.

Who could have imagined that Houdini would succeed by spending more than an hour and a half doing just one trick, in a closed room, out of sight of the audience? Where is it written in the magician's manual that the best way to become famous is to fake not only the outcome, but the event itself (Houdini made those handcuffs himself and paid the locksmith to challenge him in the first place— it only took him a minute to open them when the time came)?

Sometimes, making an original choice when there seems to be no choice at all is daunting. But this is often how the brave succeed while the masses are consigned to failure." –Seth Godin, *The Big Moo*, pp. 1-2.

Houdini was a master of pre-selling people on what they were going to see, how difficult of a feat it was, and how it was possible he might die or even not be able to escape.

The way he typically did this was by going to policemen in a certain city and throwing down a challenge. He made the event more exciting by how he sold it (they could hear him struggling but not see him) and then when he appeared he made his entrance very dramatic.

In fact, he often had to hold his breath for more than three minutes to escape from a milk can that he designed and his Chinese Water Torture Cell.

To dramatize this, he would invite members in the audience to hold their breath along with him while he was inside the milk can or upside down in the Chinese Water Torture Cell.

He advertised the events with dramatic posters that proclaimed "Failure Means A Drowning Death." The escapes were a sensation because of how he built up and used anticipation.

What can you do in your area to create a dramatic demonstration for

what you sell?

This is something you should really think and reflect about. Houdini spent more time thinking and planning out how he would promote his dramatic demonstrations than he did actually performing the magic tricks. There is a lot to be learned from this about why he is remembered today as one of the greatest magicians ever.

The late pitchman Billy Mays made this observation about the importance of a dramatic demonstration. He said: "A conclusion that the audience comes to on their own is a conclusion they'll believe and act on. No normal advertising claim can achieve that, no matter how much evidence you throw behind it. SHOW someone an "I can't freakin' believe it" demonstration, and they'll walk away convinced."

How are you using the power of dramatic demonstration? What are you doing to create more dramatic demonstration in your marketing and sales efforts? This is why capturing testimonials is so important – they are your dramatic demonstration to the marketplace that you are the best place to buy your product or service.

7.   **Master media and become known as an expert**.

The best way to do this is to create and deliver content so that you can promote your status as an expert and an authority.

Jim Palmer (GetJimPalmer.com) is a great example of positioning himself through video, podcasts, and Facebook live. He promotes himself as the dream business coach and shares valuable tips and advice through numerous media sources. He is a master of media.

Here is an assignment for you:

List all of the local media outlets in your city, town, region, and every well known media outlet that is recognized by your target market. Then, ask yourself, "How can I become known as an expert by these individuals?" Then, create the content that will help you be recognized as an expert by these individuals and institutions. Once you have one success in promotion, be sure to promote that to everyone else.

Podcast hosts are able to create celebrity by focusing on a topic and by associating with other celebrities for interviews. It has never been easier to create and post content than it is today. You can create your own web site, podcast, and write articles that can be posted online that will promote you and your expertise. You just have to start creating this content and posting it where it can be seen.

8.   Carefully develop your own reputation in the marketplace.

Don't take anything for granted. If you want to elevate your status and the status of your business, you have to promote yourself. Tell your story. But, tell it the right way. Don't do it to build up yourself and make yourself sound unapproachable.

Build your celebrity status by talking about how you have helped customers, how you are known in the community, and strive to connect with people so that they feel like they are dealing with a real person.

Invite people follow you on Instagram or other social media platforms. This is a great way for people to get a chance to interact with you and find out more about you on a personal level. People buy from those they like, know, and trust. Be more transparent and your trust will increase more rapidly with those who interact with you.

9.   Study great promoters and develop your own style.

One of the best and most controversial promoters alive today is Donald Trump. Whether you agree or disagree with him, there is no question that he is a master at getting free publicity for himself, his ideas, policies, and his brand. Unless you are a hermit with no access to any kind of media, it is difficult to go a long period of time without hearing someone talk about him or hearing/reading something from him. You can agree or disagree with his politics and his 'showmanship' but you can't dismiss how he promotes himself to get what he wants. Consider what he says about the importance of promoting yourself in his book *Think Like a Billionaire:*

"I'm always amazed when people tell me I'm a master promoter.... Promotion comes naturally from doing what you're good at. I'm good at building buildings, and that's how I promote myself—as the best builder of buildings. And everyone agrees. Neil Ostergren, a great guy who used to run the Hospitality Sales and Marketing Association, polled bigwigs in business to see what names came to mind when they thought of real estate. Mine easily came out on top." – *Think Like a Billionaire,* pp. 83-84.

Another great promoter you should study is Gorgeous George. Most people today aren't familiar with George Wagner, who was a professional wrestler during the 1940s and 1950s, who went by the ring name "Gorgeous George".

"Muhammad Ali and James Brown acknowledged that their own approach to flamboyant self-promotion was influenced by George. A 19-year old Ali met a 46-year old George at a Las Vegas radio station. During George's radio interview, the wrestler's promo caught the attention of the future heavyweight champion. If George lost to Classy Freddie Blassie, George exclaimed, "I'll crawl across the ring and cut my hair off! But that's not gonna happen because I'm the greatest wrestler in the world!" Ali recalled, "I saw 15,000 people comin' to see this man get beat. And his talking did it. I said, 'This is a gooood idea!'" In the locker room afterwards, the seasoned wrestler gave the future legend some invaluable advice: "A lot of people will pay to see someone shut your mouth. So keep on bragging, keep on sassing and always be outrageous."--John Capouya, "King Strut", *Sports Illustrated*, December 12, 2005.

The greatest sports promoter of all time was Muhammad Ali. Statements like "I am the greatest!" built pre-match hype, where he would trash talk opponents on television often with rhymes. He was a master of the power of story.

Another of history's most successful marketing geniuses was P.T. Barnum. He was an American showman best remembered for founding the circus that became the Ringling Bros. and Barnum & Bailey Circus.

Thomas Edison was an excellent promoter of his inventions. Everyone remembers Edison as the inventor of the light bulb because of the story they've heard about how he attempted more than 2,000 times to figure out what would work. As most everyone in the world knows this story, what does that teach you about the power of story? How can you better tell your story to your prospects and customers in your industry?

Evel Knievel's failures got him more exposure than his successful jumps. Knievel's nationally televised motorcycle jumps, including his 1974 attempt to jump Snake River Canyon at Twin Falls, Idaho, represent four of the twenty most-watched *ABC's Wide World of Sports* events to date. His achievements and failures, including his record 37 broken bones, earned him several entries in the *Guinness Book of World Records*. Evel Knievel (who was originally Robert Craig Knievel gave himself the more memorable name "Evel" – He was a master promoter who is best remembered for what he didn't do than for what he actually did do. What can you learn from this about the power of publicity?

Today, promoters are paid by social media platforms for posting about their products and services. Google the list of the highest paid promoters and you'll see that celebrities like Kylie Jenner, Kim Kardashian, Selena Gomez, and Cristiano Ronaldo get paid millions because they have amassed millions of followers who care what they talk and post about. What are you doing to build up your own following and promote your celebrity?

10. Write a descriptive bio about yourself that will position you as an expert and a celebrity in your chosen market niche.

Make a list of who you believe are currently the top experts and celebrities in your market. Read their online bios and consider how they promote themselves.

Now, I want you to consider the following seven questions as you reflect on these biographical statements and how you should formulate yours:

1) What do you learn from looking at the way these individuals have positioned themselves as authorities and status symbols?

2) What similar words and phrases do they use?

3) How are they promoting their fame, standing, and renowned nature to their prospects and customers?

4) What can you learn from this to apply to your business?

5) How is this different than how most entrepreneurs promote themselves?

6) Where does this leave them in a prospect or customer's mind?

7) What does this tell you about how you should be branding your business and yourself as a celebrity in your market?

Here is your assignment: Write your positioning statement to promote you as a celebrity for your business.

Use the following prompts and ideas to help you do this:

- Write your name, the name of your business, where you are located, the length of time you've been in business, and the size of your business in comparison with others in your industry.

- Write about your background: where you grew up, education, and professional background.

- Write about your involvement in your industry. How long have you been in the business? How did you become interested in the profession in the first place?

- What attracted you to specialize in your area of expertise in your business in particular?

- What services do you offer to prospects and customers in your market niche?

- Is there an area that you consider to be your specialty?

- Write about what you think has been your secret to your success in your business. What do you bring to the table that others in the industry don't (what makes you unique and different)? Make a list of your stories and insert them into videos and interviews you do. They should lead back to you, promote your expertise, and help others get to know you so they feel comfortable reaching out to you for help.

- Write about or create a video where you discuss the current trends with products people are buying from those in your industry. For example, write about trends you are seeing this year and what trends are on the horizon. Experts have definitive opinions and expertise so let others know about yours.

- Write about the best piece of advice you could give to a customer who just purchased a product from you or the biggest mistakes prospects make when planning on buying something from you

- Talk about what you enjoy most about working with your customers. This will give others a chance to see your heart. What do you enjoy most about working in your business? What is the most difficult thing about what you do (if possible, turn this into a positive – like "It is so frustrating or sad when people wait too long and can't get the very best (product or service you offer). Don't make this mistake too. Come in to our business or visit us online so we can explain how you can get the results others are getting with the product or service you offer.

- Write or talk about future goals or projects you would like to tackle in your industry.

- Write about what usually surprises prospects when they go shopping for what you offer and what people can do to avoid these obstacles.

There is great power in positioning yourself as an expert, an authority, and celebrity to prospects and customers in your market niche. Take the time to work out your strategy and put it in place. This will help you build your business and get others to promote you in ways you never dreamed possible. Believe you are worth it and take the action necessary to do this. I look forward to hearing how you've used this principle to boost your business and break through to the next level.

CHAPTER 7

BUILD YOUR VALUE SO YOUR CLIENTS PERCEIVE YOU ARE THE BEST

"Faced with the choice between changing one's mind and proving that there is no need to do so, almost everyone gets busy on the proof."—John Kenneth Galbraith

One of the biggest complaints I hear from business owners is how to avoid being shopped solely on the basis of price. Part of this problem comes from relying on the manufacturer's brand instead of your own brand and the other part of the problem comes from misunderstanding what makes up the value that causes prospects to want to buy from you in the first place.

Prospects today are looking for better deals and many businesses are lowering prices to compete on this playing field. In some cases, prospects have reduced spending capacity, but in the majority of cases, people aren't willing to part with their hard-earned money unless they see more value for their dollar first.

Where can you add more value in your business? Here are eight suggestions of how you can enhance and raise your overall value at your business:

1. Focus on increasing the intangible, personal, and unique aspects of what you do that create *real* enhanced value to your customers.

Too many business owners focus on promoting what they sell at their businesses solely based on overall intrinsic or face value. Intrinsic means "of or relating to the essential nature of a thing". Another way to look at intrinsic value is to look at what prospects expect or what is inherent when they enter a business who sells what you offer.

Most businesses position their businesses on intrinsic, expected, or face value things that have little to no differentiation. The problem with focusing on intrinsic value is that it is hard to *sustain* as a value differentiator over a period of time. This is like the example I shared earlier of the hotels with the coffee makers or irons in each room. You can't sustain these types of differentiators over a period of time for three reasons:

- What you do in your business can often be easily copied or mimicked.

- What is expected is often dictated *before* a prospect ever arrives in your marketing funnel. The experience others have had with your competitors, what they have read online, or what other people have said about you or your product in reviews matters and decisions are made *before* they actually interact with your sales team and buy.

- What a prospect "thinks" will happen at your business is based on the experiences that they have already had at other businesses and this influences the experience they will have at your business.

People value things in different ways. In order to transcend intrinsic value and raise the value of what you do, you have to focus on what the prospect values most, ***not*** what you value most. To help you understand this principle, consider the following illustrations.

For example, what is the inherent entertainment value in spending a day at Disney World, a day at Six Flags, or a day at the state fair? In each case, you are at a theme park with rides, food, and games. But the difference between how each are priced and valued is dramatically different. Why?

What is the difference between buying a polished stone from an out of the way jewelry store and buying a diamond ring from Tiffany's? If you reduce the transaction down simply to the intrinsic value of what you are getting, it is that you are buying a polished stone. That is the intrinsic value of a diamond. What allows the same polished rock to be sold for hundreds or thousands of dollars is based on how it is positioned and sold.

What is the difference between buying electricity from a utility company or from your own solar panels? If you reduce the transaction down simply to the intrinsic value of what you are getting, it is that you are buying electricity. The difference of ownership, tax credits, and environmental benefits by going solar explain why people will pay thousands of dollars for a solar system instead of continuing on with a monthly payment from their utility company.

What is the difference between buying a Tesla Roadster and a Ford Focus? Both automobiles will get you from point A to point B. The intrinsic value of transportation doesn't explain why these cars are priced so far apart. When you reduce automobiles to the intrinsic value of transportation (or getting from point A to point B), the value is reduced substantially. However, when you focus on the intangible, personal, and unique aspects of each car, the enhanced value becomes more clear (especially if you are listening to the seller of a Tesla Roadster).

What is the difference in eating at McDonald's, Ruth's Chris Steak House, or taking vitamins? The first two will give you dinner at quite different prices. If you reduce the essential intrinsic value of all three to simply eating or having nutrition, you have a completely different value altogether. The other thing that is important is that different customer groups value things differently. For example, if you are a vegetarian, neither McDonald's or Ruth's Chris are particularly appetizing options for dinner. This is why it is so important to understand who *your* customer is to your business. When you clearly understand this, it is much easier to build a value proposition that *will* mean something to those that they will pay for it.

To surpass the intrinsic value that a prospect expects, you have to focus in on the intangible, personal, and unique aspects of what you do at your business. Dan Kennedy calls this IPU (or intangible, personal, and unique) value. It is what allows businesses the ability to raise their value so they can command a premium price for what it is they sell.

Consider celebrity wedding planner and bridal fashion designer, David Tutera. He has written several books (which give him authority and expertise) and is the host of the WE TV show "My Fair Wedding with David Tutera." What is David's intrinsic value? He is a party planner. Why do people hire him and pay much more than any other wedding planner in their market? Because he is a celebrity and he has done celebrity weddings. The value of why he can command so much more in price is found in the status, the bragging rights (I got my wedding done by the same guy who did Star Jones' wedding and he has put on events for Jennifer Lopez, Elton John, Barbara Walters, and others). It is more about the experience of having him be your wedding planner and the stories you can tell your friends than it is about how good of a party planner he really is. He has done a good job of building his value instead of focusing on the intrinsic or expected value of a wedding planner. The important thing to recognize is that the value in what I've mentioned has very little to do with the product you actually get. When you position your value differently, it changes the equation. You can create significantly more interest, scarcity, and demand and a higher price as a result.

Let's take a look at Kleinfeld Bridal in New York City from the point of view of their intrinsic value versus their enhanced value which they've manufactured. The intrinsic value of buying an expensive wedding gown can be found at many other salons across the country. The reason Kleinfeld is one of the most famous and successful bridal salons in the world is because of how they have positioned themselves with enhanced value that others can't easily copy.

Kleinfeld's enhanced value is made up of:

- **The increased status and meaning of buying from them** – it means something to be a Kleinfeld's bride (this has been communicated through their TV show *Say Yes to the Dress* and their advertising). Having a different or better experience is one way you can elevate your status. When it means something to buy a certain product, you elevate your importance when you also buy the product.

- **It is unusual and rare to buy a dress from them.** It is rare because the dresses are expensive and not everyone can afford to buy them. Being able to afford a dress from them elevates your status in the eyes of others.

- **The inside look you can get if you are lucky enough to be a part of their TV show or go through the process of buying from them.** – For example, consider the psychology of these thoughts: "If I go to Kleinfeld's, I could be featured on their television show "Say Yes to the Dress" or "I'll see what it's like behind the scenes and will have a great story to tell to others (in person or on Instagram)."

- **The bragging rights you will have about having the experience of shopping or buying from them. The enhanced value is manufactured by having a better story than someone else.** – For example, "I got my dress at Kleinfeld's" "I met....[someone they've seen on the show]" "I flew to New York City and went to Kleinfeld's." Every element of the experience becomes a part of the better story you can tell others. While no one wants to admit this is true, it is human nature to take pleasure in the pride of telling a better story than someone else. Smart marketers think more about how to enhance the experiences they provide in their business so they can manufacture enhanced value in this way.

- **The psychological effect of discovering and going through the process of finding out what it means to be a Kleinfeld's bride.** People have an innate sense of curiosity about what it is like to live or experience how others do (which is why videos on what it is like to experience first class travel are so popular). Being a part of or discovering on your own what it means to be a part of an exclusive group has tremendous appeal.

Now, consider what they say on their web site. You'll notice that the underlined segments are increased value and the intrinsic value portions of the text have been italicized.

> "*For more than 60 years*, brides have learned that <u>the magic of Kleinfeld</u> lies not just in our most magnificent store; not just in our offering the *largest and finest selection of designer wedding gowns in the world*; but <u>the magic lies in the hearts of the most professional staff anywhere</u>…a staff dedicated to perform your every wish. This is the world of Kleinfeld for generations."

The web site description continues:

> **"WHY does Kleinfeld sell more designer bridal gowns than any other store on earth?**
> You are one of a kind… and so are we. Our <u>professional bridal consultants understand your individuality</u> – with <u>listening ears, a keen sense of style, and a vision of perfection</u> – they will guide you to your perfect gown…<u>limited only by your imagination</u>.
>
> *We travel the world twice a year…* to bring you the latest European bridal gowns which can only be seen in the United States at Kleinfeld… <u>No passport or travel expenses required!</u>

Every day is like a trunk show at Kleinfeld. We carry the *largest selection* of bridal gowns from each of the top American and European bridal designers... So you don't need to wait for a trunk show to find your dream gown.

Our *service is unsurpassed* with nearly <u>200 dedicated professionals</u>, including on-site stylists and bridal consultants, and custom fitters, sewers, beaders, embroiderers and pressers. Your <u>gown will receive more than 30 hours of *personal attention* that goes into sculpting it to your body.</u>

Kleinfeld is with you *every step of the way,* from the day you purchase your dress through the day you wear it. <u>The owners of Kleinfeld give each bride their private home phone number in case a bride needs special attention when the store is closed.</u>

We have been assisting brides with their gowns in Brooklyn since 1941 and we will continue this great tradition in Manhattan!"

If you notice, there is a good mix of intrinsic and increased value, but the majority of the text focuses on the increased and higher value portions of what they do. You should do the same with your business.

Now, compare that with what is on an unnamed bridal store's web site (but the principle applies with your business in your niche as well):

"What is your "Lowest Price Guarantee?" Our "Lowest Price Guarantee" is simple. If you find the exact same dress from the same manufacturer on another website, all you have to do is provide us with a link to where you saw the style for less. Here are the only qualifications: 1.) You must provide the URL address that links to the exact style on another website. Include this URL during the checkout phase (if applicable), and we will adjust the price before charging your credit card., 2.) This offer excludes items that are represented as "clearance" or "sale" merchandise and must be of like condition to the merchandise you are purchasing., 3.) Items must be

on the website of an authorized retailer for that particular designer., 4.) Auction websites, such as eBay, are excluded from this offer. We reserve the right to exclude this offer if it can be determined that the price on the other website is an error. We are not responsible for obvious errors or "typos" on our website or any other website., 5.) We do not match Internet pricing in our full service salon, but we do have additional benefits for in-store purchases., and 6.) All contract terms on orders already placed remain in effect."

The description continues:

"At _____ located at _____ you will find one of _____ (state's) widest selections of wedding dresses. *They offer a wide selection of designer gowns*, with many of them being <u>exclusive</u> only to their store. _____ also offers "in store" specials that includes discounts up to 70% off retail prices. _____ will match any competitors price as well. They can be reached at _____ or online at _____."

Which of these descriptions is more valuable in the eyes of prospects? Which has better bragging rights, better stories, and has more benefits for the consumer with their offers?

Be sure you are positioning your business in a way that enhances your value.

Now, it's your turn. What lessons can you apply to how you describe your value to your prospects on your web site? Consider the following questions to see how you can increase your value when you market and sell your product or service:

- What does it mean to buy from you? Do you elevate your customer's status in any way when they buy from you? If you don't currently do this, how could you start?

- What kind of an inside look are your prospects able to experience when they go through your process that makes them feel more important and more importantly that elevates their status in their own eyes and in the eyes of others?

- Do prospects have a better story to tell about the experience of buying from you or experiencing your product in the first 12-24 hours after purchase? Are you helping them tell a better story so they can brag about it to others on social media?

- How are you heightening anticipation and building value by the insider's look into your process? Giving people an insider's look or a passport to a different experience can heighten the value that a prospect experiences in powerful tangible and intangible ways.

Throughout this book, I have encouraged you to find and point out your differentiating factors. If you don't do this, your prospects will evaluate you solely on your intrinsic or expected value, which means they will shop for the lowest price. To increase your value, you've got to focus on the elements outlines above.

Here are some questions for you to carefully consider:

Are you building the value of your business brand to be face value or increased in a way that has a unique appeal for each individual prospect? How do you know? How can you tell?

You can tell by spotting these clues. Remember, intrinsic value states what prospects *expect* from a business who offers your product/service. Intrinsic value says:

- We've been in business for...

- We carry XYZ products (just like everyone else)

- We sell Product X to solve a particular problem

- We offer a better price than any of our competitors

You may say, well this is too hard. How can I differentiate my business when I *am* the same as everyone else? The key is to change your business to focus on your most important strengths. Think about Apple and how Steve Jobs eliminated several areas of his company to build it back to be even more successful than ever. You can do the same by choosing to focus on your area of difference and by looking for ways to inject increased value into everything that you do.

Dan Kennedy shares this example that details how value can be found in the way that two carpet cleaners go about their work. Notice the differences between the two and think about how you can apply this idea to your business as well.

"The first carpet cleaner arrives and you leave. Three hours later you come back and your carpets are cleaned.

The second carpet cleaner sends a diagnostic technician to your house. He arrives and takes you with him, inch by inch putting different colored flags in different spots. These flags tell Cleaning Technicians (who will be arriving shortly) which kinds of spot or stain removers to use. In addition, the diagnostic technician takes 'before' photos of dirtiest areas or worst stains for you to look at and compare with the final job. When the cleaning technicians arrive, the diagnostic technician gives them a briefing and points out any specific problem areas that you are most concerned about. You then leave, return three hours later and have clean carpets. The cleaning technicians then take you around and compare the 'before' pictures with the 'after' results and fix anything you aren't completely satisfied with.

Now, which one of these two has more intrinsic value? In both scenarios, your carpet is cleaned. The outcome is identical since your carpets were cleaned in three hours. What is the value difference between Carpet Cleaner #1 and Carpet Cleaner #2? The value with Carpet Cleaner #2 includes the following benefits:

- The customer is more excited.

- The customer has a story to tell all of his or her friends ("I went around and they put up these little flags all around the house...") – this is the basis of a great referral program

- In the end, the customer is happier about spending the money with the 2nd Carpet Cleaner since they feel more validated and listened to.

- The customer notices more detail about what's been done and so they appreciate the work more."

Why does this kind of differentiation matter now? The bottom line is that prospects are looking for more value when they spend their money. In their mind, they are looking for savings or more intrinsic value for their dollar. You will have to build more value into what you sell in enhanced ways to help your business grow and prosper.

The best businesses have a profound, clear, compelling, and sustainable differentiation from every other business in the marketplace. You need to invest your time in building a unique value proposition that incorporates both intrinsic and enhanced value.

Ask yourself and answer the following questions:

- What intrinsic value do you have at your business? What makes this valuable to the prospect?

- What enhanced value do you have at your business? What makes this valuable to the prospect?

- What are you going to do to build more perception of value at your business?

To help you get started with this assignment, here are a few examples of how you can build more intrinsic and increased value at your business:

- Build your value so that it means something to be a customer

who buys from you. Give your customers bragging rights – "I'm a
_____*name of your business*_____'s customer."

- Include them in a special group so they feel like they belong and
are part of a movement (something big and important).

- Use anticipation and curiosity as ways to build a better experience
and create more value. Give prospects a personalized free gift
when you meet for an appointment.

- Create experiences as part of the sales process.

**2. View and assess value differently. View it in terms of how a
prospect does and remember that value has a stated and unstated
emotional component. Tap into both to build increased value.**

In order to build value, you first have to <u>view it differently</u>. If you view
your value in an intrinsic way, that will come across in how you market,
promote and sell. If you can learn how to accurately assess value in terms
of how the prospect coming into your marketing funnel actually does,
you will be much more successful in branding your business.

If you ask most businesses how they plan to compete with their
competitors, it is usually on the basis of price. Their thinking goes
something like this: "Market share is the key to profitability and lower
prices increase market share, so let's start a price war to drive our
competition crazy (or out of business) and we'll get rich."

I love Guy Kawasaki's advice on this topic in his book, *How to Drive
Your Competition Crazy*. He says:

> "Let me try to talk you out of using pricing as a primary weapon
> against your competition. My source for this section is an
> exceptional book called *The Strategy and Tactics of Pricing* by
> Thomas Nagle and Reed Holden.
>
> According to Nagle and Holden, 'Pricing is like playing chess.
> Those who make moves one at a time—seeking to minimize

immediate losses or to exploit immediate opportunities—will invariably be beaten by those who can envision the game a few moves ahead.'

Most companies only consider pricing decisions in a closed, static space. Simplistically—very simplistically—companies think that if they lower prices, they will get more customers. Their plan for waging and winning a price war considers only themselves and customers. However, this approach doesn't take into account the reactions of competitors who may match reductions, surpass reductions, hold steady, increase prices, or increase value (for example, by bundling additional services). Thus, plans for a price war should include other companies.

Th[is] is still incomplete, however, because 'the customer' is usually a heterogeneous collection of diverse groups with different needs. This diversity should likewise be considered for pricing decisions.

Then there is the element of time—or rounds. That is, in the first round, you may lower prices and customer A may buy more, but competitor A may lower prices to match your move. In the second round, you lower prices again and competitor B may join the fray— and so on. Get the picture? Before you declare a price war, you had better consider all the ramifications of the actions and reactions of your competition and your customers *over time.*

Price 'war' is an appropriate metaphor because in war both sides usually lose if the conflict lasts long enough.

Make value, not war. A price war is simply too dangerous and I don't know any company that went broke creating too much value for their customers."—pp. 83-87.

Remember, your goal is to see value how your prospects see value. Many business owners think that prospects today only see value in price. People today think that way because they can't tell the difference between buying at from your business or buying from someone else online. Their belief is that they should get the best value and if they can't tell a difference, they will decide on the best price.

Here is an important key: **The expectation a prospect has about their shopping experience in large measure determines the value that they give to you and to what you do at your business.** If a prospect thinks they can use your business to get information (or as a try on business) and then buy online (and you empower them to do it), guess what? They will do that. On the other hand, if a prospect has a transcending experience that completely shifts how they view the solution they are seeking from you, and you are a part of that experience, they will do business with you (provided you have protected yourself and create value in meaningful and memorable ways to the *prospect*, not to yourself).

Remember, affluent consumers have come to expect *above the norm* amenities and service. Are you accommodating specific types and preferences of customers (those who prefer to make selections in private)? Do you offer catered refreshments and drinks? Do you offer complimentary gift wrapping, home delivery, and private merchandise no one else has?

Think about your business in new ways. Most business owners have a really hard time assessing and creating value since they think about it from their point of view and not from their customer's point of view. If you want to leverage your value to maximize what you sell, you have to shift your way of thinking about this.

3. Focus on a profound, clear, compelling, and sustainable differentiating point that you can build your enhanced value around.

Consider Apple computers. Their strategy for focus has been brilliant over the past two decades. Years ago, when Steve Jobs was ousted out of Apple, the company went in multiple directions and created products like the Newton and laser printers. When Jobs came back to the company, he immediately got out of those markets and focused on selling premium computers (well-made machines for the top end of the market, like luxury cars). There has always been pressure on Apple to sell dirt-cheap computers (like their competitors do), but Jobs insisted that Apple would never compete in the commodity computer market which is "a race to the bottom." For the most part, Apple CEO Tim Cook has continued with that same philosophy. Instead of taking on Dell with the cheapest possible computer, Apple made first-class products to make enough profit to keep developing more first-class products. Over time, their prices have come down because of volume and because of creating new product categories for different types of consumers.

One of the reasons why Apple has been so successful is because of their focus and also because they have focused on what increases their increased value in the minds of their customers instead of just their intrinsic value (a computer that processes data).

The enhanced value of owning Apple products includes:

- **The increased status and meaning of buying from them** – not everyone has an Apple product, except for the "cool crowd" who uses their devices (this is especially true when a new version of the product comes out since some people just have to buy the newly minted version iPhone or iPad even thought the old model they already own still works fine)

- **The inside look you can get if you are lucky enough to be one of the first to own the newest version of their latest device and the experience of going through the process of buying from them.** – Apple makes it meaningful to have the new device before everyone else. This is especially important for early adopters.

- **It is unusual and rare to buy a computer or device from them.** Today, Apple devices are much more common than when they first came on the market. It used to be rare to have one of their devices. They've kept a high value and price on their products, but they've done a brilliant job of repositioning their products into items that are absolutely necessary in the eyes of the customers who use them. Today, they have stratified their offerings so that more people can afford to buy them, but they usually have a luxury option of their products that is priced much higher than the other versions. In this case, these products become something rare that others don't or can't have (because the devices are expensive) – Apple notebooks and desktop computers are among the most expensive in the marketplace. Apple has done a masterful job of creating enhanced value behind the products they sell.

- **Customization** - Apple's products can be personalized specifically to your needs – The Apple App store has thousands of applications that can help a person's phone be completely unique to them and what they do.

- **The bragging rights you will have about having the experience of shopping or buying from Apple. The enhanced value is manufactured by having a better story than someone else.** When a new product comes out, Apple customers proudly line up to buy them and then proudly display what they have just purchased for all of their friends to see. When the iPhone originally came out, people would post videos on their social media showing them unboxing their product. Opening Apple packaging is a unique experience that also enhances a product's value. People love showing off their new devices (which is why Apple changes the look of the camera so others can see that you have the new, new thing).

- **Better stories they can tell others** – people love to promote that they were one of the first to have a certain version of a product. Many are willing to wait in line for hours because they can then tell that story to their friends. This is also the reason why people will wait in line for hours before a store opens during Thanksgiving / Black Friday sales (so they can brag to their friends that they have all of their Christmas shopping done)

To create a better offer, it has to be believable. This is one of the most important parts of value and one that most businesses don't pay enough attention to. In order to be believed, prospects want to see lots of their peers who have purchased from you AND have had a positive experience with you *before* they go ahead and do business with you

Think carefully about how you are positioning your product and how you are structuring what you are selling so that it is focused on your unique difference that appeals to your prospect. Once you've done this, you'll be leveraging your value to maximize what you sell.

4. Educate prospects better. If you aren't educating them about what makes you unique or different, they won't know.

Here is one of my favorite quotes by Warren Buffet:

"Maybe the grapes from a little 8-acre vineyard in France are really the best in the world, but I have always had a suspicion that about 99% of it is in the telling and about 1% is in the drinking."

What story are you telling? The cornerstone of your marketing plan should be to educate your prospects. You first educate them on the products you sell and what you do to bring and prepare those products for them. You should include all of the interesting details regarding the construction of the products, how you select them and what influences your decision to choose to offer them to your customers. You can post this information on your social media accounts to keep prospects up to date on what is happening in your business.

One way to educate prospects in your area is to create a booklet that you write that details *The Official Guide to Getting Results with _____ (the product you offer).* This can help build your expertise and help prospects better understand how to use your product or service.

One of the biggest marketing mistakes you can make is to fail to educate your prospects about the unique advantages your business offers to them. If you aren't telling them about what you are doing to help bring them the best products in the world, you're making a mistake.

For example, if you've reviewed 2,000 products to pick the very best options to offer, tell them how you make that choice. It will impress them that you've screened out products that don't have the quality, construction, style, endurance and dependability you know they want. Your prospects and future customers won't know these facts unless you tactfully point them out.

When you educate your prospects correctly, you will see your sales and your profits soar.

Think about you for a minute: When you buy or consider buying an item or service for you or for your business—you often don't know as much as you would like about the item. If you have unanswered questions about the item, you'll be much less likely to spend money to buy it.

When someone (a sales professional) takes the time and initiative to objectively educate you on all of the product offerings available in the area in which you are contemplating a purchase, you really appreciate it. It helps you have more trust and favor in the sales rep and in the company he or she represents.

Education is an extremely powerful marketing strategy. Educate your prospects about everything (including a few of the bad or less positive aspects of products, the risks of ordering online, etc.), and you'll sell to almost twice as many customers as you do now because of the rising trust and expertise you will gain from positioning yourself this way. Educating those you serve will help you gain an inordinate advantage over your competitors.

The other benefit of educating the prospect is that you will lead them to action. People need to be explicitly told how to act in order to take advantage of the product you are offering now. Every marketing communication that you send out should tell prospects what to do. Give them a brief education, then take them by the hand (figuratively speaking) and tell them what specific action they need to take next. Create urgency so they will act now.

Assignment: Ask and answer the following two questions:

1) What do you do at your business that prospects and current customers don't know about?

2) How can you educate prospects about these to let them know of your unique advantages?

A final thought about educating prospects. You need to make sure that they are *your* customers (the ones that you sell to). Are they really the prospects who will respond to what you sell? The goal is to focus on selling to an audience that is hungry or thirsty for what you sell. If they aren't, you won't be successful in this type of approach for building value. If they are your market, and they are hungry or thirsty, you want to focus on selling them a second helping or a second glass (or upselling them on additional offerings that will be helpful to them in getting the most from your offering).

5. Increase value by having a better offer.

To help you determine how well you are creating value and what type of an offer you have, ask yourself the following questions to see how well you are doing at increasing / enhancing your the value of what you sell:

1) **Is the need for your product obvious? Are you where they are looking when the need becomes evident in their life?**
Your goal is to be in front of a prospect as soon as they realize that they needs the solution that is provided by what you are offering.

2) **Is the need genuine?**

If the prospect you are working with doesn't need what you are selling, you will have a very difficult time creating and building any value. On the other hand, if they *must* have the product you have and they won't be able to get the results they want without it, you have a big advantage when selling. One of the most difficult scenarios for most sales consultants to overcome is the time objection or "I've got lots of time until I need this result so I'm just looking." This is a great place for you to educate the prospect *and* explain why you and your business are so important for helping them achieve the results they seek. Send out marketing notices to your prospects letting them know it is time to get the results they seek, that time is running out, and that if they don't hurry, they may end up settling for something they don't really want. It is so important to create a vivid picture in the prospect's mind to build value.

3) **Is your product or service readily available or are you the only one who is offering it?**

If a prospect can get the product they want and need and that you are selling anywhere, you have a big challenge *unless* you can differentiate yourself in a way that builds your personal value in the mind of the prospect *and* they see why she should do business with *you*. If they can't differentiate you from any other provider of the product, they will differentiate on price and you will end up being a glorified 'try-on' business (they'll find out which option or size they need and then will buy it online).

4) **Can people get results with your product or service? What proof do you offer that people can get a return on their investment?**

Depending on the product you sell, the return a prospect gets may be almost entirely emotionally based. This doesn't make the sale impossible, but it does require that you get the prospect more emotionally involved in the purchase and it also illustrates why it is so critical that you help them find a solution to the problem they have that *they* can *visualize themselves using to get the result they seek.*

5) **Are people motivated to buy? Do your prospects get emotionally involved?**

Your sales will increase when you can inject emotion into the sale. The main thing here is to help each prospect feel great about the solution you're offering to solve the problem they recognize they have, help that person ease their fears and insecurities, and help them see that *you* are the one to completely eliminate those and help them have a great experience. If you can do that successfully, you will close the sale. If you don't inject emotion into the sale and prospects don't sense any emotional triggers of why they should buy, you will not be very successful at selling since most sales are emotional.

6) **Do people need your offer now? Or is there zero urgency?**

Most prospects think they have all of the time in the world. Your job as a marketer and as a sales consultant selling the product you offer is to persuade them that they need your product now. This is all about creating urgency. Many people procrastinate today and wait longer to get what they need. It is much easier to create urgency when this is the case because they have a genuine need to get your product or service now.

7) **Is your offer compelling compared to other choices in the marketplace?**

If you aren't the best in your marketplace, what can you do to change this perception so that you are better or at least as good as your competitors? Here are several other suggestions:

- Outsell and out-market your competition

- Introduce and/or bundle accessories and gifts from downstream vendors (products they may also buy) to increase your value.

- Build your authority (if you are the best and can prove it, it makes it very difficult for any competitor to gain ground on you)

- Let prospects know what others are saying about you (especially with video)

- Educate the prospect (if nobody knows you're the best, you might as well be the worst). Most businesses aren't educating prospects so there is a huge opportunity here if you can create more informative videos so prospects want to take action

8) **Are you the highest or lowest priced offering? How do you compare with other options that are available?**

One of the most important concepts about value is to know exactly where you stand and communicate that to the prospects and customers you serve. If you want to leverage your value to maximize what you sell, you have to know where you stand and your prospects need to understand why.

Harry Beckwith in his book *The Invisible Touch* makes this observation:

> "Companies in many services essentially set their rates by studying the going, high, and low rates, and then deciding where they fall on the quality spectrum. This unfortunate practice tells their customers exactly how good the company *really* thinks it is.
>
> Ask yourself: If that's how you are pricing your services, what are you saying to your customers and prospects—that

you aren't that great?

Another problem with this pricing strategy is the Problem of the Deathly Middle. If you are the high-priced provider, most people assume you offer the best quality—a desirable position. If you are the low-cost provider, most people assume you deliver an acceptable product at the lowest cost—also a desirable position. But if you price in the middle, what you are saying—again—is: 'We're not the best, and neither is our price, but both our service and price are pretty good.' Not a very compelling message.

The premium service and the low-cost provider occupy nice niches all by themselves. If you are priced in between, however, you are competing with almost everyone. And that's a lot of everyones." –pp. 133-134.

Thinking through these questions will help you enhance the value you offer to those you serve. Then you can leverage that value to maximize what you sell.

6. Break down each interaction you have with every prospect throughout the sales process and look for ways you can add more value to them and the solution they seek with your product.

Here is my assignment to you. Think about every interaction you have with prospects who come into contact with your business. How can you enhance your value at each level?

1) Before the prospect comes in contact with you

   Ways I Can Build Enhanced Value:

2) The first 30 seconds after the prospect enters my marketing

funnel

Ways I Can Build Enhanced Value:

3) The registration or name capture process

Ways I Can Build Enhanced Value:

4) Educating the prospect on what we offer

Ways I Can Build Enhanced Value:

5) Presenting the product

Ways I Can Build Enhanced Value:

6) Closing the sale

Ways I Can Build Enhanced Value:

7) Additional options / offerings

Ways I Can Build Enhanced Value:

8) Add-On Sales

Ways I Can Build Enhanced Value:

9) Follow-Up

Ways I Can Build Enhanced Value:

10) Referral Process

Ways I Can Build Enhanced Value:

7. Build value by building and using anticipation.

Anticipation is a powerful way to create and build value. Think about a recent opening of an IKEA or the lead up to the big sales that happen at many retailers on Black Friday. People will wait in lines for hours to have a chance to get a special deal or have a chance to win something. As strange as it sounds in our "I want it now" society, anticipation actually heightens the pleasure of the experience. People who wait in line to get into a concert (or to buy tickets) and people who camp outside of stores get even more excited when they gather around others and talk about what they will experience.

The key to having anticipation be a successful strategy to build value is to ensure that the value of both the experience leading up to the end and the value of the end experience are both high. At the very least, there should be more value at the end of the experience so that the overall feeling about what happened is positive.

Think about this for a minute. If you have to wait in line to buy toilet paper or paper towels you are not too excited about it. But, if you have to wait in line to meet and get an autograph from your favorite music star or actor/actress, you feel like it was totally worth it in the end. The waiting or anticipation heightens the excitement of the experience and makes the difference.

Everyone today is in a hurry. Sometimes speeding things up makes customers happy and sometimes slowing things down makes people happier. Think about lines at Disneyland. No one enjoys standing in these lines. Yet, when the experience is over most people feel that it was worth it.

What happens when there is no line the first time you get on a ride? In this scenario, you are able to get right onto a ride. When you go back later and have to wait for an hour for the same ride, is the second ride as fun?

Let's say there is a long line and the ride is very enjoyable. Later you go back and ride the ride again. Is the second ride as fun as the first?

In both of these scenarios, which ride had the most value? Is there a lesson you can use from this example to heighten the anticipation and the experience prospects will have when they buy from you?

In this example, there are two ways to increase the value for the customer. One is to speed up the line and the second is to lengthen out the experience of the ride. Disney has created the Fast Pass program to help speed up the line and works very carefully to engineer the rides people go on so that the *length* of the experience outweighs the wait in line.

I discussed Harry Houdini and how he built anticipation for his magic shows in a previous chapter on celebrity. As I mentioned, he was a master of pre-selling people on what they were going to see, how difficult of a feat it was (and how it was possible he might die or not be able to escape). Time was the element that made the escape even more exciting. In fact, he would often go into a 'ghost house' after he had been locked up, and would read the newspaper after escaping from the straightjacket or the handcuffs. He found that if he appeared too soon, people were disappointed. He made the event more exciting by how he sold it (they could hear him struggling, but not see him) and then when he appeared, he made his entrance very dramatic. In fact, he often had to hold his breath for more than three minutes to escape from a Milk Can that he designed and his Chinese Water Torture Cell. To dramatize this, he would invite members in the audience to hold their breath along with him while he was inside the milk can or upside down in the Chinese Water Torture Cell. He advertised the events with dramatic posters that proclaimed "Failure Means A Drowning Death." The escapes were a sensation because of how he built up and used anticipation.

What can you do at your business to build and use anticipation to heighten the prospect's experience and make it even more exciting and amazing?

For example:

- Could you create a video that each prospect has to watch in your waiting or staging area that has testimonials of customers who all talk about what an amazing experience it was to do business with you before they're able to meet with a sales professional?

- Could you give them a gift box that enhances the first few moments they'll have at your store (and establish the framework for the rest of the experience and sale)?

Since prospects today are like everyone else in our society now (we want it and we want it now), think about how you can build anticipation to increase the value of the experience that they'll have in your business.

When considering what you should speed up about your business or lengthen out at your business, keep this statement from Vince Poscente in his book *The Age of Speed* on p. 51 in mind:

"When choosing the best opportunities for speeding up, consider the value of both the experience leading up to the end (standing in a line) and the value of the end (paper towels or a concert). When the value of both is small, it is a good opportunity to use speed. On the other hand, when the value of one or both is significant, speed may compromise the pleasure you get from the experience. That said, don't be fooled into thinking that speed always has to come at a price the way it once might have. Times have changed in that regard."

8. Create value by enhancing the experience with more vivid mental pictures.

"Arizona State psychologist (and best-selling author) Robert Cialdini once attended a training program for insurance salesmen as part of a research project on social influence. The attendees were given an article titled, 'Add a Picture—Make a Sale' that laid out some of the most successful selling strategies in the industry. The instructor explained this technique to his new recruits as follows:

'If you are selling life insurance, start by getting 'em alone in a quiet place and making 'em imagine that they just totaled the car. If you are selling health insurance, first make 'em suppose that they're laid up in the hospital too sick to work. If you're selling theft, get 'em to think how it would be to come home from vacation and find everything gone. And take 'em through every picture, every step along the way." – *The Art of Woo*, pp. 188-189.

What vivid pictures can you help paint in the prospect's mind to escalate the value of what you are selling him or her?

"People tend to think that things they can easily visualize are more likely to happen. If an airplane crashes or a hurricane blows ashore, the sale of flight and flood insurance goes up because people have recent, vivid images in mind that planes sometimes go down and big storms sometimes cause severe damage. Moreover, the more 'available' an idea is, the more people believe it to be true....To see is to remember, and to remember is to believe." – *The Art of Woo*, p. 189.

Here are several ways you can create more vivid pictures for prospects as you sell to them:

- *Posters* - When we were in the wedding dress business, we had posters all over our store of happy brides in dresses. We hired professional models and these vivid and stunning pictures helped brides to imagine themselves on their wedding day. The posters also depicted many of our best selling gowns. This 'availability' helped us to put ideas of potential dresses that brides could wear into their minds. This is value that we created since most other stores didn't have anywhere near the number of posters or images of brides in their store that we did. These images built our brand. What pictures could you use in your business of happy clients enjoying your product or service?

- *Ask more direct questions that help prospects picture their success as they use your product in their mind.* We've found that asking, "Can you imagine...?" or "What will it be like when...?" questions help you to do this.

- *Capture video testimonials of customers talking in visual pictures.* Ask customers to talk about how things improved once they had your produce or service When future prospects watch these videos on your web site or in your business, they will see an 'available' picture that will help themselves begin picturing their own success.

In the example I just mentioned of the insurance agents, what could you do to help your prospects better imagine themselves using your products in a vivid way?

I would encourage you to carefully consider this question and how you are painting pictures in the minds of the prospects you work with.

In today's market, you <u>must</u> be better at building value. I hope you will focus on building your enhanced value in meaningful ways and not just promoting the value prospects already expect. You have so much more that prospects and customers need to hear about from you. When you focus on pointing out the enhanced value aspects of what you do, you will leverage your value and maximize what you sell.

CHAPTER 8

PUSH FOR THE SALE WITHOUT BEING PUSHY:
HOW TO BE MORE PERSUASIVE AND ELIMINATE RESISTANCE TO CONVERT BROWSERS TO BUYERS NOW

"Push yourself again and again. Don't give an inch until the final buzzer sounds." --Larry Bird

The resistance of people to buying products and services today has increased. What used to work to get prospects to take action no longer does to the same extent. A big shift in the past decade that affects your business everyday is the resistance and opposition that prospects have developed to making a decision now. Their non-commitment to action is creating a real challenge for business owners who need to make sales now. In this chapter, I will share with you some of the changing attitudes I've observed and share with you what you can do now to be more persuasive and combat these resistant attitudes in prospects so they buy now instead of later.

I have talked with many clients over the years who stress about the loss of business from prospects who shop in their retail store and then leave without buying and buy the product online. One friend and bridal store owner told me in an email: "...Unlike maybe 5 or even 3 years ago, the Internet is a bigger problem than ever, and private label or national brands make no difference. I think for many of the 'getting ideas' shoppers, they fall into one of three groups. The first one is the girl who wants to 'shop til she drops' and wants the experience over and over again, until the eleventh hour when she finally has to make a decision. At that point, she may or may not choose to purchase at a brick and mortar store depending on her perceived budget and the 'feeling' she got from the experience, and whether service matters at all to her.

The second one is the girl who is searching for the specific dress, and if it is a national brand, she has already decided she wants to buy it from a 'real' store, (and I do find that I have a fair share of these girls, particularly with [some designers], that are not shopping for price— they want all the service). Otherwise, you have to really win her over to convince her to buy from you unless she or a friend has already had a bad internet experience.

The third type is the true internet shopper, who IMO has evolved over the past 2-3 years. She does not need a particular style #--she will just try on gowns until she finds a 'look' that she likes, and will then go searching on the Internet and buy one that looks similar to the look she liked, as long as the price is right. I think there are more of these shoppers than ever before, and they are price driven more than anything else, and it won't matter if your lines are private or not. They are just going to try on gowns, find a 'look' they like, and go find that 'look' for the cheapest price they can get it at, and no amount of good sales technique, or protecting your style number/designer information will matter to these girls, since they are not trying to find the specific dress online. And no matter who makes/designs the gown, there will always be something 'similar' to the untrained eye (hers) and that is what she will buy.

I found the third type to be very prevalent this season. I really don't know what you can do to turn around this customer, who is solely motivated by price, and, at least in my area, there seem to be more and more of them, and less of the ones that care about the pampering and service, and especially when the internet can promise turnaround/ delivery in a fraction of the time a special order from one of our stores will take."

Most business owners can identify with the frustration that my friend expressed in her email. There is no question that the attitudes of shoppers has shifted today and frustration increases when you don't know what to do in these types of situations. In my opinion, the classifications that my friend identified are really focused around two of the three types of people that are out shopping for products today. Prospects who are just "shopping for ideas" really haven't been persuaded that there is any difference between Business A and Business B and that really all businesses in that category are the same. If you're going to win in a hyper-competitive environment, you've got to change that assumption. You've got to change the conversation so that you are changing the way that people buy your products.

There are three types of prospects who buy products today. These are:

1) *Those who buy solely based on price.* This is the prospect that goes from store to store or web site to web site looking for a product at the lowest price point. That person is completely resistant to looking at or trying to find anything else that is over that price range and is resistant to any type of persuasion designed her to look at her situation more realistically. This customer is really in categories #1 and #3 that my friend identified. I teach retailers and coaching clients who struggle with this type of client and who call or enter the business looking for a super low price range to ask: "How did you come up with that number?" Most people don't know. In fact, several years ago, my wife worked with brides where she asked her that question and the bride's mother would say, "We really don't know. We just thought that is what they cost." When my wife explained what makes up the price for a wedding gown,

the mother would apologize and say, "We just didn't know. Thanks for helping us understand." They often would buy a dress that day for more than three times the price they thought they originally wanted to pay.

Here is the problem with the price buyer. These consumers in general believe that going into a retail store, shopping, getting advice from a clerk or consultant, touching and examining a product, then using a smart phone to photograph the bar code and then order it online for a cheaper price is acceptable. They don't consider it stealing from the business owner who has invested in the inventory so they can see the available options in the first place. Most younger people today feel the exact same way about 'sharing' music, entertainment, Ebooks, and even their entertainment app passwords.

Many people today feel that it is completely reasonable to take advantage of a business and it's owner's investment in inventory. They don't think about the fact that it costs money to have a place to house the inventory or pay a person to show and sell the inventory. Retailers are appalled by this attitude, yet it isn't making much difference. The retail sector continues to struggle and small and large companies are going out of business as a result. Shoppers may have redefined stealing time and overhead costs as an acceptable behavior in their own minds. It is a huge loss of revenue and in the eyes of the business owner this kind of behavior is wrong and makes them furious. If you encounter these kinds of shoppers, you must re-educate them so they understand what your business brings to the equation and why they should buy from you. If you don't, you will lose this battle every single time.

You've got to show them that they won't get what they *really* want if they buy online or from another business who is only interested in selling a product for the lowest price. In other words, you've got to shift from the *price* of your product to the *place* where they buy it. You've got to help prospects see what it means to buy from you and that it is worth the investment irregardless of the price they pay for it. This is a very important distinction. You've got to show them enhanced value as we discussed in the previous chapter.

In order to get out of the commodity business, you've got to communicate your value. It isn't about the product you sell, it is about the results they'll get. You've got to help each prospect see that you can help them get that result plus a myriad of other benefits that they won't or can't get anywhere else.

You may have competitors who sell a low priced product offering that that is 2 or 3 x less than what you charge. But, it all goes back to the results you can deliver. What is it that you know about your prospect's needs that your competitors don't know?

When you understand what a prospect wants and why they want it, you can be much more helpful and persuasive in the sales process.

2) *Those who buy when the value exceeds the price.* This customer is like the second prospect that my friend talked about. These customers want the service of the business and if your value exceeds the price in their mind, they will buy.

Live by the principle that when value exceeds price, prospects buy. If prospects aren't buying, you aren't crossing the value threshold.

An important principle about any business is that regardless of how much any product has been commoditized, there is an individual who would rather pay more if they are shown a differential in quality, time, convenience, or whatever else is most important to them. You don't have to accept the commoditization that you're seeing in your industry or business. To overcome price sensitive shoppers you've got to show them there is a difference in what they get from you versus what they get from any other competitor.

3) *Those who buy because of their relationship with you.* This customer who is the one who is most likely to refer their friends to you. They are resistant to low price offers from others because of the relationship they have with you and their trust in you as an individual. They like you, they

trust you and if they believe you can truly help and the value of what they are buying exceeds the price in their mind, you will make the sale. Affluent customers fall into this category. They are willing to spend more but the relationship has to be in place before they will buy.

I think it is important to classify these types of prospects because you have to have a different approach for each one. If you are going to win in today's hyper-competitive environment, you can't do things the way you've always done them. In order to win the sale today, you've got to play a different game.

This problem is affecting all industries where service is a component of the sale (but it is really decimating those where service isn't needed or required at all). A good example of this is with products that are now being provided by big wholesale clubs or online at amazon.com or Wal-Mart. Retailers are going out of business in record numbers because a retailer spends time getting a customer interested and then the customer ends up buying the item online or at another business that offers the best price through a limited time offer or other promotion.

Consumers today have less time and so they are looking for solutions that offer things to them quicker. Companies that can deliver on the promise of speed are those who prosper now and those who will continue to prosper in the future. People are willing to pay a price for speed.

Businesses that sell out of stock have an advantage because some people don't have time to wait. However, with Amazon's announcement that deliveries can now be upgraded to arrive in one day and in some markets within a matter of hours after an order is placed, this will continue to be a big problem for retailers who have a large overhead with big inventories and leased space.

When there are many choices, it is easy for a prospect to decide on what is most important as they consider their most important reason to purchase. However, when you are the one that defines what a prospect wants within the confines of the new realities of these changing attitudes and behaviors, you really have a big advantage.

So, let's talk about six specific things you can do to more effectively deal with today's attitudes and realities so you can overcome the heightened resistance of non-committal prospects so they want to go ahead and buy from you now.

1. Capitalize on emerging trends or be run over by them.

Here are several questions for you to consider if you want to successfully capitalize on emerging trends and win in today's competive markets:

1) What are you doing to appeal to the spend less attitude of prospects today?

Many salespeople used to offer a discount to those prospects who would make the decision to buy on their first appointment. While this worked well initially, consumers often say that the discount wasn't enough to make the decision today. They want to keep looking around and find the best deal as many of your competitors are offering similar promotions.

I've coached many business owners to re-tool their offers so that there is a direct connection to being decisive and buying on the first appointment. What kind of offer will you assemble to benefit your prospects and show why buying from you now is the best choice?

Your prospects today have a spend less attitude. You can try to change their mind and upsell them into what you are selling or you can look at ways to build your value so that your prospects feel that they are getting the best deal from you. The choice is up to you (but the rewards will go to those who win this battle of perception).

2) What can you do to appeal to the spend wisely perception (in other words getting more value before a purchase) through better experience, better deliverables (coupons or special offers from other vendors, etc.), and better follow up offers for your customers?

You aren't the only one that has to offer value. If you don't have a better offer (and I don't mean the lowest price), the better your competitor's offers look. Those who have been trained to think about buying smarter will choose to buy from someone other than you if they can't perceive a difference between your offer and that of your competitors.

Your competitors are pushing your prospects into believing that they can buy your primary product for less than you've been selling it. What are you doing to counter this?

When prospects come in and tell you they have a price range of under $500, $5,000, or $50,000 (or whatever lowball price they have heard) to solve a particular problem, are you taking the time to explain why your products and services cost what they do? Are you detailing and explaining where competitors are cutting corners to keep prices low and the impact that will have on the result they'll achieve with your product or service?

Are prospects entering your marketing funnel with the attitude that Product X should only cost $500, $5,000, $50,000 or less? If so, they will have a heightened resistance to spending anything over that.

The only way you'll be able to overcome this is to guide the prospect to an understanding of a $500 or less product looks like, what corners have been cut in its construction and different qualities of materials used to make the product you offer. The problem is that consumers are skeptical and won't believe you over any other source unless you prove why you are different.

This means that you have to be constantly educating your prospects to know why what you say is better and different than what they may be hearing from any other source.

Remember, no one will value what you do *until* you value it first. You have to promote yourself and your business. You can't wait for others to do it for you. All great promoters promote themselves first and then get others to promote them too.

This means you need to write or put information on your web site that allows you to build your authority and expertise. If you don't, you are missing out on a big opportunity to help re-educate prospects about what really goes into creating the product or service you offer.

3) What can you do to enhance the perception of speed and convenience so that the time rushed prospect is able to get what they want quickly?

Are you able to offer prospects want they want in a timely manner or do you have to send them away?

What percentage of the prospects entering your marketing funnel today are buying later? The larger this percentage, the more opportunity there is for you to convert more and more of what you sell to an in-stock option OR simply to have a better and more compelling offer.

4) What are you doing to move your business into a category of one (so that you don't really have any other competitors) and so that you can sell in a vacuum?

It is so important to question the assumptions that have driven your business from time to time. Why? Because if you don't, the marketplace may change, and your denial that it has may cause you to miss what's really going on.

Gary Hamel makes this observation in his book *What Matters Now*:

"To sustain success, you have to be willing to abandon things that are no longer successful. No strategy lives forever, and in recent years, strategy life cycles have been shrinking....Strategies die when they are:

• *Replicated*. Over time, innovative strategies become less so. JetBlue took a chapter out of Southwest Airline's playbook. Cialis and Levitra aped Viagra. And Google's Android platform in many ways mimics Apple's iOS. While some strategies are harder to imitate than others (particularly those that exploit network effects), most can be decoded by dedicated rivals.

• *Superseded*. Good strategies get supplanted by better strategies when newcomers invent more efficient ways of meeting customer needs. Digital cameras made film obsolete. Skype allowed its users to sidestep expensive international phone tariffs. Wikipedia created a free alternative to traditional encyclopedias. Sometimes a high-flying strategy gets imitated, but other times it gets shot out of the sky.

• *Eviscerated*. Powerful customers or new competitors can kill a strategy by slicing away at the profits of what was once a high-margin business. The Internet, in particular, has produced a dramatic shift in bargaining power from producers to consumers. Armed with near perfect information, customers have battered down the prices of just about everything—cars, insurance, hotels, and luxury watches. For many companies, well-informed customers are now a bigger threat to margins than well-financed competitors. Increased competition can also eviscerate profits. Historically, most industries have been oligopolies. The incumbents were protected from newcomers by regulatory hurdles, patent walls, distribution monopolies, and economies of scale. Today, these barriers are crumbling. Deregulation, the commoditization of technology, the Web's global reach, and the abundance of venture capital have knocked down barriers, and a horde of newcomers have overrun what once seemed to be impregnable fortifications." –*What Matters Now*, pp. 105-106.

Don't live in denial of what is happening in your marketplace. Schedule time to work on renewing your business to deal with these realities. If you don't, it won't get done, your business will be run over, and you will lose. I talk about how you can reinvent your business in chapter 17 of my book *The System is the Secret*.

2. Prospects today are paralyzed by choice. Are you making it simpler to buy from you than from any of your competitors?

Christopher Elliot makes this statement in his book *Scammed*:

"Is it any wonder that consumers are so confused? On one hand we've accepted the inevitability of our purchase and the bad service that often comes with it. Yet we seem at times incapable of making a decision that's right for us. That's because we the customer are not merely battered by incessant advertising, we are also maddened by the crush of choices given us. A mere 12 channels 20 years ago has multiplied into more than a thousand. Starbucks offers a multitude of possible drink combinations—more than 100,000. Crest has so many distinctive styles of toothpaste that no single drugstore could possibly carry them all.

"Researchers have found that when you go to the grocery store and see hundreds of cereals, you are suddenly afflicted by what is called decision fatigue and eventually, choice paralysis. Three things tend to happen: You can default to the tried-and-true, research for the Corn Flakes or Cheerios. You can try something new, like the new dried blueberry and flaxseed cereal. Or you can do nothing. Sometimes doing nothing is far easier. You go home and eat toast.

"We are creatures of habit, so defaulting to a comfortable choice is understandable. But that also helps one company become dominant and lazy—a business that fails to innovate therefore fails to serve its customers. Those of us brave enough to resist will eventually get beaten down by the nonstop ads, and those of us who aren't able to resist them are doomed to give the incumbents our business again. And again." –pp. 110-111.

Are you confusing your prospects with too many options so it is hard for them to make a choice?

This is a very important question to think about. I believe a big reason why a lot of prospects aren't buying on their first appointment is because they are nervous and unsure about what to do and use non-committal answers to try to escape any type of decision. They also aren't educated about how to buy your product. You've got to lead them through that educational process without being pushy.

Prospects consider your product or service with a lower than possible budget figure to see how you respond. In many cases, you try to show them products in the price points they've mentioned without understanding why the prospect is even mentioning that number much less educating him or her of why those products actually cost what they do. Change your approach and educate customers about what they *really* get for a lower priced item and *why* it is worth it to get the higher price, higher value item.

3. Create your own category of one. It is much easier to escape the limitations of a price mindset when the conversation is shifted into a vacuum where you are truly the only choice.

The best way to do this is to create a very strong personal relevance and affinity so that a prospect can't really compare what you are offering to another competitor.

A prospect can't compare what you sell when they can't find it anywhere else. You can't compete very long and protect your price, your profit, and your market share if you are offering what everyone else is offering. Be different. Carry different merchandise, but more importantly link the experience of buying from you into a conversation that makes the prospect realize that it would be a mistake to buy from anyone other than you.

Being perceived as an expert is a great way to do this. Writing is a great way to do this. You should be focused on helping prospects and customers see why you are the best and most logical choice from which to make a purchase.

You can do this by:

• Writing and gaining a connection with your target audience of prospects

• Connecting with your audience through those who already have an affinity with your audience. Who is this for you?

• Publishing videos online of you outlining the next step that allow prospects a chance to get to see you and feel your authenticity

• Becoming the most trusted authority on a specific topic in your region or area. You can decide what this is, but since trust is in such short supply, your goal is to become the go-to person in your field of expertise so that when prospects think of your specialty there is really no other choice but you.

This last point is especially true with more affluent buyers, because they are more interested in dealing with the go-to person (who've they've been recommended to, not really the product or service that is being sold). You as the seller can control this by how you position yourself and your business. If you aren't positioning yourself at all, you shouldn't be surprised when prospects seem to be making their decisions solely on price.

The real reason creating a category of one works so well is that you're really changing the playing field. You are selling in a vacuum instead of in a mall shopping environment where a prospect just goes from business to business to find out the cheapest price.

For example, many business owners today are selling the same products and offer higher and higher discounts as to why a prospect should buy from them. The trade show environment has really become crowded, but it gives a unique look at what prospects think about the process of buying your product in a contracted timeline. The more unique your position, the more important it is to sell in an uncluttered environment one-to-one instead of being clumped into the same classification as all of the other businesses in your market niche (who unfortunately are only competing on price).

4. Build your promotions to get prospects to buy on the first visit,

but have a back up plan for those who don't buy on the first visit that is still enticing enough to get them back to meet with you again.

Not every prospect will buy on the first appointment or encounter with your business. It would be nice if they did, but some won't. This happens for several reasons, but most of them happen with cautious thinkers who want the approval of someone else or really feel they need more time. Your job in these cases is to separate those who have genuine conditions for why they can't go ahead from prospects who make excuses just to avoid making a purchase now. With good sales skills, you can get to the bottom of the reason why a prospect just won't go ahead, but you've got to be the one to help make that transition and that change.

What this means is that you must have a follow-up process that you stick to and that you use without giving up on a prospect. The prospect can't perceive that you don't believe in them or their decision to make the decision to buy your product or service from you.

If a prospect senses that they can't buy from you, they probably won't. But, if they know that their sales consultant will help them overcome every reason why they think they can't go ahead to get the product they really need and love, their resistance will drop, and they will go ahead with the purchase.

This really goes back to what I talked about in point #1. If you are offering the same thing as everyone else, you shouldn't be too surprised when prospects don't take action. However, if you can truly offer something extraordinary that prospects haven't seen anywhere else, you'll be able to help prospects take action now.

Prospects aren't too excited to spend their hard earned money for an experience that is just ordinary or adequate. They want to be wowed with something extraordinary. Action is taken if they fear they might lose something by not making the decision to buy now.

Prospects have mastered the ability to convince themselves that they ought to wait. They convince themselves they need more time to explore all of the possible options because they don't really know what they are looking for or the truly simple nature of their decision. They keep looking for the magical product or service that is under $500, $5,000, $50,000 (or any low ball price point) that doesn't really exist in the way they believe.

So, if you are going to win and convert your prospect's attitudes and beliefs, you've got to place an intense focus on the prospective customer and what they want as opposed to thinking of what you want as the seller. This is a hard discipline to master because you spend a lot of time thinking about your business as a whole.

Here are some questions for you to consider about what you are selling:

Can we send individualized communications to our top 100 customers?

Am I focusing most of my efforts on the customers who matter most?

Is our share of products our prospects and customers use growing?

How can we understand what our best customers want and figure out how to give it to them?

Who bought what we were selling last week? (How can we ensure that we have more of what is selling available for those who wait to the last minute?)

How can we understand who our price sensitive prospects are, the items on which they are most price-sensitive, and the prices at which we hold and grow their business? (How can we build value in merchandise that prospects can't find anywhere else?)

How can we create or bring in a new product line that is very relevant to our highest-value customers?

Which products do our best customers need and want?

5. You can't change attitudes or overcome resistance if you don't know what is at the core of those beliefs or feelings. Ask better questions to find out what your prospects and customers are really thinking and feeling before you seek to overcome their concerns or objections.

Great questions are the tools in your toolbox to help you get better information from your prospects and customers. The problem is that prospects are reluctant and even very hesitant to share anything with you at first. In order to conquer this resistance you've must come across as a friend who cares and who is genuinely interested about the solution your product or service will provide.

Since consumers are so skeptical today you must project confidence as you do this (but not arrogance) and you must ask great questions to get a prospect talking about exactly what it is they are looking for. Once they start answering questions and sense that you really care about them, then they will open up and start letting down their guard.

Being non-committal is what people think is their best self-defense against an aggressive sales consultant who they perceive just wants to sell them something. If you can come across different and be genuinely interested in the answers to the questions you ask, you'll be so much farther ahead than a sales consultant who only seems interested in going through a pre-set list of questions.

When you get good at asking better questions, you'll be able to peel through the superficial layers. But, as with an onion, the deeper you go, the strength and size of the resistance can increase. Very few prospects and customers will reveal all of the personal factors that go into why they wants to purchase something from you. It isn't until after trust is really built that you have earned the right to go deeper and find out the reasons behind their choices and decisions.

The very best sales consultants have mastered the ability to peel through surface issues, get to the core of what really matters, and understand *why* that issue is so important. In order to get to this level of selling, it is critical that you ask great questions to collect information at deeper levels so the prospect really feels that you care and that you can help them.

Here is the point: A prospect will form their opinions about you and your business (and your ability to help them) not by what you say, but by the questions you ask.

To prove this is true, consider the following two scenarios selling an article of high end clothing (or you can substitute it with your own product):

Prospect: I'm looking for Product X (a product that you sell).

Sales Consultant #1: Great. We have lots of that product. Let's see if we can help you find one.

Prospect: I'm looking for Product X (a product that you sell).

Sales Consultant #2: That's great! Tell me, have you already started looking for Product X? What has been your experience so far?

Prospect: I've been to one other store.

Sales Consultant #2: When you were there, did they explain the four options that are available for that product?

Prospect: No, they didn't.

Sales Consultant #2: No problem. Let me show those to you really quickly as it will be really helpful to you in finding the right product for you.

[Explains 4 categories or options of Product X]

Sales Consultant #2: Have you had a chance to try all four of the options yet?

Prospect: No.

Sales Consultant #2: What options were you drawn to? What did you find out from trying that option?

Prospect: I like how I look in Product X.

Sales Consultant #2: Great. We have lots of that option here. What type of fabric are you drawn to?

Prospect: I don't know.

Sales Consultant #2: Well, there are six main types of fabrics that Product X is constructed from. They are satin, tulle, chiffon, organza, taffeta, and silk. Would you like to feel these different fabrics and get a sense for which one you like best?

Prospect: Sure.

Sales Consultant #2: Is there a particular fabric you're drawn to?

Prospect: Chiffon.

Sales Consultant #2: As you know, fabric is just one of four things that makes up the overall cost of Product X...

Which sales consultant do you think the prospect has more of a connection with?

Which sales consultant sounds more like they know what they are doing? Obviously, it is the second.

Why?

• The sales consultant is teaching the prospect something they didn't know.

• The sales consultant talks to the prospect on her level. She doesn't assume anything and she offers help in the direction that the prospect wants to go.

• The sales consultant teaches, then asks questions to get more clarity and dig a little deeper once there is a solid foundation of trust.

Be sure that you have earned trust by asking great questions and helping prospects feel comfortable around you and what you are helping them to find. The majority of prospects aren't familiar with the details of your business and the products and services you offer and this approach helps you build your expertise. It also helps lower their defenses as they sense that you know what you are talking about and how you can help them specifically.

Great questions can also help you uncover hidden objections. For example:

Sales Consultant: How do you feel this option fits in with the solution you are trying to create?

Prospect: Oh, I don't know.

Sales Consultant: On a scale of 1-10 (with 1 being you hate this option and 10 being you love it and can see yourself creating the successful experience you desire), how would you rate this option?

Prospect: 7.

Sales Consultant: Why didn't you pick a lower number?

Prospect: I don't know. I guess I really like how this option makes me feel.

Sales Consultant: What is it about this option that causes you to feel that way?

Prospect: Well, I love how I can achieve the result I want so quickly with this option.

This sequence of questions helps you discover that she is really concerned about the speed that your product offers in helping them achieve the result they desire.

Here is another example incorporating questions and gaining agreement with a wedding gown prospect:

Prospect: I don't really care for _____ on this option.

Sales Consultant: I'm glad you brought that up. What is it about _____ that is the biggest concern?

Prospect gives her answer.

Sales consultant: That's great feedback. Sounds like you really don't like _____. Is there anything about this option that you do like?

Prospect: Well, I like how teeny my waist looks in this gown.

Sales consultant: I'm really glad you noticed that. I love that about how you look in this dress too. Notice how this dress really accentuates your waistline because of....

Would you like me to grab a couple of other dresses that have this feature since we've identified how much you like it?

Prospect: Sure, that sounds great.

We could spend a lot of time talking about different scenarios here for all kinds of products. I hope that you see the value that great questions can add to the conversation you'll have with a prospect. The key is that you want to help them discover more about the product they want by asking questions that help them see what it is that they really want.

When you evaluate your sales effectiveness, look at the quality of your questions. Look at ways you could ask a similar question and get a better result and that allows the prospect to really think about what you are asking.

Remember to use softening statements to reduce resistance and help the prospect discover their own answers by the questions you ask. When you do this, a prospect will respect you more and value the experience they have with you more. Then, resistance drops and trust grows to the point that you can help that individual actually find the product they want most to achieve the results they are seeking.

Think about your last successful sale. What are the best questions you asked to get past the prospect's superficial statements? What caused the prospect to trust you enough to buy from you? Carefully think about what you can learn from that experience to help you continue to sell well.

6. Get better at handling excuses and objections that prospects have that show heightened resistance and non-commitment.

Here are several examples of excuses used by non-committal prospects and some ways to help you overcome them:

Prospect: It's my first day looking.

Spouse: We can't make a decision yet. We've got three more appointments today.

Sales Consultant: I'm glad you brought that up. Have you been to any other of our competitors yet?

Prospect: Yes. I've been to one other business.

Sales Consultant: Great. Just out of curiosity, what type of options have you found yourself drawn to? Is their a particular option that you have liked most?

Prospect: I really like Option X.

Sales Consultant: Great. We have Option X and several other options that you may not have even considered. In fact, coming to our business is literally like going to 3-4 other businesses who don't have the same selection we do.

We also offer several things that you won't find at any other business... including...

Sales Consultant: I have a special report that I've written (or our business owner has written) that details seven reasons why shopping at our business is like going to 3-4 other places. I would especially like to point out each of these seven things especially since you are considering going to several other stores so you can see the real benefit of buying the right option for you here. Can I share that report with you?

I'm going to keep looking and see if I can't find something like it online.

Sales Consultant: I'm glad you brought that up especially since I've had several customers call us lately that made that choice. They discovered that what they ordered didn't look anything like the product they thought they were getting.

Can I show you a couple of examples of disasters individuals have had when they made that choice?

Option 2:

Sales Consultant: I'm glad you brought that up. Just out of curiosity, why haven't you already made that choice? What is it that is holding you back from going ahead?

Prospect: I can't buy this product until I've looked at every other possible option.

Sales Consultant: I completely respect what you're saying. What is it that you are hoping to find that you haven't found yet?

Is there a particular option you have in your mind that you haven't seen yet?

As you know, there are only four options for this particular product...

Prospect who loves shopping and getting bids (already has received quotes from 5 or 6 other businesses), loves considering options, and loves all the options they've seen so far equally...

Sales Consultant: I notice that you've already been to several other businesses, but haven't been able to find the exact option that you're looking for. Just out of curiosity, what is it that you are really looking for? What, if anything, seems to be holding you back from moving forward with Product X?

Prospect: "Who makes this product?

Sales Consultant: I'm glad you brought that up. This particular option is from our _____ *line which we exclusively offer in the* _____region.

This product isn't available online from any other online business and as one of the top businesses offering this product in the ____ *region____*, we are honored that we are able to offer _*Product Y_* (this exclusive option here in our business).

I hope this has been helpful for you to carefully analyze what you are doing in your business to overcome the changing attitudes and heightened resistance of prospects in your industry. Don't live in denial. Make the changes now so you can create a category of one where people want to buy from you because you are really the only real choice.

Jay Abraham shows in his book, *Getting Everything You Can Out of All You've Got* the three ways to increase your sales and the power of having a 10% increase across each area and a 25% increase across each area. You can see this illustrated on the next page. Look at what happens when you focus on bringing customers back into your business and having them bring their friends with them. (See Chart #1)

If you increase these three numbers by 10%, watch what happens: (See Chart #2)

By increasing all of these values by a mere 10 percent, you have increased your revenue by 33.1 percent.

Now, let's say you increase these three numbers by 25%, watch what happens: (See Chart #3)

By increasing all of these values by 25 percent, you <u>nearly double</u> <u>your total revenue.</u>

As you can see, follow-up and increasing your business in these three areas is critically important for you to be thinking about. I would encourage you to consider every action you make at your business by thinking of the impact it will have on each of these three areas of your business. **Write or type the three questions below on a piece of paper and post it where you can see them often.** Use these three questions as the framework for making decisions and it will cause you to think in terms of results. If you do this, you will *focus on* and *do* <u>what really</u> <u>matters.</u>

1) How can you increase the number of prospects buying at your business?

2) How can you increase the transaction value for every customer buying at your business?

3) How can you increase the number of transactions that each customer makes at your business?

If you aren't marketing to those who almost bought, didn't buy, or to get additional purchases from those who did buy, you are leaving large piles of cash on the table. Systematize your follow up and marketing and you will be amazed at the results you'll see as you increase the three factors that lead to increased sales

Persuasion, and your ability to use it effectively, is a big key to succeeding as a business owner. You have undoubtedly used persuasion skills every time you have negotiated a deal, an order with a supplier, or dealt with any customer who wanted to purchase something from you. The principles of persuasion are the same regardless of who you interact with. If you are going to get better at marketing your business and selling to prospective customers, you must master the skills of persuasion.

Chart #1:

# of Prospects		Transaction Value per Prospect		Transactions Per Year		Total Revenue
250	X	$800	X	1	=	$200,000
500	X	$800	X	1	=	$400,000
1,000	X	$800	X	1	=	$800,000

Chart #2:

# of Prospects		Transaction Value per Prospect		Transactions Per Year		Total Revenue
275	X	$880	X	1.1	=	$266,200
550	X	$880	X	1.1	=	$532,400
1,100	X	$880	X	1.1	=	$1,064,800

Chart #3:

# of Prospects		Transaction Value per Prospect		Transactions Per Year		Total Revenue
313	X	$1000	X	1.25	=	$391,250
625	X	$1000	X	1.25	=	$781,250
1,250	X	$1000	X	1.25	=	$1,562,500

My goal in this chapter is to help you be more persuasive so you can sell more and get what you want more of the time.

Here are the most important principles of persuasion you must master if you want to build a more prosperous and successful business:

1. Understand the motivation of the prospect you are trying to persuade before you begin the persuasion process.

When a prospect feels safe, they will open up to being persuaded. When they feel threatened that you are trying to sell to them, they will close themselves off to any attempt at persuasion you attempt. A lot of what you do in your initial approach when they first come into contact with you (and particularly in your pre-sales efforts) will help them relax and open up to the experience you will create.

This was one of the really important skills I learned while knocking doors to sell solar panels. I was never able be persuasive about the solar panels I was selling *until* I had their attention and they *trusted* what I had to say. That has to occur in a matter of seconds because people aren't expecting you to knock on their door. You've interrupted them and they want to get rid of you as soon as possible. When they think that you're trying to sell something, they put up an instant wall and try to exit the conversation as quickly as possible.

What causes a prospect to close off to any attempt at persuasion?

It is usually an emotional reason. If you don't address it and help that person to feel safe, you will never be successful in persuading them to buy from you.

I once talked with a bride who loved a dress but just couldn't commit to buy the dress on her first visit. I stepped back and said, "I know you love this dress. What is it that is holding you back from going ahead and getting the dress you love?" She finally opened up and told me the reason that was holding her back. She told me that she had just been offered a package deal at another bridal salon that she had just been to. When she finally opened up and shared this detail with me, then we were able to have an honest conversation about how our total offer compared with what she would get from the other store. It was amazing to see her face and her shoulders physically relax when she finally told me what the real concern was. It was an emotional fear of losing out (because of the total package of what she would get including flower girl dresses that we don't offer). When I told her of a place in town where she could get flower girl dresses with the money she was saving on her dress (a $100 incentive we offered by buying on the first visit), I could see that she was open to be persuaded. If I wouldn't have known what her concern was and I kept pushing for the sale, I would have lost it (and probably never known why). As it turns out, we had a great discussion about her wedding and how the dress she loved at our store would help her create the experience she wanted. She ended up buying that dress.

The BIG lesson is this: When you feel that a prospect is closing themself off, stop selling, and start asking questions to find out what their concern really is. When you know what is really going on, you can be helpful and persuasive. Without that information, you'll be dead in the water.

One motivation or de-motivation of prospects that causes them to wait to buy is because of resistance. In other words, people don't buy on their first visit usually because they don't want the purchase to limit them from other options they could see if they waited. In order to overcome this, you must understand this motivation and sell against it (so they see that waiting will cause them to regret that decision later on). You can do this by offering an incentive for buying on the first visit. This incentive can be combined with additional bonuses a prospect will get from other vendors and your referral program on top of the product so that the total savings and benefits far outweighs waiting. This eliminates the resistance of reactance. If you don't have something like this in place in your sales process, you should put together your own incentive that will help you cut through resistance.

Most prospects aren't very good at predicting what emotions they will feel when they make a choice that doesn't work out the best for them. Many of these individuals choose to leave without buying an option they really love. A great sales consultant can be effective by sharing specific examples of what has happened to those who made the choice to buy now versus those who chose to wait. This causes prospects to actually experience the emotion of what it might feel like to lose the product they love and is very persuasive. You have to be careful here, because you don't want to come across as manipulative. The key is that you want to help a prospect in this situation truly understand what will happen if they wait.

Remember, as a professional persuader, your job is to help someone overcome their initial resistance by experiencing what the emotion of regret will feel like. The better you can do this, the more successful you will be at the art of persuasion.

A lot could be written about this, but I'll sum this up by saying you absolutely, positively MUST know the prospect you are selling to (and they must know and trust you). In other words, any sale is more about the prospect who is buying than it is the product you are selling. When you truly understand that individual and what motivates them about their needs, you will be much more successful than a sales consultant who ignores this and just goes about selling their products.

2. Believe in who you are selling to. Believe you can help that individual find a product they'll love and you will.

This seems like such a simple persuasion tactic, but it is one that we often forget. I can't tell you how many times I've talked with sales consultants about this who have been struggling with their sales.

They start complaining about the types of prospects they're working with and how they won't buy or they can't make up their minds or something like that. I've reminded them that the prospects they work with will mirror what they think about them. When you say and believe to yourself, "I like this person. I can help her find the best solution they'll love and buy today. We're going to be great friends," you go about the appointment much differently than if you have the attitude: "This person will never buy today. They brought all of these negative friends with them who don't like anything and it will just be a waste of my time." By projecting these thoughts, you can act in a way that will prevent you from being persuasive.

With every prospect you work with, you must believe that you can make a difference and act as if they already like you. When you approach a group of decision makers, say in your mind, "I like these people." It will change your view about them. You will act differently because you have chosen to smile and be their friend. When you have this attitude, it is amazing how all of a sudden everyone in the group tends to like you as well. If you've been struggling with this, it is likely because you've been feeling down or feeling some insecurity about yourself. Make the choice to flip your attitude to the positive, even if you have been having a down day (or the last prospect you worked with didn't buy). Let that prospect see and meet the most excited sales consultant they've ever met and you will open the doors of trust so you can be persuasive as you sell.

Ignore this, and you'll stumble and fall more often than not. Lighten up and learn to love something about every person you work with. It may be their smile, their demeanor, or something about them that you discover as you talk. Remember, the people you talk with on a daily basis have insecurities and fears too. When they feel they are around an ally and a friend, they'll open up and you'll be able to help them break down the wall of resistance they had when you first met.

The best way you can do this is to use the first 30 seconds to a minute that you have with a prospect to help them feel safe and that you are there to help them find the perfect solution they'll love (and thank you for helping them to find). Prospects are always on high alert when they first come into contact with who they perceive is a salesperson. If you can help them relax and see how their experience of dealing with you as a true professional will be different than anything else they have ever experienced, you'll be much more successful in opening the doors to persuasion and the sale. The goal of that first few minutes is to help the prospect feel valued, to educate them in a non-threatening way, and to help them see that you are their friend and are there to help them specifically. That sequence of questions will help you start the process of getting to know the individual you are meeting. Ask questions that allow them to talk about themselves.

Never forget that your ability to persuade is dependent upon the base of trust that you have built. Trying to persuade without having a foundation of trust won't get you many sales. Your belief in the prospect you are selling to is critical to your ability to persuade them. Your belief in them and your confidence in yourself that you can help them find the right solution are the most important bricks in the foundation of your ability to persuade.

3. Get over what you know and focus on what matters most to your prospects. You'll be much more persuasive when you focus on what they want as opposed to what you sell.

When I talk with business owners about what they are doing to market their businesses, this is one of the pieces of advice that I most often give. Sometimes, it is easy to get so caught up in what you know (because you've worked hard for that knowledge and you're excited) that you lose track of what prospects are really looking for because you're in the process of sharing everything you know with them.

A great analogy to why this doesn't work is found in fishing. If you go fishing and throw all of your expensive lures and bait into the water at the same time, what happens? You end up scaring the fish. You don't catch anything. If you want to persuade people to do business with you, you must persuade them by talking about what matters most to them, not what matters to you.

To be more persuasive, you've got to get into the mind of the prospect you are selling to. This is not an easy thing to do. But, it is the secret behind building trust and setting up an environment where you can be persuasive and help a prospect feel that you are an ally to her finding the solution to what they need. Be sure your persuasive message is in sync with what the prospect wants. When you tie this with psychological triggers, you'll be so much more successful at persuading prospects to buy from you now.

4. Focus on the prospect in front of you as though they are the only person in the world at that moment.

Are you so focused on the prospect in front of you that you aren't bothered by the numerous distractions around you? Can they sense that attention to detail or can they see that you are distracted by your phone or what is going on around you?

Research has shown that touch (beginning with but not limited to a handshake) can be a valuable tool in persuasion. If you study what great persuaders do, you'll notice this commonality among them.

Chris St. Hillaire says this of the power of touch:

"Your own use of touch has to be something that you are comfortable with and that is socially appropriate. Be careful not to cross any lines that the opposite sex might find either offensive or distracting. That said, there are many studies showing that the human touch eases anxiety, slows the heart rate, and drops blood pressure in the person being touched. The healing power of touch is a real phenomenon, and you can use it to put your colleagues at ease. It's usually acceptable to touch a colleague on the hand, forearm, shoulder or upper back. In one-on-one conversations, touching the other person's arm or hand will instantly make that person stop talking. You can do it to subtly get the other person to be quiet if he or she is talking too much, or to get the other person to stay quiet while you're making a point. In general, the person who initiates the touching is asserting power....You don't need to touch someone a lot in order to establish that you're open to friendship. One light touch on the arm while you're making a point is all it takes."
–27 Powers of Persuasion, p. 154-158.

A bridal consultant who was the top seller in our store once told me that one of her secrets to selling was that she touched her brides on the arm when she would talk to them when they were in the dress and that it made a big difference. I thought that was a weird statement, but I noticed and watched her do it and I was amazed at how she used that skill to persuade. The studies in the book 27 Powers of Persuasion have solidified my opinion that there is a reason why this works. You should make a habit now to pay attention to how great persuaders use touch and physical presence to persuade and then utilize what you learn to help you be a more effective persuader as well.

5. Credibility is the pivot point in influence and the basis behind all persuasion. To be more persuasive, you have to increase your credibility and perception of competence with those you serve.

As you work with a prospect, you have four ways to show them that you are credible. The first one is what the prospect sees you doing (or how you behave in their presence). Think about this for a minute—in the presence of a prospect what behaviors do they see? Are you bold or timid? Verbal or quiet? Aggressive or meek? Each one of these behaviors says something about your credibility to those you work with. Typically, most people see those who are bold, verbal and aggressive as being more credible than someone who is shy, quiet, and reserved.

The second way you show prospects that you are credible is by your composure. In other words, are you poised or nervous in the presence of a prospect? Do they feel like they know more than you or do they look to you for expertise and advice? Are you relaxed in their presence or tense? Are you calm as you approach the close of the sale or are you anxious? Again, prospects perceive that those who are relaxed, calm, and poised are more credible than those who behave in the opposite way. Remember, it is the perception that counts. You may be nervous, scared, and anxious, but you can't let the prospect perceive that you feel this way. Instead, you need to show that you are a competent and credible source for them to find what they seek from you. When they feel this about you, they will have confidence in you and be much more likely to be persuaded by you. This is an important consideration (especially when you are just starting out in persuading others). You may be nervous, but you can't let your fears hold you back from coming across in a way that is projects your poise and confidence.

The third way you show prospects that you are credible is your likability and how you react in social settings. Prospects respond better to sales consultants who are good-natured than those who are irritable. They would much rather be around someone that is cheerful and friendly than someone who is gloomy and unfriendly. You can come across as being likable by how you act in their presence and more importantly by how strong of a desire you have to truly help them find the right solution with the product or service they are considering.

The last way you show prospects that you are credible is by being inspiring to them and by showing genuine admiration for them as an individual. This can be projected in many ways, but if someone feels like you approve of their ideas and give them additional resources and ideas that will help them achieve their goals, they will see you as a credible source for a purchase. You can't be inspiring if you aren't excited about them and their lives. If you are tired, you can come across as uncaring and unfocused and this can shoot down your credibility in their eyes.

I remember when I was in high school and I met with a banker in our small local town in Northwest Missouri. I was trying to sell him some fundraising tickets for a dinner that our scout troop was hosting. He was a little annoyed that I was meeting with him and completely brushed me off. I never forgot how he made me feel and I never went by that bank without thinking about that experience. He wasn't inspired by our cause and didn't see me as credible. However, a good friend's father knew that banker and took his son in to see him and sell him the exact same fundraising tickets. The same banker bought ten tickets from him. That experience is a good reminder to me of why credibility is so important. My friend Robert got the sale because he had a referral and the credibility of his father to get the sale.

The more consultative and inspiring the experience of buying from you is, the more likely it is that you will make the sale. When you have credibility because of these four indicators, you will come across as a credible person and you will have properly set up the foundation so that you can successfully sell. Without that foundation, you will spin your wheels in the sales process. This is the real reason why your pre-sale marketing approach is so important. It allows you to build credibility with a prospect in ways that are meaningful to them before you ever sell anything to them.

Here are some questions for you to ask to determine how well you are projecting your credibility to your prospects in your pre-sales marketing efforts:

• Are you stressing your knowledge by educating prospects about what they most need to know about buying your product or service?

• Are you promoting your experience and what it will mean for them (that they can't get anywhere else)?

• When you communicate with prospects do you do so in a fluid manner (without using 'um' and mispronouncing words that they know)? Do you come across as being knowledgeable about what it is that you are selling or does it seem that they know more than you?

• Are you communicating clearly with them?

• Do your prospects sense that you are an expert?

• Are you likable?

• Are you inspiring? Do you borrow the credibility of others to enhance your own?

These are great questions to carefully consider as you promote your credibility. Remember, credibility is the pivot point in influence and it is why celebrity is such a powerful positioning strategy. It is what will help you build the foundation to be more persuasive.

6. Master words that persuade and use them in your sales conversations. The key is to give specific instructions or steps when directing or attempting to influence behavior.

Part of being persuasive is gaining agreement on something before you attempt any effort at persuasion. Allowing prospects the option of choice is an excellent way to begin an appointment. However, the choice should be limited to only a few options that they've chosen and that you've recommended. You don't want to overwhelm someone with too many options because it will end up being frustrating for them and for you. Then, from these choices, you can allow them to feel like they are in control because they are telling you what they like or don't like about the options they are exploring.

When a bride came into the dressing room with the dresses she chose to try on, we would always ask, "Which of the dresses you've chosen do you like the most?" Then, when she answered, we would say, "Let's try that one on first." This persuasive way of setting up the sale can help you start off the sales process with an option that they already love so you have a comparison to come back to as you consider other options.

You'll notice in that example, that I asked for her choice, but then followed it with the specific instruction to try that dress on first. I didn't say, "Which dress do you like most? Would you like to try it on first?" Why? Because more often than not, the bride will say, "No, I'll try that one on last" and you won't be able to persuade her.

Kevin Hogan says this about the importance of giving specific instructions or steps when persuading: "Decades of research reveal that specific instructions are necessary to influence and induce compliance. What does this mean to you? It means that you need to walk people step-by-step through a process that leads them to the door you ultimately want them to open. Anything short of doing this is unlikely to succeed in the short or long-term. I want to direct your attention (did you catch that?) to another technique that can be remarkably influential or explode in your face. Fear. Fear is something we are all wired to fight or flee from. Our irrational fears are those that we attempt to conquer and overcome. No one likes to experience fear. Fear literally can motivate people in ways few other things can....If you are going to use fear in a communication in order to foster change or alter behavior—or encourage someone to buy your product, idea, or service—you must also include a step-by-step set of instructions in your message in order for it to be successful.

"This formula, therefore, is: "Negative Emotions + Behavioral Plan = Behavioral Change

"To help you see how powerful this combination is when used correctly, consider this experiment that was conducted with 164 UCLA students. Here was the scenario as it was presented to them:

"You've parked your car in the lot and you are rushing to class for an important quiz you don't want to be late for. You realize on the way that you may have left your car unlocked!

"A number of the students were then told to imagine how they would feel if they went back to the car, found it was locked all along, and now had missed the quiz. Others were told to imagine how they would feel if they didn't go back to the car and instead took the quiz, only to discover afterward that the car had been vandalized. How would they feel then?

"All students were asked whether they would go back to the car or go to take the quiz. Of those told to imagine the car vandalized, 69 percent said they would return to the car and see if the doors were locked. Of those who were told they would miss the quiz, 34.5 percent said they'd go back and check on the car. The control group showed 46 percent returning to check on the car.

Kevin Hogan continues with this lesson:

"In general when the students experienced anticipated regret, they said they would take the action appropriate to prevent the regret from happening. We all know that what people say they will do and what they actually do in real life are very different things. Later research has in fact validated this fact. When people experience anticipated regret, they tend to take action to prevent the regret. As people of influence, that's a mighty important thing to remember." – *The Science of Influence*, pp. 104-106.

Now that you know this principle, you can set up the sale properly so that someone buys on the first visit and prevent what happens when someone returns to find that the product they fell in love with has been sold to someone else. Or, in the case of your schedule, you are booked out for months before you can meet with them again. You are much more persuasive when you help someone experience anticipated regret by getting them to think about what could or might happen.

Here is an example of how we used this principle when talking with a mom and daughter and they expressed the desire to keep looking at other bridal stores:

"I know you want to make the best choice and see if there is anything else out there that you like better. Can I share with you a quick story about a mother and a bride who made that choice this past week? They, like you, found a dress they loved, and thought that continuing to look around would ensure that they didn't find anything they would like better. They went to several other stores and found the same four silhouettes and cuts you've tried on here, but couldn't find anything they liked better. Meanwhile, another decisive bride came in and bought the dress she loved. When they returned two days later, the mother broke down in tears because she realized she had let another mother and daughter choose which dress her daughter would wear for her wedding. She realized she no longer had the choice, because the dress was gone and there wasn't time to order in that exact dress.

"I want you to think about this scenario carefully before you make your choice. What happens if you go out and don't find a dress you like better than this one (that you've already said you love)? Two things will happen: 1) you'll lose the first visit advantage savings, which is only available on your first visit, and 2) you could lose the dress you love most. Of course, it is totally your choice. *(Softly)* My question for you is this: Do you really want to let another bride decide for you which dress you'll wear at your wedding?"

That is a great example of using anticipated regret to be persuasive. I could share with you other examples or help you craft your own persuasive statement to push without being pushy. The choice is in their hands. You should look at ways you can use this principle to be more persuasive in your selling efforts.

Be more persuasive by detailing the specific instructions that you want someone to take after you overcome an objection and as you close every sale. If you don't give specific instructions about what someone should do next, you shouldn't be surprised when they choose to leave without buying anything.

My encouragement to you is to use these persuasive strategies to help you better sell to those you work with on a daily basis. The first few seconds of interaction you have with every prospect are so critically important. The better you get at learning how the principles of persuasion, the more successful you'll be at selling and the happier all of you will be (the prospect will get what they wants—a great product to help them achieve the results they want and you'll make the sale!) When you master these skills, you'll be able to change the behaviors and attitudes of prospects and persuade them to buy from you.

7. Use your own charm and emotions to spread enthusiasm and excitement.

It isn't enough today to just be persuasive about why you are the best choice. You also have to be persuasive with your own charm and enthusiasm to persuade prospects NOT to do something that may be a bad idea for them (such as buying a product from a competitor who doesn't offer all of the value added options that you do and most importantly, will save them time and money in the long-run). You may be persuasive when you are excited about a product solution and when they are too, but how persuasive are you when they are excited, but you know it isn't the best idea for them? A good example of this would be a prospect who chooses to buy your product online as opposed to buying it from a full service business who can offer additional value that they won't get from an online source. Are you persuasive in a way that allows your charm and emotions to come through so the prospect can sense your true empathy and desire to help them?

For example, I coach bridal retailers that when they encountered a bride who says they're going to buy a dress online, to say: "I know you want to get the best possible price on your gown. But buying a dress online isn't the way to do it. Buying a dress online will cause you to get a dress that will:

• Have wrinkles all over it which you will have to pay extra to have pressed out.

• Have loose beading or missing beads on your dress caused during shipping which you will have to pay to have fixed (most shipping companies aren't as kind to your box as you would like to think they are).

• Possibly have stains on your dress that you likely won't be able to properly remove without damaging the delicate fabric and beadwork on the dress.

• Likely arrive in the wrong size (and you may not be able to alter it to fit your figure).

• Will very likely look completely different than the picture you saw online. Many brides have experienced this much to their shock and horror and then come to us in tears hoping that we can fix the problem. Many times repairs can be made, but often at a great expense."

Then, they explain with passion about why their store offers the best choice and can prevent them from dealing with all of the heartache simply by purchasing a dress from their store. You can do the same if you will craft your approach to similar objections in this manner.

The same charm that can be used to spread enthusiasm and excitement can also be used to help your prospects avoid a mistake that may cost them big stress, worries and ultimately cost them more than the savings they thought they might be getting.

If you are drawn into a conversation with one of your prospects over a specific objection, be sure that you don't get drawn into the disagreement. Strive to objectively help the prospect see where their decision may lead and then use your charm and enthusiasm and the powerful words of third party peer testimonials to make a decision that will best benefit them.

Here are three tips to help you use your charm and emotions to spread enthusiasm and excitement:

1) If you need to think about an answer before answering the prospect, look down, not up. Looking down appears thoughtful. Looking up seems like you don't know and you're searching for the answer. Being thoughtful allows you to come across with more charm.

2) Be inclusive and reassuring as you talk with each prospect. Let them know how much you care by your attention to detail. Those who have great charm are those who take away fear through reassuring statements and eye contact.

3) Study those who are masters of the principle of charm. Study those who have great charisma. They have the ability to draw in their listeners by how they say things and how inclusive they can be.

8. There is a power in numbers. Use them to provide persuasive statistical facts to emphasize your point as you persuade.

Numbers are a powerful way to persuade. It is another way to provide third-party credibility to what you are promoting. For example, when you say that nearly 2/3 of your business comes from referrals, it is a powerful statement because it implies to your prospects that the majority of your business comes from the referrals of those who have already had a great experience with you.

Since numbers are so powerful, do you know the numbers of your business that you can promote in your marketing? You only really need one or two great numbers or statistics that can be very persuasive in your marketing. What will these be for you?

Here are a few examples of numbers you could discover and use in your marketing:

• What is your return rate of customers who come back and buy something else from you?

• How many testimonial letters or videos do you receive from customers each and every month?

• Has your business been featured in five or more news stories over the past year?

• What percentage of your business comes from referrals?

• In your pre-sales collateral, can you identify how many of your customers are decisive and buy from you on their first visit (and save money)?

Part of the reason why numbers are so powerful is because they directly tie into the psychological trigger of specificity. The more specific you can be in your marketing, the more credible it is. That's why, if you can identify the numbers to the above questions, you can put together a very compelling case for why prospects should buy from you. For example, you could say:

• ___% of all of those who buy __*Product X*__ from us also buy __ *Product Y*__from us.

• More than ___% of those who buy from us write a note or letter explaining how much they loved their experience. We love this positive feedback and look forward to receiving your testimonial letter about how we've helped you get the results you were seeking with our product(s) very soon as well.

• Our critically acclaimed business has been featured in different media publications more than 12 times this past year.

• Nearly 2/3 of all of those who buy from us do so at the recommendation of a close friend.

• 3 out of 4 customers who buy from us do so on their first visit and save $$\underline{X}$ or receive $\underline{X}$ benefit. We look forward to helping you find and save money and receive $\underline{X}$ benefit on your first visit as well.

As you can see, you can use numbers in a variety of ways to share positive aspects of how your business is promoted to your prospects. What numbers can you start using to be more persuasive in your marketing approach?

One word of caution. While numbers are very persuasive and provide evidence that your argument is correct, you've got to use good numbers. Nothing will hurt your credibility more than using bad numbers that someone disproves. However, good numbers that promote your cause can be very powerful ammunition for customers to share with their friends and to boost your overall persuasiveness. Explaining the reasons why someone should buy from you with your differences and advantages will help you build contrast so you can be persuasive in your pre-sales marketing materials.

9. Give prospects information that will help them persuade other members of the decision making process. Better yet, don't present unless all decision makers are present.

Make sure you set yourself up for success before you start the persuasion process. If you don't have all of the decision makers present, you're doing them and yourself a great disservice.

If you choose to present anyway, and they have to have the approval of someone else before they can make their decision to buy, are you arming each prospect with information that can help them make a compelling case for your product and why they should buy it from you?

Focus on giving them statistics, third-party validation, your track record, and lots and lots of experiences of others who have chosen to buy from you to build contrast.

Specificity is so important in being persuasive. Joe Sugarman makes this interesting comment on p. 143 of his book *Triggers*: "Being specific and precise in your explanations and statements is very important, in part because it can affect your credibility. Let me give you an example. If I say, 'New dentists everywhere use and recommend CapSnap toothpaste," it sounds like typical advertising lingo—puffery designed to sell a product. It is so general that it will probably cause a prospect to discount the statement you have just made and maybe everything else you say. But if I say, '92% of dentists use and recommend CapSnap toothpaste,' it sounds much more believable. The consumer is likely to think that we did a scientific survey and that 92% of the dentists actually use the toothpaste." --*Triggers*, p. 143.

Here is the important point: statements with specific facts can generate strong believability. Consider the impact of these statements:

• 71% of those who buy at __*the name of your business*__ do so because one of their friends recommended us

• There are only 3 of this product in the entire state and you are wearing the only one in your size.

• There are over 10,000 individual beads that are sewn onto this dress all by hand. It takes 38 days for one highly skilled seamstress just to sew on all of the beadwork.

• There are 72,000 nerve endings at the bottom of your feet. Our customers tell us that these shoes are amongst the most comfortable they have ever worn and that they feel like they are still walking on air when they take them off.

• Over 1,000,000 sold!

Here are 3 benefits of being more specific in what you sell:

• You are more believable and credible.

• You sound like an expert on the subject. Expertise builds trust and confidence.

• Specificity helps you eliminate skepticism and makes your message more credible and trusted.

Look at what you are saying when you sell. Add specifics to your claims. Research the facts and use the details. Numbers are a powerful trigger when you honestly research the facts and share them with those to whom you sell.

The best time to be persuasive and overcome an objection is before it comes up. Joe Sugarman makes this point in his book *Triggers* about why it is so key to bring up an objection before it comes up and how doing this really helps you close the sale later, especially if it is one that will be a major obstacle to making the sale.

He says:

"Why does this work? First, realize that you can't fool your prospect. If indeed something isn't right with what you are selling, the prospect will either know, sense, or feel it. You might think you can pull the wool over the eyes of the prospect, but in reality your prospect is a lot sharper than you think. So if you feel that there is something negative in what you are selling that the prospect might notice or respond to, bring up that negative feature first. Don't wait until later in the sales presentation—bring it up right away. By presenting a negative feature up front, you melt away that initial resistance and come across as honest rather than deceptive. The trust and respect you get from prospects will lower their defense mechanisms, and so they'll be prepared to receive the real advantages of your product or service."--*Triggers*, p. 25.

One of the most common objections that you may face is the prospect who says they can't make a decision without getting multiple quotes first. The best way to overcome this objection is to bring it up first and within the first few minutes that you begin presenting your product.

Why? Because, then when you get to the end of the process, it has already been discussed and they feel comfortable with going ahead with their purchase. They'll do this because they know others have chosen to buy that way and you are going to give them the best value, period. If you avoid doing this simple thing at the beginning, it will be brought up anyway and the prospect will go shop around more and may never be back to buy from you.

Another powerful way to arm your prospects is through a principle called "flagging." Kevin Hogan explains what this principle means and how you can use it to be more persuasive in his book *The Science of Influence*. He says: "Flagging is one specific technique that you can use to dramatically increase compliance in almost all aspects of influence.... The point of placing a flag in someone's memory is that, once it is there, it becomes part of their permanent memory and gives you a point from which to establish a key piece of the persuasion process. Here's a real life example:

"Remember, when you bought your first house? Did you want something that would be big enough for your family to live in comfortably?"

"Now, the real estate agent has no clue if this is true, but by flagging the memory of the decision to buy the house you add this specific recollection into their memory as if it has always been there. If you were to ask, 'What caused you to buy this house?' people will generate numerous possibilities internally before giving you a reason. That reason could be helpful in the persuasion process, but one thing is certain: The reason that they state probably had little to do with their decision in the first place!

"Therefore, they will be more likely to doubt the generation of their own recollection, and even though you now have a piece of information that is useful, it also has drawbacks.

"What for example? Specifically, the person may have generated a number of internal responses of their reason before saying what it was. This cause question marks to pop up in the mind and makes a further conversation more interesting but less likely to persuade.

"If you flag a memory you will get one of two responses. Either the people will accept the flag (most typical) and think in terms of comfortable, in this case, or they will rapidly tell you just why they did buy a house.

"'No, it wasn't space or comfort at all. I needed a home that was near the school.'"

"At this point you have a client with a dramatic recall (still as unlikely to be accurate). This allows you to utilize their flag in the persuasion process that has begun. Once people have a flag anchored in place, it primes mental processes to think in terms of the flag. Yes, you can bet that the nearness to school factor will be a determining factor at this point."

He continues with this key point: "You can flag another person's memory through their own generation of the flag or by planting the flag yourself. The flag should always be something that was considered by the other person at some time. If the flag is self-generated by the other person, they are more likely to internally argue or struggle with the flag because, although they originally came up with the flag, they generated other options that they considered and they might recall these other points and begin to oscillate internally.

"Imagine I were to say: 'Pick a number. I'm thinking of 61,000.' What is your number?

"Now, imagine that I say to someone else, 'Pick a number. I'm thinking of 14.'

"The responses from the two individuals are going to be dramatically different. Very few people will pick a number higher than 100 in the latter case. In the former case where I said I was thinking of 61,000, people will pick numbers in the thousands, tens of thousands, and even hundreds of thousands.

"In both cases, I primed the response by stating an anchor or flag—in the first case a big number and in the second a small number.

"The faster I ask for a response, the closer to the anchor the response will be. These numbers mean nothing but have direct impact on suggestions given to the person." –pp. 203-204.

Then, he shares this fascinating strategy:

"Let's move this interesting phenomenon into the persuasion and marketing arena. Research participants were shown apartments to rent. They were given rental fees for the apartments that varied from very high to very low. When the individuals were given high numbers, the individuals focused on the positive aspects of the apartment. When they were given low numbers they were much more likely to focus on the negative aspects. In further research, participants who are asked to accept one proposal or another are more likely to focus on the positive aspects of the proposal. Participants asked to reject one of two options are likely to focus on negative aspects of the two.

"And there are more, but it all comes down to one key concept. Anchoring is priming and it is an associative error. Whatever you mention to prime their thinking is going to cause error in the thinking toward the anchor—even when you tell someone that this is what you are doing! What does this mean in the real world?

"...Clearly, if you are selling a service for $1,000 and want to sell the most of them possible, then you should probably should set a high anchor. "What you will gain from this experience is easily worth $9,000. I could ask for half of that fee but I'm not going to. Instead I'm only going to ask only $1,000 for this experience."—p. 205.

Now, how can you use the principle of flagging and anchoring to build value and sell more of your product?

In the bridal business, I coach retailers to position their store against what brides are all familiar with (the dresses at Kleinfeld on *Say Yes to the Dress*). When brides come into their stores, they can position the experience against the price they might have thought they would pay at Kleinfeld (approximately $10,000) to the highest price dress they sell in their store. Then, a bridal consultant can help them try on gowns that are under both prices (and more within the bride's budget).

In the solar business, I coach sellers to position the investment of solar against the price they will pay to the utility companies and their ever increasing rates.

This approach also raises your value in the prospect's mind when you can give them an amazing experience and throw in a few surprises that they weren't expecting as well.

Are you using the flags of statistics, trends, or other numbers to prove why you are the best in a persuasive way with those you serve?

Are you offering third party validation through numerous and persuasive testimonials?

Are you highlighting the experience a prospect will have with you in a way that helps her to see that your track record makes you a much more reliable choice from whom they should buy?

If a prospect isn't able to make up their mind on the first visit because they don't have their spouse or other influential decision makers with them, are you empowering them with the information they'll need to make it back quickly with the right decision makers? You are responsible for imparting this information to your prospects. You can't rely on someone else to do it for you.

10. Use stimuli that grab attention and trigger decision.

I've always been fascinated by what triggers the brain to buy. When you understand triggers, you can incorporate the language patterns into the things you say to prospects as you meet with them. Every advantage matters today. A book entitled *The Buying Brain* reveals many great ideas for how you can tap into and trigger decision in the brain. The book is essentially a treatise on how and why brains buy and is a fascinating look into the newest research over the past several years and how you can utilize these findings to successfully persuade your prospects to buy now.

One of the most fascinating parts of the book is the section that explains what the brain likes and what it rejects and how to use that knowledge to market correctly. According to Pradeep, the brain is frustrated by: "Tasks that take too long to resolve, clutter, and messages that distract or don't apply" – *The Buying Brain*, p. 29.

The best kind of stimuli you can use to persuade are the kind that the brain can't ignore. The book points out three things you can use. They are:

1) Novelty. Novelty is very powerful because we are all drawn to something new. Everyone has experienced the phenomenon where a brand new product comes in and is immediately sold by a sales consultant who loves it and purchased by a customer who had never seen anything like it. This happens because of this principle. According to Pradeep, "Novelty is the single most effective factor in effectively capturing all [the brain's] precious attention. Novelty recognition is a hard-wired survival tool all primates share. Whether looking for prey or berries or suitable mates, our brains are trained to look for something brilliant and new, something that stands out from the landscape, something that looks delicious. A novel message, product, package, and/or layout is the key to penetrating their busy and selective subconscious minds. Breaking through the clutter in this way helps products stand out on the shelf and elevates a great logo from a sea of competing symbols and letters. To be embraced, a consumer touch point must first be noticed." – *The Buying Brain*, pp. 29-30.

2) Eye contact. Do you look a prospect in the eye when you talk with them and seek to overcome their objections? According to extensive research that has been done on this, "Eye contact is particularly important to a social species such as ours." –p. 30.

Eye contact helps a prospect sense your empathy and your desire to help them find the perfect solution with your product. When you evaluate how well you did in making a sale, be sure to include this as an item that you look for and analyze. Lack of eye contact also shows a prospect your insecurity. This may be due to your lack of confidence in your ability to handle a particular objection. When you are confident, you look into someone else's eyes. A lot could be said about this, but be sure to look into a prospect's eyes to grab attention and to connect with them on a deeper level.

3) Pleasure/reward images. Studies have been done where brain waves have been measured and recorded to be higher when a certain product, picture or logo is flashed in front of someone's eyes. This means that if you know what triggers the pleasure/reward circuits of the brain, you can celebrate the happiness and deep pleasure a prospect will have from achieving results with your product or service. The best pleasure/reward images you can use are the ones triggered in the prospect's imagination by the questions you ask and the word pictures you use.

Utilize these stimuli to be more persuasive as you sell. President Dwight D. Eisenhower made this great observation about leading soldiers which I think has great application to how well we persuade those we work with. He said: "I would rather try to persuade a man to go along, because once I have persuaded him he will stick. If I scare him, he will stay just as long as he is scared, and then he is gone."

Choose to be persuasive in a way that builds your credibility and gets to the heart of what your prospects really want. Then, you can persuade them to go along with your desire to help them find the perfect option in a way where you can push for the sale without being pushy. As a result, you'll convert browsers to buyers faster and will succeed in your efforts to persuade them to take action now.

CHAPTER 9

AVOID DISTRACTIONS, STAY FOCUSED, AND IMPLEMENT MORE

"Dost thou love life? Then do not squander time for that is the stuff life is made of."—Benjamin Franklin

"We have become a world of reactors, not thinkers, at a time when good thinking is so desperately needed."
--Jack Trout

The distractions an entrepreneur must face on a daily basis are staggering. It is easier than ever to be swept away in a deluge of seemingly important activities that don't result in significant accomplishment for you or your business. To overcome this, you've got to learn to control yourself and your environment. The danger you face is in knowing you could be more productive, more focused, and more consistent in your efforts. To succeed in today's marketplace, you must remain focused on priorities that yield pay and profits.

In this chapter, you're going to learn twenty-one proven methods and processes you can use to get more done. As you work to implement your list of priorities, you'll have days where you didn't accomplish as much as you hoped. It's okay. Regroup and refocus. Remember, success is built on the foundation of failure. Thomas Edison once said: "Once I have started working on a goal, I believe that it is only a matter of elimination before I find the way that will work. Therefore, I look upon every failure as a successful step that eliminates one more way that won't work." If you've experienced disappointing days that have frustrated you because you haven't been able to accomplish more, you'll love what I will cover in the pages that follow. I want to teach you the twenty-one best processes that I use to get more done.

1. Define and decide.

Each of us has the responsibility for our own lives. We have to accept responsibility for how our time is used. We have to define and decide what it is that we want.

Brian Tracy says:

"The highest-paid activity in America, and in your life, is thinking. The time you take to think about who you are and what you want is more valuable and has a higher payoff to you than any other single activity. Most people act impulsively. The phone rings, someone knocks on the door or comes in, they get an idea or the mail arrives, and they are off! The average person is like a dog that sets off to chase a rabbit across a summer field. As the dog bounds after the rabbit, another rabbit jumps up, and the dog veers after the second rabbit. Then a third rabbit appears, and the dog changes course once more. By the end of the day, the dog has been chasing rabbits back and forth around the field for hours and is completely exhausted. But the dog has caught no rabbits. This is the way most people manage their lives."

He continues:

"The opposites of complexity and confusion are focus and concentration. The most important life skill you can develop is the ability to focus single-mindedly on your most important goal or activity and then concentrate completely on achieving that goal. Work without diversion or distraction. Keep coming back to your key task. Discipline yourself to work on your highest payoff activities even when you don't feel like it."—*Victory*, pp. 179-180.

Are you taking time to think?

I think everyone can relate to chasing so many things that you feel exhausted, but haven't accomplished much. It matters that you decide what you will let take your attention and your energy. Choose priorities that will help you get the results you want. When you define and decide on your priorities you can accomplish so much more than if you just try to get out there and do everything on your own.

Remember, only you can define and decide how you will use your time. In order to implement more, you've got to view your time as a precious, finite resource that must be planned around your priorities.

Many entrepreneurs experience the frustration that comes with time because their businesses consume so much of their daily lives. Even when a business becomes successful, an owner may find that now they don't have enough time to enjoy the fruits of their labors because they are so busy. This is no different in your business or in your life. We are all short on time in almost every area of our lives. The key is to view time differently and start having it work for you.

All of us have 168 hours in every week. If you sleep 8 hours a day you have already used up 56 of your 168 hours. If it takes an hour each morning from the time your alarm goes off through showering, brushing your teeth, eating breakfast and heading out to your business, here is another 7 hours a week. We'll add another 3 1/2 hours at 30 minutes every day for the amount of time it takes to wind down, get ready for bed and go to sleep. Now there are 101.5 hours left in the week. If you commute each day to your business or job, you probably could spend another 3-7 hours every week just driving in your car commuting. Then if you are physically at your workplace 8-9 hours a day, you have used another 48-56 hours depending on how many hours you work each day and whether or not you work 5, 6, or 7 days a week.

When you factor in the time that you run errands and eat dinner, you are left with less than forty hours a week (or an average of 5-6 hours a day, to get done everything else that really matters to you). With essentially 75% of our life consumed each week by our work and other necessary activities, we are essentially left with a small percentage of time left to do things for our spouse, our children, hobbies or interests, sports, exercise, friends, personal errands, TV shows or entertainment, and I'm sure that you could add another dozen items or more that take up your remaining time.

Brian Tracy once observed: "Time is inelastic; it cannot be stretched. Time is indispensable; all work and accomplishment requires it. Time is irreplaceable; there is no substitute for it. And time is perishable; it cannot be saved, preserved, or stored. Once it is gone, it is gone forever."

In the hustle and bustle of life, it is so easy to let everything in our work or business consume our lives. When we have so much to do and too little time, it is easy to get overwhelmed and feel that we are losing control of our time. Time management helps us control the sequence of events in our day so that we can better control our lives.

However, remember that we are always free to choose what we do first, what we do second, and what we choose not to do at all. Our lives are the sum of the choices we make each day. By making better choices and better decisions we can redirect the course of our lives so that we can be happier.

One of the reasons that we sometimes fail in our time management is that we allow lesser priority activities to take precedence of higher priority activities simply because we don't plan the higher priority activities and set them in stone. When you know your priorities and plan around them, it is amazing how much more you can get done that brings personal fulfillment. Plan around your priorities and this difference in perspective on your time will help you get more done.

You will improve your productivity when you increase your clarity and focus. You may find yourself getting online and wasting time if you are frustrated, discouraged, or unclear about what you want. When you are clear about what you want, you will spend less time on routine, non-value tasks and more time on tasks with tremendous value that will help you achieve your goals.

Make up a list of all of the things you do in your business (there might be 15-20 things) that only you can do. Then determine—what is the most important thing you do? What is the most valuable use of your time right now? Whatever the answer, do that and only that. Delegate the rest.

The more clarity you have behind why you are building your business the more motivated you will be to release the internal power to accomplish your goals. Disraeli put it best: "Nothing can resist the human will that will stake its existence on the extent of its purpose."

If your purpose is to sell to the vast majority of every client in your marketplace who needs what you offer and you are passionate about that purpose, you will find you will awaken the energy to realize and fulfill your purpose. You can get even clearer in this purpose by continually asking, "And I want to do that because... or I want to do that so I can do..."

Author Steve Chandler says: "Most people are surprised to learn that the reason they're not getting where they want in life is because their major goals are too small. And too vague. And therefore have no power. Your major goal will not be reached if it fails to excite your imagination. What really increases motivation is the setting of a large and specific power goal.

A goal is just a goal. A power goal is a goal that takes on virtual reality.

It lives and breathes and provides motivational energy. It gets you up in the morning. You can taste it, smell it and feel it. You've got it clearly pictured in your mind. You've got it written down. And you keep writing it down because every time you do it fills you with clarity of purpose."--*100 Ways to Motivate Yourself*, p. 24.

The clearer your purpose, the more motivated you will be to get out and make it happen. Focus. If you can focus single-mindedly on any task, you can accomplish anything in the world. Determine that you are going to concentrate single-mindedly on your most important tasks and focus on these. Concentrated and focused effort gives you renewed energy and motivation to continue on to the next task.

2. Take the direct approach.

Brian Tracy tells this story about Operation Market Garden in his book *Victory* about the power of simplicity and the chaos that results from having too many steps. He says:

"In September 1944, British Field Marshall Montgomery convinced General Dwight D. Eisenhower that he could bring World War II to a quick conclusion if he could just have enough men, material, and paratroopers to simultaneously seize five key bridges over rivers and canals in the Netherlands and cross the Rhine River into Germany in force. At the same time, Allied tanks and infantry were to push through from the front line, relieve the airborne troops, and cross the bridges. Reluctantly, and because of political pressure from Churchill, Eisenhower allowed Montgomery to proceed with Operation Market Garden. This plan was in sharp contrast to Eisenhower's strategy of attacking along a broad Allied front, but he nonetheless allowed it to proceed. It turned out to be one of the big mistakes of the war.

"In the midst of the planning for this operation, one of the intelligence officers, Lt. General Roy Browning, observed that in attempting to take four bridges in a row, and then the fifth bridge at Arnhem, the allies were perhaps going 'a bridge too far.' This turned out to be exactly what happened.

"In one of the most complex offensive operations of World War II, thousands of paratroopers were dropped throughout the Netherlands, each group assigned to seize a particular bridge near their drop area. However, because of faulty maps and poor information, many men were dropped miles from their assigned bridges. They then had to fight their way to the bridges over hotly contested terrain, armed only with light weapons.

"The Allies received a warning that German troops were in the area, but the warning was late and was ignored. Some of the finest German infantry and Panzer Corps were refitting in the area. They were immediately put into action to counterattack the Allied troops landing all around them.

"Meanwhile, there was only one road along which supplies for the beleaguered paratroopers could be brought. Maps turned out to be inaccurate, and entire regiments got lost. There were communication problems as well as a lack of supplies and ammunition. Trucks broke down, and river crossing equipment went astray. More Allied troops were both dropped and trucked into the battle. There were not enough aircraft to deliver the troops all at once. The Germans also had anti-aircraft defenses near Arnhem that made it too dangerous for the gliders to land there; consequently, they landed seven miles away, thereby destroying the element of surprise. The Germans quickly figured out the Allied plan, reorganized their forces, and counterattacked furiously. By the time Operation Market Garden collapsed, it had been a complete defeat; costing thousands of lives and leaving the Allies right back where they started. The entire offensive violated the principle of simplicity from the first moment.

The operation was ill conceived from the start. There were simply far too many variables, all of which had to come together at once to assure success. The complexity of the operation was such that virtually no one, at any level of command, had a clear idea of what was happening, or what could be done to minimize losses or achieve victory. In retrospect, it was a foolish waste of precious human and material resources."—pp. 165-167.

What an important cautionary lesson! Trying to do too much on too many fronts will usually not end well. It is much better to be focused and clear about what is trying to be achieved. When there are lots of moving pieces, it is even more important the overall strategy is understood by all. The clearer your plans are, the easier it will be to achieve them. The other thing to remember is that business is not conducted in a vacuum. Your competition will launch counterattacks against you. It is just a matter of time before they respond to what you do in the marketplace. This means that you have to adjust as well.

3. Have the right mindset: pig headed determination.

Chet Holmes called the process of sticking to something until it is completed "pig headed determination."

When you are passionate about something, you are more likely to have pig headed determination, but it does not necessarily mean that you will get out of your comfort zone and do anything about what must be done. When you do things you've never done before, you will gain confidence and power in accomplishing the tasks you have before you. You've got to begin and see it through.

I really like what Anthony Robbins says about this in his book *Awaken the Giant Within*. He says:

"If we want to create change, we have to realize that it's not a question of whether we can do it, but rather whether we will do it. Whether we will or not comes down to our level of motivation, which in turn comes down to those twin powers that shape our lives, pain and pleasure....If you've tried many times to make a change and you've failed to do so, this simply means that the level of pain for failing to change is not intense enough. You have not reached threshold, the ultimate leverage."

He continues:

"So why would someone not change when they feel and know that they should? They associate more pain to making the change than to not changing. To change someone, including ourselves, we must simply reverse this so that not changing is incredibly painful (painful beyond our threshold of tolerance), and the idea of changing is attractive and pleasurable!"--pp. 127-128.

So, if we want to change and get more done, we have to get out of our comfort zone and do different things. Seek growth experiences outside of yourself that will stretch you and help you to grow.

You've got to have pig headed determination to succeed or you'll go right back to what you used to do. I like this statement by author Marshall Goldsmith that outlines why most people aren't better implementers in life. He says:

"As much as we all claim to want happiness and meaning in our lives (very few people say that they want to live miserable, empty lives), there's a paradoxical catch that thwarts us at every turn. I call it the Mojo Paradox and I want you to burn it into your memory:

Our default response in life is not to experience happiness. Our default response in life is not to experience meaning. Our default response in life is to experience inertia.

In other words, our most common everyday process—the thing we do more often than anything else— is continue to do what we're already doing.

If you've ever come to the end of a TV show and then passively continued watching the next show on the same channel, you know the power of inertia. You only have to press a button on the remote (an expenditure of less than one calorie of energy) to change the channel.

Yet many of us cannot do that. Quite often, inertia is so powerful that we can't even hit the remote to turn the TV off! We continue doing what we're doing even when we no longer want to do it.

Inertia is the reason I can say the following with absolute certainty about your immediate future. The most reliable predictor of what you will be doing five minutes from now is what you are doing now. If you're reading now, you'll probably be reading five minutes from now. The same is true for almost any other daily activity. If you are drinking or exercising or exercising or shopping or surfing the Internet now, you will probably be drinking or exercising or shopping or surfing the Internet five minutes from now. Take a minute to let that sink in and weigh the statement against your own life." – *Mojo: How to Get It, How to Keep It, How to Get it Back If You Lose It*, pp. 34-35.

He continues:

"Very few people achieve positive, lasting change without ongoing follow-up. Unless they know at the end of the day (or week or month) that someone is going to measure if they're doing what they promised to do, most people fall prey to inertia. They continue doing what they were doing. They don't change their behavior, and as a result, they don't become more effective."—Marshall Goldsmith, *Mojo*, p. 36.

Many entrepreneurs fall prey to this trap of going with the flow (of doing things the way they've always been done) instead of looking for new ways to improve. Here are four ways you can avoid going with the flow:

1) Improve your associations. Get around others who stretch your mind and help you see the possibilities. There is a story told that indicates how important it is to get around others who know different ways of doing things. As the story goes, one morning the family got a late start, and the six year old missed her bus to school. Though it would make him late for work, the father agreed to take her to school if she could give him directions. They left the neighborhood, and the young girl began directing her father to take one turn after another. Following twenty minutes of circuitous driving, they arrived at the school, which turned out to be only eight blocks away. Steaming, the father asked the kindergartener why she had him drive all over the place when the school was so close to home. "We went the way the bus goes," she said. "That's the only way I know."

Look for other associations who can help you learn different ways to do things than how you've always done them. You may learn shortcuts and more efficient ways to get better results. Without improved association, you'll stay confined within a self-made prison where there is only one-way to do something (which may or may not be the best way to do it). This is one of the big reasons to performers benefit from mastermind groups. If you are not already a part of one, join one that will push you and get you to associate with those around you who are making things happen.

2) When you experience discouragement and defeat, choose to bounce rather than break. Author Roger Crawford was born without seven fingers and one leg. How many in a similar situation would have broken with such a condition? He didn't. He has bounced back from this setback to become a successful tennis player and is a highly sought after motivational speaker. In his book *How High Can You Bounce?* Crawford makes this statement: "Life's problems are like small fires in a large building. If we can shut a door and confine the problem to one area, it is less likely to spread. But if all of the doors are open, the problems can feed on each other and build into one huge inferno of negativism and hopelessness. Which would you rather be, powerful or pitiful? Would you prefer to take charge and take off? Or just take it? To act or to react? Nothing can devastate us without our permission. We can choose to describe any situation in resilient language."--p. 25.

3) Break free of your comfort zone and get a better recovery rate. When you take a physical examination at the doctor's office, they usually measure your recovery rate. A nurse will first check your resting pulse rate and then have you do some type of vigorous exercise for a few minutes. Then, two minutes after the exercise, your resting pulse rate is tested again. They are looking for how quickly you've recovered or your recovery rate. People who are in good shape return to their resting pulse rate quickly. People who are not in shape often still find themselves wheezing, out of breath, and with a higher heart rate. To better deal with change and beating the status quo, you need to have a good recovery rate. If you choose to make a different decision with your business and you are paralyzed by fear shortly after you make the decision to the point where you stop or quit the progress you're making, you've experienced this type of resistance. Work at being more resilient and open to doing new things. It will help you grow quicker and get to where you want to go much faster than sticking with the status quo.

4) *Know where you are going.* The clearer you are about your own personal vision, the easier it will be to say no to competing demands for your time and efforts. We can't be like Alice in Lewis Carroll's *Through the Looking Glass*, who asks for directions in this way during her encounter with the Cheshire Cat:

"Would you tell me please, which way I ought to go from here?" she asks.

"That depends a good deal on where you want to get," the cat replies with a grin. "I don't care much where," she answers.

"Then it doesn't matter which way you go," the cat responds.

If you are undecided about the direction of your business, you will merely drift along and will likely not achieve the success you could if you would just focus in on what you need to do and do it.

Thomas Edison once said: "Sticking to it is the genius! Any other bright-minded fellow can accomplish just as much [as I did] if he will stick like hell and remember nothing that's any good works by itself. You got to make the damn thing work. I'll never give up, for I may have a streak of luck before I die."

4. Don't let obstacles stop you.

The difference between an average income and an extraordinary one is implementation. No competitor has any more time in a day than you do to get things done. Each of us has no more than 60 minutes to an hour, 24 hours to a day, or 7 days to a week. Time is the great equalizer. What matters is how you choose to use the 1,440 minutes you are given each day.

Every person has more ideas than they take time to actually implement in their lives or in their business. With the same amount of time each day, the only difference between the results people get is how it is spent and what actions are taken everyday. Some actions will produce miniscule results. Others produce massive results. Choosing where to put your time and choosing to act on the best ideas that will help you achieve your goals will be actions that will have the biggest impact in your life.

There are five big obstacles to getting more done. They are:

1. Choosing lesser priority things because true priorities haven't been established.

Stephen Covey in his book, *Principle Centered Leadership* says: "The essence of time management is to set priorities and then to organize and execute around them."

If you don't take control of your time, time will control you.

2. Failure to plan out time effectively.

Author and speaker Jim Rohn said, "Don't start your day until you have it finished on paper first."

Take time to think – at least 15 to thirty minutes each day of uninterrupted thought. You can at least take 14 minutes of the 1,440 minutes that are in each day (less than 1% of the total day) to think about and plan your day. Take a pad of paper and pencil and think on paper about the upcoming events you have, the challenges you're facing with your team, how to bring more prospects into your marketing funnels, how to help your team sell more, etc. The key is to take time every day to think and to plan. Make the decision that you won't start your day without finishing it on paper first. You will find that you will accomplish so much more if you will think on paper—even though you will get interrupted continuously as soon as you walk through the doors of your office. Do your best to get back on task as quickly as you can. This is so much easier if you have outlined what you need to do each day then if you just kind of wing it.

3. Failure to value personal time. Even if you do, there may be members of your team who do not.

You must set up the environment and the expectations you wish in order to make your goals happen.

4. There is too much to do and too little time to do it in.

We all have too much to do and too little time. Why is this true?

Every time you turn around you get more to do—you have more phone calls, more mail, more emails and more challenges to deal with in your business.

As you become better at what you do, you attract more opportunities to do it. If you're like me, it is difficult sometimes to say no, because you know that you can do something well. Since we are responsible people, we don't turn away the responsibility to do something.

5) You will never get caught up. You're never going to get everything done. No matter how good you are at time management, how early you get up, how late you stay at work, you will never get caught up. With that said, you can choose to focus on priorities that you can finish and that is what this is about. You can choose what to do with your time and then force yourself to use a better system where you can plan and then act on what must be done.

5. Get organized and work by deadlines.

Fortunately, organization is a skill and can be learned. Everyone can learn to become extremely well organized, efficient, and effective. The payoff for good planning is huge. You save 10 minutes on execution for every minute that you spend planning.

A deadline is a stop time by which something must be completed. Too many entrepreneurs have start times, but no stop time. They'll spend too much time working on something that they don't need to.

Use the timer on your smart phone to schedule a start time and an end time for what you will do. It will ring or beep when the time you've allotted is up. Then, when the timer stops, you have to stop working on that activity. To be more focused and productive, you have to have a beginning time and an end time.

I have been able to accomplish a lot in a short period of time through this method. When you set the clock, don't let anything distract you from your goal to complete the task in the next 30, 60, or 90 minutes blocks or whatever time allotment you give yourself. If you do this, you will get so much more done.

If you set aside just 50 minutes each day of productive time (and you eliminate all distractions so that this time really is productive), you'll find that you will gain 188 hours a year of intense productivity (if you just do this once per day for 5 days a week). That's nearly eight days of time that you will have spent in focused work on your goals and business. Set a goal to try this this next month. Come into work at least an hour and a half earlier than anyone else. Turn off your phone, disable your Internet access from your computer, close your email program and focus on one thing that can help you business to grow. If you will do this consistently every day for 1 week and then one month, you'll be amazed at how much more you are able to get done.

Be clear about why you are doing what you are doing. The more clarity you have and the more tied your daily activities are to your goals, the more productive you will be. Deadlines work to get things done. Use them.

6. Batch and block your work.

When you do several similar tasks together, the tasks become easier and you get them done quicker. The best way to do this is to separate out all of the tasks into batches and do them in one time block. I call this skill batching and blocking. So, you can return all of your phone calls at one time. You can send all of your return emails in a batch or write on one subject for a specified period of time. When you batch things together, you'll discover that not only do you get better at it, but you'll be able to do it quicker. I've learned this anytime I've learned a new piece of software or any new business skill. When I first start, it typically takes a little longer than I expected to learn the skill. Of course, skill development can speed up with good teachers and training. But, if there is a skill that you want and need to learn then batching those activities into a specific time period will allow you to get those actions done more quickly.

For example, when I batch audio editing files for a podcast into a specified time period with a start and end time, I found I could get it done quicker and more efficiently. If you want to get more done, this is one of the best strategies to do it. As you go through the learning curve with any new skill, you'll be able to get the core activity completed more efficiently as you do it consistently in batches and as you block the activities together in time segments.

One of my favorite stories about blocking time to get something done is from the life of Charles Lindbergh. Even his seemingly solo flight was a team effort since nine businessmen from St. Louis were his sponsors and he also had his plane built by the Ryan Aeronautical Company.

Lindbergh's solo flight across the Atlantic Ocean lasted more than thirty-three hours at a distance of 3,600 miles. That kind of focus over such a sustained period of time takes practice. Lindbergh's friend Frank Samuels flew often with Lindbergh in the 1920s from St. Louis to San Diego to deliver mail and to check on the progress of his plane, The Spirit of St. Louis. "One night Samuels woke up shortly after midnight and noticed that Lindberg was sitting by the window looking at the stars. It had been a long day, so Samuels asked, 'Why are you sitting there at this hour?'

'Just practicing,' answered Lindbergh.

'Practicing what?' asked Samuels.

'Staying awake all night.'"—John C. Maxwell, *Go for Gold*, p. 154.

What an inspiring example of batching and blocking out time! Some tasks can be batched and blocked as they are in the manufacturing process. What makes manufacturing more efficient is when a task is broken down into a specific series of steps and the person who does that task specializes in getting it done. I have been amazed when I have watched the process of how things are made at factories I've been to around the world. For example at a clothing factory, there are different seamstresses who specialize in the skills of beading, embroidery, or cutting fabric. They can complete their work much more efficiently because they have specialized in it. They are able to get it done more quickly because they become more efficient. When you have a large group of people assembled in a factory manufacturing anything, it is amazing how quickly something can be completed because of this principle.

We all know this instinctively, yet on occasion, I still try to do all of the steps on my own. You may have this tendency as well. Yet, when you delegate and have team members specialize in specific tasks, they get better and more efficient and together you are able to accomplish so much more. When I was younger, I used to go with my father to horse pulling competitions since my father is a farrier. I was amazed to watch how much more weight two Clydesdale horses could pull together than a single horse could pull on its own. You will accomplish more synergistically with others than you ever can all by yourself.

You have to work at what you want to improve. A great example for me is writing. When I first started writing, it would take me a long time to compose my thoughts and they were often jumbled together and not very cohesive. In fact, my seventh grade teacher once returned a marked up paper I had turned in with the words "You will never be a writer" at the top of the page in bright red letters. Now that I've written several books, I've thought about sending her one of them.

I've acquired the skill of writing and gotten better at it because I have worked at it for years, working on it in blocks of time specifically set out from my schedule. You must batch and block out the skill areas you want to develop as well. Once you determine the result you are after, you can build your focus to achieve success in these areas.

As I travel and I'm sure you've noticed this too, there are people who can't go two to three minutes without checking their email or looking at their smart phone. Technology can be a complete distraction if you allow it to be. Email messages can wait for a little while. They don't have to be answered immediately. It is best to get to them within 12-24 hours, but you can do this activity during one focused time interval. To avoid this tendency, you've got to work at it. You've got to consciously choose NOT to look at your smart phone when you are talking with others or when you have a quiet moment. If you don't control it, it will completely overtake and control you.

7. Work in your area of genius and delegate the rest.

Your actions and feelings affect each other. If you are doing something you aren't very good at, you won't be confident about completing it. You'll put it off. Remember to work in your area of genius. By controlling your actions and doing what you do best, you feel positive about what you are doing and more confident in completing the task that lies before you. The most important thing is to begin. If you can't do it, then delegate it to someone who can.

Goethe said: "Each indecision brings its own delay and days are lost lamenting over lost days. Are you in earnest? Seize this very minute! What you can do, or dream you can, begin it! Boldness has genius, power, and magic in it. Only engage, and then the mind grows heated. BEGIN, and then the work will be completed."

Choose to work in your area of genius and you'll confidently move towards the completion of your goal. When you are uncertain, you will hesitate. I love this statement by W. N. Murray:

"Until one is committed there is hesitancy, the chance to draw back, always ineffectiveness. Concerning all acts of initiative (and creation) there is one elementary truth, the ignorance of which kills countless ideas and splendid plans: That the moment one definitely commits oneself, then Providence moves too. All sorts of things occur to help one that would otherwise never have occurred.

"A whole stream of events issues from the decision, raising in one's favor all manner of unforeseen incidents and meetings and material assistance, which no man could have dreamt would have come his way."

Whatever it is that you want to do, begin to do it. Once you put forth the effort, you will receive the energy to complete the task.

8. Report and revisit. Have accountability partners that you check in with as often as possible to keep you on track.

Laura Vanderkam in her book *What the Most Successful People Do Before Breakfast* says:

"Numbers have consequences....If you've ever tried to lose weight, you know that nutritionists will tell you to keep a food journal, because evidence shows it works. One study of a year-long weight-loss program, published in the Journal of the Academy of Nutrition and Dietetics in 2012, found that women who kept a food journal lost about six pounds more than those who did not. Writing down what you eat keeps you accountable for what you put in your mouth. Likewise, writing down how you spend your time keeps you accountable for the hours that pass, whether or not you're conscious of them."—pp. 89-90.

If you're going to implement more, you've got to follow the principle of report and revisit. You've got to report to yourself or a coach on what you've done. I have a coach I talk to on a weekly basis who I'm accountable to. I have to report on what I did from the previous week. Knowing I'll have to report in and revisit what I committed to do helps me ensure that it gets done. I don't want to show up to a meeting I'm paying for and report that I haven't done what I said I would do. I would encourage you to have an accountability partner who you work with in this way who keeps you on track with what you want to get done. It may just be that you send an email that reports in or you have a live call where you can report and revisit what you said you would do. I've found this action extremely helpful in keeping me on track.

9. Overcome the paralyzing influence of perfection – Remember, complete is better than perfect.

It doesn't have to be perfect. It needs to be finished. Complete is better than perfect. Perfect will likely never get done. So, focus on what you can do and get it done.

President Ronald Regan told this story before he left office about *Three Musketeers* author Alexander Dumas:

"The novelist and a friend had a heated argument, and one challenged the other to a duel. Both Dumas and his friend were expert marksmen, and they feared that if they proceeded with the duel, both would die. So they decided to draw straws to determine which of them would shoot himself. Dumas picked the short straw.

With a sigh, he picked up his pistol, walked into his library, and closed the door, leaving behind him a group of worried friends. After a few moments, the loud report of a pistol echoed from the library. His friends immediately charged into the room, and there stood Dumas with the pistol still smoking in his hand.

'An amazing thing just happened,' said Dumas. 'I missed.'"--John C. Maxwell, *Failing Forward*, p. 142.

Don't let mistakes or the inability to get what you wanted done the day before kill you. Recognize it for what it was ('a miss') and move on.

10. Have consequences for delay and procrastination.

If you don't have a consequence for procrastination, you will probably keep putting it off. Since the goal here is to help you get things done, I've found that forcing myself to put off something I want if I don't get something done helps me push through the resistance that causes procrastination in the first place.

Stephen Pressfield in his book *The War of Art* says: "Rationalization is Resistance's right-hand man. Its job is to keep us from feeling the shame we would feel if we truly faced what cowards we are for not doing our work."—p. 53.

He continues: "Resistance is fear. But Resistance is too cunning to show itself naked in this form. Why? Because if Resistance lets us see clearly that our own fear is preventing us from doing our work, we may feel shame at this. And shame may drive us to act in the face of fear. Resistance doesn't want us to do this. So it brings in Rationalization. Rationalization is Resistance's spin doctor. It's Resistance's way of hiding the Big Stick behind its back. Instead of showing us our fear (which might shame us and impel us to do our work), Resistance presents us with a series of plausible, rational justifications for why we shouldn't do our work. What's particularly insidious about the rationalization that Resistance presents to us is that a lot of them are true. They're legitimate....What Resistance leaves out, of course, is that all this means diddly. Tolstoy had thirteen kids and wrote *War and Peace*."—pp.53-56.

Don't buy into your excuses. If you have something to get done and you've been putting it off, get to it now. There's no excuse for procrastination when you are clear about what you want. You've got to overcome your fear and face the fact that if you don't do the work, you're just a coward. That is a realization that I don't think anyone really wants to make about themselves. Don't let this be true about you. Do the work and beat resistance and procrastination.

Your own procrastination and resistance are preventing you from doing what you now you need to do. Put a system in place to help you overcome these debilitating behaviors.

11. Live in the now.

Your competitors can cut their price, say negative things about your product (or company) or spend more money on advertising than you can, but here are three things they can't prevent you from doing:

1) Working harder

2) Thinking smarter

3) Serving better

All three of those strategic behaviors are completely within your control and can be done when you live in the now.

I really like this statement by Daniel Drubin in his book, *Let Go of Your Bananas* about the difference between motivation and willpower. He says:

"Remember, there is a very big difference between motivation and willpower. Motivation tends to come from an outside source and is very often short in duration. I have never seen a person who relied on motivation accomplish long-term success in his or her life. However, the people I know who have the internal drive created by sheer willpower seem to be able to work miracles. They function with great clarity about their goals, certain about achieving those goals, and they continually move in the direction of their desires. Willpower comes from passion, and when you are passionate about something you will be inspired to greatness."--p. 59.

Jordan Williams, a friend of mine and mentor when I worked in the solar business, says that "discipline is more important than motivation." He would be out knocking doors at the same consistent time and then stay out until he achieved his desired outcome of three new accounts created every day. While most made excuses for getting to work, his discipline helped him outsell everyone around him. He is a great example of the principle of working now with discipline.

This is so true in your business and in your life. When you do what makes you feel good about yourself, you will do more of it. As you know, the best time to make a sale is right after you've made a sale. Successful actions give you the motivational energy to complete another successful action. Living in the now will help you implement more now.

12. Beat resistance.

You can change if you aren't happy with where you are. You can overcome setbacks, defeats and failures. Failure is not fatal. However, you've got to beat the resistance to change by changing the software in your mind. Dr. Henry Cloud makes this observation in his book *Boundaries for Leaders*:

"Resistance to change is a fact of life. If you want change to take hold, you must have good boundaries to contain the forces that are working against your effort." –p. 216.

You've got to create those boundaries in your thoughts and emotions. So, choose to begin each day with the attitude that when you walk out to work with prospects and customers each day, you will astonish them. Don't be boring. Don't be predictable. Be different. Take control of your business. Refuse to be controlled by fear. Stop internalizing your disappointments, defeats and discouragement, and letting your emotions prevent you from doing what you are capable of at your business. We all fail. Yet, we can rise from these failures to accomplish new and amazing things.

Leonardo da Vinci said: "Obstacles cannot crush me. Every obstacle yields to stern resolve. He who is fixed to a star does not change his mind."

13. Know your weaknesses and plan accordingly.

Unfortunately, many people today (and you may be one of them) let their weaknesses stop them from accomplishing more. They paralyze themselves and their growth by letting their weaknesses control them and by being fearful of the future.

Andrew Matthews in his book *Being Happy* said: "As the things that we love and most fear will tend to occupy our thoughts much of the time, so will we tend to attract those very things."

Consider these examples of this:

• Have you ever totally ruined a new suit of clothes the very first time you wore them? Just as you were thinking to yourself, "I don't want to dirty this lovely new shirt or blouse," you spill your drink or something all over yourself.

• Or have you ever heard someone say: "I drove a beaten up old wreck for seven years and never even scratched it. As soon as I got my new car, people started driving into the back of me, sideswiping me and running me off the road."

Then he makes this statement:

"I spoke earlier of the woman who had five accidents in seven years. At last she realized that she has dwelt so much on her fears that she has attracted what she did not want. Even if we say to our mind, 'I don't want 'A' to happen, we will gravitate toward 'A'. Our mind cannot move away from anything only toward something."

He concludes: "Focus on what you want. Dwelling on your fears will bring them upon you."--*Being Happy!*, pp. 70-73.

On top of attracting what we fear into our lives, we also face the challenge of overcoming our weaknesses. We have to be the leaders here – since as playwright Lister Sinclair once observed: "A frightened captain makes a frightened crew."

14. Know what motivates you and reward yourself accordingly for completion of a task.

When you fail to keep a promise to yourself because of laziness or a lack of desire, you weaken yourself and your motivation for the future. For your own growth, it is just as important to keep the promises you make to yourself as you do for others.

Give yourself a reward for completing part of what you're working on. Take a sip of your favorite drink after you've done something, or give yourself one bite of a cookie. Perhaps you set the reward as eating lunch after you've finished the task you're working on. Or you allow yourself a Hershey's kiss or some other treat. Maybe your motivating reward can be saying: I am going to go out tonight with my spouse if I can get _____ done.

Remember, you are more likely to get something done if you promise someone else that you will do something by a certain period of time and then have to report to them whether you did it or not. Then, reward yourself once that action is completed.

For example, if you set a goal to lose weight and you don't go to the gym, after you have told yourself you will, you lose self-respect. When you do what you say you will do, you will feel a great sense of accomplishment and peace of mind. When you do what you say you are going to do, you create more energy to do it again.

You will find that you will have more energy and will stay motivated by putting positive things into your mind so that you can encourage those around you to be more motivated as well. You'll never be great at implementation unless you can motivate yourself to do something. Sir Edmund Hillary, the first person on the top of Mount Everest said: "Strong motivation is the most important factor in getting you to the top." Wise words.

15. Know your limitations and do work in blocks that correspond with your energy levels.

To get more done, you've got to know your limitations. There are times in the day when you are more energetic so arrange your day so that your most difficult and important challenges coincide with your peak energy levels. Charles Givens in his book *SuperSelf* says: "Every person has a specific time of the day when we are most effective. If you have ever referred to yourself as a morning or a night person, you are already aware of your peak performance period. It is the time of day when you have the greatest clarity of thinking, have the most creativity, the most confidence, and the most energy. Research has shown that the average person experiences four periods of performance during the course of a sixteen-hour day. These are: 1) Three hours of peak performance; 2) Five hours of good performance; 3) Six hours of feeling as if they are not operating on all cylinders, 4) And two hours of complete exhaustion."

During our peak performance times, we can accomplish and produce more results than during our off- peak times. Your goal should be to determine when your peak hours are and then do your highest priority, most focused activities during this time.

Do you currently plan your activities and your day around your peak performance hours? If not, start today.

Are you aware of your peak performance hours, but only occasionally schedule your activities around them? You will be much more productive by changing your schedule in this way.

Make a list of the activities that you do at your business each and every day. Divide these into two categories: 1) activities that require peak performance and 2) activities that can be done in off-peak hours and then stick to only doing activities in each area during the appropriate time. It is amazing how much more efficient we can be if we utilize our time effectively this way. To help you start with this list, here are a few ideas:

Activities that Require Peak Performance	Activities that Can Be Done in Off-Peak Hours
Marketing campaigns for the business	Bill paying
Decision making for the business	Going through the mail
Preparing for training meetings for staff	Phone calls, Sending/Receiving Emails
Analyzing reports and determining what products to offer	Errands (going to the bank, picking up supplies, etc.)
Reading	Sending thank you cards to customers who have bought from you
Thinking about the direction of your business and how to improve	Meeting with vendors
Meetings with team members about performance and improvement	Meeting with salespeople from various manufacturers or advertisers
Setting goals for the business for the month or year	Going to the post office to drop off direct marketing pieces to be mailed out
Selling	Listening to a podcast

Once you determine your peak performance times, do your best to stick to doing only those things during that time. It will make a huge difference in your productivity and effectiveness and ensure that you implement your most important tasks more quickly.

16. Establish your priority of the moment and get the most from those moments.

Now, this minute, is all of the time that we have. If we can learn to manage ourselves minute by minute, the hours and days will take care of themselves. As John Maxwell says, "Today matters."

I once observed a group of entrepreneurs who brainstormed and listed all of the things they wanted to get done that they felt were their most important priorities. Then, they went through the list twice more prioritizing those lists until they had one area of focus. Then, they went to work on that one priority with complete focus. It was a great lesson to me how taking the time to focus and decide made all of the difference in how quickly something was implemented. Don't diffuse your focus into too many areas (some of which may be in conflict with one another).

There is an old saying that "if you have too many priorities, you have none." This concept really goes into the idea of batching and blocking. You can only work on one priority at a time. So, choose wisely. What will help you get to your goal quickest? You've got the same amount of time as anyone else. If you want to implement more, you've got to focus so you can use your time wisely.

Ralph Waldo Emerson once asked, "What would be the use of immortality to a person who cannot use well a half an hour?"

Periodically, ask yourself: Am I making the best use of my time now?

To determine your most important priority, think on paper. Make and use lists. All of us know that we are much more effective when we think through our day on paper first. We don't do this more often because it is easier to begin and get distracted on other activities than it is to take five minutes to plan out your day first and focus on these things systematically throughout the day. Take time to plan out the next day before you leave work for the day. If you didn't do this, spend 10-15 minutes first thing to plan out what you will do that day.

The biggest reason why we don't work off of lists very well is because we have too many things on the list in the first place and it is easier to get distracted by easier things than it is to focus on all of the many activities on the list itself.

Chet Holmes said it very well: "The key to being productive is to stick to the six most important things you need to get done that day. You'll find that when you have a long list, it becomes the management tool for your time. When you want to feel productive, you go to your list and just pick something and do it. It feels good. When you have a long list, you generally do the easier, less productive tasks just to trim down the list. At the end of the day, you find that the most important things on the list didn't get completed because they are either the hardest, the most time-consuming or both. Long lists also mean that you will never finish your list. There is a negative psychological impact to not finishing your list. But there is an enormous psychological boost to crossing off that sixth item on your list, especially when all six of them were the most important things you needed to do that day. So here's the rule: list the six most important things you need to do and, by hook or by crook, get those six things completed each day. That doesn't mean you don't keep a side list of running items that need to be done. When you plan each day, you can go to your long list and use that as a menu of items from which to build your list of the six most important things for that day." –*The Ultimate Sales Machine*, p. 14.

When you plan, write down the six most important priorities you need and will get accomplished the next day before you go home. When you get interrupted, do your best to get back on task as quickly as you can. Remember, productivity is about control.

A great way to help you or your sales consultants overcome the tendency to not use their time effectively is to put a dollar figure on the value of their time. Help your sales consultants figure out how much they want to make per hour and then ask: "Is what I am doing right now earning me $__ /hour? If not, what can I start doing to make $___/hour?

You can help your sales consultants know the value of their time by what they do in it. Require them to fill out a Daily Productivity Work Sheet so they start measuring their day in terms of accomplishments instead of time passed.

Ralph Waldo Emerson said: "Guard well your spare moments. They are like uncut diamonds. Discard them and their value will never be known. Improve them and they will become the brightest gems in a useful life."

17. Focus on one thing at a time. Multi-tasking is a myth. You'll get more done when you focus.

We have all heard that multi-tasking is an essential and important part of getting things done. Unfortunately, multi-tasking is what causes us to be less productive than we could be if we would just focus on one thing for an extended period of time.

Multi-tasking is a so called "skill" that many individuals claim they have and do well. The definition of multitasking on Wikipedia is an interesting one. It says that "Human multitasking is the performance by an individual of appearing to handle more than one task at the same time." The distinction here is "appearing". There is a difference between "appearing" and actually doing.

There is a really interesting book written on this topic called *The Myth of Multitasking* by Dave Crenshaw. His thesis in the book is that "multitasking or switchtasking" reduces your efficiency (doing things right) and effectiveness (doing the right things) because it constantly switches your mental focus.

Listen to what he says: "When most people refer to multitasking they mean simultaneously performing two or more things that require mental effort and attention. Examples would include saying we're spending time with family while were researching stocks online, attempting to listen to a CD and answering email at the same time, or pretending to listen to an employee while we are crunching the numbers. What most people refer to as multitasking, I refer to as "switchtasking." Why?

Because the truth is we really cannot do two things at the same time— we are only one person with only one brain. Neurologically speaking, it has been proven to be impossible. What we are really doing is switching back and forth between two tasks rapidly, typing here, paying attention there, checking our "crackberry" here, answering voicemail there back and forth back and forth at a high rate. Keep this up over a long period of time, and you have deeply engrained habits that cause stress and anxiety and dropped responsibilities and a myriad of productivity and focus problems. It's little wonder so many people complain of increasingly short attention spans!"–*The Myth of Multitasking*

On the other hand, research has shown that those who stay focused on one thing for a specific period of time are able to get much more accomplished than someone who is trying to get multiple things done at the same time.

One of the biggest lies we can tell ourselves is that we are great multi-taskers. Don't get sucked into believing this lie. Now, you are probably saying, "But, James, I really am good at multi-tasking." Even if you could be good at multi-tasking, those around you at your business are probably not. But, if you feel like that, listen to the results of this study and what it means for you at your business:

"Beginning in 2004, [Gloria Mark] persuaded two West Coast high-tech firms to let her study their cubicle dwellers as they surfed the chaos of modern office life.

One of her grad students, Victor Gonzalez, sat looking over the shoulder of various employees all day long, for a total of more than 1,000 hours. He noted how many times the employees were interrupted and how long each employee was able to work on any individual task.

When Mark crunched the data, a picture of 21st-century office work emerged that was, she says, "far worse than I could ever have imagined." Each employee spent only 11 minutes on any given project before being interrupted and whisked off to do something else. What's more, each 11-minute project was itself fragmented into even shorter three-minute tasks, like answering e-mail messages, reading a Web page or working on a spreadsheet. And each time a worker was distracted from a task, it would take, on average, 25 minutes to return to that task." --Clive Thompson, The New York Times, October 16, 2005, http://www. nytimes.com/2005/10/16/magazine/16guru.html?ei=5088&en=2864 cc65d74cefb8&ex=1287115200

Can you believe that? When people get off task, it takes an average of 25 minutes to return to that task because they are constantly interrupted. Think about the consequences of this in your life and at your business. And, this study was conducted before all of the many apps and distractions that come with our phones. One of the things I continually work on with the top entrepreneurs I coach is this area of carefully measuring how productive they really are. Most entrepreneurs I've interviewed on this topic have privately admitted to me that they are not as productive as they could or should be. They all attribute it to being constantly interrupted or distracted.

Tony Schwartz in his book *The Power of Full Engagement* says that "the greatest power of the human mind is the ability to focus on one thing at a time." The problem with distraction and interruption is that it causes us to lose our natural ability to focus. This is a very difficult habit to overcome. It is so much easier to log on and check our email and let others control what we do. This causes us to be reactive in our businesses instead of proactively determining and doing what needs to be done.

Get control of yourself. Don't fall for the lie that multi-tasking makes you more productive. In reality, it spreads you thinner so that nothing really gets done as well as it could if you would just focus on one thing single-mindedly for a period of time.

Here are some questions for you to consider:

• Do you feel that you are good at multi-tasking?

• How many times in an average day at your business do you find that you are interrupted?

• How often do you find yourself trying to juggle multiple projects at the same time?

• What one idea have you gotten from what I've shared so far can you start using at your business to become more productive?

Take the time to think through these questions. Most of the things that you do in your business require your focus. When you take your mental focus off of one thing to focus on another, it is certain that you will make mistakes and not accomplish as much as if you would just focus on one single thing at a time.

18. After working in a focused block or when you feel fatigued, take time to regenerate your energy.

Charles Givens says: "At the opposite end of Peak Performance Periods are those hours in the day when you feel totally fatigued and not much good for anything. Have you ever said to yourself, 'I'm just too tired. I'll do it later?' That's an indication you've stepped into total fatigue time. Fatigue seems a natural excuse for inaction; when repeated over time, it leads to a pattern of personal ineffectiveness. Get tired, and you are often stopped to overcome fatigue and reduce the number of totally fatigued hours you experience each day." –*SuperSelf*, p. 275.

He recommends the following to overcome fatigue:

1) Drink plenty of water. When you feel fatigue beginning to set in, drink two to three glasses of water and then repeat the process again in

fifteen minutes. Loading up the body with water activates the lymphatic system and flushes out toxins, including lactic acid, which is a main physical cause of fatigue. You will feel the effect within five minutes. You will also be running to the rest room more often, of course, but the fatigue-reducing effect is remarkable.

2) Breathe deeply and sit up straight. Take ten deep breaths. Breathe in deeply and quickly to the count of two, completely filling your longs. Hold for two seconds, then exhale slowly to the count of four. Do this breathing exercise while sitting or standing. You will increase the supply of oxygen in the blood, which then carries it to your brain, causing you to feel more alert. You will actually feel it happen in an instant.

3) Do some quick exercises. Do ten push-ups or jog in place for thirty seconds. Exercise will help eliminate fatigue by quickly increasing your heart rate, which slows down dramatically when you become fatigued.

4) Trigger your adrenal glands. There is a point in the palm of your hand which, when rubbed for twenty to thirty seconds, will trigger your adrenal glands to pump adrenaline in your system, making you feel more alert and alive. The point lies approximately one inch below the base of the longest finger of each hand, in your upper palm. You will feel a bump, which is part of the bone, at the correct place. Place your thumb on that point and, pressing fairly hard, rub in a circular motion for twenty to thirty seconds. Do the same thing with the other hand, and within a minute you will feel a sense of alertness and renewed energy. Do this whenever you experience fatigue or when you wake up drowsy from a deep sleep or a nap. I use this strategy two or three times every day.

5) Refocus on your goals and objectives. A powerful mental antidote to the onset of fatigue is to remind yourself why it is important to stay on track. Since by now you are filling your day with prioritized activities, think about how your current activity is important to your goals.

6) Use short naps to overcome fatigue. The mind and body can actually

replenish their abilities and strength with as little as a fifteen-to-twenty minute nap during the daytime. I have used the napping technique as a fatigue-buster ever since I was a kid and read about Thomas Edison's practice of lying down in his laboratory for frequent naps."—pp. 277-283.

These six strategies are great ways to regenerate your energy when you feel fatigue. I have used all of them. It is hard for me to take a break because I just like to keep going and going. However, I've found that when my energy wanes, I feel much better and can continue on to complete a task to completion by regenerating my energy in these ways. We all need to be better at exercising and "sharpening the saw" as Stephen Covey puts it in his book *The Seven Habits of Highly Effective People*. Schedule more time to sharpen your saw. If you don't, you will accumulate stress, tension, and anxiety in your life.

Some of the direct results of high levels of continuing stress are emotional outbursts and explosions, migraine headaches, high blood pressure, ulcers, skin rashes, insomnia, depression, lack of energy and fatigue, tension headaches, heart attacks, nervous twitches, fear, worry, and apprehension, and clumsiness.

You don't want those things in your life. So, eliminate stress by following these four suggestions:

1) Exercise. Exercise allows your muscles to go through alternating cycles of tension and relaxation. Forcing your muscles from an abnormal state of tension to a more natural state of relaxation helps to alleviate stress. We all know we should exercise more. Start exercising at least 20 minutes every other day until it becomes a habit. It will help you to eliminate tension and be more productive throughout the day. And, you will feel great about yourself!

2) Eliminate negative influences from your life. It is amazing how much negativity there is in the news or when you are around some people. Choose to be positive and be around positive people and influences. It

will help reduce the stress of working at the store each day – especially if you've had a frustrating experience with someone.

3) Read good books. Take time to read an uplifting book that can inspire you. I have found that biographies are a great way to be inspired. It is inspiring to read about how great individuals have accomplished so much because of the encouragement of others. Stopping to read also helps you think about how you can improve your life.

4) Listen to positive people or motivational speakers / teachers. There are plenty of audio books or podcasts available today that can help you learn new business skills and encourage you. It is amazing how listening to an uplifting recording can lift your spirits after a stressful day.

19. Work in a clean, uncluttered environment.

Clutter saps your discipline, your time, and your energy.

Here is a great definition of clutter: If you haven't looked at it in a year, if it is changing color or fading, if people in your business make fun of it, or if you don't know why you saved it in the first place, it is clutter and you should get rid of it.

If you have been overcome with clutter in your business or in your office space, consider these four things to organize your workspace:

1) Clear your desk.

Direct mail entrepreneur Joe Sugarman once wrote a book explaining his five rules for success. One of his five principles was, "End every day with a clean desk." He made this a rule throughout his organization. This policy forced all employees to work more efficiently and complete their work by the end of the day. It made a major contribution to success.

Brian Tracy in his book *Time Power* talks about how he introduced this rule into his company. He told everyone that they were expected to clean up their desks and leave them neat and orderly at the end of each day. When they argued with him, he told them that if they didn't follow this rule, he would go from office to office and throw away everything on their desks into a waste basket to be taken away that night. He said that he only had to follow through on this threat once before everyone realized that he was serious.

One of his managers (who was probably the messiest in his company) gave every excuse he could for working in a cluttered and chaotic environment. Brian refused to listen or compromise and after one week the manager came to him and apologized for being so argumentative. He said, "All my life, I have thought that I worked better in a messy environment. In the last week, I have accomplished two to three times as much as I ever accomplished at work before. I am absolutely astonished at how much more I get done when everything is put in its proper place throughout the day."

What kind of difference could cleaning up your office space mean to your productivity?

Here is a good exercise for you. Stand back from your desk or work area or if you are really brave your front desk that customers see when they enter your business.

Ask yourself: What kind of person works at that desk?

What kind of business has a desk or front counter like this?

Honestly evaluate yourself through the eyes of a neutral third party. What do you really see?

In a recent survey of senior executives, it was found that 50 out of 52 said they would not promote a person with a messy desk or a cluttered work environment. Even if that person was producing good work, these executives said they would not trust a position of responsibility to a person who could not get organized. We all can do better at this. Take some time to organize your office this week.

Make the change and everyone will see the difference.

2) Assemble everything you need before you start.

Just like a good cook gets out all of the necessary ingredients to prepare a dish before he or she begins, or a master craftsman arranges all of his tools, assemble all of the tools of your trade before you start working on a particular job. If you have to place an order with a manufacturer, be sure to have everything you need before you make the call. If your desk is clean and you are organized you'll be able to find everything so much faster and get it done so much quicker.

3) Handle paperwork that crosses your desk right the first time.

It is amazing how much clutter can occur just from stacking bills, mail, printed out emails, orders, Post-It Notes, etc. It is best to take action and handle papers only once as I've already mentioned.

If you choose to file something, ask yourself this question: "What would happen if I couldn't find this paper?" If the consequence is negligible, you may want to consider just tossing it.

It has been found that 80% of papers that are filed are never needed, used, or seen again. Don't create more clutter in your file cabinets just because you are filing.

If you do file things, be sure to have an organized way of filing things. A shocking statistic that I read is that as much as 30% of working time today is spent looking for misplaced items. These are things that have been lost because they have not been filed correctly. Strive to file documents electronically so that they are easier to search and find.

Create a system that works well for you. Throw away what you don't need. It is amazing how much stuff we accumulate. Several years ago, I visited my Grandfather's office after he passed away. It tooks years to organize and get rid of files that he accumulated his entire life. Don't let this happen to you. Throw away what you don't need.

4) Tear out pages of magazines and articles that you read and file them so that you can use them later. John Maxwell talks about how he has filed everyday for nearly 50 years and as a result he now has the material to write two books a year. Don't keep magazines lying around your office. Only keep what is valuable and then discard the rest. It will help you to stay much more organized and will give you the material you need to help you train your team. It will also be a good example to those you work with that you expect others to do the same.

20. Repurpose.

One way to get more done is to repurpose something that has already been done into a new format. For example, if you've written a special report, you could take that same content and use it again as a newsletter article, blog post, podcast episode, part of an Ebook, or even an email education campaign. Each of these uses may be seen by a different audience.

21. Visualize the completion of the task.

Your thinking must be positive, specific and detailed in order for you see and seize what you want. A great book that goes into a lot of detail about this subject is John Maxwell's book, *The Dream Test*.

Here are a couple of things that you ought to visualize each day:

• What kind of business you have (size, amount of sales, etc.)

• Doing what needs to be done to reach your daily goal (We will hit $_____ today – you can even visualize the amount showing up in your bank account the next day). When you imagine yourself doing what needs to be done in a successful, positive manner, you will be motivated to do it and make it happen.

• Your reasons (why you do what you do). As Brian Tracy said: "Reasons are the fuel in the furnace of achievement."

To visualize the completion of the task, expect the best of yourself and think positive thoughts about what you want to achieve. To visualize success, you've got to stop thinking negatively or thinking about failure. I would encourage you to go on a 21-day diet of watching or reading any kind of news. It wouldn't hurt to eliminate scrolling through social media posts for a week so you can see the difference in how you feel. Instead of filling your mind with the negative thoughts of others, fill your mind with ideas or things you can do to improve yourself and your business. Here are three suggestions to help you better visualize the completion of the task:

• Fill your mind with your own self-suggestions. Self-suggestion is an important part of self- motivation. So, fill your mind with thoughts such as: "I am cheerful." "I make things happens at my business." "I am the best salesperson in the world." "Every prospect I meet wants to buy our product from me on our first visit." "My business is successful and growing every day."

• Write positive quotes or thoughts on a 3 x 5 card, a little notebook, or as a note on an app on your phone. Carry it around with you and reflect on what you've written down or typed.

• Let go of your limitations. To move to a new area of growth, you've got to let go of what you were doing. This can be scary, but is essential. In baseball, you can't steal second base if you never take your foot off first base.

Visualizing what you don't want will hold you back and prevent you from accomplishing what you want. Instead, be clear about what you want, write it down and then mentally see yourself completing the task in front of you. Remember, you can't get to the next level without letting go of where you are now.

Feeling overwhelmed is a bad habit. It is easier to stop doing something because you get overwhelmed then it is to break down what needs to be done and work on it one step at a time.

I had a business coach who taught me this lesson. I was once in the process of learning a new design skill. It was challenging and I wasn't very good at it. My coach taught me: "I see you getting that glazed look in your eye. You've got to stop feeling overwhelmed. Look, I'll teach you how to do this, step by step, but if you can't get past this feeling of being overwhelmed, you'll never learn this skill."

That is great advice. None of us can get better at improving our business skills until we charge forward to learn the skill instead of making excuses for why we can't. All of us are busy. All of us have more to do than time to do it in. We all have the same 24 hours in a day.

If you want to implement more, you've got to choose your individual priorities and be committed to work on those items you've identified as most important each day. Focus on systems that will improve your business. Focus on priorities that pay big dividends. You can learn skills that aren't currently easy and do what you need to do to grow and get better. Breaking down your day into time blocks with start and end times has been so helpful to me and I know it will be for you as well.

I hope you've been inspired by these twenty-one proven ways in which you can implement more in your business. You can learn more about my productivity systems in chapter 16 of my book *The System is the Secret*. Remember, the difference between those with an average income and an exceptional income is implementation. Choose to be a finisher and an implementer. You can do it!

CHAPTER 10

AVOID DESTRUCTIVE MANAGEMENT MISTAKES THAT WILL HINDER AND STOP GROWTH

"There is nothing so useless as doing efficiently that which should not be done at all."
–Peter F. Drucker

Business owners and managers face numerous challenges in leadership in order succeed in business today. I personally have dealt with many of these challenges in my own businesses and I am frequently asked about what to do in certain situations by entrepreneurs and managers when they talk about the biggest headaches and nightmares they are dealing with on a daily basis.

Here are a few of the biggest nightmares and headaches business owners face that keep them up at night:

1) Negative reviews and the fear that they may turn off future customers and not feeling like you have any power to change them or make a difference (especially when they are false and untrue).

2) Dealing with lawsuits and insurance claims from someone who is hurt by your product or someone who falls and is injured in your business.

3) Dealing with employees (a whole book could be devoted to this topic). With all of the things there are to worry about, there are a lot of issues that stem from employees that cause a lot of business owners to lose sleep. Having employees walk out on your business on a busy day is something I've had to deal with and believe me, it is not a fun experience. This happened once when I was thousands of miles from my store in China and all of the employees left because they were upset at something their manager did. In addition, you sometimes have to deal with employees who steal from you by not working when they are on the clock, with the theft of cash from your business, or employees who've become burnt out and affect your productivity and results. Another issue is dealing with employees who leave and then file for unemployment. I once read a book that detailed the thirty riskiest employees to fire that detailed some pretty frightening scenarios.

4) Things you didn't plan on having to deal with – As an example, some retailers and businesses have told me that they have had to deal with credit card processing companies and chargebacks who are requesting additional insurances and security because another business in their industry has closed. These companies don't want to be left on the line dealing with chargebacks.

5) Discovering a brand new competitor or a giant in your industry is moving into your neighborhood and taking your business. I have visited numerous times with business owners who have had big competitors move in and who have taken much of their business. In some cases, these business owners haven't just lost sleep. They've lost their businesses. The emergence of web sites selling direct to the public and other Internet vendors continues to be a big concern as well. A company that can spend millions or billions of dollars to expand into a new market where you've been successful can advertise aggressively and take even more of

your business in the future.

7) Wondering or worrying about how you will make payroll for your employees or what you will have to do because you can't pay yourself (or you have to wait to pay yourself).

8) Finding out that a competitor has stolen your ideas and is profiting off of them.

9) Worrying about the amount of money you've put into your business <u>and</u> you aren't sure you'll ever see a return on your investment. On top of that, you may see businesses in your industry go out of business which causes you worry that this might be your future too.

10) Feeling that your business is consuming all of your time and is affecting your relationships with your loved ones.

11) Seeing sales decline and not knowing what to do about it.

12) Watching tried and true marketing practices that used to work and then finding out that they no longer do (especially when you spend money you don't really have).

13) Seeing other businesses in your industry that are doing better than you and feeling discouraged or depressed about it (not sure about what you should do).

14) Watching your expenses go up and wondering how this will affect your bottom line.

15) Worrying about employee theft of inventory or losing inventory to fire or destruction from other natural disasters.

16) Discovering that an employee you've trusted and depended on has burned out and is no longer working out for your business. Or, even worse, that they've decided to start their own business to compete with yours.

17) Loss of data from computer crash.

The list could and does continue. With just that list of potential nightmares, it could keep us all up worrying and wondering what to do. But, if you're going to overcome the fear of being paralyzed, you've got to feed your mind the right kinds of things and be focused on the positive. I really like this statement by Darren Hardy in his book *The Compound Effect.* He says:

"If you want your body to run at peak performance, you've got to be vigilant about consuming the highest-quality nutrients and avoiding tempting junk food. If you want your brain to perform at its peak, you've got to be even more vigilant about what you feed it....Controlling the input has a direct and measurable impact on your productivity and outcomes.

"Controlling what our brains consume is especially difficult because so much of what we take in is unconscious. Although it's true that that we can eat without thinking, it's easier to pay attention to what we put in our bodies because food doesn't leap into our mouths. We need an extra level of vigilance to prevent our brains from absorbing irrelevant, counterproductive or downright destructive input. It's a never-ending battle to be selective and to stand guard against any information that can derail your creative potential....Left to its own devices, your mind will traffic in the negative, worrisome, and fearful all day and night. We can't change our DNA, but we can change our behavior. We can teach our minds to look beyond 'lack and attack.' How? We can protect and feed our mind. We can be disciplined and proactive about what we allow in." –*The Compound Effect*, pp. 120-121.

If you are to succeed amidst the difficulties you face in running your business, you've got to get up and about the business of solving your challenges instead of being paralyzed by a seemingly endless myriad of management nightmares. You've got to be up and doing instead of getting bogged down by discouragement and difficulty.

My hope is that I can share with you some ideas and actions you can take to resolve several the most difficult and challenging management nightmares and headaches. Then, you can feed your mind with a positive approach to what can be done to overcome these situations when they come up for you.

Many business owners find comfort in talking about their problems when they get together. It is easy to whine, complain, and share bad news. It is even easier to accept mediocrity when you associate with others who are where you are or who are doing worse than you are. However, if you want to be the best, you've got to associate with those who are where you want to be.

All entrepreneurs face challenges as managers and leaders. The key to overcoming them is to focus on solutions instead of just venting about what you're frustrated and unhappy about. You can't beat resistance if you let yourself become overcome by it.

So, let's get into some solutions to fifteen of the most challenging management and leadership mistakes that you may be facing in your business.

1. Failing to pay attention to indicators or feelings of team members.

Finding and keeping great employees can be a challenge for even the most seasoned leader. Employees that are great today can burn out over time. A key skill that all leaders and managers must develop today is the ability to recognize key indicators that influence when a change should be made. With technology today, people are almost always accessible. This accessibility can prevent people from disconnecting from from stress and work. People need physical and mental breaks from work or they will burn out. Your ability to recognize and pay attention to the indicators and feelings of great employees who need a break will help you have greater retention and productivity from those who work around you.

I grew up around horses. My father has been a farrier, or horseshoer, for nearly sixty years. I learned a lot about horses growing up around them, but I learned the most by watching my dad interact with them. He was often brought in to help horses that had gone lame to get better, or to become sound. Horses go lame for many reasons and require the expertise of professional farriers and veterinarians to keep them performing at their best.

Dan Kennedy once observed: "I own racehorses. At any time, 15 to 20 of them. I have day-to-day, hands on personal contact with them. It is impossible not to form relationships with them, to bond more to some than others, to care about them, and to miss them when they leave the stable. Each horse has his own unique personality. Some are antisocial, but most are not only social but real characters. They are equine athletes, each trying his best to perform successfully. Most give it their all—for you. I also drive professionally in more than 100 harness races a year, and I always keep several of the racehorses to drive myself. With these, the bond can be even greater, as I and the horse are competing out there as a team. When I have retired horses, I have gone somewhere private and wept. There are several I miss often, even though they've been gone for years.

"With that said, they can never become pets. This is a business. They are professional equine athletes and I own the team. I must trade players, I must force players to retire, if I am to keep my team competitive and my business solvent. Beyond that, the ultimate truth of owning, training, and racing horses is: they ALL go lame. As the saying goes, it's not a question of if. It's a question of when....One way or another, at some point, they all go lame. If their lameness cannot be quickly and affordably resolved, then they must go." –*No BS Management of People and Profits*, pp. 39-40.

This is a hard lesson for many to learn and act on. It is hard to let someone go that you know well. The longer they have been with you, the tougher it is. I once had to replace three managers for different businesses over a period of two years. It wasn't fun. It involved tremendous heartache.

When an employee burns out, I've noticed three consistent themes. These are:

1) They ask for more money for their position without a corresponding increase in their own results.

2) They ask for more time off because they are exhausted and tired.

3) They find fault with other team members. They point fingers at others and their failings instead of recognizing their own.

When you see these three things, you know that a problem is looming. It is best to recognize these signs for what they are. You need to take action. In some cases, it means giving your leaders a break. In others, you must begin looking for those who can get you where you need to go.

I have had many conversations with business owners who have waited too long to make a change and then finally have done what needed to be done because they had no choice. It is better to have the courage to act before you have to. Only you can control what happens in your business with your employees and team.

Fred Smith makes this observation in his book *Learning to Lead*:

"No one wants a reputation as a hatchet man. But as a last resort, you must be willing to fire people or relieve them of a particular responsibility. It is more important for the staff to know that you will than that you do. It shows you are committed to your mission and are willing to prune those who will not contribute to it.....Whenever I am tempted not to act in a difficult personnel situation, I ask myself, 'Am I holding back for my personal comfort or for the good of the organization?' If I am doing what makes me comfortable, I am embezzling. If doing what is good for the organization also happens to make me comfortable, that's wonderful. But if I am treating irresponsibility irresponsibly, I must remember that two wrongs do not make a right." –pp. 103-104.

I really like that statement. Are you doing what makes you comfortable or are you doing what needs to be done for the good of your business? That is a good question to reflect on when you are struggling with a difficult decision about whether to keep someone or let them go.

Holding onto someone for too long who is burned out will cause you to burn out faster than anything else. You must replace those who are no longer contributing to your business. You will worry, feel stress more often, and worst of all, watch your results decline (which will cause even more stress and worry). Have the courage to recognize burnout for what it is and give your best leaders opportunities to take a break throughout the year to avoid burnout.

One of the biggest struggles I have dealt with has been around employees who have lost the energy, excitement and drive they once had. This has likely happened to you as well. You've got to watch this closely OR it will come back to haunt you.

Monitor performance and morale. Be aware of the moods and attitudes of your team members. Fill your team's motivation buckets with encouragement, praise, and helpful assistance. In other words, let them know how they are doing and help them when and where they need a helping hand.

Sam Walton, founder of Wal-Mart once observed: "Appreciate everything your associates do for the business. Nothing else can quite substitute for a few well-chosen, well-timed, sincere words of praise. They're absolutely free and worth a fortune."

It is so important to pay attention to the moods and attitudes of everyone around you.

Great managers know that most people's motivation buckets leak like a water bucket full of shotgun holes. The key is to be sure that you are filling their buckets with things that are important to each individual team member. This also means that you have to constantly be filling your own bucket or you won't have anything to pour into people.

Ineffective leaders who have lots of turnover are more like big, long dippers that reach in and constantly drain people's buckets. They do this by taking credit for the success of others and a long list of other behaviors that de-motivate rather than motivate.

Most of the frustrating experiences I felt when working for others came from this management blunder: taking credit for what I had contributed and constantly draining my motivation bucket.

Are you ever guilty of this?

Do you pay close attention to the feelings of your team members?

Do you know when you need to be encouraging and give a motivational training session and how to balance that with hitting the targets and goals you need to achieve?

This distinction is a fine line, but it is the difference between accomplishment and defeat, the difference between high morale and low morale. If you don't do this well, you will find that you are likely losing those around you.

John Maxwell in his book *Leadership Gold* makes this point:

"As leaders, we'd like to think that when people leave, it has little to do with us. But the reality is that we are often the reason. Some sources estimate that as many as 65 percent of people leaving companies do so because of their managers. We may say that people quit their job or their company, but the reality is that they usually quit their leaders. The company doesn't do anything negative to them. People do. Sometimes coworkers cause the problems that prompt people to leave. But often the people who alienate employees are their direct supervisors." --p. 145.

Pay more attention to the mood and feelings of each team member. This is especially true with millennials. You must understand what motivates them and help them to feel that they are a part of something that they can connect and contribute to in a meaningful way. If you try to manage people the same, you will fail. Learning to be a better leader and attracting people to you is a skill that you can develop and be better at in your business.

2. Losing control or influence with a project or team member.

This is a nightmare that many business owners don't want to admit or talk about. I once had this happen with a manager at one of my businesses. Since I wasn't always in the store, she sometimes made decisions with members of my staff that I didn't know about. The net result was that she ended up hiring a few individuals who were loyal to her (and who protected her) instead of being loyal to the business and to my wife and I. When I ended up firing her, I ended up losing our entire team and had to start hiring again from scratch. This was my fault because I was busy and wasn't paying enough attention to it as I should have.

If you want to have influence with members of your team, you've got to lead them by what you do and how you do it. You can't expect people just to follow you.

Let me give you several examples of indicators that you may have lost control in your business:

• You find that team members are protecting or covering for each other instead of talking with you about what is going on (showing up late, not doing what needs to be done, etc.)

• You go on a business trip and find out that your manager or assistant manager dealt with a situation in a way that you wouldn't have and they didn't consult you about it (and it cost you money)

• When vendors or individuals call, they don't talk to you but ask to speak to someone you've delegated. That is fine for them to be working together except for when you find out that the decision the two of them have made is something that impacts you in a negative way financially. For example, several years ago, I heard from a friend in the bridal business that they discovered that one of their employees was receiving inventory of dresses and then shipping them to another store and getting kickbacks from the store who was receiving the dresses. They were very upset when they found out this was happening. You can delegate things at your business, but you can't abdicate responsibility about what must be done. When a manager or assistant manager has to go into the back room to have a conversation with someone who is calling and they are nervous when you are there and they are talking on the phone, that is a big indication you need to be paying more attention to what they are doing. Nip problems in the bud before they become bigger challenges that could cause you to lose control of what is happening in your business.

• Some employees create black boxes around systems or processes that only they know about. You feel like you can't fire them because they are the only one who knows how to do something you've delegated to them. The truth is that you were the one who originally delegated out what needed to be done so you can learn it again and by getting involved in a process again (if you have to fire someone or if they choose to leave), you can get things back on track again.

The important lesson is this: You don't want to create an environment of fear, but it is critical that there is an environment of respect in your business where everyone knows what is expected and what they need to do.

I really like this advice and rule that Richard Goldstein, the chairman and CEO of International Flavors and Fragrances, Inc. shares about this: "It is important to keep in mind that empowering someone does not mean that you allow them to act in a vacuum. People who are empowered to do their jobs must also know when to seek the counsel of others. How do you know when to consult with others? It's simple. If the decision you are about to take is reversible, or if the cost—financial or otherwise—of a potential mistake is affordable, then I say go for it. If, on the other hand, the decision is irreversible and the cost of a potential error is considerable, then it is probably prudent to consult with others first." –*Leadership Secrets of the World's Most Successful CEOs*, p. 111.

So, how do you know whether you should be a control freak or trust others to take on new projects and assignments? Well, you've got to trust those you hire and give them the ability and authority to get things done, but they also must be accountable for results.

3. Overcoming resistance to initiating or implementing a new business strategy.

When changes are introduced, there is usually resistance, confrontation, or conflict that results. Most inexperienced leaders try to get their way by pushing through challenging issues with force and by pulling rank. This can alienate those whose help you need to succeed. When it doesn't work, they often give up and settle because they don't want to ruffle feathers or cause contention.

I've heard of this challenge from many entrepreneurs and managers over the years. They hear a great idea and then present it to their employees. Later, when asked how an idea is working, they say: "Well, no one at my business liked that idea" or "No one felt like that would work." As a result, no action is taken. Everyone resists doing something that is new for the first time. Yet, if you are to succeed in dealing with tough management issues, you must be willing to make a stand and confront those who aren't doing what you've asked them to do.

When you've dealt with difficulty with others, what do you do? Have you settled with some problems for too long? Are you ready to confront the tough issues and start making a difference? If so, you should follow the approach John C. Maxwell outlines in his book *Winning with People* on pages 111 through 116 which I will paraphrase here.

1) Tackle the problem head on.

2) Meet with those who can help you overcome the problem. If you need to confront someone about their poor performance, do it. Delaying the confrontation you don't want to have won't help you get where you need to be.

3) You may not find agreement, but that doesn't mean you can't come to an understanding of what needs to be done.

4) Let's say you've asked one of your team members to do something while you go out to run an errand. When you return, it hasn't been done. Instead of questioning that person's motives, you should tell him or her what you see and describe your feelings without accusation. Explain why what you asked to be done was so important to you and ask what came up that prevented it from getting it done. Then, encourage them to get it done. This approach works a lot better than saying, "Why isn't this done?" in an accusatory tone.

5) Give the individual you're meeting with a chance to respond to what they feel is going on. This will tell you a lot about the person you're leading. Do they realize there is a problem? Do they know what to do? Do they know how to do it? Is there something that is preventing them from taking action?

6) Once you have their perspective, agree to an action plan of what you want to make happen in the future. Agree on a way forward together. Then, outline what you will do together going forward. The biggest problem with confrontation without resolution or a way forward is that you will only be frustrated going forward. You've got to lead and have a vision of what you want to have happen.

Expectations are critically important. Everyone must understand what you expect.

Do each of your team members know what they are expected to do? Are they held accountable for what must be done? If not, there is a big disconnect here. No one wants to leave at the end of the day and feel like they haven't accomplished anything of significant value.

Each team member you hire has been hired to accomplish a task. Are you providing them with the tools to help them excel at their profession? Do you know what holds them back and what they can change to be more successful in their efforts? I recently had a conversation with a friend of mine who told me that she felt extremely frustrated in her job because she was hired, but wasn't trained on what she was supposed to do. She had ideas, but didn't feel like anyone really cared to hear what she had to say and more importantly wasn't receiving any help to implement those ideas or better reach the goals of the business. Don't make this mistake. When you hire someone for a specific role, make sure they have what they need to succeed.

One of the most impressive ideas I got from the book *Good to Great* by Jim Collins is that you need to put your best people on your biggest opportunities, not your biggest problems. Prior to starting our first business, I had a boss who consistently put me on solving problems within the business (instead of going out and developing new business and selling more – which was where my strength and passion really was). I eventually quit the company because I didn't enjoy being drug down by seemingly unsolvable problems (that I didn't have any real authority to solve anyway). I have thought about this big lesson with those I have hired and worked with since. I strive to look for areas of strength and make assignments or delegate tasks where I feel that individual will have the biggest impact. This element of work life is so important. People want to do what they already do well instead of constantly be asked to do something they don't like or don't do well.

Adrian Gostick and Chester Elton report this shocking statistic in their book *The Invisible Employee*:

"An astounding 65 percent of Americans reported receiving no recognition for good work in the past year." They also quote a study conducted by *The New York Times* which reported that:

- 25% of employees reported being driven to tears in the workplace

- 50% call their place of work a place of 'verbal abuse' and 'yelling'

- 30% are regularly given unrealistic deadlines

- 52% have to work 12-hour days to get their work done." --*The Invisible Employee*, p. xiv.

I really feel very strongly about the power of encouragement and recognition. I worked for a short time for a man who never encouraged me and who took credit for my work. I despised the work environment. I have never forgotten how I felt. As a result, I constantly want to praise and recognize the work of our excellent team members. Ask yourself: When was the last time you praised one of your team members? Resolve to do this more often.

When you genuinely care about your team members, they will work harder with you to accomplish the goals you've set. If they don't feel like you really care about them, they won't give their all.

For the most part, people want to be better. They just rarely encounter someone who cares enough to help them become what they want to be. Years ago, a former employee wrote and expressed appreciation for the training she received when she worked for my wife and I. She told me that since she worked for us, she hadn't had a single boss who took the time to help her learn new things or who really encouraged her personal development.

Have the courage to ask for the opinions of others. Everyone loves to feel heard and you can facilitate this by asking for feedback before or after training meetings. Ask your leaders what they feel is a topic that is most important for you to address. It is so valuable to hear their input and I believe everyone will appreciate and value your training more as a result.

Make sure you build a team whose members are *all* committed to doing the work. There is nothing more discouraging than being around someone who isn't accomplishing much. Top performers don't like being around mediocrity. If you can ensure that they are in an environment that rewards quality work and doesn't appreciate mediocre work, they are motivated to achieve more and accomplish more as a result. If you keep someone who isn't selling well, what message does that send to the rest of the members of your team? If you are never evaluating the performance of those you work with, you are sending a message that growth and progress really aren't that important to you. Be sure you emphasize and reward what you want repeated.

4. Getting everything done with limited resources is challenging. To succeed, every member of your team must be in sync.

These days it seems like everyone has to do more with less. This is a big management challenge that keeps a lot of people up at night worrying or wondering how they will do this.

I've always been impressed with Michael Dell of Dell Computers. Years ago, I read this statement about his management philosophy and it really impressed me.

"When Michael Dell promotes employees, he gives them fewer responsibilities, not more. That may sound wacky, but the strategy—which Dell calls 'job segmentation'—has been key to ensuring his company's growth hasn't led to flameout. Dell says: "When a business is growing quickly, many jobs grow laterally in responsibility, becoming too big and complex for even the most ambitious, hardest-working person to handle without sacrificing personal career development or becoming burned out."—*Business Leaders and Success*, p. 135.

If you're going to get everything done that you've got to do in your business, you've got to bring the best efforts out of individual team members. The ability of a team to work in harmony and in an synchronized effort is a goal that is worth striving for. How do you synchronize the efforts of so many different personalities so you can get everything done even if you just have a few team members who are helping you out? This is a great question and one I have thought about often. I am reminded about this principle when I watch the Olympic sport of synchronized swimming.

David Cottrell says: "Synchronized swimming, an Olympic sport since 1984, has always fascinated me. The only way to describe it is to call it upside-down ballet. It's beautiful to watch but also very demanding for swimmers, requiring fitness, stamina and flexibility...As I've watched synchronized swim competitions, I've wondered how a team can stay perfectly in sync, especially when the team is performing upside-down and underwater—neither of which is natural for most human beings. Yet Olympic-caliber synchronized swim teams work in unison to create a breathtaking performance. On world-class synchronized swim teams, each member must clearly understand every nuance of the choreography. All members must also know their individual roles, when to perform each move, and how each of them personally contributes to and affects the entire team's performance. When every swimmer is in sync, the performance can be spectacular. But if even one team member were ever out of sync, chaos would result."

Cottrell continues: "The same thing happens in business. Synchronization is absolutely fundamental to your organization. When all elements of your organization are in sync, its performance can be energizing, spectacular, and profitable. But without synchronization—if even one aspect of the organization is out of sync—people lose focus and stagnate. Before you know it, forward movement comes to a halt. The result can be chaotic—and often unprofitable too!" –*Monday Morning Motivation*, pp. 53-54.

I've thought a lot about this challenge. It is amazing what you can do when everyone is working together toward a common goal and conversely, it is astonishing how quickly momentum can be lost when a few decide to do their own thing at the expense of someone else on the team. When this has happened in our business on two different occasions, we had to fire those who were doing their own thing (because it caused a lot of stress amongst the other employees who were focused on what was happening as a part of the team goal). In one case, a top selling sales consultant started stealing sales of other consultants and claiming that they were hers. In the other case, one of the consultants started talking behind the back of another consultant about how terrible she was and tried hard to get her fired. Her real motivation was to eliminate another good seller so that she could rise quicker and sell more. In both cases, the drama that accompanied these situations caused a loss of momentum and obviously disrupted the synchronicity of our team efforts that we had been experiencing in a big way.

From these experiences, I've realized that the best way to get your team working together is to have a combination of individual goals and team goals. Simplify what you expect of each member of the team (based on their individual skill level and contribution) and reward what will help you get the greatest results.

Are your objectives clear? Does each team member understand what their key objectives are and how they can accomplish them?

If not, it shouldn't be a surprise that they have a hard time sticking to them over a period of time. When the objective isn't clear, confusion usually reigns. I once worked for a company where the CEO would come to us each and every week and give us a new objective. One week, he wanted us to focus on selling one product and then the next month, he wanted us to focus on selling something different. It created a lot of confusion amongst the sales team. I eventually went to him and told him that I could get a lot more done if I could just focus on one product area that I was really good at selling. I recommended and said that it would benefit the team if they could be separated into different areas of specialization and focus instead of trying to be great at selling everything. As a result, we broke into specialized groups and saw our overall revenues increase.

If you are experiencing ups and downs in your business, think about how a strategy of specialization could help you and your team to focus on your most important priorities (and the most profitable areas of your business).

Albert Einstein once said, "If you can't explain it simply, you do not understand it well enough."

Do you know what your area of specialty is? Do each of your team members? Are they well trained within that specialty to successfully accomplish the tasks you have given them? How are you rewarding team members for what they accomplish?

We often have team goals where everyone on the team benefits when we hit certain optimal targets. For example, a bonus offered for everyone on the team when optimal goals are reached can be a great incentive. Allow members of your team to be highly motivated not only by the rewards of their individual performance, but also by the rewards they can receive if they each do their individual parts to make the team goal happen. When each team member is working in sync, it is amazing what happens.

Is your team working in sync or is it in chaos? As the leader, you're the one who controls the direction and the velocity in which your business moves forward. If what you want and what your team is doing is not in alignment, you must change direction and get back in sync. Then, you'll be able to accomplish what you originally set out to do.

5. Getting so caught up in putting out present fires that you don't take time to think about your direction and where you are heading in the future.

If you're going to grow your business while dealing with management nightmares that keep you up at night, you've got to spend more time thinking about the future and what is happening in your business. Then, you've got to take action towards the opportunities you see instead of spending all of your time putting out fires and dealing with the present difficulties you are facing.

How often do you spend time planning your day?

How well do you think through what needs to be done in advance?

Everyone can benefit from spending more time planning, yet it is easy to make excuses about why you don't have time to do so. You must make the time. Start before anyone else arrives, don't answer the phone, and think on paper about the upcoming events you have, the challenges you're facing with your team, how to bring more prospects into your marketing funnels, how to sell more, etc.

When people get busy, they tend to wing things. The first thing we typically stop doing is taking time to think and to plan. To be a great leader and manager, you need to set your vision and articulate it to others. If you don't articulate what is important to you, you will get distracted and lose focus. You may know what your priorities are and they may be something you think about all of the time, but if you don't talk about them and help those you work with understand what is important to you, they likely won't act on your priorities.

Bob Boylan tells this story:

'Walt Disney was walking through Disney World before its completion, with a small group of his department heads. Suddenly he stopped, pointed to a specific area, and said, 'I want 10,000 fireflies over there!'

The head of construction asked, 'When?'

Notice that the man did not say, 'But, Walt, where could I possibly find 10,000 fireflies?' or 'Wouldn't 5,000 be sufficient?'

He then makes this point:

"Perfection, absolute top quality, was the value here. Just do it, please. The man said, 'When?' No second guessing, just 'when?' He understood that for Mr. Disney, perfection was the value—a value the man himself obviously also bought into.

In order to have this fit, however, it's important that your potential followers understand your values—what's important to you. You need to clearly define this for them. That's the first step." --pp. 15-16.

How do the members of your team know what's important to you?

Do you clearly articulate your vision so everyone understands their priorities or is this vague and confusing to those who work in your store?

Bob Boylan makes this interesting observation:

"In most organizations, few employees can answer the question, 'Where are we headed?' In fact, a recent Booz, Allen & Hamilton study revealed that only 37 percent of senior officials think other key managers clearly understand business goals.

"Well, that's not so good. However, it's normal. How does this happen? Because no clear direction has been established by the leader.

"Or if one has been established, it hasn't been communicated forcefully, or memorably, enough for people to know where they are headed." --p. 45.

He continues: "Vision is the second step to leadership. Without it, there is no focus. A good vision grabs. Its passion helps transform purpose— where you want to be—into action almost automatically."--p. 50.

Do you know where your business is headed in the future?

Have you communicated that vision with everyone around you or do others feel that you are just trying to hold on to what you've currently got?

That is a brutally tough question – but one that is important to ask –

because it indicates what you are communicating about where you are headed.

If you bumped into a person on an elevator who could help you achieve your goals, how would you describe your business and what you stand for in thirty seconds? How would you act? Would you mumble out an answer or clearly articulate where you are headed?

If you can't clearly articulate what you stand for, those around you won't be able to do so either. Know and clearly articulate what you stand for.

Where are you heading? Where do you want to end up? These are important questions that you must take time to stop and think about. In all of the hustle and bustle of your business, are you taking time to readjust your direction and get on track to where you want to go? If not, you will likely end up in a much different place than what you thought when you started.

My encouragement to you is to take a half day or a day each month when you sit down and think. Get away from the business and turn off your cell phone. Be somewhere where you won't be interrupted. Think about and plan your future by projecting yourself five years into the future. Imagine your business is exactly where you want it to be (it is perfect in every way). What does it look like? Write down your answers to the following questions:

- What is my take home income?

- What is our business gross revenue?

- What is our net revenue?

- What reward will I give myself if we hit our goals?

- What would I have to start doing now in order to make this vision a reality?

- What do I need to stop doing?

By taking the time to go through this exercise, you will put yourself in the top 5% of business owners in your industry. It is time for you to be proactive about what you want from your business.

6. Keeping your team focused on your daily, weekly and monthly goals without losing morale (especially when numbers are down).

When goals aren't reached it affects everyone on your team. In order to beat these discouraging moments, you've got to bounce back and bounce back quickly.

Stop beating yourself up over the past. When, you've missed a goal, take these three steps: 1) reset, 2) refocus, 3) recommit.

There comes a moment of truth when you bring up what isn't working and talk about it with those on your team. You have to put the challenges you're facing in context by helping them realize the past is past and that today is a new day and the time to focus on what you will be done today that can be controlled. I've found that having a contest, a spiff, or a bonus for hitting a certain goal can also spark and renew excitement to get everyone believing again.

To hit your goals, you've got to pay attention to them daily. You've got to look towards the future. Most owners are so busy reacting to what happens in their businesses day by day, that they don't take time to proactively set goals and determine where they really want to be. As a result, they end up in a different place than they thought they would.

If you want to be a BIG success in any business, you have to take the time to plan out where you are going and what you will say "no" to in order to get there. In other words, you have to be so clear on what you will do that you will not be distracted from anything that will prevent you from getting there in the quickest amount of time.

That doesn't happen without time and focus. Take time each week to think about your goals and the future of your business.

When you find yourself in a crisis, review the ideas I discuss in chapter 14 of *The System is the Secret* for Crisis Management Systems. When you're in the midst of a crisis, you've got to take the initiative and get the buy-in from your team to pull out of a nosedive and land prior to taking off again.

Think more about your opportunities. You may find it works best to schedule a half day once a month to go to a secluded spot where you can't be interrupted. If you don't schedule time to think, you'll be directed in areas that aren't where you want to go.

Don't just get bogged down in the crisis. Lay out a plan, get busy, and start again. Stay focused on the results you seek. Nothing beats low morale like success.

7. Know how to delegate. If something isn't done that you've delegated, recognize the opportunity to train, teach, and begin again.

As your business grows, you get busier with administrative issues. By delegating these out, you are able to take more time to think and act on big picture items that will help you get where you want to go.

If what you've delegated didn't get done, it is due to one of two reasons:

1) You didn't do it right – the person you delegated the project to didn't clearly understand what was to be done.

2) The person you delegated it to couldn't complete it for a lack of skill or motivation (they weren't the right person to delegate it to in the first place), or they just didn't have enough time with everything else they're already doing.

When delegating:

• Explain clearly your expectations

• Have a deadline when you expect it to be completed

• Ask for frequent updates

• If the deadline isn't met, reset it, re-explain what is to be done and delegate it again

• If you've made a mistake in who you've delegated the task to, you can take it back or you can choose to better train the person you assigned to do what you wanted done.

When you make a mistake with delegation, admit it and move on.

8. Know when to hire a manager and divide up roles. Put the right parameters in place to ensure that such a transition goes smoothly.

When you need more help, I've found these steps are helpful in determining who the leader should be, and how you should make that transition:

1) Identify what needs to be done.

2) Consider who would be best at the job.

3) Divide out responsibilities appropriately.

4) Demand accountability and results.

5) Watch and learn from who rises above your expectations.

6) Ask for daily and weekly reports.

You've got to stay connected and keep everyone on your team up to speed with changes that are being made. One question I've been asked often: What do you do when members on your team say they are too busy to send you a status update of the critical success factors that you want to measure?

You've got to explain why their report is so important. They've got to be accountable to reporting in and letting you know what they've done. If they're too busy consistently, you need to sit down and figure out what is preventing them from doing it. Maybe some responsibilities need to be shifted around.

Learn to delegate. If you don't, you'll kill yourself or go crazy.

J. Willard Marriott said: "Don't do ANYTHING someone else can do for you."

Most entrepreneurs really resist this. They are afraid to let anyone else do something because they are afraid it might not be done right.

The reason you don't delegate more is NOT the talent level of your team. It is because of you. If you have employees who can't do the work, that is your fault. If you don't trust them, that falls on you as well. If they are not properly trained, guess what, it's you again.

Start delegating. Here is how to do it.

• Determine what to delegate – many times it isn't delegated properly because we don't understand what we want done clearly ourselves.

• Adjust for the individual – follow up accordingly

• Explain the 'big' picture

• Set expectations

Make sure your team member / manager / receptionist / marketing assistant, etc. reports back – if they haven't completed the task properly – reassign them and allow them to finish the task

Don't take the work back – consider delegating anything that someone can do 70% as well as you. This will allow you to focus on higher level tasks that others can't do as well as you.

Ask:

• What have I been doing that I could be delegating (to free up more time to work on more high priority activities)?

• What are your highest value activities?

• What am I doing right now that someone else could do?

• What can ONLY I do?

If you want to successfully manage and market your way through today's economy, you have to better manage your business and team members. When you do so, you will find your efforts synchronized and you'll accomplish more together than you ever could on your own.

If you're going to get better results from each member of your team, you've got to understand what drives or motivates them. Dwight Eisenhower once observed: "Leadership is the art of getting someone else to do something you want because he [or she] wants to do it."

Here are several ways you can motivate and inspire those around you at your business:

• Involve your team in major decisions.

• Listen to them—they often have the best ideas.

• Know about them and members of their families.

• Listen more to what is important to them. Many times people will motivate themselves if you just ask great questions and listen.

• Give thank you notes and gift cards out to those on your team who really go the extra mile. Notice the little things that others do to make your customers smile and reward them accordingly.

• Assign your best performers to become mentors to those who may be struggling. Let them help struggling team members fill their motivation buckets by helping them succeed.

• Give your team access to helpful training materials. Training is an ongoing process. Have a library at your business of books, online training courses, and articles that can inspire them to fill their own motivation buckets.

• Let your team know how they are doing towards achieving your goals. Have group rewards when you reach your goals on a monthly, quarterly, or yearly basis.

One of the best things you can do to inspire and motivate your team members is to catch them doing things right. As you encourage and recognize the accomplishments of those around you, morale and performance will improve, especially if you tie the recognition to the accomplishment of critical success factors that will help you reach your goals.

As Thomas Jefferson once said: "Nothing can stop the man [or woman] with the right mental attitude from achieving his [or her] goal; nothing on earth can help the man [or woman] with the wrong mental attitude."

Catch your team doing things right and reward them accordingly. Be sure you are rewarding results and accomplishments and not just activity. Being present at work is not the same thing as consistently performing and getting results at a high level during work.

Remember, the things that get rewarded get done so be sure you are rewarding accomplishment and not just activity in your business.

9. Be decisive. Don't take too long to solve a problem, make a decision, or resolve a conflict.

In my book *The System is the Secret*, I outline four types of challenges that come up in a business. These are:

1) Anticipated Changes - these could include situations where:

• You know you need to add additional inventory at certain times of year.

• You know an employee will be leaving because of a move, pregnancy, etc.

• You know what months are slowest in your business so you can prepare ahead to market for these slower times.

• You know when you are busting at the seams and need additional space to take care of the new customers coming in (if you're growing at 25% a year or more, you'll will need more room soon).

2) Sudden & Unexpected Changes - these could include situations where you have:

• A key employee who decides to leave or has to leave because you've fired them for incompetence

• A call from your credit card processing company to inform you that they will be freezing your merchant account preventing you from accessing funds

• Just realized that an employee has been stealing from you or that inventory has been stolen from you over a period of time.

• A situation where your computer crashes and you lose your computer data.

3) Crisis (Forced on You Changes) - these could include situations where:

• You have a cash flow crunch and discover that you may not be able to make payroll or you'll have to cut your own payroll to make things work.

• Customer service issues come up that cost you money and your reputation.

• You have any type of crisis involving members of your family .

• You get a negative review online from a customer that causes you stress (especially when it is wrong and not true)

• You see your expenses go up without a corresponding increase in sales.

4) Competitive Changes - these could include situations where you discover that:

• A big competitor or industry giant just acquired one of your biggest customers or will be moving into your area.

• A competitor starts to offer a product that you've been doing well with and starts taking sales away from your business.

• A key employee leaves to work for one of your competitors.

• A competitor is copying something that you are doing that is working for you.

• A competitor bad mouths you online.

When any of these situations or challenges of any kind (especially when you or one of your team has made a mistake that will cost you money), it is best to ask yourself the following ten questions so you can get the facts:

1) What is the situation exactly?

2) What has happened from different perspectives?

3) How did it happen?

4) When did it happen?

5) Where did it happen?

6) What are the facts?

7) How do we know that these facts are accurate?

8) Who was involved?

9) Who is responsible for doing (or not doing) the things that set in motion the challenge we are facing today?

10) What can be done to ensure that this situation doesn't happen in the future?

It is helpful to ask these questions because sometimes we make assumptions that get us into trouble before we know all of the facts. It is best to question your assumptions, determine what would happen if they were wrong before making any concrete decisions about doing something different.

On more difficult decisions, consult with your inner circle or management team to advise you in the key actions you should take. You may seek help from an outside source on more dramatic challenges that you face. After getting the information together, make and stand by your decision.

If you are still worried ask yourself, "What prevents me from seizing this opportunity or making this decision?" Then, act and do what needs to be done. Leadership is about making tough decisions.

Look for others to help you and move forward. You don't have to face your challenges alone.

Remain in control even when things become challenging. Tom Landry, former football coach of the Dallas Cowboys, made this great observation: "Leadership is a matter of having people look at you and gain confidence, seeing how you react. If you're in control, they're in control."

People watch what you do and then adapt their behavior to match what they see. When your words and actions aren't congruent, people are more likely to follow the behaviors of what they see.

Lead by example and be decisive. Failing to take action when action must be taken is a recipe for disaster. It is easy to lose focus on what really matters and concentrate on the most urgent things instead. This mistake happens when you get bogged down on your biggest problems, not your biggest opportunities.

Make sure you are saying no to the things that can distract you. Remember, the things that distract you from making the critical decisions in your business aren't necessarily bad – but the problem is that over time you drift away from what really matters.

10. Condoning incompetence. Refuse to accept mediocrity.

Why do business owners or managers allow incompetence? It is usually because of one of two reasons:

1) They hope it will go away if it is ignored.

2) They are afraid or unwilling to confront others who have made a serious mistake.

If you see someone doing something that you don't like in your business, here are seven steps to how you should confront the problem:

1) Bring it up immediately. If you ignore it or wait to get to it later, you probably never will. Inaction will condone the behavior you don't really want. Dick Vermeil, former NFL coach of the Kansas City Chiefs and Philadelphia Eagles once observed: "To not confront poor execution and behavior is to endorse it. To not reinforce good execution and behavior is to extinguish it."

2) Discuss the issue in private. Never, ever confront someone in a public area where others are privy to what you are discussing. The basic rule is this: criticize in private, praise in public.

3) Control your own emotions. When we are angry, our blood leaves our brain. This is a natural instinct since the flight or fight response reroutes blood to the limbs to run away or fight. When the blood leaves our brain, we don't think very well. As a result, we may say things that we don't mean. If you get upset, step away from the situation until you can regain control of your emotions.

4) Be specific about the behavior or action that you did not agree with. Document the issues that have been on your mind and share specific details about the action you disapprove of.

5) Be clear about the standard (what you expect).

6) Set goals for a new direction. This is the most important part of your discussion. Express your confidence that they can do what needs to be done.

7) Schedule a follow-up visit to review their progress.

Those who are competent have the following four characteristics:

1) They are committed to excellence.

2) They never settle for average.

3) They refuse to be mediocre.

4) They pay attention to detail.

The best members of your team will perform with consistency. To be successful, you need A players and competent professionals to surround you. Never condone incompetence.

11. Forgetting your role as a leader. You'll usually regret decisions if you are trying to be a buddy, not a boss.

David Cottrell once observed: "If your goal is to get everyone to like you, you will avoid making tough decisions because of fear of upsetting your friends."

I can't tell you how many times I have heard business owners and managers tell me about difficult problems they have because of this issue.

When you act decisively and treat everyone the same with regard to your expectations, you are much more likely to have long-term effectiveness as a manager. Making exceptions for one individual will soon lead to making exceptions to others and pretty soon there will be absolute chaos with your system of rules and procedures.

One of the worst things that can happen to your authority as a leader is when a team member becomes a great friend and then starts taking advantage of that relationship. It starts innocently enough, but pretty soon they start showing up late for work, goofing off instead of working, and stretching the standard you have set. They expect you to look the other way since you are friends.

When this happens, you have to get over your personal emotions and do what is best for the business and let that person go. It is okay to be friendly with everyone who works with you and for you, but you can't let others on your staff feel like you give preferential treatment to one person over another.

The longer you prolong such a decision, the tougher it will be on you and on them. Part of being a leader is making tough decisions and making them in a timely fashion. Don't postpone for years what you know you should have done earlier because you are afraid of upsetting your buddy, instead of being the boss.

The most important part of hiring someone is to define the relationship (between you and them) when they are first hired. Many business owners have hired friends, relatives, or family before. If you choose to hire a friend or family member, remember that you will have to choose at some point between being their boss and their buddy. It is very difficult to be both and have a relationship that others on your team will respect and not resent.

The Bottom Line: treat everyone the same. It does not matter if the employee is a janitor or your star salesperson, a receptionist or the one in charge of your marketing; everyone at your business should be treated the same when it comes to adhering to published policies and your performance expectations.

12. Not establishing standards and sticking to them.

Jim Collins in his book *Good to Great* makes this great point about the importance of standards and sticking to them. He says:

"The good-to-great companies probably sound like tough places to work—and they are. If you don't have what it takes, you probably won't last long. But they're not ruthless cultures, they're rigorous cultures. And the distinction is critical. To be ruthless, means hacking and cutting, especially in difficult times, or wantonly firing people without any thoughtful consideration. To be rigorous means consistently applying exacting standards at all times and at all levels, especially in upper management. To be rigorous, not ruthless, means that the best people need not worry about their positions and can concentrate fully on their work." --p. 52.

One of the benefits of having standards and sticking to them is that everyone rises to the standard or they don't. This makes it easier for you to make adjustments in your personnel if someone is not hitting the standard.

There are two parts of this: one is actually setting a standard and two is making sure that you stick with the standards. If you don't stick with your standard, pretty soon it becomes meaningless and can be demotivating to the people who actually do reach it, especially if there is no consequence for those who don't.

I like what Jim Collins says:

"The only way to deliver to the people who are achieving is to not burden them with the people who are not achieving." --p. 53.

You can set standards for:

• Sales per hour

• # of sales per day, per week, per month, per quarter

• # of new leads created

• # of outbound phone calls made each day

• # of new accounts created / converted

• Sending out a thank you card for every purchase made

• Getting a testimonial from every customer you sell to

• Any other number that will help you better track results.

The key is to look at the critical success factors that you know lead to a sale and then measure and reward those activities.

Another big area where you need to have standards is to prevent time theft, which is becoming a bigger problem all of the time.

I really like this statement by author and speaker Dan Kennedy:

"In the workplace, people need to grasp that they are there to work... whatever they're doing is your business as long as they are doing it at your business on your business's clock."

I'm not trying to be rude, but the point is that your business is a workplace that should be a place of work and productivity, not spending time on the Internet and texting friends.

If you have employees who would rather spend time working on their projects rather than working on the business of selling and helping your prospects and customers, it is time to replace those individuals with those who will help you and the other members of your team get the work of each day completed.

No one wants to pick up the slack of those who are ineffective or unproductive. Do yourself and those you work with a favor and let go of those who will not comply with the standards you've set.

David Cottrell makes this point: "The single greatest 'demotivator' of a team is to have members who are not carrying their load. It takes courage to address issues honestly and then let people go when that's necessary. Your emotions are involved, the employee's short-term livelihood is involved, and it is a tough conversation to have. But, if you have provided someone every opportunity for success and yet his [or her] performance fails to meet expectations, summon your courage and allow him [or her] to go where he [or she] can be successful. It is not a personal mistake of yours, nor is it the employee's mistake—the job is just not right for him [or her]."--p. 47.

When everyone understands and follows the rules, it is amazing how much more productive you really are.

Bill Glazer, a mentor of mine who once owned two successful menswear stores in Baltimore, Maryland makes this statement about the importance of measuring everything that is important at your store and then posting it for all to see:

"Think about what happened the last time you went to a professional baseball game. The first batter walked to the plate and the big electronic screen posted his name and all his relevant statistics. It gave you his batting average, how many home runs he had hit, how many games he had played, and a host of other statistical information.

Why did they do that?

For one thing, it is a way for the people in the stands to evaluate the quality of the player.

Also, it serves as a motivation for the batter. Don't you think that he wants to have really great personal statistics up there on a huge screen for thousands of people to see, including his manager, his fellow players, and the team owner? If he has pride, it's got to motivate him to try to do better.

Most entrepreneurs and people in management don't really know how well [individual team members] are doing. For example, when I was in retail, I found that most retail store owners would track each of their salesperson's sales. That's good, but it's not enough.

The only way you are going to find out is by measuring everything that's important.

Some people think that's wrong. They don't measure much of anything. They tell people, "Just go out there and do the best job that you can."

That's wrong.

It's wrong because doing the best job that you can may not be good enough. Just like in baseball. If everyone on the team is batting between .225 and .310, a .115 player is not going to be in the lineup even if he is doing the best job he can.

That's why you need to measure everything that's important.

Think of all of the different things that, when measured, can give the result you want and exactly what is acceptable performance."—*No B.S. Management of People and Profits*, pp. 177-178.

He continues:

"Every day at my retail stores we posted our EPR (Employee Productivity Report). We wanted to know how everyone was doing, and equally important, we wanted the salespeople to know how they were performing."

He listed 15 different categories. These are:

• % OF TOTAL DAY: The percentage of the total sales that every salesperson sold for each specific day.

• $ DAY: The dollar amount that the salesperson sold each day.

• UNITS: How many items the salesperson sold each day.

• RECEIPTS: How many different receipts the salesperson generated each day.

• AVERAGE SALE: The average amount of each of the salesperson's transactions.

• UPT: The average number of units of each transaction.

• AVG DAILY $: The average amount of each sale for each day.

• PROJ. 4 WEEKS: Based on the salesperon's performance to date, what his projected sales volume would be.

• KIT PHONE: How many 'Keep-in-Touch' phone contacts the salesperson made that day with his previous customers and how many appointments he made. (NOTE: More than 30% of our sales were by appointment…in a menswear store).

• KIT WRITE: How many 'Thank-You' notes the salesperson wrote that day to customers who recently purchased from her.

• KIT APPS: How many appointments showed up for that salesperson that day.

• KIT APPS $: How much total sales the appointments generated for that day.

• EMAIL: How many email addresses the salesperson gathered that day.

• REFERRALS: How many referrals the salesperson received from her clients that day.

• CC: How many store credit card accounts the salesperson opened that day.

I modified these for our bridal store and measured fifteen areas of productivity and have coached many retailers to do the same. Here are these fifteen areas:

1) % of Total Day's Sales

2) Sales / Day

3) Sales / Hour

4) # of Dresses Sold

5) # of Accessories Sold

6) Average Sale Amount

7) UPT (Units per Transaction)

8) # of Phone Calls to Brides

9) # of Thank You Notes

10) # of Appointments who Came to Store

11) # of Pre-Sales Activities (preparing the next day's appointments)

12) Email Addresses Gathered

13) # of Referrals Received

14) # of Written Testimonials Received

15) # of Video Testimonials Received

As you implement any version of a measurement program, you will probably have the experience that he and I and most likely you have had as well. He says:

"When we first put this program into effect, it met a lot of resistance. Salespeople told us that it wasn't right for other people to see their performance. Funny thing was that these were the same salespeople who had lower performance.

We found that in a short period of time, two very interesting things happened.

First, we experienced some turnover by the underperforming salespeople. These were the same people who should have gone. They were not the right fit for the job.

Second, the performance of the salespeople who remained rose significantly. What we discovered was that good salespeople are naturally competitive. They'll try to be the top in each category measured. The chart that we posted showed each of the 15 categories of statistics was updated daily and was right outside my office. Every day our sales associates walked by, stopped, and studied the chart. They liked it because they knew exactly how they were doing and where they stood."--p. 179-181.

Remember, you must inspect what you expect. Measuring performance in key areas will help you achieve your goals faster than trying to control results.

13. Failing to evaluate performance and train for improvement.

One of the most important things you do as as a leader is to evaluate how well team members are doing at their jobs.

Jim Collins in his book *Good to Great* says: "Managing your problems can only make you good, whereas building your opportunities is the only way to become great."

One of the most important opportunities to manage is the performance of each of your team members. Part of this is setting a standard of performance for the job you hire them to do. People will rise to your expectations. What do you expect?

Create an expectation and hold team members accountable to reaching their daily and weekly goals.

As the old saying goes, "If you can't measure it, you can't manage it."

Be sure you're investing in the training of those who will help you make your business work day in and day out.

Even if you are a small business and you are the only person who works in it, it is vital to ask yourself: How much do I invest in myself, my training, and my development?

Many business owners and managers justify not putting much time and effort into training by asking: "What if I train this individual and they leave?"

Instead, the question that should be asked is: What if I don't train this individual and they stay?

Training and developing those on your team especially in the area of selling is the best way to ensure improved sales, profits, and market share. Poorly trained sales consultants often want to be more effective but just don't know how. When you give employees the tools they need to be more effective—through training—you help them, but you also help your business.

Here are several benefits of training. Training can:

• Improve loyalty of your team. When you train someone, you show that you care about them. Train members on your team with the belief that the things you are teaching and training them will help them through their lives, not just while they work for your business.

• Improve morale.

• Reduce turnover since those who are better trained and equipped to succeed will make more and will be even more excited about working with you

• Reduce sales costs because you have a higher close ratio

• Reduce hiring costs over time

• Improve communication at all levels (everyone will know what to do)

• Improve the loyalty of your customers because of the experience they have with someone who is properly trained

The only time training is really a cost (instead of a powerful investment) is when it isn't done very well, it is done too late (after a mistake costs you money), or when it isn't consistent or reinforced. We need to be reminded more than we need to be instructed.

How do you know if you have had an effective training meeting? The answer can be summed up in two words: Performance improves.

Meetings tend to be very ineffective and uninspiring if you try to cover too much in too little time and if you consistently have ineffective meetings.

Here are five suggestions to help you have better training meetings at your business:

1) Stay focused on the topic at hand. Don't let discussions or practices get out of hand with off topic conversations.

2) Control distractions, side conversations, and interruptions. Don't answer your cell phone or business phone while you are having your training meetings.

3) Let those attending a meeting know what it will be about in advance. Ask them to contribute in some way. Involvement goes a long way to making training meetings more effective and powerful.

4) Make your training meetings mandatory. It is difficult to have a training meeting if everyone is not there. Start and end on time. Have monetary consequences for individuals on your staff who are late.

5) Evaluate how effective your meetings are. Are you getting results after the meeting? Are individuals implementing what they are being taught?

One of the greatest teachers I have ever met, Gene Hill, once taught me this lesson. He said, "Great teachers don't just cover material. They uncover understanding."

That is how an inspiring training meeting should be. It should uncover understanding. When someone leaves one of your meetings, they should be fired up, motivated, excited, and confident because they have been trained and inspired. You will know if you have had a good meeting because performance will improve.

Coach K said in his book *Leading with the Heart*:

"How much I speak to players on our team is important, but they'll forget a lot of what they hear. It's also important to make sure they watch and observe through action and video. Usually, the team will remember more of what they see. But the most critical aspect of our team training is what the guys actually do and what they understand.

So we perform all kinds of gamelike drills over and over again. Such repetition is designed to refine physical habits. And it is key to ensuring that a team will perform well in a real-life situation—because the group will not only hear and see what we tell them, they'll actually execute what we tell them."

Then he says this: "Whenever I go into a practice session with my team, I go in fully prepared. I put together a one-page handwritten lesson. I decide not only what points I want to get across, I also pick different places where I will talk to them—in the locker room, in the middle of the court, on the bench, under the basket, and so on. I choose a variety of spots in order to change the environment so the guys will stay attuned and aware. That way they'll be more likely to retain some of the things I tell them. I also determine how I will talk to the team. If I have a seven-minute drill planned, I can't take four minutes to explain it. And while I don't want to rush my explanation, I want to get it done in about a minute so they spend six minutes 'doing' rather than only 'hearing.'

He finishes with this thought: "A leader may be the most knowledgeable person in the world, but if the players on his team cannot translate that knowledge into action, it means nothing. In other words, it's not what I know, it's what they do on the court that really matters." --Mike Krzyzewski, *Leading with the Heart*, pp. 88-90.

Isn't that great? You have the responsibility to transfer what you know into what your team does by how well you conduct your training. Have effective training meetings that uncover understanding and inspire and motivate your team to do what needs to be done.

14. Catching the fatal and very contagious pronoun disease (or 'disease of me'). Be careful that it doesn't happen to you. Stay

humble.

The fatal pronoun disease we are talking of is the one that begins every sentence with the word: "I."

Don't let this mistake happen to you. Remember what Vince Lombardi, NFL Champion coach of the Green Bay Packers once said:

"The achievements of an organization are the results of the combined effort of each individual."

I have always been impressed by Vince Lombardi, who was the coach of the Green Bay Packers from 1959 through 1967. When he took over as head coach, the team had just suffered its 13th losing season and in 1958 their record was 1-10-1. I've always been intrigued by great leaders or coaches who have been able to come into difficult situations and turn things around. The principles behind the leadership it takes to regain momentum are the same regardless of if it is a football team or a team of sales consultants.

Bart Starr, quarterback for the Green Bay Packers said this of Vince Lombardi's opening meeting with the team:

"Gentlemen, we are going to relentlessly chase perfection knowing full well we won't catch it because nothing is perfect. We are going to RELENTLESSLY—and he really hammered the word RELENTLESSLY—chase perfection because in the process we will catch excellence. He paused for a moment, walked even closer to us, and said, 'I'm not remotely interested in being just good.'" –Chris Havel, *Lombardi, An Illustrated Life*, p. 5.

Do the actions you take at your business reflect this kind of commitment? Do team members know that you are not just interested in being good, but that you are in the relentless pursuit of being the very best?

"Lombardi began getting what he wanted by assessing the Packers' current roster and deciding who could and could not help the team win. This required a man of vision who knew what his team would look like, and how an individual player's skill would fit into the overall scheme." –p. 27.

Before the start of their training camp, Lombardi told his players:

"Gentlemen, we're going to have a football team. We are going to win some games. Do you know why? Because you are going to have confidence in me and my system...By being alert you are going to make fewer mistakes than your opponent...By working harder you are going to out-execute, out- block (and) out-tackle every team that comes your way."

When the meeting was finished, Starr immediately called his wife, Cherry, and said, 'Honey, we are going to begin to win.'"

And begin to win they did. Part of this came from how Lombardi built his team. Defensive end Willie Davis said:

"Defensive players would motivate each other with reminders that a subpar effort could earn them a meeting with the coach...When we lost, it was painful, and when we lost, I thought of him first before my own problems with it. And that's why in my opinion we became winners. We were a team. There was nothing attractive about losing, and if there was he made it quickly dissipate." –p. 47.

Everyone on your team makes a difference. No one person is any more important than the other on the team. When someone starts feeling and acting that way, it will dramatically affect your environment.

Here are ten ideas to help you get rid of the 'disease of me' and encourage your team members to work together:

1) Encourage members of your team. Your team members need genuine, sincere, and authentic encouragement. People will follow you when you encourage them.

2) When you hire someone, learn their name quickly. As Dale Carnegie said, "A person's name is the most important thing in the world to that person."

3) Be more interested in making people feel good about themselves, than making people feel good about you.

4) Smile more and live with a positive attitude.

5) Listen more than you talk and learn to ask excellent questions. Part of good listening is the ability to ask good questions.

6) Be observant and learn to read people. Study what people do, and then ask yourself why they do it. Discover what motivates each member of your team.

7) Be willing to say "I'm sorry" first. When is the last time you sincerely apologized to someone above you, at your level, and someone below you? I once heard Brian Tracy teach that we should always be willing to say: "I'm sorry. I was wrong." Many people are afraid to say these words, yet they will help you get past the disease of me faster than anything else.

8) Always go for the win/win scenario. Never make a deal unless both sides win. Never.

9) Share the credit and the praise. When there is success, share the rewards with members of your team. Be sure to give the praise publicly so that everyone can hear you (especially when someone has a big win).

10) Adopt a windows/mirror philosophy of life. Look out the window when others succeed and point out those who have made a difference instead of introspectively looking at the mirror and thinking about how good you are. The only time you should look in the mirror is when things don't go well and you are looking for what to change.

Finally, to get rid of the disease of me, remember that the letter "I" is not found in TEAM.

15. Not having your own outlets to help you overcome being overwhelmed, frustrated, or discouraged. If you don't, you will likely take out your frustrations on those around you.

There are so many things that you are responsible for as a manager and leader that it is easy to get overwhelmed. When you consider all that you have to do, it is understandable that you will get frustrated and discouraged. This typically happens because you have too much to do and too little time to do it in.

You may feel that it is difficult if not impossible to catch up on all that you have to do. In business, it is like there is a conveyer belt of challenges coming at you all the time. The list of things to do doesn't stop. The only way to succeed is to decide what you won't do. Break up your tasks and work on them in 90-minute blocks of focused effort.

When you are overwhelmed with all of your responsibilities, remain positive and tackle one challenge at a time. If you are frustrated or disappointed, your customers shouldn't be able to tell. A prospect should only see enthusiasm, excitement, and the professional demeanor of someone they can trust and who they know has their best interests at heart. Everyone on your team should see the best from you as well.

My hope is that you will use what you've learned here to develop a great team of leaders around you while avoiding the leadership pitfalls I've outlined in this chapter that will slow, hinder, or stop your growth. If you recognize and understand how to navigate these leadership situations, you'll be able to successfully navigate your way through challenging times so you can manage and lead your team onward towards greatness.

CHAPTER 11

USE LEVERAGE AND DIFFERENTIATION TO STRENGTHEN YOUR BUSINESS ADVANTAGES

"Give me a lever long enough and a fulcrum on which to place it, and I shall move the world."--Archimedes

I want to share a story that is found in Brian Tracy's book *Victory* that illustrates the power of leverage and in this particular case showcases something the Allies knew that helped them defeat the German army during World War II.

"The Germans...had a secret weapon, the Enigma machine. This incredibly sophisticated device allowed the Germans to communicate worldwide with a code that was impossible to break. Each encoded message was encrypted differently from each subsequent message when it was run through the Enigma machine. Because of this, there was no consistent code to be broken by the Allied powers. The German intelligence services and military commanders could send and receive top-secret messages worldwide with no fear of detection.

"However, an incredibly fortunate event took place early in the war. The Allies were able to obtain an Enigma machine and secretly transport it into England. The existence of this machine in Allied intelligence became one of the biggest secrets of the war and was not revealed until well after the war was over.

"The Allies set up a separate intelligence unit at a large estate called Bletchley Park forty miles north of London. This unit was fully staffed by intelligence experts with the highest top-secret clearances possible in the Allied military. These code-breakers and translators worked day and night throughout the entire war intercepting German communications, deciphering them, and making them available to the key commanders and relevant parties.

"This intelligence breakthrough was a major reason for the Allied victory in Europe. The capture of an Enigma machine and the codebooks that went with it gave the Allies a critical edge that enabled them to ultimately prevail over a formidable military force....Sometimes, one piece of information is all that is necessary to give the advantage to one force or the other." –Brian Tracy, *Victory*, pp. 102-103.

What kind of power or leverage would you have if you knew what your competitors were going to do before they do it?

Obviously, you can't have that exact power, but thinking about the story of the Engima machine, helps us understand the power of anticipating what others will do and then acting on that knowledge. Such knowledge gives you a tremendous edge or leverage point.

A more valuable question is: What kind of power or leverage would you have if you could think about and anticipate shifts in the market before they happened?

Such information would be invaluable. The important point from both questions is that leverage gives you an advantage. All you really need and want in business is an advantage in some way. In this chapter, I'm going to share several leverage points with you to help you gain an advantage in your market. To do so, I want to help you look at the best assets you have at your business and carefully consider how you can better leverage them to help you get what you want.

Another way to better understand the concepts of leverage and assets is to look at the character of Mickey Mouse. Mickey Mouse was originally a cartoon character used in short cartoons in movie theatres. Since then, that same asset has been leveraged many ways through comic books, books, videos, movies, cartoons, clothing, toys, theme parks, a cable TV network, Disney+, and licensing for untold numbers of products. You can see how one idea has been leveraged across a wide variety of media to get even more benefit and value than was originally anticipated.

This is such an important idea because very few business owners in general really understand how to leverage their assets for maximum benefit. My goal in this chapter is to help you better understand how you can leverage what you already have to help you build and expand your business brand.

First, I think it will be helpful to better understand the definition of the word leverage.

Leverage is the exertion of force by means of a lever, or an object used in the manner of a lever. A mechanical advantage can be gained in this way. Another definition of leverage is the power to influence a person or situation to achieve a particular outcome. Other words used to describe leverage include: influence, power, authority, weight, sway, pull, control, say, dominance, advantage, pressure, clout, muscle, teeth, or bargaining chip.

I think I really first started to understand this concept when I read a book by Robert Kiyosaki entitled *Retire Young, Retire Rich* shortly after we opened our first business. The book is all about the types of leverage that business owners can use to grow their businesses.

In the introduction, Robert Kiyosaki makes this statement which greatly impressed me the first time I read it. He said:

"Leverage is the reason some people become rich and others do not become rich....Because leverage is power, some use it, some abuse it, and others fear it." –*Retire Young, Retire Rich*, p. xiii.

He continues: "The reason less than 5 percent of all Americans are rich is because only 5 percent know how to *use* the power of leverage. Many who want to become rich, fail to become rich because they *abuse* the power. And most people do not become rich because they *fear* the power of leverage."

He also defines leverage as the ability to do more with less. He says:

"In the broad definition of the word, the word leverage simply means the ability to do more with less. When it came to the subject of work, money, and leverage, rich dad would say, 'If you want to become rich, you need to work less, and earn more. In order to do that, you employ some form of leverage.' He contrasted that statement by saying, 'People who only work hard have limited leverage. If you're working hard physically and not getting ahead financially, then you're probably someone else's leverage.'" –*Retire Young, Retire Rich*, p. 33.

Another way to understand leverage can be found in fishing. When fishing, you can use your bare hands, a fishing pole, or a net. Which one has the most leverage and will allow you to catch the most fish in a short period of time?

As you grow your business, you can use other people's money as leverage by going into debt. You can use other people's time by employing other people. You can profit from other people's relationships by utilizing the relationships others have with those to whom you want to sell. You can use your time differently than others. You can choose to build a business in your spare time or you can watch TV, go shopping, read, or do any number of things. Why is it important to understand the words "leverage" and "asset" in conjunction with growing your business?

The key is that you can't do it all alone through your own work. You have to create assets and leverage them to help you grow beyond your own capacity. I would like to cover four ways you can use leverage to help you build and expand your business and six multipliers that will give you a bigger crowbar so you can get more leverage.

1. Use the leverage of your mind to entertain the realm of possibility of how you can grow your business.

The most powerful leverage you have (regardless of the size of your business) is in your mind – because you have to entertain the realm of *possibility* before you can embrace it as your new *reality*. This is why it is so important to associate with and learn from others who stretch your realities – they help you see what is possible (and grab onto those new realities like a crowbar that removes the obstacles) instead of being stuck in the same old ways of doing things.

Robert Kiyosaki makes this statement about leverage:

"The number one leverage is the leverage found in your mind because it is where your realities are formed."-p. 55.

The realities of our own minds can hold us back from accomplishing more. To help you understand this idea, consider the belief or reality that existed for many people before the Wright brothers helped others see that human beings could fly. The popular idea at the time was that "humans can't fly." It wasn't until the Wright brothers used the leverage of their minds to envision another possibility that they were willing to work to find a way. Once they embraced the new reality that it was possible to fly were they willing to step out and do something about it.

Another example is when Roger Bannister broke the four-minute mile barrier. At the time, the popular belief and reality for most people was that it was impossible for any human being to run a four-minute mile. Most people believed that the human heart couldn't withstand such exertion and that it would explode if anyone attempted to run this fast. What is important about what Roger Bannister did is that he believed he could break the four-minute mile *before* he did. He embraced this new reality in his mind and used the leverage of his mind to work and train so that he could break the four-minute mile. Then, once he did it and proved it was possible, others were able to do it as well.

2. Understand and leverage the assets you have at your business in ways that help you maximize your potential and power.

To grow your business, you need to better leverage the assets you have. Your own individual assets aren't enough.

To help you better understand how you can leverage your business assets, I've listed the biggest assets any business has (regardless of size) below. I'll also ask you to think about both sides of the leverage spectrum and why one business has more power and leverage than another (with the same asset). I'll also ask you to carefully think about how you can better leverage these assets in your business.

Take the time to carefully think about what I am going to ask you here. You won't ever develop these assets and use them to gain more leverage unless you embrace the new realities of what I'm trying to share with you. Then, and only then, will you move past belief to take action and develop these assets into better leverage points to launch your business to a higher level.

1) Your brand identity and all of your intellectual property (business name, brand identity, logo, etc.)

Which has more power and leverage?

- A business that relies on the manufacturers of the products they offer to brand them

  OR

- A business who builds their own brand and then leverages it in many ways.

Why?

How can you better leverage this asset at your business?

2) Your status as an celebrity specialist who has expertise

Who has more power and leverage in your business niche?

- A celebrity, authority specialist who has a massive social media following that will buy or do what they recommend
  OR

- You or any competitor that isn't well known or thought of as an expert or authority?

Which business has more power and leverage?

- The best known brand in your market niche
  OR

- A copy cat business who tries to compete on price?

- Why?

How can you better leverage your expertise and manufacture your celebrity?

3) Your processes and systems

Which has more power and leverage?

- A business with no processes and systems
  OR

- A business with well thought out processes and systems that anyone can run (without you having to be there all of the time)?

Why?

How can you better leverage your processes and systems?

4) Your brand reputation in your market

Which has more power and leverage?

- A business that is known for what products they offer
  OR

- a business that is known for the experience customers have when they buy there?

Why?

How can you better leverage your brand reputation in your business?

5) Your sales consultants and team

Which has more power and leverage?

- A well trained sales consultant who sells three out of every four prospects
  OR

- A poorly trained sales consultant who sells one out of every four prospects?

Why?

How can you better leverage your sales skills and processes in your business?

6) Your customers (who have already purchased from you)

Which has more power and leverage?

- A business who is content to just sell one product/service
  OR

- A business who consistently invites and sells to customers who buy not only one product, but everything else they will need to utilize that product and achieve the results they seek? On top of that, this business asks for referrals after *every* sale and gets them.

Why?

How can you better leverage your current customers in your business and better ask for and get referrals?

7) The territory you hold with certain product lines

Which has more power and leverage?

- A business with no exclusive product lines (offers what everyone else including Internet vendors does)?
  OR

- A business who offers what no one else has and offers what can't be found online?

Why?

How can you better leverage your territory and product exclusivity at your business?

8) Your connections (people customers in your area should know but don't)

Which has more power and leverage?

- A business who introduces customers who buy from their business to the top downstream vendors in their area (and charges these vendors for this opportunity)
  OR

- A business who knows top downstream vendors, but doesn't take the time to introduce their customers to them (because they are too busy or because customers will meet these vendors on their own) anyway?

Why?

How can you better leverage this asset at your business?

9) Investments (Inventory)

Which has more power and leverage?

- A business with limited inventory that doesn't have a lot of depth of selection or sizes
OR

- A business with an extensive depth of inventory so that customers can experience products / services that fit their unique specifications?

Why?

How can you better leverage your inventory (products and time) in your business?

10) Your relationships with key vendors and suppliers.

Which has more power and leverage?

- A business who barely knows their key vendors
OR

- A business who really gets to know their key vendors and spends their time and money (through purchases) to build better relationships?

Who do you think gets more attention when challenges come up?

How can you better leverage your relationships with vendors and suppliers in your business?

11) Advertising and cross promotional opportunities with other businesses – Will others pay you to be in front of your customers

(who they want to sell to as well)?

Which has more power and leverage?

- A business who gives access to their customer database for free (handing out business cards and flyers to customers just because business owners dropped by)
OR

- A business who helps build bridges between someone else's customers and other businesses that want to be in touch with those customers (and who charges for the opportunity)?
Why?

How can you better leverage your customer list to benefit other advertisers and promoters at your business?

In each case, one business has power and more leverage over other businesses because of how they view and utilize the leverage points in their business. You must do the same.

3. Find and use multipliers which will give you a bigger crowbar and even more leverage.

A multiplier is something that allows you to increase the benefit you would get out of the same thing by looking at it differently. Well placed and executed multipliers can have a huge impact on the amount of leverage you can utilize as you grow your business.

Here are six examples of multipliers which provide leverage:

1. Utilizing current resources in creative ways and seeking opportunity where others don't.

How can you better utilize your resources? Are there opportunities that others don't see or benefit from in the market?

My children find it hard to believe that there was time when TV went off the air at midnight with colored bars and a monotone sound. Today, television has found tremendous leverage by selling infomercial time during these same off peak hours that used to air absolutely nothing. Fortunes have been made by television stations who have sold this time to advertisers who want to sell their products via stories and numerous testimonials to an audience that can't sleep or just returned from working all day.

Numerous companies have successfully used reality television to brand themselves and their businesses. Chip and Joanna Gaines used HGTV's *Fixer Upper* TV show to build a massive following and home and lifestyle brand Magnolia. Mara Urshel, Ronnie Rothstein, and Wayne Rogers have done the same for Kleinfeld Bridal with the hit TV show *Say Yes to the Dress*.

This works because the TV shows helps create celebrities out of the business owners and members of the staff so that you accelerate the speed at which trust enters a transaction with the business. You can build your brand of your business to millions of viewers (current customers and future customers that may never have been exposed to them in any other way). In addition, you can make the *experience* of buying your product something that prospects want to have (prospects will fly to a retail location from around the world for the experience) – this enhances the bragging rights of those who later buy from you.

What Disney + has done with its archive of current and past films is a great example of this principle. Not only do they have a huge catalog of films (betweeen their own studio and the recently acquired Twenty-First Century Fox catalog of films), they've created new shows to generate a huge amount of monthly cash flow from an existing asset. They are leveraging this content to take on Netflix.

Who wants access to your customers, your unconverted leads, and other assets that you're not currently using? When you sell access to the customers you have acquired to other business professionals who want to sell them their services, you are using your business as a leverage point to make money. These entrepreneurs pay to have access to those with whom you already have access and have a relationship of trust.

Another unexploited opportunity is that of looking at different distribution models. Is there another way you can get prospects to look at your service?

What are you doing with your unconverted leads? These are prospects who have been into your marketing funnel or visited with you, but haven't purchased anything from you yet. There is always a big opportunity here because most entrepreneurs don't follow up with these prospects very well.

Here is a question that you should carefully consider:

What current resources or unexploited opportunities exist at your business?

Here are a few examples of ways I've coached other retailers who have a physical space to capitalize on and leverage current resources that aren't being used to their full potential:

- Special offers between 12 pm and 3 pm (Double the value of a few promotions during slower times similar to what Sonic does with its 50% off drink specials in the afternoon during their off peak times)

- Special offers on a traditionally slower day of the week - creates excitement and gets prospects into the business.

- A special offer when all decision makers come in for an appointment Monday – Friday

- A special offer if a prospect books a follow up appointment at the time of their first purchase for the next product offering in your sequence

- A special offers to move older products - this can be sent out to

a select group of customers who would have bought, but have
limited budgets

Think differently about what you already have. How can you exploit
your current resources? Some of these may seem obvious, as in the case
of Disney +, but others may require some thought and testing.

2. A different and improved way of selling.

Pre-selling your prospect will prepare those who enter your marketing
funnel and encourage them to set up an appointment to visit with you.
You should carefully consider this improved means of selling as well and
ask yourself: What are you providing to a prospect to prepare them to
buy from you *before* you meet with them?

A great example of this is a plastic surgeon who deliberately delays
consultation appointments so material can be mailed out to the
interested prospect. Everything in the packet that is sent out (which
includes two DVDs and a questionnaire is designed to pre-sell the
prospective buyer on why the plastic surgeon is the best and only choice
for the type of surgery she is considering. The packet also contains a
copy of the plastic surgeon's book (which sets her up as an expert and an
authority). Finally, there is a phone script where the receptionist follows
up and gives out assignments to the prospect before she arrives at the
consultative appointment. The real goal is to ensure that the prospect
watches the first DVD (which is loaded with testimonials and answers
to questions she might have including a brief overview of what she can
expect from the process to eliminate her fears and concerns). She is also
instructed to fill out the questionnaire and bring it in with her.

In Chapter 5, I discussed the importance of selling experiences, not
products. Disney has done this with their theme parks and millions
come back every year because of the experience they have there with
their family. Car dealerships have been selling experiences for years, even
allowing an experience with the car before you buy it through a test
drive.

Focus on the experiences you create. Look for new ways and places where you can introduce surprises to your prospects and customers. You can also introduce unique experiences when you bundle additional products and other payment options, and even by selling membership in an Insider's Club concept where you move from transactional selling to a continuity based selling model.

3. Sales mastery.

How deeply do you study and practice the selling process?

To master something implies that you are working at it all of the time. You aren't content with what you knew before. You keep learning and figuring out what works, and what doesn't.

Several years ago, I spoke at a seminar where I asked the business owners in attendance to identify how many of them were asking for the sale more than once when they were selling. Our informal survey revealed that many of their salespeople weren't even asking once for the sale. I told them that our sales consultants were trained to ask for every sale at least five times with each prospect. Because we require this, we make more sales (and most of our sales happen on the third request). If you are only asking once or not at all, you will not make the sale.

I have a friend who owns a software company that requires his salespeople to practice and know twelve different ways to ask for the sale now. They have found that their average prospect buys on the seventh request, but since the salespeople all know at least twelve ways to close the sale, they continue until the prospect buys. There is more resistance in selling today, and if you aren't asking more, you are losing a lot of sales. You are getting the prospect three-fourths to almost all of the way sold and then letting her leave so that they are nearly over their resistance to buy. Then, they ends up buying from the next company that pitches their product to them. Your competitors are thankful because you have worn down the prospect's resistance for them so it is easier for them to make the sale because of your efforts.

Don't make this mistake. Train your consultants to ask for the sale at least five times with every sale they make. Require each sales consultant to write down how many times they asked for the sale on their sales report that indicates what they *could* have done to make the sale. Without fail, the prospects who aren't buying are only being asked once or twice. This helps the sales consultants to see the importance of persisting and overcoming the prospect's objections until they buy. Train your sales consultants to persistently ask for the sale at least five times. When you do, you'll see your sales and closing percentages go up and you'll be ecstatic about the result.

Train your sales team on what they must do when the phone rings or when someone begins a sales interaction with them (whether that is online or offline). What difference in results is there between a team of trained sales consultants over those who have little to no training and wing it when that interaction begins?

4. Game changing elements.

Throughout this book I've been covering game changing elements that will help propel your business forward. Disney offers great examples of how they constantly work at improving their current business. Disney opened his theme parks with was a different pricing strategy than what was employed by most amusement parks at the time. Instead of charging for each individual ride, Disney charged a single admission price prior to entry at their parks which includes the price of all of the rides. By doing this, they are able to ensure that purchasing rides doesn't get in the way of you buying everything else that they want to sell to you.

Disney is also a master of studying the flow of customers and how they move within their parks. They are constantly monitoring how many people stop at each intersection, what they do when they are there, what they stop to buy, etc. They study all of this with the purpose of increasing the amount each person spends there. And their efforts have paid off. In 2007, the average Orlando Disney World visitor surpassed the average Las Vegas visitor for the amount of money spent in eight hour period. Disney is worth studying because they are masters at how they separate people from as much of their money as possible while having those same individuals be thrilled about spending it.

Domino's Pizza changed the pizza business with speed and certainty of delivery. What game changers are you introducing to your customers that are giving you a sustainable advantage?

There are numerous trends to consider that may very well morph into game changing elements in the near future. One of these is fractional ownership. This is where a number of people own a small piece of a big thing. This concept has been used to sell time shares, condos, private jets, and most recently really expensive jewelry. For example, thirteen women who had never met before each contributed $1,200 to buy a 15-carat diamond jewelry necklace which none of them could have afforded to purchase on their own. They each get to wear it for a month at a time and send it from place to place throughout a year. Additional trends to consider include the trend of having things be all inclusive as is done now with vacations and businesses who focus on being a one-stop shop.

My question to you is this: What will *you* do with the trends you observe happening in your market?

Leverage is a powerful idea you can act on to accomplish more. Not one of us accomplishes anything without the help of others as Thomas J. Stanley points out in his book *The Millionaire Mind.* He says:

"It's rare that anyone becomes successful without the assistance of others. A group of individuals, no matter how gifted, is not a team at all. How many running backs became All-Americans without their linemen opening up opportunities? Zero. Becoming wealthy in America is very similar. I have never met one affluent person who takes complete credit for his economic successes. Most will give credit to their spouse, key employees, mentors, and others. No man or woman is an island, whether the context is sports, business, or building wealth—nobody gets to the highest peaks without the help of others."—*The Millionaire Mind*, p. 37.

Those who reach the highest realms of success employ the leverage of others to help them get there faster. My hope is that you'll use the ideas I've shared with you here to leverage your business to even greater success. Be sure you carefully consider new opportunities or better capitalize on existing opportunities you may have forgotten about or aren't implementing as well as you could.

CHAPTER 12

STOP PLAYING SMALL AND SELLING YOURSELF SHORT - CREATE THE BUSINESS YOU WANT AND DESERVE

"Organizations that are out of balance become stuck—unable to move forward. What's more...those organizations that remain stuck, become dead."
–Keith Yamashita & Sandra Sparo

It is easy to get stuck in business. When you get stuck, you may feel trapped and not sure what to do to get out of the rut you're in. Things may have been cruising along just fine for a long period of time and then all of the sudden or gradually over time, something happens that causes you to lose your momentum. When this happens, you can remain stuck on a plateau, and feel frustrated that you are stuck where you are.

As we end this book, I want to encourage you to stop playing small and selling yourself short so you can create the business you really want. I'll outline some of the specific things you need to pay more attention to if you're going to create the business you want and deserve to achieve your dreams.

George Bernard Shaw once said: "The reasonable man adapts himself to the world; the unreasonable one persists to adapt the world to himself. Therefore all progress depends on the unreasonable man."

With the negativity of politics and general pessimism about life, many have set aside or given up on their dreams. They've thought about getting out of business and may be looking to do something else. If you've been feeling down for whatever reason, it is time to stop playing small and start your dream engine again.

It's hard to break free of the negativity and toxic environment that cloud your mind with the barrage of messages that are constantly thrown in front of you. But, it is absolutely necessary if you are to break free from your limitations and accomplish your dreams. In order to achieve what you want, you've got to focus. You can't focus when your mind is all over the place, worrying about things over which you don't have any control. Instead, you've got to channel your attention into what you want and what you *can* do now to make things happen.

To help you to break free of the toxic negativity that has been in your mind, I've got an assignment that I would like you to work on. For the next seven days, spend 20 minutes reading a book that teaches you a business skill that you would like to learn instead of spending 20 minutes looking at the news online or scrolling through social media pages that don't bring you any closer to your goals.

Then, at the end of each reading session, answer one of the following seven questions. Or, answer all seven questions in one sit down session. Take at least three minutes for every question. If you need to, put a timer on a clock and then spend at least three minutes on every question. In the time it takes you to answer these seven questions (21 minutes), you'll be well on your way to re-igniting the passion and excitement behind your dreams. Then, in the remainder of this chapter,

I'll share ideas to help you do what needs to be done to get back on track.

Here are the seven questions and the exercise that should take you at least 21 minutes to complete:

1) What were my dreams when I was a child around 10 years of age? What and who did I want to be?

2) What have been the greatest moments of joy and fulfillment in my life?

3) What are the greatest sources of joy in my work?

4) What activities do I absolutely love in my personal life?

5) What are my greatest talents and natural abilities?

6) What is the single most important thing I would like to accomplish in my career?

7) What is the one most important thing I would like to accomplish in my personal life?

What did you learn from completing that exercise?

Each time I go through this exercise, I am reminded that I get to choose how I spend my time and which talents and abilities I want to develop. One of the big reasons why many business owners choose to play small and sell themselves short is because they allow themselves to succumb to resistance. They intellectually accept the idea that they want to earn more, but they can't overcome the emotional resistance that prevents them from doing what needs to be done. In other words, they get trapped into staying small because they fail to act due to their own inner, emotional resistance.

Inner resistance is what holds many back from going bigger and achieving more. There are four common causes of this inner resistance. They are:

1) Issues with money

Many people disrupt, stop or repel the flow of money to them because of their own inner, emotional resistance to money. If you want to be more successful, you've got to understand why money moves from one place to another and how you can get more of it to flow to you.

Most people have an internal thermostat for money that dictates how much money they make. When I first got into sales, I saw this with salespeople. Some would sell a lot at the beginning of the month or the end of the month. If they hit their goal early, they left early and didn't come back to the office until the following week. Are you moving up the thermostat in your mind so that you can think bigger and stop thinking / playing small?

2) Sensitivity to what others think and say about you.

Achievement makes those around you (especially if they aren't accomplishing much) feel uncomfortable. They often lash out with criticism and gossip in order to make themselves feel better about what they haven't accomplished in comparison to you.

Control your own thinking. Don't worry about what people are thinking about you. The truth is most people aren't thinking much about you at all. They are only thinking about themselves. Being worried about what they think or lowering your ambitions won't help you achieve what you want. It is better to get around others who stretch your thinking and imagination instead of being around others who pull you down through your association with them. If you're experiencing this kind of resistance in your life, perhaps it is time for a new group of friends or associations.

3) Fear of being in over your head.

It is easy to get overwhelmed by what you don't know or by unfounded fears that prevent you from taking action. This resistance is preceded by thoughts such as: "I don't want to become successful, because then people might try to take advantage of me or sue me" OR "What will people think or say about me now that we're doing so well?" OR "I don't want to have to pay more...have more employees..., etc."

The truth is that people aren't necessarily happy for you when you do better. Your competitors sure aren't happy about it. But, your close friends may not be happy with it either because it makes them feel insecure with who they are and the fact that they've been left behind.

4) Self sabotage

This happens when you realize you are unwilling to pay the price to build a bigger business, but are also unwilling to admit it. As a result, you procrastinate or do things that are completely opposite of what will help you accomplish your goals.

Being clear about the resistance that may be holding you back can help you avoid it. Being clear about what you want (your dreams) can give you the motivation to do the work that must be done on a daily basis. It takes focus and work to detox your mind from negativity and small thinking. Some people associate with those who are where they are instead of getting out of their comfort zone to get what they want.

It isn't enough to just be a bigger dreamer and to detox your mind from the constant negativity you face each day. You've also have to work a plan that will help you achieve your goals. The game of being successful in business has gotten tougher. This means that those who will win going forward are those who are the toughest. If you are to succeed, you'll have to be at the very, very top of your game. Coasting along and hoping things work out is not an option.

Here are eight strategies that can help you stop playing small and get back on track with your business.

1. Know and make decisions by your numbers.

There are three big areas that I want to discuss where you should be evaluating your performance by numbers. These are what you are selling, who you are attracting to buy from you, and how you are using your time.

First, let's talk about what you are selling. Carefully analyzing your numbers for your actual sales results will help you see opportunities and see what isn't working that you may otherwise have missed.

Second, you should evaluate who you are actually attracting into your business. There are four types of prospects that you can attract into your business:

1) High value, low likelihood of repeat transactions.

2) High value, high likelihood of repeat transactions.

3) Low value, low likelihood of repeat transactions.

4) Low value, high likelihood of repeat transactions.

You'll notice that there are two types of transactions (high value and low value) as well as two types of repeat transactions (low likelihood of repeat transactions and high likelihood of repeat transactions).

Many businesses today complain about having prospects come into their marketing funnel who only want to buy a product under a certain low dollar amount and not buy anything else. By marketing to and attracting more affluent prospects into your business, you can ensure that you have more high value with a high likelihood of repeat transactions.

Where is your focus? Are you stuck attracting the wrong kinds of prospects or are you attracting high value prospects who will buy from you multiple times over the course of their lives?

You need to focus on determining who your high value customers are for your business. These should be:

• A prospect with a high transaction (and profit) value who is ready to buy now.

• A prospect who will be spending more of what you sell (and where there may be additional sales opportunities monthly, quarterly, or yearly)

• A customer who has already purchased something from you in the past (who will buy something else if they are marketed to in the right way)

• Those who can convince others to buy from you (those who are actively promoting your referral program through social media.

Work harder at attracting high value, high likelihood of repeat transactions customers into your business.

Third, how are you using your time? If you are going to go for your dreams and make more money from your business, you've got to put dollar value constraints on your time. In other words, you can't allow yourself to get caught up in activities that don't pay you the money that will help you reach your income targets.

If certain activities are permitted to consume more time than what they actually pay you for, you will end up missing your income targets. Too many business owners get caught up doing things they think or believe they must do that don't really end up bringing money into the business. Most business owners get caught up in activities instead of accomplishments that yield a financial return. You can't allocate more time to an activity if it isn't yielding results.

Choosing what not to do is as important as choosing what you will do. Focus on the critical success factors each day that will yield the biggest dividends and delegate other activities that will take you way from doing these things.

2. Raise your prices and / or the margin of what you're selling.

I'm always intrigued by what Disney does with their prices. When many are shrinking and cutting their prices, Disney is continually raising their prices. This allows them to continue to be profitable as their costs rise. Ignoring this reality will hurt you. The big lesson here is that Disney is focused on aiming more at affluent clientele and not worrying about the loss at the bottom.

You can be charging more than any other business in your area for certain products. At least 5-10% more of prospects in your market niche would pay more for certain products and services that are selling. In other words, not all customers are equal. How you sell and the stratification you provide in your business shifts your potential and your profits.

With each new version of an iPhone, iPad, or iWatch, or computer notice how Apple employs the following six strategies to help them sell at a higher price:

1) Create a Place - I would encourage you to watch any keynote video where a new Apple product is introduced (particularly ones where the late Steve Jobs was showcasing the product). Notice how each video showcases the excitement of people buying the previous version of the product and how the focus is all about creating a place.

2) Create your own language - Starbucks changed small to Tall and Large to Venti. Changing the name shifts the entire argument about price – because there is no way to create contrast or comparison. This is a very smart idea. What language can you create in your business to shift the conversation from price to value?

3) Reputation – Your story creates demand and intrigue (Apple does this brilliantly when they launch any new product). Are you telling stories about what you sell to help build your reputation and more importantly create demand and intrigue by how you tell the story? For example, by showing the demand for people who want to buy the new iPhone on its launch day, the excitement for the person watching the video increases to the point that they also want to buy it. If you study how Bantaicivitcoffee.com, sells their coffee for approximately $179 for

less than a pound (12 ounces), you'll notice that it does so with intrigue. They talk about this coffee and how it is made. More importantly, people think about what this coffee could actually taste like if it is made from the poo of Asian palm cats (civits). Studying how they sell their product using intrigue and create demand by positioning themselves as being the best is an exercise that is worth studying.

4) Status – How do you rank in comparison with other businesses who sell what you do? I think this is the most powerful lesson to be learned from watching a new Apple product launch video. It means something to buy a new Apple product to many customers. This is why some will wait up until midnight to buy the new device on its initial launch day or wait in line for hours to be one of the first who gets a product.

Kleinfeld Bridal has done a great job of this. It means something to buy a wedding dress from them. Elon Musk has done this with the Tesla automobile. It means something to buy an electric car from Tesla. What are you doing to enhance the status you give to your customers when they buy something from you?

5) Celebrity – This can be done by linking yourself to celebrities who build up your brand. One of the things Apple does well here is that they make the customer the celebrity by how they position their employees to give those who have been waiting in line high fives as they approach the counter to make the purchase.

6) Demonstration of your unique value

A keynote speech introducing any of Apple's new products does a masterful job at this. Not only do they showcase the product that is being launched, they also showcase the value of the device and most importantly everything else they get from Apple that makes it even better. When thinking about your business, how are you providing a demonstration that convinces and persuades?

It is better to target prospective customers for whom price is not the key motivator. Bring them into your marketing funnel for reasons other than price.

Everyone seems to be offering bigger discounts today. Some mistakenly think that since everyone is doing this, you had better lower your price too. Price cutting is a self-inflicted wound. It isn't worth it to bleed yourself out to make unprofitable sales. It is better to focus on a different segment of the market or get out of a commoditized business.

Remember, the overwhelming number of your prospects and nearly all affluent consumers are swayed predominantly by price only when there is nothing else that is very compelling or intriguing about what you are offering. It is your responsibility to craft a compelling reason why prospects should buy from you.

Avoid competitive environments. Instead, develop and maintain a unique relationship with your customers and offer them something they can't get anywhere else by appearing in a category of one.

The goal is to sell in a competitive vacuum. If you sell the same product as everyone else and it can be found online, you deserve to get beat. Bottom line: If you invite commoditization, you'll get it.

You want to develop a personal relationship with every one of your prospects so that they trust you and want to do business with you.

Stop trying to win over cheap prospects. Instead, focus on helping prospects who want more than the cheapest price. Implement sales processes that make price a non-issue.

It is worth investing time and money into elevating your status in the minds of the prospects in your area. Manufacture your own celebrity, become a trusted expert and authority figure so that you attract more affluent prospects and they believe that you are the best choice for someone in their situation.

What's working in your business now?

When I consult with companies about how they can improve their business, I typically go through the following exercise to find hidden opportunity in their business. I invite you to consider how you can improve each of these areas in your business as well.

Leads and Lead Sources

Where are you new leads coming from?

What are your three best sources?

What steps are you going through to pre-sell these prospects on why you are the best choice?

What are your three least effective lead sources? Why are you still using those sources?

Appointments

If someone sits down with you for an in-person or phone consultation, what are you doing to follow up with them if they don't buy?

What is causing these prospects to wait before moving forward?

What systems do you have in place to ensure that they are invited to make a purchase from you?

What three ways could you ensure that a prospect's concern is answered before they leave your appointment?

o

o

o

Here are three ideas to help you get started:

o Invite the prospect to visit with you or a sales manager covertly disguised as an evaluation meeting to help a brand new sales consultant

(you can try to find out the prospect's last objection and overcome it)

o Have the sales consultant ask for the sale at least 4 times

o Give the prospect a special report designed to answer the last objections.

In the bridal business, I wrote a report called "3 Big Fallacies that Prevent Brides from Getting the Dress They Love." In the solar business, I wrote a special report entitled: "The 9 Most Shocking And Outrageous Myths About Going Solar." These articles were designed to overcome the last objections a prospect might have about going ahead. When I would get to that point in the sale, I would give them the report and then ask one last time, "I know you really loved the option we discussed and that you tried out. What, if anything, would prevent you from going forward now and receiving the benefits we discussed?"

In each case, people would finally open up and share their last objection and we were able to close the sale.

How could you use this idea in your business?

Prospect Who Requests Information, But Doesn't Want to Meet

Many prospects today may request information, but aren't ready to commit to an appointment. You could also classify prospects in this category as those who want to look around, but aren't committed to a serious discussion about buying what you sell.

Here are some questions for you to consider:

What is causing these prospects to resist your appointment?

What is the biggest headache about shopping for your product? How can you eliminate those hassles and make the process of buying simple and easy?

One of the best examples I have seen that addresses this is from a bridal store in Westport, Connecticut called The Plumed Serpent Bridal. Their tag line is: "The least complicated thing about your most complicated day." That tagline really explains the importance of removing hassles for customers.

Does the information you give to prospects help them see why you are the only *real* choice?

What are three ways that you can help these prospects overcome this resistance?

o

o

o

Those Who Buy From You On the First Visit

How can you get this customer back into your store to buy again?

What three things can you do to establish a pattern of purchasing so the customer wants to come back and do more business with you?

o

o

o

Prospect Who Buy From You on a Return Visit

If prospects do return and buy from you, what is the average length of time between when they leave and when they return?

What could you do to speed up their return (since the longer the prospect waits, the bigger the likelihood that they won't buy from you)?

What three things could you do to incentivize the prospect to return and buy from you?

o

o

o

Prospects on Your Lead List Who Are Lost (Don't Currently Receive Follow Up)

What follow up systems do you have in place to ensure that you aren't losing any of the leads you've acquired?

In what three ways could you improve your follow up process to better capitalize on the leads you already have?

o

o

o

The key for being successful in each of these areas is to be clear about the desired outcome. Then, you can work your way backwards so that you can come up with a better system which will yield the results you seek.

In order to strengthen your business in these areas, you've got to be willing to ask the hard questions that will help you consider your weaknesses in new ways so you can improve them.

The better you can assess how you are doing in these areas, the more successful you'll be at discovering breakthroughs that will help you be more successful at growing your business.

Be different. If you aren't offering a different and compelling product to a prospect, then they will continue looking. That means you've got to be better at selling you and what it means to buy from you.

As we've already discussed in chapter 8, prospects are more resistant to buying on their first visit and if you don't have ways to overcome this resistance, you will lose the sale. Prospects who are scared of letting go of their money must be sold to differently. In other words, you need to be selling more of who you are and what it means to buy from you instead of just selling a product (which is what most businesses are trying to sell). You never just want to be another option for buying your product or service.

Be where your prospects will see you and where it means something to be seen.

To better understand your customer and to help you elevate your status and illustrate your expertise, answer the following questions:

Where are your best prospective prospects?

What do they read?

What do they watch?

What do they listen to?

Where do they go and congregate?

Where else can you be that is relevant to your prospects?

Where else can you place yourself that elevates your status, importance, and demonstrates your expertise?

Where could you be seen in your market area to help you establish more prominence?

Who or what can you associate yourself with that your best customers pay attention to, respect or are involved in?

As we wrap up this chapter, consider these eight questions to help you avoid playing small and selling yourself short.

1) What is the cost of playing small and not really going for your dreams?

2) What has that cost you so far in your life? What does it cost you spiritually? Emotionally? Financially?

3) What would it continue to cost you if you were to carry on playing small and not really going after your dreams? What would it cost you over the next year? Over the next three years? The next five years?

4) What would it ultimately cost you in your life? What would you lose out on? What would you miss out on? What's the ultimate price that you would have to pay for selling yourself short, playing small, and not going for your dreams?

5) What do you stand to gain by stepping up and making the commitment today to play full out, follow your heart, and live your dreams?

6) When you have what you really want, what will that allow you to be, do, or have?

7) What's most important to you about achieving your dreams in life?

8) How committed are you to doing whatever it takes to achieve your goals?

Anyone can get stuck on a plateau and be frustrated with the lack of results they have. Some businesses get stuck after they've been working in their field for a period of time. What matters is choosing to do something about it and to work on creating more momentum now.

Here are six specific actions you you can take when you feel stuck to accelerate and gain momentum to grow your business to new heights.

1. Be very clear about what you want. You usually get stuck when you start drifting and aren't clear about your destination. Spend 14 minutes each morning planning where you want to end up at the end of each day.

Drifting with the status quo or just going with the tide can give the false appearance of motion without direction. Drifting is dangerous because you feel as though you are making progress (and sometimes you are), but you will never get to your desired goals with the speed and momentum you could if you focused in on the actions required to get you to where you want to go.

Are you clear on the result you want to create? When you are, you will do the work necessary to put the systems into place to make sure that the results you want will happen. When you are clear about what you want, and you build a plan and then you go out and do the work, you will gain more and more confidence in what you are doing.

Choose to take action and get better each and every day. Remember, change begins with language. This is what the inner game is all about. You can tell yourself whatever story you want. Are you telling a story about what you really want?

Plan out an optimal day. Ask yourself: What two or three items (if I do them) will have the greatest impact on my business today?

Michael Hyatt developed the Full Focus Planner to help people better plan their days and get things done. He calls this activity the Daily Big Three. No matter what else happens in your day, you come back and get these activities done. You can get more information about Michael's excellent planning system at https://fullfocusplanner.com

If you will better plan out your day, you will see a difference in the results you actually get each and every day. Be clear about what you want and you will make it happen.

James Kilts, former CEO of Gillette talks about the importance of clarity in his book *Doing What Matters*:

"Most business leaders are hardworking and well intentioned. Yet despite their best efforts, they get in trouble because they lack the clarity of vision and certainty of purpose necessary to confront the reality of their business situations. It's often an inadvertent failure to face the truth fully and honestly. It existed at Gillette as well as Nabisco. And from my discussions with other CEOs, I know that this 'doomsday' scenario plays out at hundreds, if not thousands, of companies. Although I will describe the Circle of Doom's manifestations at a corporate level, it is prevalent at all levels within companies."—p. 193.

He continues: "At times, the slide into the Circle of Doom is the unfortunate by-product of success. A company enjoys several years of strong growth and even stronger earnings. Everything is going right—a bright, motivated management team is in place; the leadership process is functioning well; new products are successful; economic growth is robust; and competitors are quiet. Earnings growth of 15 to 20 percent annually seems like a slam dunk....So a wager is made, and lost, and companies start their descent into the Circle of Doom. It always starts with unrealistic growth targets that are, at best, a long shot to be met.... In order to meet the anticipated growth and keep momentum strong for the future, companies must spend capital and aggressively build overhead structures. Sharp increases in the planned rate of sales mean a larger supply of product will be needed, which in turn means new production capacity will be necessary—a new production line or maybe even a new factory. Since adding capacity takes lead time, capital has to be allocated in advance of the increased sales in order to start the planning and move the organization into high gear.

"...[Then] when it appears that the unrealistic targets are beyond reach, then the companies throw even more money at their problems. Perhaps some high-value cents off coupons will stimulate sales....These stopgap efforts may work for a while. But, ultimately, reality comes knocking. No amount of wishful thinking can create sustainable growth. Sales begin to slide, and so do profits. To increase revenues, prices are raised. But that further erodes sales, and market shares start to drop as consumers balk at the big price gaps between your products and competitive brands. So to prop up the bottom line, marketing budgets are cut. The rationalization goes something like this: Our brand is so strong that reducing the marketing budget by one-quarter and dropping the savings to the bottom line won't even be noticed. We have high consumer loyalty that will carry us through. It is far better to bolster the company's bottom line than it is to have some extra ad impressions.

And when that isn't enough, companies start what's called trade loading. They jam products into their customer's warehouses at cut-rate prices with special terms and conditions, which again helps to delay reality. Yet the outcome is never pleasant."—pp. 193-197.

Here is the sequence of what happens in the Circle of Doom in an industry:

• Unrealistic objections (goals with no strategy to make it happen)

• Invest in additional inventory requiring more capital (and possibly overhead with employees and space)

• When sales targets aren't met, business owners panic and cut prices in order to make whatever sales they can or to create cash flow.

• Profits are down and it is hard to pay the bills so owner invests in a different product line with potential of having greater profitability and increasing their prices (also requires more capital outlay) – this becomes an even more severe problem when the addition of a new line isn't also paired with the deletion of another line.

• Amount of money spent on marketing is cut because there isn't enough profit or all additional capital is now tied up on merchandise in a warehouse.

• Decline in new customer acquisition results in fewer sales.

• Prices are cut through sales to generate cash flow (what Kilts called "Loading the Trade")

• Business owner feels frustrated and stuck – decides to set higher goals without putting the systems in place to make goals a reality – tries to get big wins without making small wins first. As a result, they go back to setting unrealistic objectives of what can be sold.

• The loop continues spiralling downward into even lower and lower profitability until the business either goes out of business or is sold to another owner who thinks the business will be fun and enjoyable (who doesn't understand what is required to make the business profitable).

When you get into the Circle of Doom, it is difficult to get out without a clear strategy and a lot of hard work. It takes focus working on the systems that will help you achieve the goals you want to actually stop being stuck with what is going on.

To escape from the Circle of Doom and to get unstuck, you've got to have an escape plan. You've got to have realistic goals, improved organizational discipline (especially in marketing and sales) and stronger financial management.

That is great advice. It is so important to have clarity, but to have realistic goals and real targets. I believe in setting minimum, target, and optimal goals for this reason. The minimum goal is at the minimum the real target, but you incentivize your team to hit the target and optimal goals because those are what we really want to achieve. Yet, even if you have a setback, you know you have still had growth if you only hit the minimum goals.

Being stuck can happen for a number of reasons, but being unrealistic is right up there near the top.

Let me give you an example. I once had a business owner approach me after a seminar and tell me that she wanted to hit the goal of $1,000,000 in sales and she wanted to know what to do. I asked her a few questions and discovered that she was doing less than 10% of that number in her business at the time. She told me that she wanted to hit the goal in a year or two. I asked her about what she was willing to do to hit the goal. She didn't want to change anything but she just wanted the sales to magically happen and asked me what my secret was to making this happen in our business. I told her there wasn't one magic secret and that a lot of work was involved. She wasn't interested in doing all of the work. She just wanted to know the secret formula to making the goal happen. I think this is what Kilts means by setting unrealistic, unsustainable growth targets. You aren't going to hit targets without working hard at all of the fundamentals of business.

Jim Collins talks about this principle in his book *Good to Great*. He calls the process of building momentum The Flywheel Effect and he calls the Circle of Doom, the Doom Loop. Here is how both of these cycles work in the process of achieving a goal. First, you decide to achieve a goal (financial goal for the business, improve customer service issues, build a web or email strategy, sell more products, etc.)

Then, you take a specific action towards achieving the goal. The first gains seem incremental. It takes tremendous persistence to keep on going when you are not seeing an immediate result or very little improvement or benefit for your business.

Obstacles come up and threaten to derail your forward momentum. You are about ready to break through to a new level and increased momentum. Keep going. This is the worst place to give up, yet this is sadly where many people do lose the momentum they've created.

Then, finally over time, you break through to the next level and start gaining momentum to grow even more. Then, you start over and continue the cycle.

Be clear about what you want. When you find yourself drifting away from your clear objectives, stop, regroup, and get back on track.

2. Change your focus from goal orientation to systems implementation.

I read a really interesting statement about the power of systems in *How to Fail At Almost Everything and Still Win Big* by Dilbert artist Scott Adams. He said: "Throughout my career I've had my antennae up, looking for examples of people who use systems as opposed to goals. In most cases, as far as I can tell, the people who use systems do better. The systems-driven people have found a way to look at the familiar in new and more useful ways. To put it bluntly, goals are for losers. That's literally true most of the time. For example, if your goal is to lose ten pounds, you will spend every moment until you reach the goal—if you reach it at all—feeling as if you were short of your goal. In other words, goal-oriented people exist in a state of nearly continuous failure that they hope will be temporary. That feeling wears on you. In time, it becomes heavy and uncomfortable. It might even drive you out of the game.

"If you achieve your goal, you celebrate and feel terrific, but only until you realize you just lost the thing that gave you purpose and direction. Your options are to feel empty and useless, perhaps enjoying the spoils of your success until they bore you, or set new goals and reenter the cycle of permanent pre-success failure.

"The systems-versus-goals point of view is burdened by semantics, of course. You might say every system has a goal, however vague. And that would be true to some extent. And you could say that everyone who pursues a goal has some sort of system to get there, whether expressed or not. You could word-glue goals and systems together if you chose. All I'm suggesting is that thinking of goals and systems as very different concepts has power. Goal-oriented people exist in a state of continuous pre-success failure at best, and permanent failure at worst if things never work out. Systems people succeed every time they apply their systems, in the sense that they did what they intended to do. The goals people are fighting the feeling of discouragement at each turn. The systems people are feeling good every time they apply their system. That's a big difference in terms of maintaining your personal energy in the right direction.

"The systems-versus-goals model can be applied to most human endeavors. In the world of dieting, losing twenty pounds is a goal, but eating right is a system. In the exercise realm, running a marathon in under four hours is a goal, but exercising daily is a system. In business, making a million dollars is a goal, but being a serial entrepreneur is a system."—pp. 31-32.

He continues:

"For our purposes, let's say a goal is a specific objective that you either achieve or don't sometime in the future. A system is something you do on a regular basis that increases your odds of happiness in the long run. If you do something every day, it's a system. If you're waiting to achieve it someday in the future, it's a goal.

"Language is messy, and I know some of you are thinking that exercising sounds like a goal. The common definition of goals are a reach-it-and-be-done situation, whereas a system is something you do on a regular basis with a reasonable expectation that doing so will get you to a better place in your life. Systems have no deadlines, and on any given day you probably can't tell if they're moving you in the right direction.

"My proposition is that if you study people who succeed, you will see that most of them follow systems, not goals. When goal-oriented people succeed in big ways, it makes news, and it makes an interesting story. That gives you a distorted view of how often goal-driven people succeed. When you apply your own truth filter to the idea that systems are better than goals, consider only the people you know personally. If you know some extra successful people, ask some probing questions about how they got where they did. I think you'll find a system at the bottom of it all, and usually some extraordinary luck."

"...Consider Olympic athletes. When one Olympian wins a gold medal, or multiple gold medals, it's a headline story. But for every medalist there are thousands who had the goal of being on that podium and failed. Those people had goals and not systems. I don't consider daily practices and professional coaching a system because everyone knows in advance that the odds of any specific individual winning a medal through those activities are miniscule. The minimum requirement of a system is that a reasonable person expects it to work more often than not. Buying lottery tickets is not a system no matter how regularly you do it."—pp. 33-34.

What a great insight! When you view what you do in your business everyday in this light, it shifts your focus on building and acting on systems that you can control that produce the results you want. In reality, both goals and systems are required. You need to have a direction, but you also need to have a specific plan of attack for what you will do to make the goal happen.

For example, consider two business owners. One focuses on setting goals and the other focuses on setting up systems for achieving a specific target of a sales revenue number of $3,000/day. Look at the difference:

1) Business Owner Owner A is goal oriented. She sets a goal for $3,000 in sales each day. She is frustrated every day her goal isn't hit.

2) Business Owner B is systems oriented. She sets a goal for $3,000 in sales each day and has the following systems in place:

• She has a Lead Generation System that brings in 6 prospects / day so a minimum of 3 products at an average of $1,000/day can be sold with a 50% close ratio. She has a training system to work at getting her close ratio to 70-75%.

• Each of her sales consultants makes a minimum of 2 outbound phone calls/day and she has 5 consultants. That equals 10 calls / day which equals 5 appointments/day; 30 appointments/week in a 6 day week.

• She has a system that generates inbound leads by mailing out at least 5 postcards / day. With her 5 consultants, that means she could theoretically have 25 possible appointments scheduled. With her system and follow up, she expects at least one qualified lead or appointment/day to result from this system.

• She has a system that generates leads daily from her web site and numerous systems to direct traffic to her web site.

• She generates leads daily from marketing system including utilizing Google Ad Words, her blog, her web site, trade shows and other events.

• Each sale at her business results in an upsell because of follow up systems (converting every prospect buying a product to a follow up appointment where additional items can be sold).

• She has a referral strategy in place to get referrals from past customers (generating 5-10 leads/month).

• She has a system of cross-promotional offers with other vendors that results in new leads every week.

I could go on with more systems that she has in place, but the point is this: This business owner is happy when systems are followed because the owner knows this will consistently lead to success. They may have a disappointing day, but with consistent systems in place, the results take care of themselves.

Are you focused on your goals or on your systems? If you would like more help with systems development, I encourage you to get my book *The System is the Secret* available on Amazon.com.

3. Refocus on your goals, not your problems.

Problems and challenges can distract you from achieving your goals. Some of these problems can keep you up late at night worrying about what to do. The reality is that when you find yourself feeling stuck and discouraged, you are probably focusing on the problem, not the goal. Lee Milteer taught me these five suggestions to reflect on when considering obstacles you face in your business.

1) Refocus your attention on the goal. See yourself with the goal already achieved. What does it feel like to have accomplished your goal? Make your mental image as vivid and detailed as possible as you imagine the feeling of accomplishment.

2) See your problem from a distance. Make the picture small. See the problem as a challenge—an opportunity to use your creativity. Look down on your problem from a mental mountaintop.

3) Recall past successes. Bring the confident feelings back to your mind as you recall these successes. Hold those feelings in your mind as you vividly picture the accomplishment of your new goal.

4) Review what happened just before you got stuck. Is there something different you can do at that point; is there another direction you can take that will help you get unstuck?

5) Examine your goal again. Ask yourself these three questions: a) Is it reasonable? Does it fit your self-image—your talents and training? b) Does it conflict with other goals? (For example, spending more time with your family and doubling your income may be goals that are conflicting— they both require your time. Consequently, it will be very difficult to achieve both.) If it does conflict, modify it or the other goal to resolve the conflict. c) Do you need to be more flexible? If you are stuck on a particular stepping stone, maybe you need to get rid of it and create an alternative steppingstone.

Going through these questions is a great way to refocus on your goals.

4. Start. Get going. Look for little wins that will give you forward progress.

Achieving momentum starts with creating forward progress. Getting started is often the most difficult part. It's like the law of inertia: an object in motion tends to stay in motion, and an object at rest tends to stay at rest. Momentum is what happens when you get moving.

A train moving at full speed will smash right through a brick wall and keep moving; however a single rock place properly can prevent a stopped train from getting started. So in the early stages of creating momentum if problems or obstacles come your way, do whatever it takes to get past them and move forward. That same problem will become easier as you see more and more success.

Take some time to write down the obstacles or barriers that may prevent you from gaining momentum at your business. Creating momentum is not easy. It takes hard work and effort, but once you have momentum, it can change your business. Be persistent. It is easy to lose heart and focus when you are building momentum, but it is the little things consistently done over and over that will take you to new heights.

Momentum is like a chain reaction or dominoes falling. Once the first domino falls, it is hard to stop all of them from falling.

Momentum, by its nature, requires a lot of upfront pushing to get the ball rolling. It takes time and effort to build up momentum.

John Maxwell explains: "It takes a leader to create momentum. Followers catch it. And managers are able to continue it once it has begun. But creating it requires someone who can motivate others, not who needs to be motivated. Harry Truman once said, 'If you can't stand the heat, get out of the kitchen.' But for leaders, that statement should be changed to read, "If you can't make some heat, get out of the kitchen."--*The 21 Irrefutable Laws of Leadership*, p. 171.

To get unstuck, you've got to understand what creates momentum, what stops it or slows it down and how you can work to maintain and sustain the momentum that will help you rise out of a plateau that you may have been experiencing.

So, how do you get unstuck from lost momentum? Here are five steps:

1) Recognize that you are in a slump. Take a time out. Rethink, re-energize and refocus on your business. Talk to those who support you—mentors in the business, friends in other businesses, family members, etc.

2) Remind yourself of a major accomplishment. Select a recent month's sales figures, or a notable victory in your life that made you feel great. Replay it vividly in your mind. Talk about it. Look at photos, thank you letters from customers, or comments from others about the success you experienced. Understand that you are a talented person. You've proved it before and you can do it again.

3) Get back to the basics. One of the main reasons for breaking momentum is that you're not practicing the fundamentals that got you to where you are in the first place. Take some time to have a reality check about your current situation.

Are you doing the easy things instead of the activities and developing the systems that will guarantee you the results you are looking for?

4) Take a break if you're physically or mentally drained. Recapture your energy before you start up again. Don't spend too long here or you'll lose your momentum entirely.

5) Work your way out of the slump. Life and your business are full of cycles. They don't last forever so take one day at a time. Remind yourself, "This too shall pass." The best way out is through. As Winston Churchill once stated, "If you're going through hell, keep going."

5. Take responsibility to steer the momentum. Don't expect anyone else to take the reins and make it happen. It is your job to steer and increase momentum.

John Maxwell says: "Momentum always has a direction. Most people in an organization are carried by that momentum and have little impact on it. But leaders cannot afford to surf momentum; they must steer it."-- *The 21 Most Powerful Minutes in a Leader's Day*, p. 269.

It is a lot easier to steer momentum while you are in motion then it is when you are at a complete standstill. Do you need to change the direction of your business? Are you gaining or losing momentum?

I've learned that times of transition in your business are the most critical times for continuing and sustaining momentum. These can happen when you have a change of leadership. They can happen following a really good month where you start to slide into a bad month. Remember, good leaders can sustain momentum. Great leaders can increase it.

Where are you at right now? Do you need to sustain momentum or do you increase it? It takes a specific set of skills in leadership to increase momentum. You've got to be able to set a new vision, incentivize those who are helping you to achieve the vision, offer encouragement and be willing to get in the trenches and get your hands dirty too. The help of an outside coach or mentor to guide you through such times can be invaluable.

To steer and increase momentum, you often need to break new ground and set new records. You can't just rely on what you used to do in order to sustain what you did last year.

You know you have momentum when you run over obstacles in your path like they were nothing. Momentum is when things happen easily, where one success follows another and forward growth comes quickly. Anticipate the obstacles you will face and your momentum will allow you to move past mistakes quickly. When your team members learn from their mistakes they will sell more and achieve more, and they will do it at a higher level. If something isn't working don't ride it all the way around the doom loop. Adapt quickly and you can pull out of a bad situation.

When the flywheel of momentum starts to turn, pay attention to clues, connections, and opportunities that are presented to you so that you can anticipate obstacles, learn from your mistakes and adapt quickly to succeed.

Remember, your job as the leader of your business is not just to sustain momentum, but to increase it. It is hard to do this if you are always at the grindstone pushing everything forward yourself. Eventually, you will lose your energy, your drive, your enthusiasm, and you will drop out or drop dead. Stephen R. Covey calls this "sharpening the saw."

Abraham Lincoln once said, "If I had eight hours to cut down a tree, I would spend six of them sharpening my axe." Find ways to eliminate the things that drain your energy. Find outlets that inspire you and help put you in a good mood.

Refuse to be bored by the mundane in life. As writer Paulo Coleho observed: "We can become blind by seeing each day as a similar one."

John Maxwell said: "Momentum can make or break your organization. Learn to use it to your advantage and you can take your people anywhere."--*The 21 Most Powerful Minutes in a Leader's Day*, p. 264.

6. Sustain and build momentum. It starts slowly but with consistent focus and time, you can accelerate out of any business plateau that you may currently be on.

The most difficult part of getting unstuck is getting started. Once the ball gets rolling it seems that projects often take on a life of their own and carry themselves through to the finish. Choose to be a person of action.

If you've felt stuck in your business as a result of shifts in the marketplace, I hope you realize that you don't have to be stuck there forever. It is a choice to break free of negative momentum and start doing the things that will help you get back on track.

Don't get so bogged down with your obstacles that you fail to spend time on your opportunities. True leaders see opportunities where others see only problems. Be a leader and look for the opportunities at your business so that you can accelerate out of any business plateaus you may been on and start climbing again up the ladder of success.

What will you do with the opportunities you've been given? What will you be able to say about what you've done at this time next year?

There will always be challenges in any endeavor as you grow and move upward, yet there is a tremendous amount of excitement and optimism when you do so. I hope the ideas I've shared with you here will be things that you will act on each and every day.

Always be looking for ways to create shortcuts and incorporate these game changers into your business. They will help you cut out unnecessary steps that will help position you as the leader and the best provider of your product or service.

CHAPTER 13

DEALING WITH A CRISIS AND CONTROLLING YOUR EMOTIONS

"Crisis reveals what was already in us." --John C. Maxwell

You will experience crisis in business. Some of those may be events like the coronavirus pandemic or other forced on your crises that you weren't planning on happening in your daily routine. As you read this, you may still be dealing with the aftermath of the coronavirus outbreak and the quarantine that went along with it. A roaring economy slowed or came to a halt across virtually every industry for a period of time. The true impact of this event may not be known for many months and years, but the biggest challenge that comes up in a crisis situation is about how your thinking is affected by what is happening around you and how it will affect you. When a crisis comes up in your business, especially one that is out of your complete control, it is easy to panic and lose perspective. In many cases, you will have to rethink how you run your business.

Several years ago, Brian Tracy wrote a book entitled *Crunch Point: The 21 Secrets to Succeeding When It Matters Most.* I first read this book when it came out and I've referred back to it on multiple occasions including during the great recession and again as I was writing this chapter. The book is full of great ideas of what to do when you have tough times in your business (because everyone has them). In this chapter, I'd like to share principles I've learned from this book and other life experiences and then share several specific things you can do to come out of a crisis.

Brian Tracy says in the introduction to this book:

"No matter who you are or what you are doing, every person and organization experiences problems, difficulties, unexpected reversals, and crises that knock you off balance and must be dealt with right away. It is estimated that every business has a crisis every two to three months that, if not handled quickly and effectively, can threaten the very survival of the enterprise."

He continues: "But when the going gets tough, the tough get going. It is only by facing the challenge of a crunch point that you demonstrate to yourself and others what you are really made of....By their very nature, sudden challenges, problems, and crises come unbidden. They are unwanted, unexpected, and often serious in their implications. They also are unavoidable and inevitable. You can never stop them completely. The only part of the challenge-response equation that you can control is your response. All that you can determine is how you are going to respond to the inevitable ups and downs of business and personal life. Your response is under your control."

It is easy to get discouraged or beat down when one problem after another seems to wear you out or wear you down. It can be easy to lose control of your thoughts and feelings and be overwhelmed by whatever crunch point or crisis you are experiencing in your business or personal life.

Brian Tracy says:

"The natural tendency when things go wrong is to react or overreact in a negative way. You may become angry, upset, disappointed, or afraid. These stressful thoughts and negative emotions immediately start to shut down major parts of your brain, including your neocortex, the thinking part of your brain, which you use to analyze, assess, and solve problems and make decisions. If you do not immediately and consciously assert mental and emotional control in crunch time, you will automatically resort to the fight-or-flight reaction. When things go wrong, you will want to either counterattack or retreat, neither of which may be the right strategy in a crisis situation."

During the aftermath of the recession that started in late 2007 and early 2008, Mark S.A. Smith shared with me this about what he does when he experiences a stressful event or moment in his business. He said: "When you feel overwhelmed immediately do these three things:

1) Stop and take a breath. Unless you're in the middle of a life or death situation, you can take five minutes to take a break. You can't be resourceful when you feel overwhelmed, so stop and get your feet on the ground.

2) Make a list of what you know about your situation. Look for information and resources that you can use to move forward. One of the biggest opportunities: renegotiate the deadline to get more breathing room.

3) Identify the next logical step. You don't have to have every step identified, just the next one. You'll be delighted to find that what you need lines up at the right time. Movement relieves overwhelm.

The best way to beat overwhelm is to learn to say, "No!"

I think that is fantastic advice. It also helps to look at every problem or crisis that comes up in your business as a valuable lesson or an opportunity in disguise. While this is much easier said than done, it does help to deal with challenges when you are simultaneously looking for the valuable lesson in every setback or difficulty.

It is hard to know in the midst of a challenge how things will work out. It can be stressful and you may feel fear and worry in the midst of difficulty. However, being paralyzed and not doing anything won't help you move forward. Sometimes the answer to our challenges and crises are not what we want to hear, but the lessons in the tough situations can help us get out and make the changes necessary to get our businesses back on track.

Brian Tracy has a four part "worry-buster formula" that I have used often when I have encountered a difficult situation. Here is his formula:

1) "Stop and identify the worst possible outcome of the problem or crisis. Be perfectly honest with yourself and others. Ask, 'What is the worst thing that can happen in this situation?'

2) Resolve to accept the worst, whatever it is, should it occur. This action calms you down and clears your mind. Once you have mentally decided that you can live with the worst possible outcome, you will stop worrying.

3) Determine what you would do if the worst possible outcome occurred. What actions would you take?

4) Begin immediately to improve upon the worst possible outcome. Identify everything you could do to minimize the damage or reduce your losses. Focus all your time and attention on achieving the very best outcome you possibly can." --*Crunch Point*, p. 12.

When I've realized that being paralyzed by fear doesn't do much to help me overcome my problems, I can move forward with purposeful action to fixing the challenges I'm facing. I would recommend the same formula to you.

I've heard it said that the answer to most of the problems that a business faces is a great offer. In other words, if you invite a group of prospects to take action now, what will the financial result be for you and your business? I'm will discuss more about this later in the chapter when I outline what you can do now to make the most of your next 90 days as you come out of a crisis.

In my book *The System is the Secret*, I outlined four types of challenges that come up as crisis situations in a business and some examples of each one. The third one is a crisis that is forced on you. These are things that you are blindsided by that you have little to no control over that you can dramatically impact your business. These could include:

o Coronavirus panic (cancellations and decreased revenue)

o Cash flow crunch – not being able to make payroll (or having to cut your own payroll out)

o Customer service issues

o Any crisis in your family

o Products or raw materials arriving late because of supply chain issues and dealing with the aftermath or loss of your customers

o Negative review by client online that causes you stress (especially when it is wrong and not true)

o Seeing expenses go up without a corresponding increase in sales

When you experience any kind of challenge (especially when you or one of your team has made a mistake that will cost you money), it is best to ask yourself the following ten questions so you can get the facts:

1) What is the situation exactly?

2) What has happened from different perspectives?

3) How did it happen?

4) When did it happen?

5) Where did it happen?

6) What are the facts?

7) How do we know that these facts are accurate?

8) Who was involved?

9) Who is responsible for doing (or not doing) the things that set in motion the challenge we are facing today?

10) What can be done to ensure that this situation doesn't happen in the future?

Sometimes, we make assumptions that get us into trouble without getting all of the facts. It is best to question your assumptions and even determine what would happen if they were wrong before making any concrete decisions about doing something different.

When you make a BIG mistake that causes you to lose money or your business experiences something shocking that you weren't expecting (like the panic surrounding the coronavirus pandemic), you go through the five stages of grief as outlined by psychologist Elizabeth Kübler-Ross. These are the same stages you go through when you lose someone close to you. When you understand these emotions, you can better bounce back from the disappointment and frustration you feel when something doesn't go your way in your business.

These stages are:

1. **Denial** – basically what happens here is you are shocked because you can't believe what is happening is happening to you. It wasn't supposed to happen and you recognize that it will now seriously disrupt you and your business. In denial, you mentally try to shut out what you are feeling and pretend that it really isn't happening.

2. **Anger** – once you realize that the situation is indeed happening (such

as having to have all of your employees work from home, considering the lost revenue for your business, losing a valuable employee, or finding out about any mistake that will cost you money, the natural tendency is to lash out in anger against someone else that you feel is responsible for the setback that you are experiencing). When you do this to members of your team, we may say things we really don't mean and which we can't take back.

3. **Blame** – anger turns into blame very quickly where you try to track down the person that caused the problem in the first place. Sometimes in really bad situations, someone may end up getting fired.

4. **Depression** – when the reality sets in that you can't avoid the setback takes place, it is common and easy to get depressed and tremendously discouraged. You feel let down, cheated and betrayed by someone else. Very often, you may feel sorry for yourself (especially when you look around at others and see that they don't seem to be experiencing the same challenges that you are). In the case of the coronavirus, most everyone else is dealing with the same challenges you are.

5. **Acceptance** – At some point, you realize that the setback has happened and that it doesn't do anymore good to be angry about what is going on. You accept what happened and start looking to the future again. In some cases, this may take several weeks or months before this feeling is reached.

The thing I would mention about these five stages (and why it is important to understand them) is that when you recognize what stage you are in, you can take control of your emotions and get through the next step. This isn't easy, but it is a lot harder if you don't have a road map to guide you through the challenges. The key action is to learn to control your emotions so that you can do something productive towards overcoming the crisis or challenge in front of you,

Brian Tracy says that "when a crisis occurs, there are four things you should do immediately.

1) Stop the bleeding. Practice damage control. Put every possible limitation on losses. Preserve cash at all costs.

2) Gather information. Get the facts. Speak to the key people and find out exactly what you are dealing with.

3) Solve the problem. Discipline yourself to think only in terms of solutions, about what you can do immediately to minimize the damage and fix the problem.

4) Become action-oriented. Think in terms of your next step. Often any decision is better than no decision." –p. 31-32.

The process for making any of the types of decisions mentioned above are triggered when:

• You are dissatisfied with a situation and you start asking "What If" questions. Michael Hyatt at the onset of the COVID-19 coronavirus crisis in the United States asked: "What does this make possible?" as a great question to consider at the onset or in the midst of crisis.

• You discover an opportunity and begin investigating how it could affect you

• You meet a talented or exceptional individual

• Looking and thinking about ways to turn some kind of challenge into an opportunity

Many have a difficult time deciding to START because of:

1) The paralysis of analysis

2) Being overcome by fears

3) Having a stronger belief in others more than self (He/She could do it, but I never could...because...)

4) Personal excuses

Many business owners have a difficult time deciding to STOP for the same reasons.

If you are going to get more done at your business, you've got to decide AND act. Those who are most successful decide and get into motion right away. There is little or no time gap between decision and action. They get to implementation right away.

It takes persistence to change and grow through a crisis. Successful entrepreneurs in any industry are risk takers who persist and do whatever it takes to overcome the challenges they face. As I've studied the lives of those who have succeeded in business, I've noticed that those who make things happen have a desire to take control of their destiny and are willing to step out on a limb in order to do so.

It also takes an ability to control your emotions. It means overcoming worry, fear, and anxiety. This is not easy to do. We've been dealing with these emotions for a long time as members of the human race.

In the spring of 1948, nearly three years after the end of World War II, Dale Carnegie published his classic book *How to Stop Worrying and Start Living.*

In Chapter 3 of the book, he tells this story:

"Many years ago, a neighbor rang my doorbell one evening and urged me and my family to be vaccinated against smallpox. He was only one of thousands of volunteers who were ringing doorbells all over New York City. Frightened people stood in lines for hours at a time to be vaccinated. Vaccination stations were opened not only in all hospitals, but also in firehouses, police precincts, and in large industrial plants. More than two thousand doctors and nurses worked feverishly day and night, vaccinating crowds. The cause of all this excitement? Eight people in New York City had smallpox—and two had died. Two deaths out of a population of almost eight million.

"Now, I had lived in New York for many, many years; and no one had ever rung my doorbell to warn me against the emotional sickness of worry—an illness that, during that same time period, had caused ten thousand times more damage than smallpox.

"No doorbell ringer has ever warned me that one person out of ten now living in these United States will have a nervous breakdown—induced in the vast majority of cases by worry and emotional conflicts. So I am writing this chapter to ring your doorbell and warn you.

"The great Nobel prize winner in medicine, Dr. Alexis Carrel, said, 'Businessmen who do not know how to fight worry die young.' And so do housewives and horse doctors and bricklayers."—*How to Stop Worrying and Start Living*, p. 40.

We could add every profession and every industry in today's times. I'm not comparing the current COVID-19 situation with this story in its severity. I just think the response to fear that he details here is something that we are facing today as well. Viruses are contagious. Fear, panic, hysteria, calm, empathy, kindness, and love are also contagious. We choose which one we will spread by our thoughts and actions.

Dr. Carrel's advice that "those who do know how to fight worry die young" is a great reminder to all of us. The best way to conquer fear or worry is to take action. In his book, Carnegie says: "Inaction breeds doubt and fear. Action breeds confidence and courage." In this time, that is great advice. Take action in the direction of your goals and dreams today, tomorrow, and always.

As you work at taking action in the midst of a crisis, I invite you to consider the actions you are going to take to pull out of the crisis and make things happen in your business. Here are seven suggestions:

1. Start with your intention.

When you make the decision to pull out of a crisis, you have to have an intention to make things better than they were. A great coach taught me that your intention is everything. If your goal is to go running first thing in the morning, he said that the key to doing it is to set up everything the night before manifesting your intention. So, you would put out your exercise clothes, socks, and shoes and put them right by your bed so when you went to bed and set your alarm clock, you knew that when you woke up, you would be ready to go to your workout.

What will you do to manifest your intentions that you are serious about really doing the right things that will lead to your results? What will you do to ensure you won't get distracted with anything that will pull you off of your goal?

2. Take simultaneous actions, not sequential ones.

In unprecedented situations, you don't know exactly which thing you do will bring the greatest results. Instead of waiting to find out, take simultaneous actions. As you monitor what is working, you'll discover what is working best. Then, put more of your effort there. In the midst of a crisis, with things changing on an hourly or daily basis, it is best to have a Plan A, B, and C and be working towards making them each happen. Anticipate trends and direction. Work on your opportunities, don't just react to what's going on around you.

Be quick and agile. Respond to a crisis quickly. Minimize the time between your decision and action.

3. Increase your effort.

Take massive action. Implement quickly. When you look at anyone who is super successful, it is no surprise. Just look at everything that they're doing.

In the midst of a crisis, it is time to operate at peak levels with increased effort. If you want the next 90 days to be the most productive you've ever had, you've got to act like you have never acted before.

Anybody can do anything for a period of time. You can be a peak performer for 90 days. Think about what would happen if you did that.

You can raise your effort for the next 90 days and cut out time wasters and only focus on things that will bring you sales and bring you money.

As I mentioned earlier, in times of crisis, it is natural to turn up our performance to ensure that we get the results we want. Here are eight areas where you must raise your effort in the next 90 days:

1) Your most important profit generating items in your business – what is selling best and what is helping you make the most profit now? If you only focused on selling those items (and incentivized your prospects and customers to buy them), could you sell even more of them over the next 90 days?

2) Your best team members - Who are the 20% of your team that produced most of your results (80%)? What should you do to reward them and help them buy into your 90-day challenge? What incentives or rewards will you put in place to get them excited about what you are doing?

3) Your core marketing activities - What are the three to five things that are working best right now to bring in prospects? In other words, if you found out today that you could only do one things to get prospects into your marketing funnel, what would that core marketing activity be? Then, over the next 90 days, work on amping up your efforts in that area (or at the most 3 areas) so you can bring in the right kinds of prospects now. This doesn't mean you stop doing the other marketing things you've already got in place. What you are doing is focusing on what is working best and amping up your performance in those areas. For example, if you are spending $X a month on Google Ad Words now, and that is bringing in customers, why not double or triple that over the next 90 days?

4) Sales strategy – What is working best for you to close the sale now? What seems to get your sales consultants excited and your prospects excited to buy now? Put your best sales strategy in place to ensure the maximum number of dollars to enter your business every day.

5) Profit centers – What 20% of your business is generating 80% of your profits? What can you do in the next 90 days to ensure that you are selling more of what is making you the most money?

6) Top Customers – who are your top customers? Who has already come back and bought something else from you? What can you do to get those customers back to buy something else from you in the next 30 days? The key question: How can you get more of your customers who have already purchased something from you in the last 90 days to buy something from you again in the next 30 days?

7) Your own skills, qualities and attributes – What is the one thing that you and only you can do that would have the biggest impact on making the next 90 days your most productive ever? Does that mean you should be out selling yourself at least two appointments per day (or 3 hours a day)? Does that mean that you go out and generate ad revenue for your business three hours a week?

8) The key result areas of your business – what is your daily goal in order to make your 90-day challenge possible? Where are you the strongest right now? Where are you the weakest? Where should you put your focus in the next 90 days? What one thing could you do in the next 24-48 hours that would strengthen and reinforce your weakest key result area?

Transformation is possible for you. It is up to you to decide that you will persist through any difficulty you are facing now in order to make a major transformation in the next 90 days.

James Whitcome Riley once wrote: "The most essential factor is persistence, the determination never to allow your energy or enthusiasm to be dampened by the discouragement that must inevitably come.

4. Create a manufactured why.

Sometimes, a crisis can create your why. When your back is against the wall, it is easy to motivate yourself to do what needs to be done. If you aren't up against the wall, then you need to manufacture your why.

Most business owners wait until a crisis to actually get down and create optimal results. Well, there is a big one here now with all that has happened and is happening as a result of the coronavirus panic and its aftermath.

What would happen instead if you manufactured a why that got you out doing things differently than you ever did them before?

In order to get yourself to perform at peak levels, you need to create a why that will motivate you.

The key is that if the why is not compelling enough, you will give up to soon. That's the beauty of having a 90-day challenge. You will work like crazy over the next 90 days on your key result areas because you have your why reason.

Where are you heading? Where do you want to end up? These are important questions that you must take time to stop and think about. In all of the hustle and bustle of dealing with the present crisis, are you taking time to readjust your direction and get on track to where you want to go?

If not, you will likely end up in a much different place than what you thought when you got into this business. Why not make the next 90 days your best ever?

Why not manufacture your reasons why you will make the next 90 days exceptional?

Ask yourself the following questions:

• What will be my why?

• What reward will I give myself if we hit our outrageous goal in the next 90 days?

• What would I have to start doing now in order to make this vision a reality?

• What do I need to stop doing that is wasting my time and taking me away from doing what I must be doing to hit this goal?

It is time for you to be proactive about what you want from this business. Get out there with your why and make amazing things happen.

I love these words from poet Edgar A. Guest:

"The easy roads are crowded

And the level roads are jammed;

The pleasant little rivers

With drifting folks are crammed.

But off yonder where it's rocky,

Where you get the better view,

You will find the ranks are thinning

And the travelers are few.

Where the going's smooth and pleasant

You will always find the throng,

For the many—more's the pity

Seem to like to drift along.

But the steps that call for courage

And the task that's hard to do,

In the end result in glory

For the never-wavering few."

When you have a reason why and can clearly articulate that purpose to others, you will find that you will attract better individuals to your team. The secret to fast growth and making the next 90 days coming out of a crisis absolutely amazing is to remember that people want to be around those who know where they are going and everyone wants to be a part of something bigger.

Your sales consultants and every member of your team will buy into your vision for your business when they buy into you as a leader and they see that you clearly understand why you are committed to your business and the next 90 days of intense effort.

If they constantly hear you grumbling about everything that is wrong with your business instead of staying focused on where you are headed, they will lose faith in what you and they are doing. Be the kind of leader who knows exactly what you stand for and those who surround you will also stand up with you to help you accomplish the goals you have for your business.

5. Pick an outrageous goal that inspires you.

Don't pick an average goal. Pick something that will totally inspire you and cause you to stretch. A goal that will give you the juice and the motivation to go the distance.

What will cause you to not get bored, but actually get excited again about your business?

What will get you up every morning with a smile on your face thinking about what you are going to do?

Maybe your outrageous goal is to have $50,000 or $100,000 (or ten times that) set aside in your business reserves savings account at the end of 90 days AND to take the trip you've always wanted this summer. This is money you can use to help you get through a difficult crisis in the future.

Let's say that your outrageous goal is that you are going to personally contact 100 prospects and invite them to buy something from you. Let's say that everyone else on your team also sets the same goal.

Make this a game. Who will get there first? You can play this game one of two ways. You could play it to see who is the first person to actually contact 100 prospects or you could play it as who is the first person who actually talks to 100 prospects and invites them personally to do business with you now with a specific offer with an end date to get the offer (which creating urgency).

Either method will get you immediate action and activity into your business, but the second one will have a better long-term result. In other words, for one of your 100 prospects to count, you have to talk with or interact with a prospects in a live fashion in some way (in other words a voice mail is a start, but you only get to count the prospect as one of your 100 when you actually talk to him or her or receive a message back from them that they are ready to set up an appointment to talk with you about what you offer).

Set a reward that the first sales consultant who gets to 100 documented contacts with 100 prospects to will get a $100 bill or the one who exceeds $100,000 in sales will get one hundred $100 bills. Then, let the contest begin. You can create excitement by focusing on what matters now.

You could also change this up and have the requirement be that 50 of the prospects have to be new customers (who haven't purchased anything yet) and 50 of those you meet with have to be customers who bought one thing from you and are now scheduled for an appointment to consider something else you offer that can be beneficial to them.

Or perhaps, your goal could be: "Over the next 90 days, I'm going to bring in personally to the business (through selling to prospects or selling advertising in my business an additional $100,000."

This means that you will bring in at least an extra $1,111.11 every day over the next 90 days. Is that doable? Yes. Will it be challenging? Yes.

What will you need to do differently every day to make that goal happen? Simply put, you will need to schedule yourself at least one more appointment on average every day and making an additional sale every day. You should also set the goal to be the first one to call 100 customers who have already bought something from you and how you can help them grow their business.

What would happen if you reached that goal? What would happen if two or three other members of your sales team hit that goal?

What could your reward be? Maybe you pay an additional $1,000 bonus plus a trip to a specific destination when it is safe to travel again for a couple of days. You decide what the reward will be. But, get excited about whatever you decide to do.

Will you take up an outrageous challenge to dramatically change your business in the next 90 days?

You get to set the goal, but the more outrageous the goal and the reward is, the more your team members will step up to the challenge and you'll be amazed by the results.

What will your outrageous goal be? Set it and watch that goal inspire you over the next 90 days to exceptional productivity and results.

Use the advantages of technology to get in touch with customers and get them talking about you so that they want to do business with you. Use more technology to get prospects in touch with you.

Due to technology, it is now easier to communicate a focused message than ever before. Many struggle with technology because they don't have a structured focused message.

The goal here is to automate your sales process. If you can do more of your marketing AND sales through technology, that will free up yours and your bridal consultants time so that your revenue goes up and your time spend selling and marketing will go down.

6. Have an accountability partner who you can work with who will tell you what you need to do.

If your phone bill didn't have a due date, when would you pay it?

If your mortgage didn't have a due date, when would you pay it?

Accountability is a very important part of results.

What accountability mechanisms do you have in place that help you perform at your best (so that you are always working at peak level?

How can you perform at peak performance if you don't have an accountability mechanism?

For example, if you set the goal to lose weight, the following accountability mechanisms can keep you on track:

• Food calorie counter app tracks what you're really eating. If you go over, you have to exercise.

• A set time to work out each day which you have to report to someone you did (coach, partner, etc.)

• Having a high intention to lose weight – you put constraints in place to ensure that this time you won't get off track (Putting out your workout clothes the night before and planning your routine when you first wake up or when you get home is a BIG part of intention)

• Having an accountability partner who can keep you on track and help coach you to ensure that you are working at a peak performance level.

What accountability mechanisms will you put in place to ensure that you achieve the results you want?

7. Focus ONLY on doing revenue producing activities over the next

90 days. Pay for performance, not perspiration.

If you are going through a challenging time right now, realize that fear, panic, and worry was not going to make will not make your situation any better. Worrying is not going to help you create money or sales. When you are singularly focused on achieving results through revenue producing activities, you won't waste time doing anything else.

There are three main revenue producing activities in your business:

1) Generate new leads.

2) Schedule appointments.

3) Close sales.

That's it. Three things. If you and every member of your team start focusing more on ONLY doing activities that produce revenue, guess what? Your business will begin to transform itself. Money will start flowing into your business again. You can turn your situation around and rebuild your business to be what it needs to be or transform it to the next level.

Have the intention to produce the best result you've ever had in your business in the next 90 days. What is that for you?

What will you do over the next 90 days that will help you peak perform?

To succeed at achieving your 90-day challenge goal, you need to manage by the three Ps – Persistence, Perspiration and Performance. I got that idea from Michael Feuer in his book The Benevolent Dictator. I think it is a very valuable idea and one that you should employ at your business.

A word of caution:

Henry Ward Beecher once wrote: "The first hour is the rudder of the day." The way you start each day in the next 90 days has to be different from what you've been doing the last 90 days.

If you are getting up and checking Facebook or getting online and filling your mind with negative things from the news, it is time to stop for the next 90 days. Instead, begin each day with intention. What do you need to do the night before (like setting out your exercise clothes) to manifest your intention that the next 90 days is going to be different, that it is going to be amazing?

In the next 90 days, you need to treat yourself like an Olympic athlete who is only focused on one goal: winning.

You define what you want. Then, manifest your intention by starting your day off right. Focus on what you want and make sure you only do what will help you reach your goal. Then, at the end of the day, ask: What did I do today that will help me get closer to my goal? If you got distracted, you have to put ground rules in place so you can get on task tomorrow and not let that happen again during your 90 Day Challenge.

Spend a few minutes every morning reflecting on your goal, making assignments for yourself and members of your team that you will do in order to get what it is that you want. There is no excuse for not making the most of every day for the next 90 days.

Refuse to get angry or upset when things go wrong during the day. Instead, ask yourself: What will I do next to get back on track towards accomplishing our outrageous goal in the next 90 days?

If you hear disappointing news, bounce back quickly and refocus on the critical success areas that you know will yield results.

In the next 90 days, choose to eliminate criticism, condemnation, or complaining from your vocabulary. These actions weaken you and you don't have time for that. You need to talk more and focus more on what you want in the next 90 days.

Plant more seeds every day if you want to reap a harvest. If you don't like your harvest, you didn't plant enough seeds in the right places. To see growth, you need an immediate campaign now to get more seeds planted and growing.

If you're not reaping a harvest in your business it's likely that you didn't plant enough seeds last season. To make sure this doesn't happen again, plant more seeds now and every day.

Far too many spend too little time everyday working on their marketing and filling their marketing funnel and planting future seeds for growth. This next 90 days as you emerge from your crisis is going to be different. Your next 90 days is going to be amazing.

Don't make excuses. Just go out and make it happen.

I love this statement by Dr. C.E. Welch:

"Many fail because they quit too soon. People lose faith when the signs are against them. They do not have the courage to hold on, to keep fighting in spite of that which seems insurmountable. If more of us would strike out and attempt the 'impossible,' we very soon would find the truth of that old saying that nothing is impossible. Abolish fear, and you can accomplish anything you wish."

A crisis will happen in your business in the future. It doesn't matter what it is. It is your job to beat the crisis by your thinking and focused action. You can do it.

LESSONS ABOUT DOING WHILE DEALING WITH DISCOURAGEMENT AND DEFEAT

"How you think about a problem is more important than the problem itself. So always think positivbely."
--Norman Vincent Peale."

In this epilogue, I'd like to share some final thoughts on dealing with crisis situations, and how to deal with defeats, setbacks, and discouragement. Every entrepreneur faces tremendous disappointment, defeat, discouragement, and even failure at different points of their career. No one enjoys going through difficulty or disappointment. When you look back at your experiences, you can be reflective, but you have to live in the present. It is important to live in the now and take actions to make a better future. In fact, your experiences in business may have been filled with disappointments and with things you never would have imagined would have happened when you started. I'd like to share some lessons and thoughts I've learned about how to control your thinking and emotions so you can take the actions necessary to get your business to where it needs to be.

John Maxwell says the following about adversity:

"Adversity and the failure that often results from it should be expected in the process of succeeding, and they should be viewed as absolutely critical parts of it."

Consider the inspiring story of horse jockey Eddie Arcaro. He won more American Classic horse races than any other jockey in history and is the only one to have won the U.S. Triple Crown twice.

However, he began his career with 250 straight losses before he had his first win eight months later. "On January 14, 1932, a month before his sixteenth birthday, Arcaro won his first race. He steadily improved under [horse trainer] Clarence Davison's tutelage, but in 1934 Arcaro cracked his skull, fractured two ribs, and punctured his lung after tumbling off a horse in Chicago. With Arcaro sidelined for at least two months, Davison sold the rider's contract to Calumet Farms. Arcaro recovered quickly and resumed racing. Four years later, in 1938, he captured his first Kentucky Derby win. In 1941, ten years after he had been told he would never be good enough to be a jockey, Arcaro became only the fifth jockey to capture the U.S. Triple Crown, riding Whirlaway in the Kentucky Derby, the Preakness Stakes, and the Belmont Stakes. History repeated itself in 1948, when Arcaro won the U.S. Triple Crown astride Citation. During his thirty-one year racing career, he rode in 24,092 races, won 4,779 victories, placed in the top three 11,888 times, and posted a record 554 stakes victories. Arcaro's skill earned him the nickname 'The Master.' He was inducted into the Official National Thoroughbred Racing Hall of Fame in 1958, three years before he retired from the sport. He once observed: 'You have to remember that about 70 percent of the horses running don't want to win. Horses are like people. Everybody doesn't have the aggressiveness or ambition to knock himself out to become a success." – *The Secret of Success is Not a Secret*, p. 17-18.

That is a great story about the importance of perseverance when beginning anything new. It takes a lot of courage and managing your thoughts and emotions to get through multiple disappointments and failures on the way to success. Dan Kennedy said this about disappointments: "I recently saw the woman who owned Secretariat, a Triple Crown winner who absolutely destroyed the field in the Belmont his year, and was one of the greatest racehorses who ever lived. She was asked about what her level of confidence had been after the Derby, after the Preakness, before the Belmont. She said that she never got too optimistic because 'this is a business made of disappointments.' She was much younger in the pictures with Secretariat, elderly in this interview, and wise. She smiled cheerfully when she said it. It was not a gloomy pronouncement. It was simple recognition of a reality. If you can't handle a lot of disappointment, you probably aren't getting to the winner's circle....In any case, it is a resilient attitude that is mission-critical to successful performance in most things. Difficulty and disappointment must be managed, which also means managing your thoughts and emotions." --13-34, p. 1.

Everyone learns much more from failure than they do from success, but no one wants to have to have difficulties or adversities. We would all rather skip these all together, yet this is where we learn the most. The truth is that we learn more from our failures than our successes.

You shouldn't lose faith when challenging moments arise. That doesn't mean you don't think about quitting. The key is to keep going. When I've had a challenging day, I often think about the words to Walter Wintle's famous poem "If You Think You Can". He said:

"If you think you are beaten, you are;

If you think you dare not, you don't.

If you'd like to win, but think you can't,

It's almost a cinch you won't.

If you think you'll lose, you're lost,

For out in the world we find

Success begins with a fellow's will;

It's all in the state of mind.

If you think you're outclassed, you are;

You've got to think high to rise.

You've got to be sure of yourself before

You can ever win a prize.

Life's battles don't always go

To the stronger or faster man;

But soon or late the man who wins

Is the one who thinks he can."

George Horace Lorimer said: "Because a fellow has failed once or twice, or a dozen times, you don't want to set him down as a failure til he's dead or loses his courage—and that's the same thing."

If you've experienced any fear, disappointment, discouragement or defeats in your business as things have shifted in the marketplace, take heart—you're not alone. Everyone who has ever accomplished anything has experienced the emotions of fear, loss, rejection, frustration, and discouragement from bad mistakes or worries. Each of these emotions can have a paralyzing effect on your mind and prevent you from taking the actions you must take.

I've read many biographies over the years and one principle that stands out to me is that all entrepreneurs experience failure.

Consider Sam Walton who started Wal-Mart. Early in his business

career, biographer Vance Trimble said the following about his entry into
Bentonville, Arkansas following the failure of another store he opened.
He says:

"The junior department store lasted just a couple of years, Sam Walton's
first expansion—and first failure. However, the Ben Franklin store was
a definite and brilliant success....The fantastic way in which Sam built
up and enlarged his sales volume beyond anything that had been done
before by a Newport five-and-dime caught the eye of his landlord, P.K.
Holmes Senior...[He] was amazed by, and more than a little envious of,
the high flying Ben Franklin Store. In the spring of 1950, P.K. Holmes
Senior called at the store to have a business talk with Sam Walton.
What the landlord had to say sent a stunned and distraught Sam flying
to his lawyer's office. 'My God, what's the matter?' said Fred Pickens Jr.

'My lease! My lease!,' said Sam Walton. 'It's up at the end of the year!'
'Well, just renew it. You've got an option to do that—I suppose.' The
lawyer watched Sam Walton, the thirty-two-year-old merchant 'genius'
of Newport, lower his head and stare glumly at the rug, shuffling his feet
in agitation.

'No,' said Sam Walton weakly, 'I don't.'

Fred Pickens Jr. rushed to the rescue and began trying to negotiate a
renewal of the lease. It was critical for Sam. There was no other suitable
and available location for a Ben Franklin store in Newport. If he
couldn't hang on to his Front Street location, he'd be out of business.
The lawyer offered Holmes Senior higher rent; he didn't accept. He
tried to interest the landlord in various different terms but kept running
into a stone wall. Then, finally, he grasped the real situation.

'It's no good,' he told Sam. 'I hope to God the next time you take over
a lease from somebody, you check to make certain it contains a proper
renewal clause. They're not going to let you keep the store. The plain
truth is they want Douglas Holmes to run a Ben Franklin in that
building! You've shown the whole town what a money-maker it can be.'

Fred Pickens Jr. watched the color drain out of his client's lean face.

'Looks like you're finished,' he said.

"The lawyer saw Sam clenching and unclenching his fists, staring at his hands. Sam straightened up. 'No, Fred,' he said. 'I'm not whipped. I found Newport, and I found the store. I can find another good town— and another Ben Franklin. Just wait and see!'

Then, he decided to move his store to Bentonville, Arkansas (which is still the headquarters of Wal-Mart today). However, "Bad luck was still stalking Sam Walton. The storm clouds that had hovered over the square on his arrival nine days ago returned malevolently. A violent downpour began May 9—the first day he had taken possession of the Harrison Variety store.

" 'It was the worst rain in the history of Bentonville,' Sam recalls. 'Twelve inches in twenty-four hours! Of course, the store's old roof leaked. I had to rush around covering all the counters with oilcloth and plastic to keep the merchandise from being washed away—really!' As soon as the weather cleared, Sam leveled the wall, enlarged his store, installed new shelves and counters, as well as fluorescent lights, and hung out a big new sign: WALTON'S 5 & 10c.' In the Benton County Democrat he announced a one-day remodeling sale for Saturday, July 29, with free balloons for 'all the kids.'...Sam Walton had pulled off his entry into Bentonville...[but] he used up all the money he was bringing out of Newport. [He] was down to zero again."

The announcement in the paper when they left Newport said:

"It is with regret that we are preparing to leave Newport, and our many friends and customers. Being unable to renew our lease, we are moving to Bentonville, Arkansas, to make our future home. As of January 1st, the Ben Franklin store will be under new ownership and management. We sincerely appreciate your friendship and patronage during the past five and a half years and assure you it has been a pleasure and a privilege to have been of service to you. Once again, friends, 'THANKS FOR EVERYTHING.' –Sam and Helen Walton" –*Sam Walton*, pp. 54-64.

This is just one example of how Sam Walton persevered through failure to success. Since all entrepreneurs experience failure of some kind, I want to talk with you about what you can do to control your thoughts and emotions and work through the adversities you face on the way to success.

Dr. Henry Cloud says: "I have not met a leader who thinks perfectly rationally 100 percent of the time. All humans have a tendency toward goofy or distorted interpretations of events and other people's motives, especially under extreme stress. All of us have our insecurities, and those touchy buttons that, when pushed, cause our thinking to go awry and our fears to be magnified. The key is to know your own particular style of kookiness. Once you know your own patterns, you can recognize them and change them. While there is no limit to the variations on distorted thinking that affect performance, there are some patterns that crop up more often than not. These include: overidentification with results, indecisiveness, conflict avoidance, and resistance to change." – *Boundaries for Leaders*, p. 209.

When you're going through stressful times, it is easy to let fear overwhelm and paralyze you. Dr. Henry Cloud makes this observation in his book *Boundaries for Leaders*: "The problem is that the brain is wired to avoid pain and anxiety. Over time, when you continue to avoid things that cause you fear or anxiety, such as a CEO's fear of letting someone struggle, a pattern builds up, causing you to respond almost automatically to any situations that would cause you that anxiety. As a leader, you cannot allow a pattern of fear and avoidance to rule you. If you are afraid of making a mistake, you will never make bold moves. If you are afraid of upsetting or disappointing people, you will never be able to deal with underperforming employees. As a leader, you have to act (or not act), despite the fear, but never because of it."

He continues:

"In my experience, many great leaders go through a three-stage process when it comes to facing their fears. First, they fear it and put it off. Next, they push through the fear, make the decision, and it is painful. And finally, they wonder why they waited so long to make it after the pain is gone and they have resolved the problem. As these stages are internalized, and they become aware of them, seasoned leaders find it easier to make these hard calls. But as long as you don't confront these uncomfortable feelings, your emotions will control your actions. Grow past the fear! Look at what you are afraid of and get to the bottom of it. Is it failure? Is it loss of approval? Is it fear of confrontation? Is it fear of causing someone distress? Is it fear of change? And remember: You can have fears without being 'fearful.' 'Fearful' is when you let your fears make your decisions for you, so...don't let fear make your decisions for you! Having fears is normal. Being 'fearful' is dysfunctional. Fearful leaders—that is, those who respond out of fear—are the worst leaders, period.

"So, feel your fear, name it, accept it, talk it over with those you trust, and then choose to do the right thing, no matter how uncomfortable you feel. People are waiting on you! Lead! Who cares how you feel?! Do what is needed and work through the feelings later." –pp. 212-213.

This is so important. When facing your fears, you've got to do something over which you have control. You may not know everything to do, but you can do something everyday to improve your situation and get things turned around.

This directly affects you because when you allow your thoughts to run rampant in any way, your brain freezes up and tells you to basically do nothing since your brain thinks that 'it won't make any difference.'

Dr. Henry Cloud says:

"Your brain thinks that since you have no control over what is making you feel miserable, it might as well give up trying to have any control at all. How does this happen? To understand it, you have to remember what caused it in the first place: a lack of control over things that affect your well-being....In a learned helplessness situation, the brain can make a big thinking shift in how it tells your entire system to respond. It just goes passive and shuts down. Initiation stops. Creative thinking stops. The search for solutions stops. Problem solving stops. Trying new options stops. It's game over, or at least on pause. That is learned helplessness in a nutshell. Your brain thinks, 'Nothing I can do.' But, as if it could get no worse, it does. Later research showed that without some kind of intervention or reframing, this kind of passivity will become even more pronounced and predictable in a thinking style. Seligman put this thinking style into three categories, the 'three P's,' which are: Personal, Pervasive, and Permanent

He continues:

"The three P's are ways that people explain things that happen, and this thinking style shuts them down. It usually begins with a single event. Say a salesperson calls a client to offer a new product, and the client says that he is not interested. Someone without optimism would think, 'Oh, well. Guess that client doesn't need it, or he has a brother-in-law he buys from, or he is an idiot, or has another plan,' or some other explanation like that. And then the salesperson moves on and calls the next client, as if life is still normal and making calls leads to sales. But the person with learned helplessness thinks in a very different way, with the three P's now dictating how he experiences this episode. He explains the event (the client saying no) very negatively in three ways:

1. First P: He 'personalizes it.'

"Instead of explaining the reason for the 'no' as something due to external events having nothing to do with him, he explains it in relation to himself, in a negative direction. 'I am such a lousy salesperson. I am a loser. I am not convincing when I talk to clients. I have no credibility.

No wonder they aren't buying anything from me.' Bottom line: 'It is because I am bad in some way.'

2. Second P: he sees it as 'pervasive.'

"Instead of seeing this as a specific, isolated event, just one client, he generalizes it to 'everything.' It goes from a single event to a pervasive reality. 'It isn't just this client...all of my clients think that about me. In fact, it isn't just my clients. It is this whole business I am in, and this whole industry. And it is not just this product....none of our products are that good. And it is not just work. My friends really don't like me either. In fact, it really is my whole life. It's all bad.' The single event has been interpreted in a negative way that pervades the whole picture. Everything begins to look negative. Bottom line: 'Nothing is going well.'

3. Third P: He sees it as 'permanent.'

"Instead of seeing this event as a single event in a single point in time, he sees it as permanent. He thinks it will continue happening this way: 'It is not going to change. It will always be this way. The good days are gone. We will never make our numbers again,' he reasons. The thinking says the current negative event is not something that will eventually pass but has become 'the way it is, and the way it will be.' It is the 'new normal.' In short, there is no hope, and no reason to hope. Once the time dimension of thinking becomes negative, the future is all but certain. 'Tomorrow will be bad too.' Bottom line: 'Nothing is going to be any different. So why try?'

Dr. Cloud continues:

"So think about this formula and the implications for business. If people feel like they have no control over any outcome, and all of the outcomes are going to be negative, and everything about what they are doing is bad, and it won't ever be any different, because they are incapable losers and the market environment is hopeless too—then not much good is going to happen. They have learned that they are helpless and there is nothing they can do about it. What happens then?

"They feel awful, their relationships suffer, and their performance tanks. Their brains change too. In the midst of the financial crash and the following year, I found this syndrome to be present in several industries, from real estate to financial services to health care to consumer products. The reality of the negative external situation, the financial meltdown, was rewriting people's internal software, and they were becoming very different people. Even previously high performers were being affected and acting as if there was nothing they could do. Until... they discovered they could rewrite the software. When we make this discovery, everything changes for the better.

"It also explains why one salesperson may feel paralyzed and not hit his numbers while another colleague may have the best year of his career, in the middle of the same bad market. How does that happen? They are thinking very different thoughts:

"The first one is thinking: 'No client would want what I am offering because I have no credibility after the crash. Look at how my clients' portfolios are doing. I am not doing well at any part of the business, and besides that, the market is bad and it is not going to be any different tomorrow. This is just the way it is going to be.' The result? Virtual inactivity, or low-energy activity, resulting in no new business, and no increasing business from existing clients.

"But the second person starts to shift his thinking. It occurs to him that he has a couple of hundred clients. And a lot of them were not happy with him, but it was not his fault, it was the market drop. So he doesn't personalize the situation. Instead he has an aha moment: if any of his clients were upset with him, and potentially looking for a new broker, that means there are thousands and thousands of clients out there upset with their brokers and looking for a new one!...All of a sudden, the world looks like a very, very positive place to be. The potential for growing business has never looked better. Lots of people are eager to make a change. Everyone becomes a prospect. As a result, he gets very busy calling and meeting people, asking them if they would be interested in hearing his strategies for surviving the downturn. His business begins to thrive like never before.

"Same market as the first guy, very different results. The reason: very different software." –pp. 111-115.

Have you let fear unleash negative thoughts in your life that are paralyzing you with the "three P's"? If so, Dr. Cloud has this reminder and advice:

"...If negative thinking is present in your teams, culture, and organization, you are allowing it to be there. So begin by taking a personal audit and asking yourself to what degree have you become a victim of negative thinking—your own and others. Has the market or any other force caused you to begin to experience any of the 'three P's?'

• Personal: 'What ever made me think I could be a leader? The reason we are stuck is that I am not up to the task. What ever made me think I was good enough to pull this off?"

• Pervasive: "It seems like everything I am working on is failing. Nothing is going the way I need it to go."

• Permanent: "It is not going to change."

"Some of these statements might seem extreme, but they are all subtle variations that can linger in your head and still do damage. Your attitude and your way of thinking are contagious. If you think something can be done, then so will your people. If you don't then neither will they. They will feel your energy and see your activity either way."—pp. 116-117.

Have you got caught up in the trap of the "three P's" where you begin blaming yourself with negative thoughts which paralyze you from taking control and doing what must be done? If so, you need to recognize it, and consciously change your thinking so you can get back on track.

In the remainder of this chapter, let's talk about six specific actions you can take to get a very different outcome now.

1. Stop blaming yourself for where you are now. This action only paralyzes you further. Instead, begin rewriting your inner software by shifting how you think about yourself. If you've made mistakes, experienced failure or are facing criticism, don't let it affect what you do.

In *The Secrets Thoughts of Successful Women*, author Valerie Young makes this point:

"No one likes to fail....In one way or another you've spent your entire adult life trying to avoid stumbling. In the imposter world there is no such thing as constructive criticism—there is only condemnation. To not make the grade in some way only serves as more proof that you're a fraud. And to receive less-than-positive feedback from someone else— well, that just makes it official.

"...Taken together, failure, mistakes, and criticism constitute another piece of the competence puzzle. How you think about and handle these inevitable parts of life has enormous impact on how competent and confident you feel. See for yourself:

Answer Yes or No

• When things go wrong, I automatically blame myself

• When I make a mistake, I have a really hard time forgiving myself

• I often walk way from conversations obsessing over what I said—or 'failed' to say

• I remember every dumb thing I ever said or did

• I take even constructive criticism personally, seeing it as proof of my ineptness.

"If you answered yes to the majority of these statements, you are most definitely not alone. And by you, I mean you and practically every other woman in the world." –pp. 137-138.

Then, Young points out the major difference between men and women with how they respond to failure and criticism. She says:

"Perhaps the biggest difference has to do with where males and females ascribe blame. It's well known, for example, that despite doing better academically in the early school years, girls have less confidence in their intellectual abilities. Partly this has to do with the tendency for females to blame failure on a lack of ability. Males do just the opposite. They credit themselves for their accomplishments and point to outside reasons for failure—the teacher didn't give us enough time to study, the test was too hard, the referee was unfair.

"It's known as self-regarding attribution bias. Basically, it's the difference between thinking that rises in your stock portfolio are a result of your savvy financial instincts and blaming losses on bad luck. A cartoon I once saw said it all. A woman struggling to zip her pants says, 'Yikes, I must be getting fat!' A man in the same predicament says, 'Hey, there must be something wrong with these pants!'

"It's easy to laugh. But if you happen to be the one constantly pointing the finger at yourself, you've got a major problem. For starters, where you place the onus of responsibility for a failure directly impacts your options for managing it. Say you deliver a presentation and it bombs. It's one thing to assume ownership of the failure by admitting that you skimped on prep time. It's quite another to believe that you performed poorly because you're incompetent. In the first scenario the solution is clear: Prepare more next time. If, however, you believe things went badly because you are fundamentally inept, then you have no recourse for improvement. It's why when faced with the prospect of failing a course, female engineering students are likely to leave the program altogether, while their male peers are more likely to repeat the course and continue to pursue their degree.

"When you personalize failure or criticism in this way, you also allow them to mean more about who you are as a person. So when your boss or your advisor tells you that your work is inadequate, what you hear is 'You're inadequate.' You may be so accustomed to reading too much into things that even kudos can be interpreted as criticism. Like the graduate student who after successfully passing her oral exam was told by her advisor, 'You couldn't have done any better.' At first the student took it for the compliment it clearly was. On further reflection, though, she decided that what he really meant was, 'Given your intellectual capabilities I guess that's the best we could expect from you.'" –pp. 139-140.

Do you have this tendency? Do you choose to see things with a negative slant where you internalize what is happening to you and continue to think about it until it negatively affects your behavior?

If so, the good news is that you can rewrite the software of your mind by changing your thoughts. You don't have to settle for the behavioral patterns you've found yourself slipping into over the past several years. You can choose to look differently at yourself and your business.

Valerie Young says that the best way to remind yourself that you are doing this is to carry a Q-tip around with you and remind yourself that it stands for Quit Taking It Personally. She says: "Tape a cotton swab to your bathroom mirror, tuck another inside your desk drawer or bag to use a visual reminder. Realize too that just because you feel inadequate doesn't mean that you are inadequate. I can practically guarantee that sometime in the next twenty-four to forty-eight hours you will have the opportunity to feel stupid just like the rest of us. It's called life. Again, the words you use really do matter. You'll be amazed at how differently you feel simply by changing your response from 'I am so stupid!' to 'Boy, did I feel stupid.'....The moment you realize what's happening, silently shout STOP! Repeat this as often as necessary...When the self-blame game begins, consciously call upon your more logical self for a 'second opinion.' In other words, the instant the thought my proposal was so lame enters your mind, check in to see what the other side thinks. With emotions out of the picture, allow your rational mind to counter with 'I'm sure it was better than I'm giving myself credit for.'" –pp. 149-150.

That is great advice. Rewrite the software of your mind by how you think about and talk to yourself. Focus on what you want that you can control.

One of the biggest traps we fall into as small business owners is that we focus on what is happening to us and external problems in our industry that we don't have a lot of control over. Individually, we don't have a lot of control over what is happening in the stock market or the day to day fluctuations in our economy. Instead, we should do as achievers do—focus on what we want to produce and cause to happen. Focus on the causes that will create the effects you want. You are in control. You determine what happens. Work on the areas you can control. Focus on the critical success factors that will lead to the results you desire and you will be successful even in times of uncertainty.

2. Everyone experiences adversity and failure. It isn't fatal unless you allow it to be.

Former Chicago Bears coach Mike Ditka once said: "Success isn't permanent and failure isn't fatal."

John Maxwell shares this story: "Years ago when Bear Bryant was coaching the University of Alabama's football team, the Crimson Tide was ahead by only six points in a game with less than two minutes remaining in the fourth quarter. Bryant sent his quarterback into the game with instructions to play it safe and run out the clock. In the huddle, the quarterback said, 'Coach says to play it safe, but that's what they're expecting. Let's give them a surprise.' And with that, he called a pass play.

When the quarterback dropped back and threw the pass, the defending cornerback, who was a champion sprinter, intercepted the ball and headed toward the end zone, expecting to score a touchdown. The quarterback, who was not known as a good runner, took off after the cornerback and ran him down from behind, tackling him on the 5-yard line. His effort saved the game.

After the clock ran out, the opposing coach approached Bear Bryant and said, 'What's this business about your quarterback not being a runner? He ran down my speedster from behind!'

Bryant responded, 'Your man was running for six points. My man was running for his life.'

Nothing can motivate a person like adversity....If you step back from the negative circumstances facing you, you will be able to discover their positive benefits. That is almost always true; you simply have to be willing to look for them—and not take the adversity you are experiencing too personally.

If you lose your job, think about the resilience you're developing. If you try something daring and survive, evaluate what you learned about yourself—and how it will help you take on new challenges. If a bookstore gets your order wrong, figure out whether it's an opportunity to learn a new skill. And if you experience a train wreck in your career, think of the maturity it's developing in you....Always measure an obstacle next to the size of the dream you're pursuing. It's all in how you look at it." –*Failing Forward*, pp. 115-118.

In a nutshell, everyone experiences challenging times at one time or another. Even if you've been successful at one thing for a long period of time, you may be overtaken by aggressive competitors if you keep doing the same things.

In other words, you can't be a follower and expect to be a leader in your industry. You have to see the overlooked opportunities around you in your market and take action to create the results you want.

The only way this will happen is if you really want to change and if you allow yourself to change. This is hard because as John Maxwell once observed: "Leaders only grow to the threshold of their pain."

He also says that change is a challenge because:

• Few people really like it.

• Most people don't know how to do it correctly.

• Only some people know it is essential for growth.

Failure is a part of growth. That doesn't mean it is easy or fun. It is a tragedy when failure happens, but it isn't fatal unless you allow it to be.

3. Reach your potential by paying the price every single day. Do something everyday.

What opportunities may you be missing because you are not willing to pay the price to change?

Are you missing opportunities because you are happy with the status quo and are oblivious to what is happening around you in the marketplace?

Even if your business is doing very well, you always have to be willing to make changes.

Ray Kroc, the leader who led McDonald's to massive growth, said: "As long as you're green, you're growing. As soon as you're ripe, you start to rot."

The problem is that most people would rather embrace the status quo than reach outside of their comfort zone to make improvements. Yet this is the key to beating disappointments, defeats, and discouragement. You have to be willing to make changes. It is when you strive to make changes in your business that you will encounter resistance from other members of your team and sometimes even from yourself. What price are you paying every single day in the following three critical areas of your business?

1) Increasing the Number of Customers Buying at Your Business

As an assignment, sit down and write 20 ways you can bring 10% or 25% more customers into your business this month. Have a contest with your team to see who can come up with the best and most unique ideas. Vote on what you think will be best.

2) Increasing the Transaction Value for Every Customer Buying at Your Business

If you aren't selling as much as you would like, ask yourself why?

Are you upselling something with every product or service you sell? If not, why?

If you did, what kind of a difference would that make to your business?

When selling, have your consultants break down their goals into steps and daily manageable tasks.

- How much do you want to sell? (daily, weekly, monthly, annual basis)

- How much you want to earn?

- What activities do you have to do on a daily, weekly, monthly basis to achieve goals?

- Sales are proportionate to contacts. If you want to make more sales, generate more leads.

The bottom line is that if you want to get better at selling, you have to study the subject. The key component to increasing your sales is identifying your limiting step.

Ask: What one thing if I improved at would have the most dramatic effect on my sales?

What one thing if I did would help me sell more to every customer who buys something from our business?

3) Increasing the Number of Transactions that Each Customer Makes at Your Business.

This is a function of follow-up. What kind of system do you have in place to contact the customers who have already met with you once?

How are you inviting customers to come back in to make additional purchases?

Put systems in place that will allow you to increase the number of transactions that each customer has with your business. Develop a referral program that gets more customers into your sales funnels.

4. Be a student of other successful, innovative, and profitable ideas that people in other industries are using to grow their businesses.

Become a student of marketing. Read books on ads and marketing campaigns and why they work or don't work. One of the best books I've ever read on ads is entitled *Cash Copy*. It details what works in print ads and what doesn't. The author, Jeffrey Lant, goes through hundreds of examples of real-life ads and he points out specifically what makes an ad work.

Two other books that you ought to read on this topic are *The 22 Immutable Laws of Marketing* by Jack Trout and Al Ries and *Influence: The Psychology of Persuasion* by Robert Cialdini.

5. Break out instead of break in. Try different approaches. Be unpredictable. Don't fall into boring routines.

Ask yourself, "What are our potential customers looking for they can't find elsewhere?" Offer that in a creative way and people will flock to your business. The best way to break out is to find and execute breakthroughs. Breakthroughs happen because of our mindset. People who have this kind of mindset and attitude make breakthroughs. People who don't never see the opportunities in the first place.

What overlooked opportunities are you sitting on?

Make a list of breakthroughs you have noticed in other industries and keep adding to it over time. Create a file of some of the best marketing approaches you've seen.

6. Reflect more on your business and look for opportunities. Too often, you are too close to the little details and don't step back often enough to see the big picture. When you take time to think about your business more, you'll see bigger and better opportunities.

One of the foundational principles of producing better results is to know yourself and your business inside and out. The more you think about your business and the things that make businesses successful in other industries, the more insights you will have.

You can change if you aren't happy with where you are. You can overcome setbacks, defeats, and failures. Failure is not fatal. However, you've got to beat the resistance to change by changing the software in your mind. You've got to create boundaries in your thoughts and emotions. Take control of your business. Refuse to be controlled by fear. Stop internalizing your disappointments, defeats, and discouragement. We all fail. Yet, we can rise from these failures to accomplish new and amazing things.

The future is bright for those who implement the principles outlined in this book, to those who listen and adapt to the needs of prospects in the marketplace, and who increase their value with every transaction so their clients have amazing experiences they'll never forget. I look forward to hearing of your successes as you implement these game changers in your business. Get in the game and go for it!

ABOUT THE AUTHOR

James Karl Butler is a serial entrepreneur who has built four companies from the start-up phase to over a million dollars in revenue. He is the author of eighteen books. He grew his first retail bridal store from $0 to over $1,000,000 in sales in three years and grew another retail business from $0 to over $1,000,000 in just over 18 months.

James has helped some of the most respected and largest retailers and businesses across the country to grow their sales and shatter their previous sales records. He is a celebrated systems and marketing authority who speaks and trains business owners how to create rapid and sustained growth in their business.

He is the author of the best-selling book *The System is the Secret.* He inspires entrepreneurs to take action in their businesses through applying the principles in his books and podcasts. He offers a coaching and training program to a worldwide audience of entrepreneurs providing insights and systems-based training designed to help business owners grow their businesses to the next level. He and his wife Heather are the parents of five children.

You can follow him on Instagram at @jameskarlbutler or reach him at jameskarlbutler@gmail.com.

Made in the USA
San Bernardino, CA
06 July 2020